Booker T. Washington

Recent Titles in Black History Lives

W.E.B. Du Bois: A Life in American History
Charisse Burden-Stelly and Gerald Horne

Thurgood Marshall: A Life in American History
Spencer R. Crew

Barack Obama: A Life in American History
F. Erik Brooks and MaCherie M. Placide

Harriet Tubman: A Life in American History
Kerry Walters

Zora Neale Hurston: A Life in American History
Stephanie Li

Rosa Parks: A Life in American History
Darryl Mace

Jackie Robinson: A Life in American History
Courtney Michelle Smith

Booker T. Washington

A LIFE IN AMERICAN HISTORY

Mark Christian

Black History Lives

BLOOMSBURY ACADEMIC
NEW YORK • LONDON • OXFORD • NEW DELHI • SYDNEY

BLOOMSBURY ACADEMIC
Bloomsbury Publishing Inc, 1359 Broadway, New York, NY 10018, USA
Bloomsbury Publishing Plc, 50 Bedford Square, London, WC1B 3DP, UK
Bloomsbury Publishing Ireland, 29 Earlsfort Terrace, Dublin 2, D02 AY28, Ireland

BLOOMSBURY, BLOOMSBURY ACADEMIC and the Diana logo
are trademarks of Bloomsbury Publishing Plc

First published in the United States of America by ABC-CLIO 2021
Paperback edition published by Bloomsbury Academic 2026

Copyright © Bloomsbury Publishing Inc, 2025

For legal purposes the Acknowledgments on p. xvii constitute an
extension of this copyright page.

COVER PHOTO: Booker T. Washington, 1910.
(Peter P. Jones/Library of Congress)

All rights reserved. No part of this publication may be: i) reproduced or transmitted in any form, electronic or mechanical, including photocopying, recording or by means of any information storage or retrieval system without prior permission in writing from the publishers; or ii) used or reproduced in any way for the training, development or operation of artificial intelligence (AI) technologies, including generative AI technologies. The rights holders expressly reserve this publication from the text and data mining exception as per Article 4(3) of the Digital Single Market Directive (EU) 2019/790.

Bloomsbury Publishing Inc does not have any control over, or responsibility for, any third-party websites referred to or in this book. All internet addresses given in this book were correct at the time of going to press. The author and publisher regret any inconvenience caused if addresses have changed or sites have ceased to exist, but can accept no responsibility for any such changes.

Library of Congress Cataloging-in-Publication Data
Names: Christian, Mark, author.
Title: Booker T. Washington : a life in American history / Mark Christian.
Description: Santa Barbara, California : ABC-CLIO, An Imprint of ABC-CLIO, LLC, [2021] | Series: Black history lives | Includes bibliographical references and index.
Identifiers: LCCN 2021023106 (print) | LCCN 2021023107 (ebook) | ISBN 9781440872488 (hardcover) | ISBN 9781440872495 (ebook)
Subjects: LCSH: Washington, Booker T., 1856–1915. | African American intellectuals—Biography. | Washington, Booker T., 1856–1915—Influence. | African American educators—Biography. | Tuskegee Institute—Biography. | African American leadership—History. | African Americans—Politics and government. | African American civil rights workers—Biography. | African Americans—Relations with Africans. | African Americans—Social conditions—To 1964. | African Americans—Intellectual life.
Classification: LCC E185.97.W4 C47 2021 (print) | LCC E185.97.W4 (ebook) | DDC 370.92 [B]—dc23
LC record available at https://lccn.loc.gov/2021023106
LC ebook record available at https://lccn.loc.gov/2021023107

ISBN: HB: 978-1-4408-7248-8
PB: 979-8-2163-9666-6
ePDF: 978-1-4408-7249-5
eBook: 979-8-2160-5510-5

Series: Black History Lives

For product safety related questions contact productsafety@bloomsbury.com.

To find out more about our authors and books visit www.bloomsbury.com
and sign up for our newsletters.

*To the four Adas integral to my life journey. For my two grandmothers, my mother, and especially my daughter: Ada Christian, born November 29, 2006.
All gone, but not forgotten.*

Contents

Series Foreword ix

Preface xi

Acknowledgments xvii

Chapter 1
Historical Context *1*

Chapter 2
Childhood in Bondage and Hampton Institute *19*

Chapter 3
Tuskegee Institute and Family Matters *41*

Chapter 4
The Atlanta Compromise and Beyond *65*

Chapter 5
Of Dr. W. E. B. Du Bois and Others *99*

Chapter 6
Africa in His Mind and Practice *143*

Why Booker T. Washington Matters *179*

Timeline 211

Primary Documents 217

Bibliography 257

Index 267

Series Foreword

The Black History Lives biography series explores and examines the lives of the most iconic figures in African American history, with supplementary material that highlights the subject's significance in our contemporary world. Volumes in this series offer far more than a simple retelling of a subject's life by providing readers with a greater understanding of the outside events and influences that shaped each subject's world, from familial relationships to political and cultural developments.

Each volume includes chronological chapters that detail events of the subject's life. The final chapter explores the cultural and historical significance of the individual and places their actions and beliefs within an overall historical context. Books in the series highlight important information about the individual through sidebars that connect readers to the larger context of social, political, intellectual, and pop culture in American history; a timeline listing significant events; key primary source excerpts; and a comprehensive bibliography for further research.

Preface

When a scholar is asked to tackle the life and times of any historical figure, there is inevitably a degree of trepidation one encounters. However, when it comes to a person as complex and elusive as Booker T. Washington, it is even more daunting. Above all else, he was a private man. To delve into his life is to open up oneself to an extraordinary individual who lived in unusual times. The Southern states were viciously racist during his lifetime, but he endured and prospered. Washington was born into enslavement but eventually rose to the heights of affluent society. He was a man who would be in the company of celebrities for a tea party with Queen Victoria at Windsor Castle in England. He was a man who dined at the White House with President Theodore Roosevelt. And yet, he was also a man of African American heritage who took the daily slights and injustices of racialized discrimination in his stride.

Washington's biography/history as an African American straddles the historical periods of enslavement, emancipation, and reconstruction, and it draws to a close midway through the second decade of the twentieth century. Within the larger context of Black history, Washington is a largely misunderstood figure, often relegated to the status of an "accommodationist" and "conservative" who gave up the political and voting rights to white supremacy in the South. Viewed disparagingly as obsequious to the white powerbrokers, he was unfairly dismissed by future generations. For decades after his death in 1915, he was overlooked, until Louis Harlan, a white Southerner, published a major two-volume biography. Along with his widely regarded study, Harlan, with Raymond Stock, edited fourteen volumes of Washington's business and private correspondence papers between 1972 and 1989. Harlan dedicated almost four decades dissecting the life of Washington, and most of what is known in terms of a fundamental analysis of Washington largely stems from Harlan's tremendous contribution to scholarship.

Louis Harlan's work could be described as an attempt to lift the veil from the mystery of Booker T. Washington. Although it is largely a lifetime of work by a biographer, there is still room for further excavation and interpretation into this momentous life. Harlan, it can be stated, is fair in most of his assessment, but as a reader one comes away thinking that Washington was devious and vindictive to his enemies and kind to his family and friends. Harlan erroneously suggests that the "Tuskegee Machine" that Washington led was at times underhanded, and its tentacles reached into halls of power whereby any African American with ambition had to kowtow to his way of thought (Harlan 1972, 254–271). This theme is constant in Harlan's analysis, and one ends a reading of his work thinking rather subconsciously negatively about Washington. Indeed, at the very end of this mammoth scholarly project, when the reader gets to the death and mourning of Washington, Harlan ends his study with an odd reference to "pick-pocket" thieves on the day of the funeral and the suicide of a faculty member. He writes, in summing up the momentous mournful day, "Ironically, pick-pockets appeared to work the crowd at the railroad station, and soon after the funeral excitement a faculty member who had earlier suffered a nervous breakdown jumped to her death from a high window on the campus" (Harlan 1983, 457). What a strange and negative manner to end an almost thousand page, two-volume, biography.

A generation passed before a more positive account of Washington's life was published by another white historian, Robert Norrell. His biography, *Up from History: The Life of Booker T. Washington*, published in 2009, gives Washington's life greater meaning and humanity, yet it still stays within a white liberal frame of reference that remains within a standard of past scholarship, and there is little investigation or interrogation of W. E. B. Du Bois's aversion toward Washington.

This biography, however, intends to go deeper and actually critique Du Bois more profoundly than what is usually offered by scholars. The fact remains that Du Bois is viewed as a godlike figure in Black history. Moreover, in terms of his contention with Washington, it is akin to a boxing match whereby Du Bois is Muhammad Ali and Washington a Great White Hope. Never does Washington get a punch on his opponent, maybe the odd jab. But the scholarly world has more or less confirmed Du Bois as the greatest and Washington as a washed-up has-been. Hence, there needs to be a reappraisal that at least allows some nuanced and closer scrutiny of the erudite Du Bois.

One should ask, What was the behavior of Washington's enemies that made him defend himself in clandestine ways? Is it not standard for a human being in a leadership role to defend him- or herself against perceived adversaries? Clearly there was never any violence on behalf of Washington against a rival. Yet he was a man who lived in the "eye of the storm" of white supremacy. It was a hellish time between 1890 and 1915 for African Americans. He lived and led like a man with his head in a lion's mouth. One false move in the South could have got him assassinated or lynched and his Tuskegee Institute burned to the ground.

This biography is unlike the common retelling of a subject's life, instead providing readers with a deeper comprehension of the broader influences that shaped Booker T. Washington. Basically, one cannot understand fully his life experiences, particularly his interactions with both white powerbrokers and his African American underlings and peers, without some focus on the nuances in these complex relationships. Additionally, it is important to consider the political and cultural developments that had crucial relevance to the decisions Washington had to consider in his role as a leader of Tuskegee Institute and perceived of African Americans generally in the late nineteenth and early twentieth centuries.

A perspective that is central to this biography is the notion that Booker T. Washington has been "fossilized" as a historical figure. For many scholars there is nothing more to learn from his life; all has been revealed—this point of view could not be further from the reality. Indeed, there is much to reconsider about his life in terms of how his rivalry with W. E. B. Du Bois has basically been interpreted as Washington being for "industrial education" and Du Bois being for "higher education"—the crux. Yet it is hoped that the author will debunk this simple dichotomy and relegate it to the dustbin of scholarship. The interaction between Washington, Du Bois, and others will be covered, and new ways of analyzing these interactions will be revealed. For sure there was much contention and disagreement on how best to push forward the African American experience. However, there were also friendly relations, cooperation, and collaboration between Washington and Du Bois that have been rarely highlighted.

There are numerous other biographies that have fleshed out Washington's life and times, including Michael Rudolph West's scholarship, which preceded Norrell's work (West 2006). However, West focuses primarily on the theme of "race relations" and how Washington navigated this aspect of his life's work. Some scholars doing studies on a historical figure have a specific focus that they want to highlight and examine. It is in the interest of all to be candid about one's motivations as an author assessing the life of another human being. Biographies are at best subjective to the interpretation of the writer and open to scrutiny, and rightly so. Therefore, when one considers the importance of biography as it intersects with history, there is a need for both the writer and the reader to step outside of her or his own history and cultural experience.

A renowned African American writer, Ishmael Reed, wrote an introduction to a new edition of Washington's famed 1901 autobiography, *Up from Slavery*, and succinctly makes a strong argument for a reappraisal that speaks more readily to Washington's life and unique cultural experience.

Reed writes, "Booker T. Washington deserves a reassessment, unfettered by the biases of Northern elitist African-American intellectuals and comfortable white radicals who would only have been satisfied if Washington had engaged in a wild suicidal shoot-out with whites—who outnumbered the black population three to one—so that they might use his martyr's photo to further their causes. He was opposed by those who disagreed with his economic theories. Yet one hundred years later, theirs remain untested" (Reed 2010, xxi). Therefore, this biography intends to add something new or beyond the usual narrative that has endured for decades without critical insight or an alternative response.

Ishmael Reed, above all, speaks to the profound misunderstanding and unfairness that surrounds Washington and his legacy. It is important for the reader to pay attention to the actual reality of how vicious white supremacy was in the time he lived, how dangerous it was for a man or woman of color to stand up for their rights, and how perilous it would have been to openly show dissent to the white power structure if one had a foothold in the community and responsibility for the livelihood of others. Washington knew from experience how any threat to the status quo could harm his attempt to improve the lot of African Americans in the Southern states. It was easier for those intellectuals based in the North, where the violence of racism was not as caprice, to pontificate for civil and human rights at a safe distance. Yes, one from the North could find it more comfortably safe to denounce anyone who walked like a fox on ice while challenging racism and disenfranchisement in the South. But the fact remained that hundreds of courageous men and women died with a rope around their necks doing such. This period in the Black Belt was not a time to simply call out white supremacy willy-nilly. One had to do so with a degree of tact if one was to outwit the evil nature of men who killed with ease those who offered dissent. Washington was not a coward; he was a man of vision and was someone who was endeavoring to build a future for his people from the bottom up.

This is not to dismiss Harlan or any other biographer who leaned too easily toward the Northern intellectuals' interpretative perspective, while downplaying the actual threat Washington encountered on a day-to-day basis. Washington had to employ a strategy for uplift that worked without causing unnecessary conflict or without raising the angst of white racism to the degree that brought forth violence to Tuskegee Institute. Younger scholars in a sense will have fresh eyes on this period of history. Hopefully the reader will be able to come away from this biography with greater insight than doubt about the efficacy of this important historical figure. Indeed, Washington has largely been disparaged and unable to defend his legacy because after his death his main rival lived on for almost half a century.

W. E. B. Du Bois was a prolific writer and was able to cement his perspective without reply from Washington, who lay in his grave in the grounds of his beloved institution that he had grandly built up during a thirty-four year tenure. During his lifetime, Tuskegee Normal and Industrial Institute would often be named by its shortened version: Tuskegee Institute. Some decades after his passing in 1915, it would be renamed Tuskegee University, and it still remains today as an immense part of his legacy. What needs to be added to his legacy is a more nuanced version of his life and times—one that does not render him a fossilized figure but allows the reader to view a side to Washington that broadens his appeal to a new generation in the 2020s and beyond. This is the aim and promise herein: new insights into the life and times of Washington.

Chapter 1 examines the historical context of the nation just prior to his birth that covers the challenges and dynamics in how he emerged. Chapter 2 recounts his childhood years and the struggle he had to obtain a rudimentary education. It also covers his pursuit of further education at Hampton Institute under his mentor, General Samuel Chapman Armstrong (1839–1893). Chapter 3 considers his experiences establishing himself in Tuskegee and his experiences in the building of a renowned institution of vocational and general education. It also examines his family matters, the joy, and the pain of grief and loss, while continuing to strive against all odds to establish Tuskegee into a renowned education establishment. Chapter 4 leads the reader into his famous address at the 1895 Cotton States and International Exposition in Atlanta, Georgia. The speech would become known as the "Atlanta Compromise," and it catapulted him into national fame. Moreover, it surveys his creation of the National Negro Business League (NNBL) in 1900. Chapter 5 assesses his major rivals and the manner in which he had to navigate through this critical aspect of African American leadership, while not losing his white, liberal philanthropic funders. Chapter 6 reflects on a much undervalued area of his world, that of Africa and its potential. He operated in a time of the "scramble for Africa" in 1884 and beyond. Washington was up against insidious European forces that exploited the continent, its peoples, and its profound mineral resources. Nevertheless, Washington endeavored to make tangible contact with a number of African leaders of grassroots struggle for liberation and economic development. Even today, this is a scantily researched area in the life of this omnipresent man in the affairs of African Americans and Africans on the continent. Therefore, there is an effort to highlight this aspect of his life's work through the studies of scholars who have covered aspects of African-Tuskegee relations. The final chapter considers Washington's legacy and offers a new paradigm for studying his life for future scholars interested in delving into a fascinating life in American history. There follow a timeline, primary documents, and an extensive bibliography for further reading and study.

Acknowledgments

I want to thank the Black History Lives editors at the ABC-CLIO publishers who engaged me to take on this erudite challenge: Kevin Downing, Michael Millman, Kim Kennedy-White, Angel Daphnee, Nicole Azze, and Erin Ryan. Special thanks to Erin for keeping me on track and for the solid support.

There are also many people to thank who know me, who do not know me, and whom I would like to know that inspired me to complete this biography of Booker T. Washington. For many years I took on board the trite and disparaging view of a man who survived enslavement and then the nadir in African American history to leave behind an institution that would rise from a shack to a multimillion-dollar-endowment university situated in the Deep South: Tuskegee University.

I want to thank the wonderful president of Tuskegee University, Dr. Lily D. McNair, who allowed me to stay on the campus for a week in the month of April 2019. Dr. McNair is the eighth president in the institution's history. It was during part of the Spring Break that I stayed on the campus, so I did not get to meet her in person. Through email exchanges with her secretary, Ms. Veronica Cook, we set up my arrangements to stay. In hindsight, having researched his life, I think this is what Booker T. Washington would have done had I requested to come to his establishment of learning on a fact-finding mission. During my stay I wanted to "get a feel" for the man and the famous grounds. The staff and students I met were all very cordial as I walked across campus reflecting on what it must have been like to have lived and worked there in the 1880s to early twentieth century. What a beautiful campus it is, with the Carnegie Library building still standing as an administrative office, but no longer a library. The students I spoke to during 2019 were friendly, energetic, and contemporary African Americans—I'm sure some were from the broader African Diaspora too. Cars went past me with the latest rap music bellowing. I wondered smiling how Dr. Washington would have chastised these students! How times have changed.

The Oaks, where he lived with his family, still stands as a tourist attraction on the campus. I wandered inside in awe of its historical significance as the young and confident African American man from the tourist office narrated the history of the house. I did see signs of decay in this marvelous house with ceilings in definite need of repair. This is unacceptable, and I do hope the National Park Service can find substantial support for this National Historic Site. The guide, Mr. Sedric Wytch, did a wonderful job enthusiastically explaining the history, and I would like to acknowledge here the service he and others provided. I would like to thank Dr. Tyrene Wright for her insights on the African aspect of Booker T. Washington history; she is an alum of Tuskegee University, which is special, and a living example of Booker T. Washington's legacy.

I would like to thank the School of Arts & Humanities at Lehman College—City University of New York for a travel grant that allowed me to visit Tuskegee University, and thanks to some of my colleagues and the underpaid administrative staff who have been supportive in my endeavors, not in any specific order: Dr. William Seraile, Dr. Marie Marianetti, Dr. Jaye Jones, Dr. Ghelawdewos Araia, Ms. Barbara Glover, Mr. Lowery McClendon, Ms. Julette Sanchez, Dr. Carole Weisz, Mr. Joe McElligott, Dr. Gillian Bayne, Mr. Hank Williams, Mr. Michael Deas, Ms. Marimer Berberena Alonso, Dr. David Badillo, Dr. Forrest Colburn, Ms. Jean Geiger, Ms. Sabrina Heywood, Mr. Willis Attico, Ms. Veronica Mason, and Ms. Jazmine Miller. Special thanks to the Lehman librarian, Dr. Janet Munch, who helped me track down various rare sources with ease.

To the students I have benefited from teaching in my decade at Lehman College; many have gone on to be successful professionals: as teachers, social workers, nurses, and other professionals. Most come from the Bronx and Harlem, along with those from Latin America, the Caribbean, and African continent. They have largely embraced my Black British humor, and that is all I could ask for when teaching such an often deeply emotional subject matter. African American, and in general Africana, history has been a labor of love for me now for over three decades. It continues to stimulate my intellectual curiosity. There is nothing more pleasing than finding hidden Black history. This biographical account will hopefully shed a number of unexplored areas relating to Booker T. Washington, which is largely due to my education in the disciplines of Africana Studies and Sociology.

My mentor Dr. William E. Nelson Jr. (1941–2013) from The Ohio State University (OSU) continues to inspire me like many other intellectual warriors who have passed on. Dr. Nelson built the Department of Black Studies at OSU from 1969 until his retirement in 2009. He was also at one time the president of the National Council for Black Studies and of the African Heritage Association. Just like Booker T. Washington, he made something out of nothing for future generations to benefit from. At the time of both their lives, they were probably not as appreciated as they should have been. I hope this small contribution is a testimony to all those thousands of lives who have struggled for the liberation of Africana peoples worldwide, while suffering the slings and arrows of misfortune.

Finally, I would like to acknowledge a few of my longer-term colleagues, friends, and family who have endured my ideas on Pan African history over the years: Nkosi Nantambu, Michelle Spooner, Christel Temple, Patricia Reid-Merritt, Clenora Hudson-Weems, Molefi K. Asante, Leland Ware, Terry Mills, Mark Giles, Stephanie Y. Evans, Martell Teasley, David Canton, Michael Tillotson, Richard Benjamin, and Eric Lynch. To some of my family Christian members: Cabral, Ada, Nevada, Ivan, Franco, Kevin, Janet, Rita, Jenny, Tina, Pam, and Victor. To the memory of those passed but not forgotten: Ada, Gladstone, Rupert, Roger, Denny, and Ian, to name a few. To the many nephews and nieces. Again, I thank everyone, and all errors are solely mine in this book of a great man in time and place.

1

Historical Context

To comprehend the life and times of an important historical figure, there should be an understanding of the time and place from where the person emerged. Indeed, the intersection between a biography and its historical juncture is crucial to understanding what such a person, man or woman, experienced. In essence, we each enter the world at a time and place not of our choosing; we are held captive to the whims, notions, and structure of whatever society we are born into. This is an important point to make as we journey through the life and times of a man born into enslavement and who grew to become a de facto leader of African Americans.

Without doubt, the life of Booker Taliaferro Washington (1856–1915) is both fascinating and complex. It is definitely worth the attention of anyone interested in understanding African American history from the mid-1800s to the early part of the twentieth century—the United States of those times was certainly remarkably different than the twenty-first century version. In short, the Southern states were still largely agrarian, and the Northern states were rapidly embracing the industrial forms of labor that produced commodities at a much faster rate. The world was rapidly changing, and it would take an extraordinary person to emerge from enslavement to become a prominent principal of an institute of learning, an excellent fundraiser, an outstanding orator, and a man who endeavored to bring hope to millions of his people through self-reliance. He accomplished all of this while dealing with a viciously violent Southern racist environment that

> ### FREDERICK DOUGLASS (1818–1895)
>
> Frederick Douglass escaped enslavement in 1838 by fleeing to New York from a Maryland plantation. As a fugitive he would become a spokesperson for the abolitionist movement. His first autobiography, *Narrative of the Life of Frederick Douglass, an American Slave*, published in 1845, explained the horrors of bondage. Douglass toured Great Britain, lecturing with the book, addressing crowds of two thousand and more. He returned to the United States in 1847 a free man after funds were raised by British abolitionists to pay off his slaveholder. He would go on to be the voice of freedom for African Americans still in bondage up to 1865 and the Thirteenth Amendment to the Constitution that abolished slavery. In the post–Civil War era, Douglass continued to work for the betterment of his people, including women, and for equal rights for all. In 1892, he gave the commencement address at Tuskegee Institute, stressing to the students the need for "thrift and commonsense" and requesting the white world "give us a fair chance, but be sure *do* give us a fair chance."

ultimately wanted the African American population unequivocally disempowered. Indeed, during the initial twenty-five years of his life (1856–1881), he essentially encountered physical and mental hardship, grief, and poverty that most ordinary mortals could not have endured. Without being overly emotive, the reader of this biography should be inspired by the depth of human endurance and perseverance that this larger-than-life figure represents.

At the time of Booker T. Washington's birth (April 5, 1856), there was a strong abolitionist movement in the United States, and its ultimate goal was to end the long night of enslavement for African Americans. Frederick Douglass (1818–1895) had escaped enslavement from Maryland and fled to New York as a young man, and by the mid-1850s he had developed into a major spokesperson for his people and their quest for freedom. Douglass was a very bold and courageous speaker who did not bend in his conviction that enslavement was a curse on the American republic. He did all he could to denounce the evils of chattel bondage that denied the freedom of about four million African American souls (Blight 2018).

There were strong allies among whites, and the leading abolitionist was William Lloyd Garrison (1805–1879), who had aided the development of Douglass as an orator and writer in the abolitionist cause. Both Garrison and Douglass led the assault on the institution of slavery well before Booker T. Washington had entered the world. Douglass and Garrison were brave souls, fighting against tremendous odds because the "peculiar institution," as it has been referred to, was profoundly supported by powerful white men who had vested financial interest in keeping it a profitable enterprise. Yet the times were changing, and the challenge to slavery as an economic system was increasing. Abolitionists fought hard against its expansion, which ultimately led to greater conflict and turmoil.

By the late 1850s, the United States was heading for a civil war with the supporters for and against enslavement getting increasingly agitated in regard to their respective causes. Those who supported it had long profited from the unpaid labor of African Americans for almost 250 years, and now it was their livelihood at stake. They had known no other life but the subjugation of another people for their economic

Frederick Douglass (1818–1895) was the undisputed leader of African Americans from the 1850s until his death in 1895. He was a brilliant orator, writer, editor, and activist in the struggle for African American liberation. (Library of Congress)

WILLIAM LLOYD GARRISON (1805–1879)

A staunch abolitionist who worked to end slavery, William Garrison was born in Newburyport, Massachusetts. In 1830, he established an abolitionist paper, *The Liberator*. In 1832, he helped form the New England Antislavery Society. He met a young Frederick Douglass in 1841 at one of the antislavery meetings. Douglass was asked to give an account of his experiences of being enslaved and won recognition as a brilliant orator. Garrison acted as a mentor to Douglass until he grew "too big" and developed his intellectual independence as a writer and orator. Douglass established a newspaper with another African American abolitionist, Martin R. Delaney (1812–1885). The *North Star* was established in 1847, and its slogan was "Right is of no Sex—Truth is of no Color—God is the Father of us all, and we are all Brethren." Douglass always gave kudos for Garrison's mentorship in his days as a fugitive who, but for the assistance of his mentor, could be sent back into enslavement anytime.

William Lloyd Garrison (1805–1879) was a staunch abolitionist who led the movement against enslavement in the mid-nineteenth century. His paper, *The Liberator*, was widely used to highlight the cruelty of the system. Garrison was instrumental in helping Frederick Douglass gain public recognition. (National Archives)

benefit. Indeed, in terms of racial equality, the whites in the Southern states specifically had been nurtured to regard African Americans as lesser human beings. Yet as Dr. Martin Luther King Jr. would often state, "No lie can live forever" (Carson and Shephard 2002, 131). For many readers this may be difficult to understand in the twenty-first century, but the depth of enslavement and the oppression of African Americans were more or less total in the 1850s. Its legacy is still very much part of contemporary society (Feagin 2014). During the enslavement era, the system enveloped the young Booker T. Washington's mental sky. For those who wanted enslavement abolished by any means necessary, there would be no compromise. The abolitionists viewed it as an evil scourge that had to be eradicated without delay. To take away the freedom of another human being and turn he or she into a piece of property to be treated no better than an animal was abhorrent to the average abolitionist. Enslavement had to go and the sooner the better. These were very testing times, and slavery as an institution created a lot of division among the Southern and Northern states. One of the key reasons for the Civil War was over the right to either expand or limit the extension of the peculiar institution into Midwestern and Northern states (Stampp 1956).

During this period of American history, the states that promoted enslavement were largely politically against the states where slavery did not exist. Free men and women of African heritage had few rights to liberty and the pursuit of happiness. But in 1857, when Dred Scott tested his

Dred and Harriet Scott, from *Frank Leslie's Illustrated Newspaper,* June 27, 1857. Dred Scott sued for his and his family's freedom and lost, leading to the famous Dred Scott Decision of 1857. (Library of Congress)

right to citizenship and freedom having moved to a free state, the Supreme Court decision in *Dred Scott v. Sandford* denied African Americans any right to citizenship. Indeed, this Supreme Court decision, under Chief Justice Roger B. Taney, effectively established all African Americans, free and enslaved, as noncitizens with no rights that could be respected under law. The outcry from abolitionists was substantial, and it pushed the nation closer to a civil war. There were numerous rebellions, and some of the most widespread and serious ones occurred in 1856, the birth year of Booker T. Washington (Stampp 1956, 137). One of the most famous assaults on enslavement was led by a white abolitionist, John Brown (1800–1859). He detested the enslavement of African Americans and did all in his power to put an end to it. He advocated for armed revolts among the enslaved against their slaveholders. This was very controversial, and it led to the spread of fear and anxiety among those who supported slavery.

John Brown's raid on Harpers Ferry, Virginia, in October 1859, was meant to secure an arsenal of weapons to arm enslaved people in order to cause mayhem on local plantations. Although the raid struck fear across the slaveholding states, it ultimately failed, and John Brown, along with a number of his coconspirators, was put to death by hanging on December 2, 1859. Nevertheless, this incident led to more abolitionist support to end the long night of enslavement. Combined with the Dred Scott Supreme Court decision, the raid on Harpers Ferry created an impasse between

Roger B. Taney (1777–1964)

Chief Justice Taney was in office from 1836 to 1864 at the Supreme Court and was raised on a tobacco plantation where enslaved African Americans did the labor that created a wealthy existence for his parents and siblings. He was a staunch slaveholding supporter and the key justice behind the Dred Scott decision. It is an often overlooked fact that Justice Taney's background was inextricably interwoven with the slaveholding class. Indeed, he was the son of tobacco planters from Maryland. He was the chief justice on the Supreme Court from 1836 to 1864. Justice Taney led the Supreme Court as proslavery advocate for more than three decades. Often Chief Justice Taney's significant role goes unnoticed as the case is known merely as the "Dred Scott decision," which hides the depth to which proslavery was etched into the minds of at least seven of the nine Supreme Court judges during the buildup to the Civil War (1861–1865). Historically, the Dred Scott decision is regarded as one of the key factors that led to the war.

Dred Scott (1799–1858)

In March 1857, the U.S. Supreme Court ruled 7–2 that all African Americans living in the United States, enslaved as well as free persons, could never become citizens due to them being deemed property. Dred Scott maintained that he and his spouse should be granted their manumission because they had resided in Illinois and the Wisconsin Territory for four years where enslavement was unlawful. Along with establishing the non-citizenship of all African Americans, the ruling also invalidated the Missouri Compromise of 1820, thereby permitting slavery in every federal territory. Scott died of tuberculosis about eighteen months after the decision. He had gained his freedom in May 1857 after his owner, John F. A. Sanford, was paid a price for his freedom.

John Brown (1800–1959)

John Brown was an abolitionist and leader of the Harpers Ferry, Virginia (now West Virginia) raid on the federal armaments store, October 16–18, 1859. A staunch believer in the freedom of African Americans, Brown advocated armed rebellion among the free and the enslaved in order to overthrow the slave system. In all about twenty followers were in the group led by Brown, and among them were two of his sons who would perish. It is known that he asked the African American abolitionist Frederick Douglass to take part in the raid, but he declined because he felt it had little chance of success. Soon after the raid began the local area was alerted, at the end of which seventeen lost their lives and John Brown was captured with another six members of his group. All were eventually put to death by hanging. The Harpers Ferry rebellion sent shock waves through the Antebellum South and the slaveholders now knew that the abolitionists would stop at nothing to end slavery. John Brown was martyred for the antislavery cause, and today is largely viewed an American hero. Before he was executed on December 2, 1859, for treason, he left a note with one of his guards that read "I, John Brown, am now quite certain that the crimes of this guilty land will never be purged away but with blood." Although the raid failed and was largely condemned, it is regarded as one of the key incidents that led to the Civil War about sixteen months later in April 1861. John Brown had much support among the Christian faithful.

those who wanted slavery abolished and those who wanted its expansion. The Civil War was an inevitable consequence in the growing tension between slaveholding states and those states that did not allow enslavement.

Booker T. Washington was three years old in the spring of 1859. His short life had already intersected with tumultuous changes. This was the era nearing the end of slavery whereby he and his family would eventually be impacted. No enslaved African American family escaped the unforgiving human cruelty of chattel slavery. This is something that can get lost in the fog of history, the actual day-to-day existence. Far from the "happy darkies" stereotype exemplified

John Brown (1800–1859) led a slave rebellion with a group of men, along with two of his sons, on the federal arsenal in Harpers Ferry, (West) Virginia. The aim was to emancipate enslaved African Americans and spark a rebellion that would end slavery. This historical event is regarded as a leading catalyst to the Civil War (1861–1865). (National Archives)

in the works of the renowned white Southern historian U. B. Phillips (1929), who is largely regarded as a proslavery historian, it is clear that there was differential treatment toward the enslaved from plantation to plantation. However, the atrocity of the enslavement system certainly outweighed any perceived "benevolence." Indeed, one only has to read the autobiographical accounts of Frederick Douglass (1994) and other writers of slave narratives who have shared their firsthand accounts of how grim it could be to live within the confines of servitude. The idea that some masters were less cruel than others seems rather myopic given the inhumane conditions endured by the average African American on a plantation in the Antebellum South.

Crucially, the reality of enslavement had to be harsh for all those on the receiving end of its worst elements. Enslaved people were not allowed to read and write and did not have the freedom to build a family. Fortunately, Booker T. Washington grew up with his mother and siblings on a small plantation. It was only by chance that he was not separated from them in childhood. Most often children were separated from their mothers at a very young age so that no bond could be formed between the mother and child. What is known through the published slave narratives are accounts ranging from abject cruelty of masters to masters who treated their enslaved persons with a degree of care. Cynically, some suggest any care given was merely to protect the value of the person, who was by law property to be sold on an auction block at the caprice of the master. The separation of families occurred most often in this manner with one or two members being sold to other plantations in order to raise funds for the plantation owner. It was a business, and the enslaved were regarded as commodities within this enterprise. The significance of enslavement history to the life of Booker T. Washington cannot be estimated easily, other than to state it fundamentally shaped his life and his work.

In April 1861, the Civil War broke out between the Confederates and the Union Army. Booker T. Washington's home state of Virginia was among the secessionist states; those that broke away from the Union between December 1860 and May 1861 were in order of secession: South Carolina, Mississippi, Florida, Alabama, Georgia, Louisiana, Texas, Virginia, Arkansas, North Carolina, and Tennessee.

There are a number of causes that led to the Civil War. While enslavement is generally cited as the main reason, other social, political, and cultural differences between the North and the South also contributed. Some of these differences created a greater rift between the North and the South that ultimately instigated the Civil War. First, there was the issue of states' rights, which had long been an issue ever since the writing of the Constitution. There had been opinions about how much power the states should have versus how much power the federal government should have. During the buildup to the Civil War, the Southern states felt that the federal government was taking away their rights and powers to expand the institution. So, it was always a thorny issue between Southern politicians and those Northerners who wanted ultimately to see the end of enslavement. However, it would be a stretch too far to suggest that the Northerners cared universally for the empowerment of African Americans. There was never, in fact, a desire for full citizenship, which would be a battle that would be ongoing into the twenty-first century.

In addition, by the 1850s, the economies of many Northern states had moved away from agriculture to favor industrialization through factory work. Many people in the North worked and lived in larger urban cities like Boston, New York, and Philadelphia. However, the Southern states continued to preserve a large agricultural economy, and this was based primarily on enslaved labor. While the North no longer needed outright bondage, the white South relied comprehensively upon the enslaved for their continued prosperity. This dilemma caused a great many Southerners to feel insecure about the potential loss of their livelihoods, if indeed enslavement was to be abolished. The tension between the Southern and Northern perspectives grew even stronger with the Dred Scott decision of 1857 and the John Brown Harpers Ferry rebellion of 1859. Nevertheless, clearly at the core of the South's concern was the continuation of their way of life with enslavement at the heart of the economy. Certainly the South depended on African Americans for their labor to produce the crops of cotton, tobacco, rice, and other commodities on plantations. Yet the growing abolitionist movement in the North was not going to be denied their quest for social justice. Simply put, the

Roger B. Taney (1777–1864), the son of plantation owners, served as the Chief Justice of the United States from March 1836 to October 1864. A staunch advocate for enslavement, he delivered the majority opinion in the Dred Scott Decision of 1857 that deemed African Americans non-citizens of the United States. (Library of Congress)

abolitionists wanted the enslavement of humans to be made illegal throughout the United States.

To further add to the angst of Southerners, the election of Abraham Lincoln in November 1860 brought forth the disintegration of the Union. Growing resentment reached a point whereby South Carolina seceded. Abraham Lincoln was a member of the new antislavery Republican Party and represented the death knell to the proslavery advocates. He also achieved the election victory without even being on the ballot in ten of the Southern states. They sensed that Lincoln was ultimately against the expansion of slavery and his politics were not for the Southern cause, even though he had never openly stated an abolitionist approach to the African American experience. Lincoln's main concern was always to keep the United States together; he was pro–United States and anti-secessionist. His priority was to ensure the continued and sustained development of the Union, not necessarily to end the long night of enslavement. The latter

---

ABRAHAM LINCOLN (1809–1865)

Abraham Lincoln was responsible for the Emancipation Proclamation that freed all enslaved African Americans that resided in rebellious states during the Civil War. He wrote the Proclamation in the September of 1862 and it came into existence on January 1, 1863. All enslaved would not be freed until the Thirteenth Amendment was ratified in April 1865. Yet, the Emancipation Proclamation would prove a death knell to the institution of slavery that had stained the moral fiber of the United States for almost 250 years. The long night of captivity and bondage was finally brought to an end through the Civil War. It is difficult to state the importance of President Lincoln because he oscillated in his opinion. Ultimately he did not want slavery to expand, but his prime objective was to save the Union from disintegrating. Historians differ over his moral standing in regard to the social status of African Americans. Clearly, he uttered words that deemed him unfavorable to the equal status and preferred ideally to have African Americans emigrate through the American Colonization Society (ACS). His wishes were proved to be ill thought as the likes of Frederick Douglass rightly contended that African Americans had helped build America and therefore had a right to its benefits. The assassination and death of President Lincoln on April 15, 1865, meant that history would not be able to tell how he would have embraced the social freedom of African Americans as it unfolded. His successor, President Andrew Johnson (1808–1875) proved to be an ally of the Southern racist elements and an enemy to African American liberation. He supported the Southern states that enacted the Black codes to curtail African American freedom and his support for white supremacy was implicit in all he did in office. Overall, Johnson is regarded as one of the worst presidents to hold office.

came as a consequence of the Civil War; it was not the main aim of Lincoln at the outset (Bennett 1999). This is not to disparage or belittle Abraham Lincoln, he was fundamentally a man who would do without enslavement, but he was also a politician endeavoring to navigate through extremely choppy political waters. The ebb and flow of those waters were dangerous, unpredictable, and inevitably would take his life before he could enjoy the benefits of his hard work to save the Union and abolish enslavement throughout the nation.

Frederick Douglass understood that Lincoln moved very slowly in his first years in office and that he even preferred African Americans to leave and find a home back in Africa under the American Colonization Society (ACS).

Abraham Lincoln served as President of the United States from 1861 to 1865. He was responsible for the Emancipation Proclamation of 1863 that freed enslaved African Americans in Confederate States. The 13th Amendment of 1865 finally abolished enslavement. (Library of Congress)

Lincoln ultimately, Frederick Douglass stated, "was preeminently the white man's president" (Blight 2018, 6). Though Douglass had respect for Lincoln's courage and legacy, he believed African Americans could not be deemed anything more than his unwanted "stepchildren" in the midst of a brewing civil war. This point is instructive because it encapsulates the essence of the African American experience of never quite belonging to the nation that brought them to its shores—forever the outsider striving to belong yet encountering resistance with each and every step toward establishing true liberty. The Civil War would prove to be an important step toward liberation, though it took a number of bloodshed years and almost seven hundred thousand American lives in the process.

As the Civil War developed, Virginia seceded on April 17, 1861; Booker T. Washington was just five years old and enslaved at the time. In his most famous autobiography, *Up from Slavery*, he writes, "Though I was a mere child during the preparation for the Civil War and during the war itself, I now recall the many late-at-night whispered discussions that I heard my mother and the other slaves on the plantation indulge in. These discussions showed that African Americans understood the situation, and that they kept themselves informed of events by what was termed the 'grape-vine' telegraph" (Washington 1986, 8). This gives a clear indication that Booker T. Washington's early life intersected with how his family embraced the advent and reality of the Civil War. The fact that the majority of African Americans were not allowed to learn to read or write did not stop them from finding ways to communicate. Regardless of the harsh realities of enslavement, those under its yoke found ways to survive and continue to create hope. Communication between enslaved peoples in the South came through movement between towns and plantations, through word of mouth, or through the house slaves taking in the conversations at the dinner table at the master's house. The degree to which a human being can find ways to cope with oppression is remarkable. One can only wonder how was it possible to keep faith in living when each day could force a family apart or engender a whipping for the most menial of transgressions. The sting of the lash for insubordination was a common cruelty during those times, and it was most often done in the presence of the entire enslaved plantation community in order to induce fear into their hearts and minds.

The Civil War brought the South to its knees economically when it concluded on April 9, 1865. Booker T. Washington had just turned nine years of age. With there being approximately four million newly freed African Americans needing sustenance, it was a time of great change for the nation. What would happen to his family? How would they survive? It was indeed a time of great anxiety mixed with the exhilaration, because to be free, truly free, was a human aspiration felt by all enslaved men and women. No human being will gladly suffer enslavement because there is something in all human spirits that wants to expand and to grow. This is the essence of what it is to be human from the moment of birth. However, having been born into a system that dehumanized one's being, it would have been difficult for many to adjust to a new way of living. It is akin to the prisoner who has been locked away for many years, even from birth, and then suddenly set free in one's twenties, thirties, or older. How does one cope? Well, this and the earlier questions were faced by the Washington family as the dawn of freedom arrived in 1865.

Less than a week after the end of the war, the nation had to come to grips with the assassination of President Abraham Lincoln. The Great Emancipator was held in esteem by African Americans. Many freed persons felt that their future looked ominous without the presence of

President Lincoln to guide the nation on a steady path toward reconciliation and unity. The immediate aftermath of the Civil War is regarded by historians as the Reconstruction Era. The reconstruction primarily included the rebirth of the Southern states that now included the freedom of four million souls. How would their freedom be integrated into the new South? What were the key problems that had to be faced? This was a short period "in the sun" for African Americans, and it lasted a mere twelve years from 1865 to 1877.

The Reconstruction Era is briefly defined as the age when the federal government intervened in the political and social affairs of the vanquished Southern states and attempted to redress the deep-rooted inequalities that were encountered by the newly emancipated African Americans. There were three key amendments to the Constitution that were aimed at securing citizenship rights for African Americans: the Thirteenth, Fourteenth, and Fifteenth Amendments. The Thirteenth Amendment abolished enslavement throughout the United States; the Fourteenth Amendment established citizenship irrespective of one's racial or past life in servitude; and finally, the Fifteenth Amendment granted to all citizens, regardless of racial heritage, the right to vote. However, and incredulously, it still left out women who could not exercise their freedom to vote for over a half century till 1920. Black women during and after enslavement, specifically, would continue to carry a heavy burden in their communities. It is an undeniable fact that the collective pain, agony, and emotional anguish felt by the women of African American heritage cannot be estimated. Booker T. Washington's mother, Jane Burroughs, is but one example of the untold stories of Black women that will be shared in the following chapter.

The Reconstruction period would be a time for optimism, and the Washington family, like all African Americans, had to find a way to embrace the new life experience of freedom from enslavement. There were newly elected African American officials to state legislatures, and schools were established by the Federal Freedman's Bureau, which oversaw the transition of four million souls from enslavement to freedom. Historians note that former African American Union soldiers who had fought in the war took education very seriously and flocked to school in order to learn to read and write (Kelley and Lewis 2000, 273). There were never enough schools supplied and maintained to cater to the ever-growing, and illiterate, African American population. Booker T. Washington would be a person to help fill the void in providing much-needed educational opportunities for his people in the Southern states, but this would be the period from the 1880s to 1915.

Because the era of Reconstruction was so short lived, lasting a mere twelve years at best, it did not provide enough material welfare for African Americans to get ahead in any meaningful way. As it has been pointed out, at the end of the Civil War, the masses of African Americans were "desperately poor, and poor in a way that we do not easily grasp today.... He was without clothes and without a home. He had no way to rent or build a home" (Du Bois 1992, 598). Food was scarce. They had to either beg for it or resort to theft of it; it was either this or starvation to death. Matters were made worse by new forms of law enforcement to keep the movement of African Americans stifled and without real freedom. Moreover, to use Alabama as an example, not long after the war ended, a law was enacted "making it illegal to sell, give or rent firearms or ammunition of any description to any freedman, free Negro or mulatto" (172). These kinds of laws sprung up during the initial years of "freedom" for African Americans and are largely hidden from history.

In particular, the introduction of "Black codes" by many Southern states between 1865 and 1866 curtailed African American mobility, freedom,

A free black man being sold to pay his fine, in Monticello, Florida, from *Frank Leslie's Illustrated Newspaper*, January 19, 1867. The sketch illustrates events which happened under the Black Codes, a series of laws passed by Southern states which imposed severe punishment upon African Americans who broke labor contracts, including being sold for up to one year's labor. Many Northerners considered it another form of slavery. (Library of Congress)

and physical movement from one location to another throughout the South (Kelley and Lewis 2000, 242). They could be arrested at whim if unable to produce valid documentation that proved their employment status. If found to be unemployed, they could be detained under a vagrancy law and put to work under a peonage system that had a person work until a "debt" had been paid. Effectively it was another form of enslavement that was employed by unscrupulous plantation owners to gain the free labor of African Americans. Based on the flimsiest of charges, an African American man or woman could lose their newfound freedom and be bound in debt or prison.

This system developed into an elaborate euphemism called "convict contract leasing" whereby anyone imprisoned from the post–Civil War era

---

BLACK CODES (1865–1866)

Sanctioned in 1865 and 1866, the laws were intended to substitute the social controls of enslavement that had been detached from the Constitution by the Emancipation Proclamation and the Thirteenth Amendment. The Black codes had their origins in the slave codes that had formerly been in effect to stifle the freedom of free African Americans during the era of enslavement from 1619 to 1865.

The Black codes were designed to intimidate African Americans. For example, they could not: change an employer without permission; ride freight cars without a ticket; consort with white women; if found to be loitering, they could be deemed a vagrant, which was illegal. Petty crime could lose one's freedom for life. Some African Americans were kidnapped and forced into labor campus by unscrupulous law men who created a "crime" in order to take the freedom of an African American.

Blackmon (2008) explains the system created by white Southerners to outwit the Northern Yankees after the Thirteenth Amendment was ratified. There was a constant threat to the limited freedom African Americans held in the early post–Civil War years. Once the Union Army left the Southern states in 1877 after Rutherford B. Hayes was elected president, the threat to African American freedom was evermore present. Labor was needed for the building of railroads, in mines, and on the former plantations. The Black codes effectively incarcerated many thousands, while ensuring millions of dollars of profit for these former Confederate states: Alabama, Mississippi, Louisiana, Georgia, Florida, Texas, North Carolina, and South Carolina (Blackmon, 2008, 8). This indicates the longevity of enforced labor that brought much wealth to those who instigated the system. It would take decades into the twentieth century before the Black codes were largely eliminated. To this day it is still for the most part a hidden history. Clearly, the Black codes is a profoundly disturbing chapter in the long legacy of involuntary servitude masked in supposed lawbreaking.

up to the onset of World War II (1941) could be exploited as cheap labor, which was no different than during the time of enslavement (Blackmon 2008, 7–10). Thousands of African Americans "freed" from enslavement fell into the convoluted crime traps of the Black codes that would inevitably take away their imperfect liberty. Moreover, the rise and fall of arrests and incarceration tended to coincide with the need for cheap labor in the Southern states' economy (Blackmon 2008, 7).

Though the enslavement era had endured for almost 250 years and was abolished with the Thirteenth Amendment, the Black codes, violence, and intimidation prevented African Americans from truly enjoying the pursuit of happiness and the American Dream. In 1866, the Ku Klux Klan (KKK) was established in Tennessee by an ex-Confederate soldier, Nathan B. Forrest (1821–1877). The KKK terrorized African Americans throughout the Southern states in order to suppress their voting opportunities and job prospects, preventing them from rising into more stable communities. Terror was the key to keeping them suppressed and disenfranchised. The aim ultimately was to restrict their power in society and to stifle any attempt in developing an economic foothold. The KKK specifically targeted those who supported the Republican Party, the party of Lincoln, and the Emancipation Proclamation. They specifically targeted African Americans and white schoolteachers who were the bedrock of educational opportunities through the Freedman's Bureau. Anyone who did not yield to white supremacy would be under fire and suffer many forms of intimidation or death itself (Kelley and Lewis 2000, 243).

The Reconstruction Era, while it engendered pockets of hope, also saw the rise of discrimination and bullying that forced many African Americans into other forms of servitude. To grapple with this history demands a level of critical thought that effectively challenges the simplistic narrative that "Lincoln freed the slaves" and the worst was then over for African Americans. This is fundamentally untrue. Life on the path to freedom was only just beginning. The Washington family were just one of thousands lost in a sea of poverty, insecurity, and an uncertain future. The reality of hardship would continue for millions of the formerly enslaved. It would take an ambitious leap of faith and be rather myopic to suggest that life was infinitely better in a materialist sense now that the system of enslavement was abolished. Certainly, on a psychological level it may have lifted the spirits of many, but on the physical level of day-to-day survival, the struggle was just beginning. Those millions who went on to raise families and eke out a life in the early years of freedom did so under great hardship and sacrifice. Long-held views of racism and superiority of the former masters did not abate; on the contrary, these opinions increased. Racism sustained in various forms, as did exploitation in terms of labor and its value to the white supremacists of the South (Du Bois 1992, 670).

The white Southerners had made immense profit from enslaved Africans, and they continued in unscrupulous ways to gain more revenue from their cheap labor after the Civil War ended, especially once the Union Army left the Southern states. Effectively the Southerners had a free reign to do as they pleased with the African Americans after 1877. White supremacy was firmly established after Reconstruction ended with the withdrawal of Federal troops after President Rutherford B. Hayes had compromised with the South's political elite. In doing so, he abandoned African Americans of the South who needed a strong arm protection from the federal government. The renowned historian, Rayford Logan, puts it succinctly: "White supremacy was more securely entrenched in the South when he [Rutherford B. Hayes] left the White House than it had been when he entered it" (Logan 1997, 35).

In briefly considering the historical backdrop to the life in which Booker T. Washington was born into in the mid-1850s, the reader should be able to gauge comfortably that this was not a pleasant time in the history of African Americans. In hindsight one can look back and ask "How could this have taken place?" or "How could humans be so cruel?" These questions are for the present and future generations to ponder. The task now is to consider the outset of Washington and his start in life. If we are to appreciate the human spirit and its longing to express itself unhindered by the vicissitudes of mental and physical oppression, then we are able to comprehend the visceral nature of existence. Each generation has, in some sense, built its foundation from the previous. We cannot ever in true conscience believe that "we stand alone" absent from the past. What has gone before can hold sway on the minds of the living without much hindrance. That is why biographies are more than useful in giving a glimpse into the past lives that weigh on the present like ghosts. Therefore, having a degree of insight into the period that led to Washington's birth and shaped his surroundings is more than a useful exercise in forming historical memory. Clearly, no other generation of Americans has had to endure the horror of enslavement and a civil war combined. In fact, it is likely that no future generation will have to experience such an inhumane set of circumstances. It was into these circumstances that Booker T. Washington was born, and they informed a life dedicated to the uplift and liberation of his people from ignorance, self-hatred, injustice, and poverty.

2

Childhood in Bondage and Hampton Institute

Booker T. Washington never knew the white man who was responsible for his birth. It is speculated that he worked on a nearby plantation and that he was a local man. Like the majority of African American boys and girls born into enslavement before Washington, there were merely vague notions of who impregnated the enslaved mothers. Sexual abuse or forced compliance was an everyday occurrence, and the life of an average enslaved woman was punctuated by the possibility of rape or unwanted attention from a white slaveholder, overseer, or a son of both.

Booker T. Washington, in his most noted autobiography *Up from Slavery*, did not know the exact year or date of his birth: "As nearly as I have been able to learn, I was born near a cross-roads post office called Hale's Ford, and the year was 1858 or 1859" (Washington 1986, 1). This confusion over birth years and dates were a significant certainty in the lives of the enslaved. Very few births were logged correctly by the impassive slaveholders. Indeed, they would ordinarily deem the enslaved as property, akin to the possession of a horse or a cow. The historical name for this form of an asset is "chattel"—or the ownership of property other than real estate.

Biographers have since largely agreed that Washington was born in the spring of 1856 (Harlan 1972, 3; Mathews 1948, 3). However, those connected to the Booker T. Washington family estate and legacy have taken April 5, 1856, as his official birthdate. Apparently this date was supplied on the testimony of Booker's older brother, John; he testified having seen the birthdate in an old Burroughs family Bible. Moreover, the birthdate of April 5, 1856, was then adopted by the estate of Booker T. Washington posthumously (Harlan 1972, 325). The conundrum of piecing together the history of a formerly enslaved historical figure is commonplace in slave narratives. For example, the renowned African American abolitionist Frederick Douglass (1818–1895) did not know his exact date of birth either. For decades historians thought of it being somewhere in 1817, but archivists later found a ledger stating he had been born in the month of February 1818 (Blight 2018, 9); as with Booker T. Washington, the precise day and time of his birth is still somewhat of a mystery. This was the reality for the majority of enslaved African Americans during the era of enslavement. A family could also be torn asunder at the whim of the master. Indeed, many enslaved families were often separated and individual members sold off to other plantations near and far. No provision was allowed for the feelings of the closest relatives to the person being sold to another plantation. It was no different from selling a horse or any piece of property to the highest bidder. It was just business, and the human aspect was not a consideration. The emotional trauma involved in such brutal separations was unfathomable.

However, Washington was fortunate to have contact with his mother from birth up to her death in 1874, when he was eighteen years old. His mother's name was Jane Burroughs, and along with her children, John, Booker, and Amanda, she was owned by a slaveholder, John Burroughs. Jane's sons, John and Booker, were both considered fatherless. Amanda was likely the offspring of a local enslaved man named Washington Ferguson, whom Jane would later marry. The plantation they lived on was relatively small in size compared to the many larger ones in the vicinity, with a total of ten enslaved African Americans. The plantation was located near Hale's Ford, Franklin County, Virginia, in the Blue Ridge Mountain region. The proprietor, James Burroughs, and his wife Elizabeth Burroughs were more akin to a farming couple. Their social backgrounds did not suggest an aristocratic way of life, like that of the larger stereotypical plantation owner depicted in movies like *Gone with the Wind* (1939). They appeared to have been in the mold of farm-like settlers in terms of social class, much like yeoman farmers (Harlan 1972, 6). Yet they were slave owners who invested in the system of enslavement, and according to their inventory, the Burroughses had invested quite a lot of money into the ten African Americans they held in bondage. The inventory from the Burroughs estate of 1861 is instructive in terms of depicting how enslaved African Americans were valued, and it also indicates the smaller-sized plantation that Booker T. Washington grew up on. Washington's worth was calculated at $400 in 1861 (an adjusted inflation rate of $400 in 1861 is worth over $12,000 in

2020). Besides Booker, the inventory states the names and values of the other listed enslaved persons from the Burroughs plantation as follows:

1 negro man (Munroe)	$600
1 negro woman (Sophia)	$250
1 negro woman (Jane)	$250
1 negro man (Lee)	$1,000
1 negro boy (Green)	$800
1 negro girl (Mary Jane)	$800
1 negro girl (Sally)	$700
1 negro boy (John)	$550
1 negro boy (Booker)	$400
1 negro girl (Amanda)	$200

The preceding inventory forms a glimpse of what is known of the Burroughs estate (Harlan 1972, 8). Jane Burroughs's history is rather vague in terms of her entire background, but it is recorded that her age was forty in 1860 and that she was married to Washington Ferguson, who was from a neighboring plantation and enslaved. There is no definitive evidence of Jane's parentage other than she may have also been the product of a nearby tobacco factory owner who hired enslaved men and women for labor on his plantation (Harlan 1972, 5).

The cabin that Jane and her children occupied was about fourteen by sixteen feet in size, with a dilapidated door that hung precariously on damaged hinges. For windows, there were merely openings in the walls, with no glass cover to guard from the elements. The family huddled on the dirt floor for whatever comfort they could muster. In the center of the cabin floor, James Burroughs had dug a large hole, covered by wooden slats that stored sweet potatoes for his house. During the summer, the temperature could be unbearable, with the external and internal heat combined due to the large furnace used for the purpose of cooking. Likewise, the winter brought draughts of cold wind from all areas of cabin, while the burning furnace then converted into a source of much-needed warmth compared to its unwanted heat in the sweltering summers.

In his autobiography, Washington describes summertime being of intense heat due to the constant cooking that Jane necessarily had to perform to keep the plantation folks fed. He further explains that he and his siblings "slept in and on a bundle of filthy rags laid up the dirt floor," describing how he never slept in a proper bed during his first nine years of life as an enslaved boy, and he had no recollection of ever sleeping in a clean bed during his upbringing (Washington 1986, 5). Again, this indicates a very harsh environment for a young child to endure, but it was the norm for the majority of enslaved persons.

Jane cooked for the Burroughses' household anytime they wanted food, and she also had the responsibility of feeding the enslaved on the plantation, usually corn and pork. She spent many long hours of the day toiling under the worst conditions and with a distinct lack of adequate cooking equipment. She was up before dawn and was not able to concentrate on her family's needs until late in the evening. Her life was unbearably harsh; as a single parent on the plantation, she had to take care of her three young offspring under the most rigid of conditions. The Burroughses' demand on her time also meant that she unintentionally neglected her own children. Indeed, her children had to fend for themselves during the daylight hours while their mother cooked meals for the entire plantation. The meals for her own family consisted largely of leftover scraps from the slaveholder's household meals.

By character, Jane was a very kind and affectionate person, full of love for her children, as best as she could offer it. As Booker recalls, "The early years of my life, which were spent in the little cabin, were not very different from those of thousands of other slaves. My mother, of course, had little time in which to give attention to the training of her children during the day" (Washington 1986, 4). Understandably, there is the inevitable impression of maternal neglect due to the harmful reality of a system that encouraged it. Yet, it could have been far worse if they had been separated or sold off, as were many thousands of enslaved under the peculiar institution.

As a young enslaved boy of about seven years, Booker T. Washington was already experiencing the harsh conditions of enslavement. In his autobiography, he explains his experience of carrying corn every week to a mill about three miles from the plantation on horseback. This task brought on great anxiety for the young child because he had to carry a bag of corn heavier than himself and balanced on the rear end of a horse. On each journey, it was inevitable that the corn would slide off the horse due to the uneven weight. With the corn being far too heavy for him to place back on the horse, he would have to wait for a kindly passer-by to aid him. Often it would take hours for someone to come by, and the time spent waiting brought tears to his eyes and fear to his heart. He knew as time passed that he would have to explain his tardiness to the master and that this could lead to a severe scolding or flogging. Also, he dreaded the trek back to the plantation from the mill in the dark of night. The road back to the plantation was lonely, and the woods were replete with soldiers who had deserted the war. There were stories of African Americans having their ears cut off by deserters, and young Washington feared the same fate as he traveled outside of the plantation on errands (Washington 1986, 6).

The closest Washington got to being educated in his first ten years was to carry the school books of the master's children on their way to school.

Booker hungered for schooling even at this very young age, as he peered through the schoolhouse door watching the lesson. As he puts it, "The picture of several dozen boys and girls in a schoolroom engaged in study made a deep impression upon me, and I had the feeling that to get into a schoolhouse and study in this way would be about the same as paradise" (Washington 1986, 7). He had a clear appetite for learning. During this period of enslavement, thousands of African American children were not allowed to read or write, or to engage in any form of education. Those who did manage to learn to read and write surreptitiously were the exception to the rule. They also did so at great peril to their lives, for if it were found out by the slaveholder, they could be severely physically punished, maimed, or even killed. As a child, Booker did not realize the depth of this reality; he merely wanted to learn, and it was a burning fire inside his mind and soul at a very young age. Nothing could dim the passion he held for an education, and to him it was akin to paradise to be able to study and become literate.

Despite a lack of formal schooling, Washington was a perceptive child and one who soaked up everything around him. For instance, he recalls never having sat down with his family at a table for a meal together in a civilized manner. Booker states, "On the plantation in Virginia, and even later, meals were gotten by the children very much as dumb animals get theirs. It was a piece of bread here and a scrap of meat there" (Washington 1986, 9). He remembers that the enslaved human beings all ate rather like animals, scavenging for scraps of food haphazardly. When he had grown in size to take orders, aged five years onward, he was told to go to the "Big House" at mealtimes to fan away flies from the master's dinner table. The fan was operated by a pulley, and he was there at the intimate times when the Burroughs family ate their meals. Booker took in the table conversations, and he soaked it up; he was a child who had deep perception and precocity, especially when the topic turned to freedom and the war updates. He absorbed, matured, and grew beyond his tender years, while toiling with aching arms at the master's table.

During these sessions in fanning away flies from the meal table of the master's house, Booker's mouth watered at the thought of eating the ginger cakes on display. He vowed to himself that if he ever gained his freedom, one of the first things he would do is to secure and eat a ginger cake (Washington 1986, 10). The experience gave Booker an insight into how whites lived, ate, and conversed over dinner. He witnessed another world that was completely separate from the lives of the enslaved. And the meals were far outside the average diet of the enslaved, which, on a fortunate day, was usually the leftover corn bread and pork. Booker witnessed an array of food on the table, and a seed was planted in his mind that this could one day be his experience too. Now and then his mother would surreptitiously bring something back from the Big House that had not been eaten or had been partially consumed to share with her children.

Booker did not have a pair of shoes until he was about six years of age. His first pair were wooden at the base, with a rough piece of leather on the top. They were cumbersome and noisy to wear that created, what he considered, a self-consciousness in his appearance. Yet the most awful aspect of clothing he wore when enslaved was a flax shirt. A very rough material that scratched his bare skin. Most enslaved persons had to wear such material as clothing. It was cheap and common attire that Washington had no choice but to put on. There was simply nothing else to put on, and he had no power in the matter anyway. His elder brother, John, to limit his suffering, would wear in any new shirt to keep his younger brother from having to endure too much skin irritation. Washington never forgot the generosity of his elder brother and spoke highly of him throughout his lifetime. This is also true of his younger sister, Amanda, who was close to both her brothers throughout her life. In addition, not long after enslavement was abolished in 1865, Jane took in a young boy who was an orphan, naming him James B. Washington and adding him to her family. Though poor, Jane still had the heart and mind to take in another child who would have surely perished had she not (Washington 1986, 37).

Washington's first awareness of potential emancipation and the freedoms that might come with it arrived when his mother awakened him early one morning. That day, Jane huddled her three children together and prayed ardently for Abraham Lincoln's armies to be victorious. This had an indelible impression on six-year-old Booker, who could not fathom how the enslaved were able to keep up with the knowledge of the war if indeed so many were illiterate. He did not comprehend at such a young age the power of the African griot tradition whereby communication came from word of mouth, drums, and the stories of thousands of runaways and abolitionists. There were many underground resisters to enslavement, African American and Euro-American, who detested the institution. Many fought hard for the end of enslavement, so it is not surprising that word got to Booker's mother and surrounding plantations regarding the circumstances and pace of the war. As he stated, "Even the most ignorant members of my race on the remote plantations felt in their hearts, with a certainty that admitted of no doubt, that the freedom of the slaves would be the one great result of the war, if the Northern armies conquered" (Washington 1986, 8). Often the mail also carried news with it, and the task of collecting mail usually fell to an enslaved man, who gathered it from the post office. Ordinarily he would hear news about the war from the discussions at the post office, from newspapers, and other forms of communication stumbled on. The phrase "I heard it through the grapevine," made famous by a Marvin Gaye song, comes from the days of enslavement. The grapevine is a person-to-person communication system that passed on gossip and other news until the word of an incident becomes common knowledge among the community in question. This is often how the enslaved public thirsting for freedom heard about their chances of securing it.

Though cruel and unforgiving as enslavement was, Booker T. Washington insists that he bore no ill will toward white people. He writes in a manner that is akin to an interracial interpreter trying to heal wounds and create an understanding toward his background and that of the enslavers. He writes, "During the Civil War one of my young masters was killed, and two were severely wounded. I recall the feeling of sorrow which existed among the slaves when they heard of the death of 'Mars' Billy. It was no sham sorrow, but real" (Washington 1986, 12). From his recollection, the white boy Billy had been gracious on the plantation and often begged for mercy if one of the enslaved were to be flogged or punished. In other words, he had a kind heart and tried whenever he could to ease the burdensome life of the African Americans on his father's plantation.

Washington tends to recollect with tenderness the time when two other white boys from the slaveholder's family came back injured from the war, and it appears incredulous in retrospection. He states that the enslaved would feel sorrowful and "even beg for the privilege of sitting up at night to nurse their wounded masters" (Washington 1986, 13). While the Civil War was taking place to end enslavement, on Booker T. Washington's plantation, the enslaved were vying over who could take care of the wounded masters of the Big House and help nurse them back to health. Washington explains that this was merely because these young white boys were kindly to the enslaved. There is something rather poignant about this reality, that even during the worst kind of cruelty in making one human being a piece of property, those under its evil can find the humanity to still find sorrow in the plight of the slave master and his offspring. In hindsight, the production of his autobiography, and the manner in which he employed it back in 1901 and later as a fundraiser among white philanthropists, makes this aspect of his life on the plantation rather skeptical. Indeed, it is a rare occurrence to have enslaved African Americans mourn the slave master or his offspring. Maybe Washington wanted to show his readers that he held not one iota of bitterness toward whites. In this regard, he knew that it would be a strategy to disarm and allow for friendship. He grew to be a very shrewd man who maneuvered in territorial political waters. He tells a story of enslavement that does not yield to bitterness or rancor. As would become clear, he was certainly not a man who held animosity toward anyone, even though he had to in later years find ways to combat those who wanted him to fail in his work and institutional building.

When freedom finally arrived in 1865, the certainty of it all came as an overwhelming reality. What would they do now, and where would they go?

How would they survive, and where would they live? The songs of freedom, spirituals that the enslaved often sung, now had a greater significance. Freedom was no longer a fantasy, as Washington writes about his people, "Now they gradually threw off the mask, and were not afraid to let it be known that the 'freedom' in their songs meant freedom of the body in this world" (Washington 1986, 20). There was great responsibility now on the shoulders of the emancipated. This had to be thought through and planned carefully, and no enslaved person had ever had to do such. There was something frightening about freedom that could not be explained easily. Washington puts it this way: "It was very much like suddenly turning a youth of ten or twelve years out into the world to provide for himself" (21). This was his feeling about the end of enslavement and what now faced his family and his people in general. For his mother, it was simply a matter of keeping the Washington family together, and all else would fit into place as time would permit.

By 1865, Jane had married Washington Ferguson, the stepfather of her two boys, and the likely father of her youngest, Amanda. He lived on a neighboring plantation but could only visit them about once a year. But when the war began, he ran off and made his way to the new state of West Virginia. There he set up a home and was working in the salt mines in Malden, about five miles from the state's capital, the city of Charleston in West Virginia.

As soon as freedom had been acknowledged, Washington Ferguson sent for Jane and the children to join him in Malden. The journey over mountainous terrain with only a cart and a few household items was arduous for the family. They lacked food, and their clothing was inadequate, yet they persevered, knowing that their long-term freedom compensated for any short-term struggle. The trek took several hundred miles and was largely done by walking. Eventually they reached their destination in the center of the salt mines of the small town. Washington Ferguson had already secured employment in the salt mines. However, the cabin he had for his newfound family was not much better than the one they had occupied on the plantation in Virginia. Freedom may have been provided by the Thirteenth Amendment, but poverty and hardship remained in their lives and in those of the former four million enslaved souls. The area in which the Washington home lay was in the midst of a group of cabins. The stench was often unbearable, as the area had no sanitary rules. It was a poverty-stricken community with all the vices that are usually associated: gambling, prostitution, brawling, and criminality. On top of the hardship, the mother had taken in James, the young orphan. The fact that his mother took in this child, having three other children to feed, is again testimony to her kind heartedness that Washington always referred to in his references to her.

Booker Taliaferro Washington took his last name from his stepfather, and his first two names were given to him by his mother. The last names of enslaved African Americans usually followed the line of the slaveholder. Renaming, or the adding of names to one's persona, was a common occurrence after emancipation. Booker T. Washington was the name henceforth of the once enslaved boy who would grow up to be a famous man and a leader of his people. The meaning behind his first two names deserves some explanation. An early biographer, Basil Mathews, put forward the theory that the name Booker is akin to a Nigerian Muslim name "Bukar" and that it derives from the first Caliph of Islam, who succeeded Mohammed, Abu-Bakr. Mathews (1948, 5) argues that it is a very common name in that area of West Africa. It is known that many African words crossed the Atlantic with the millions of African souls that were captured and brought to the Americas. It is feasible that "Bukar" became "Booker" in the cross-fertilization of cultures. Africans who came in bondage were not empty vessels; they carried with them culture, intelligence, skills, emotions, and ideas. Africans retained words too, and symbolism; they were strong peoples from various African cultures. It is a theory of naming that makes a great amount of sense.

The fact that millions of Africans survived the horrors of the middle passage and the day-to-day assaults on their humanity is testimony to their collective will power. Too often the Africans that were brought specifically to North America are described in monolithic terms as if Africa is merely a country and not the vast continent it actually is. In point of fact, on African retentions, the renowned anthropologist Melvin Herskovits's book *The Myth of the Negro Past* (1941) argues that many African cultural retentions remained in the culture of African Americans long after they had settled in the United States. He countered the argument that Africans lost all their cultural heritage within the enslavement experience. Naming was just one aspect of African cultural retention, and it is highly possible that the name Booker is in some way related to the Nigerian name Bukar, as the pronunciation is exact. Apparently his second name, Taliaferro, was a name his mother gave him soon after he was born and then dropped. It belonged to a white man living on a local plantation. His mother may have been forced to give up the second name or at least keep it clandestine, hence the Booker T. This gives another indication that his biological father was a local white man who had a brief encounter(s) with his mother. It is more than likely that the meeting would have been one of force rather than consensual. African American women in bondage were extremely vulnerable to the advances of the slaveholder and those connected. Any white man could take the innocence from an African American woman in such an oppressive environment.

Once Booker's family settled into Malden, Washington Ferguson put Booker and his brother John to work alongside him in the salt mines. Though difficult and involving many hours of labor per day, it is in this capacity that Booker's world opened up slowly to the possibilities of learning to read. This feeling began to grow more fervent in his mind, and his main ambition then, as a boy of ten years, was to be able to read newspapers. Yet he could not in his present predicament find a way to learn how to read, as his surroundings did not allow for such a notion to become a reality. No African American around him could read; his mother and siblings were illiterate, along with his stepfather. Education did not come easy; his stepfather would not allow schooling, because he needed to draw as much income from the labor of his two sons. Booker first worked in the salt mine, which he could endure even though it was arduous from 4:00 a.m. until early evening. He was soon moved to the coalmine that provided fuel for the salt-furnace. He dreaded this labor because of the dirt, danger, and difficulty in cleaning oneself after work had finished. It was also dark and dismal inside the coalmine, which was divided into sections. The months spent in the coalmine gave him the fuel to work as hard as he could so never to experience such arduous toil again. He also learned that one should only measure success not by the position one has reached in life but instead by the impediments one has overcome and endured to gain success. As a young boy he was developing a philosophy for life akin to the Horatio Alger tales, those that spoke of the rags-to-riches lives of young boys who lived impoverished lives but rose to be secure in a middle-class lifestyle.

As mentioned earlier, one of the central aspects in his personality was the absence of bitterness. Washington never held onto anything that would disturb his ability to get ahead in achieving his goals. He believed in hard work and sacrifice, never giving in to negative thought that would inevitably hinder his energy and focus. Moreover, there is nothing in his utterances of his past that speak to not having pride in his African American heritage. He was a man who wanted the best for his people—yet he harbored no ill will toward whites. This aspect of his life is rather commendable given the harshness of his upbringing (21). His ambition to receive an education never waned; his mother knew he was passionate about it too. In her tenderness and limited resources, she did all she could to not cloud the mental sky of her child. She managed to get hold of a basic spelling book, which Booker cherished and was determined to master. He vowed to be able to read what was in books and newspapers, as they held a special kind of magic in his mind (27).

His stepfather finally gave in to the gentle persuasion of Booker's mother, and the boy was allowed to attend school in the evenings after he had finished his work in the mine. It was far from easy, but it was a good first step on the journey of a thousand miles. Washington made the most of the slight elementary education he received by continuing to soak up the messages around him that spoke of a larger world. While working in the coalmine, he overheard two miners discussing the reputation of a great school for African Americans somewhere in Virginia. His ears tingled, and he got closer to the chatter in the dismal surroundings of the cold and damp mine. Apparently it was a school for deprived souls of his heritage set up after the Civil War by the Freedman's Bureau to assist the newly emancipated. Hampton Normal and Agricultural Institute was the school. Booker was disturbed with inner excitement at the thought of such an institution. He vowed there and then to find out where it was and how he could find a way to make it there. The thought of an education at Hampton haunted him day and night after listening to those two miners. The work in the mine continued on for a few more months, but the idea of going to a school for his people never left him. It developed into a private obsession as he thought about a future that took him away from the dreariness of his present predicament.

While working one day, he heard of a job vacancy available from the coalmine proprietor, General Lewis Ruffner, and his wife was from the North, or a "Yankee" as they described her back then in West Virginia (43). They were looking for a new servant to work in the house as a cleaner. Disregarding her reputation in being a rather severe task master, especially with young boys, young Washington considered anything would be better than his current occupation. He asked his mother to put his name forward, and he was accepted for the house servant position. The salary was five dollars per month. Due to her strict reputation as a stern woman with no time for foolishness, he shivered with nerves in her presence. After a few weeks he worked out her psychological nature better and learned her likes and dislikes. Mrs. Ruffner was a stickler for tidiness and kept everything neatly in its place. She was an orderly freak, and anything out of its place would create a storm of annoyance. Everything had to be right; no dust or disrepair would be tolerated. Booker recalls being in the employment of Mrs. Ruffner for about eighteen months (44). He learned the art of cleanliness and puritanism. He credits her for his orderliness and intolerance of litter and uncleanliness. She passed on the lesson of personal hygiene that stuck with him as he prepared for a life in education. Indeed, while being a house servant, he spent part of his time attending school, mainly in the evenings after all his chores had been completed. He hired anyone who could teach him something about reading or math. Mrs. Ruffner was sympathetic to his ambition in achieving an education. He speaks of developing his first home library and collecting books while working under her watchful eyes.

In 1872, at age sixteen, without genuine support for his idea to go to Hampton, he set out with a few dollars on a journey into the unknown. His mother was always supportive of her son's ambition, but in his reflection of the time, he felt she thought it being a "wild goose chase" traveling so far to

Hampton. Her health was very poorly at the time of his departure, and he wondered if ever he would see his mother again. With all this angst in his mind, he ventured into the unknown on his quest for a formal education. Not having enough money for the entire journey, he was only able to catch a train from the Charleston station. This was the newly built Chesapeake and Ohio Railroad, which took him only half way toward his Hampton destination. The entire journey was approximately five hundred miles; after the train journey, he took a stagecoach through the mountain terrain. As it stopped for the evening break, the white passengers were ushered to a hotel for recuperation until daybreak, but Washington was not allowed in due to his African American heritage (47). Cold, hungry, tired, and broke, he lingered around the area until daybreak. The next day he continued his journey on foot, catching the odd ride from a kind-hearted spirit until he reached Richmond completely exhausted. The smell of food from the stands only made matters worse, as he could not afford to buy anything to eat. This was a test of his endurance, and it would not be the last. He was still about eighty miles short of Hampton Institute, so weary that he had to spend another night in the cold, sheltering under a boardwalk (49).

The following morning he spotted a ship unloading its cargo and asked the captain if he could earn some money for food. Fortunately he was able to secure temporary labor unloading pig iron for the Richmond foundries. He recalls being able to eat a hearty breakfast, which he regarded the best he had ever eaten in his young life. He lost count of the days he worked unloading, and to save his pay he continued to sleep under the boardwalk he had commandeered. After a few days he thanked the captain for his kindness and set out to complete his journey (50).

It is difficult to imagine what would have happened to him had the universe not opened up the opportunity for him to earn some money for food and to carry on his trek to Hampton Institute.

He eventually arrived at Hampton dirty, disheveled, and in need of a shave and wash—not a sight for a head teacher, Miss Mary Mackie, who looked at the ragged youth with hesitation and doubt. He hung around for a few hours while she admitted other, more respectable looking, students. Washington recalls being asked by her to clean a classroom and that he felt that it was a do-or-die situation, his entry exam. He dug deep into the training received at the Ruffners' household and cleaned that room as if it was his very last hope in life. Miss Mary Mackie came in to inspect his janitorial skills, wiping a handkerchief across tables and benches checking for dust; he passed the test. Feeling like he had reached the Promised Land, Washington embarked on his three years of education at Hampton Institute (53). He largely paid for his tuition through his role as janitor; clearly he impressed as an efficient and reliable "house boy" in the company of whites. Indeed, his experience on the plantation, and in the Ruffners' household, and now at Hampton Institute led to one key learning outcome: how to please white people. It was an invaluable lesson in the life he would lead, because a man of color in the South had to walk like a fox on ice in order to survive. Any sign of being "uppity" could have dire consequences for an educated African American male specifically. If learning the art of diplomacy in putting whites at ease was a necessity, then Booker T. Washington had earned a doctorate in it by the time he graduated from Hampton Institute. It was also here that he met a white man whom he would idolize as a mentor and possibly as a subconscious father figure (Harlan 1972).

General Samuel Chapman Armstrong (1839–1893) was the founding principal of Hampton Normal and Agricultural Institute. He was a thirty-three-year-old general from the Union Army and one of the youngest in his rank.

As the founder of the Hampton Institute, American Civil War veteran Samuel Chapman Armstrong (1839–1893) made an important contribution to the education of both African Americans and Native Americans. His school served as a model for others, including the Tuskegee Institute, started by his most famous pupil, African American leader Booker T. Washington. (Library of Congress)

He was born to a Christian, Presbyterian, missionary family. His initial encounter with the young Washington was impactful; he writes about General Armstrong being "a great man—the noblest, rarest human being that it has ever been my privilege to meet" (54). This is high praise, and it endured throughout his life; he never waned from his devotion to his mentor. Harlan (1972, 58–59) alludes to the relationship being paternal, with Washington subconsciously adopting General Armstrong as a surrogate father, the male parent he had never known. The sad part about this is the fact that Armstrong was fundamentally a racist who believed in the inferiority of people of color. Harlan cites a journal article written by Armstrong depicting the need to bring morality and character to those from "the weak tropical races." Crucially, at best, young

Washington found a person who could nurture his morality and character for hard work, thrift, and discipline. But ingrained in this relationship was a deeply rooted paternalism that tends to be a propensity in many white liberals. One can understand, possibly, the impression this man had on a young African American male trying to secure an education. Clearly, he would not have comprehended the depth of psychological harm such paternalism could do to an individual and his or her self-confidence. Yet, Washington at this stage in life had an understanding that whites held the power. They had the prerogative on how things were to be organized and run. He was poorly educated at this time and was desperate to succeed in gaining an education. General Armstrong would no doubt have been encouraged to witness his paternalistic methods being accepted and imbedded in a young man who would become his star pupil at Hampton Institute over the next three years, from 1872 to 1875.

What is important to consider in this scenario relates to the basic relationship between "good whites" and people of color in their quest for human dignity. On reflection, from the standpoint of the twenty-first century's third decade, what Washington experienced does not particularly empower young African American males of today, or even generations prior. Why? Fundamentally, if we are considering the essence of growth into African American manhood that respects oneself as a man of worth, one cannot embrace what paternalism promotes: an inferiority complex. White liberals have a massive impact on the empowerment of people of color in society; they had it in the time of Washington, and it is prevalent today. A majority of school teachers still tend to be white and middle class. This was the same situation that Washington encountered in the nineteenth century. In Armstrong he saw what he considered to be the "noblest"

GENERAL SAMUEL CHAPMAN ARMSTRONG (1839–1893)

General Armstrong, the son of missionaries, was raised in Hawaii. He joined the Union Army and rose quickly in the ranks from colonel to general during the Civil War, and he commanded the 8th Colored Infantry Regiment. After the war he worked for the Freedman's Bureau and established Hampton Normal and Industrial Institute (now Hampton University) in 1868. This was originally a vocational school that taught newly freed African Americans, and later American Indians, trade skills and discipline with a heavy dose of ascetic Christianity. Armstrong would become Booker T. Washington's mentor when he joined the Institute in 1872. Washington spoke very highly of Armstrong's impact on his life and his values as an educator. For instilling a disciplined approach to life and the building of character Washington largely gives Armstrong credit.

of humanity. Yet we know through archival evidence that General Armstrong was a man who considered Washington a social inferior, and not in his image. That is a hard pill to swallow when one reflects on how deeply devoted Washington was to the man whom he deemed so highly.

In a sense, Washington was admiring the missionary zeal of men like General Armstrong. To be sure there was a distinct need for men and women of good conscience to aid the suffering of the millions freed from bondage. Yet, paternalism also impedes mental progress and an ability to lift oneself up from the quagmire of racialized discrimination. In *Up from Slavery* his account of General Armstrong borders on fanatical delusion. He writes on his admiration for him, "General Armstrong . . . was but a type of that Christlike body of men and women who went into Negro schools at the close of the war by hundreds in lifting up my race" (57–58). In hindsight, if one considers such an attitude as General Armstrong's, is it empowering to have such missionary zeal absorbing the mind of a young African American male? Even if we step into 1872 and imagine the situation objectively, it is one of inferior-superior relations. Washington was a sixteen-year-old who was grateful to any kind of assistance and was willing to accept that white people, according to his psyche, at that time were superior. He had been conditioned to understand how to inculcate a genuine admiration as long it benefited his uplift. One could deem this form of adulation as misconceived due to the dire condition Washington found himself, which was close to destitute. He viewed Armstrong as a savior, not a racist who believed in the superiority/inferiority of human beings.

The irony in this, however, is the indisputable fact that Washington was very proud of his racial heritage. He would not have changed this even if he could, and that is also the importance of his life. He understood that his people were in a lowly social status due to the evils of enslavement, but he did not view this as a long-term situation. For him it was about getting "up from it" and not allowing the past to keep one in this predicament. Some would call this wishful thinking and somewhat naive, but the fact of the matter is that it worked for him and he proved that one could rise from a lowly status and achieve incredible success. At Hampton Institute, he learned in his role as a janitor by being around the teachers and, of course, by studying the manner, style, and deportment of Armstrong. Washington's precociousness was able to fully bloom as he absorbed the ideas of what came down to learning a puritanical Christianity. The curriculum at Hampton Institute consisted of both academic and vocational training infused with religion for moral grounding. There was an emphasis on learning a trade in order to give students a means of earning a living once they left and entered society. Washington developed a habit of reading the Bible daily for inspiration and spiritual guidance. He also found it a useful text in developing one's knowledge of literature and how to express oneself in an erudite manner. He wore secondhand clothing and barely survived the costs of staying in the school, but with the help of Armstrong and others he developed into the kind of student they would be proud of: a sober minded and emotionally sensitive African American.

During breaks in the academic year, students would leave Hampton Institute to go back to their homes for summer, but Washington was too poor and could not afford the expense. These were times when he would become a tad homesick for his family and community in Malden. He was one of the youngest students at Hampton Institute during his time there, and he states that some were as old as forty years of age (61). Therefore being young was both a blessing and a curse. Being youthful he absorbed knowledge quickly, but having no economic wherewithal it did not allow for an ability to travel easy. So he spent every spare hour studying and preparing himself for the future. The school days were twelve hours in duration at Hampton Institute, with the students rising at 5:00 a.m. to clean, make up beds, and prepare breakfast. Then it was time for classes for academic and vocational training. The school intake grew exponentially during the time Washington was there that they had to extend the dormitories by erecting tents. As an obedient student, Washington volunteered to sleep in one of the tents, though the winters proved extremely harsh with the cold winds drafting through the gaps in the tent. It was in all senses a boot camp led by a former Civil War general who espoused a Christian philosophy and practice akin to the Protestant Ethic (Weber 1992).

In 1875, he graduated as valedictorian. Three years had been well spent under the missionary zeal of Armstrong and his faculty; Washington had immense respect for the methods employed at Hampton Institute, and it would be the model of education that he would later develop at Tuskegee Institute. It is difficult to estimate the extent to which Washington imbibed the lessons he took from studying under Armstrong. Evidently, there developed mutual respect between the two over the years. Armstrong went out of his way to support the young Washington, whom he saw as the ideal Hampton Institute graduate. However, Armstrong's key role as the son of missionaries was to make his formerly enslaved charges as close to the white Christian as possible in nature and disposition.

A year before his graduation, Washington's mother passed away after suffering from ill health for a long time. He wrote in *Up from Slavery*, "This seemed to me the saddest and blankest moment in my life" (70). He loved his mother dearly, and one of his ambitions was for her to live long enough to benefit from his success. This was not to be, and he had to shoulder the grief of losing her in such a manner for the rest of his life. One of his mother's greatest wishes was to see her children educated and doing well in the new world of freedom—it was not to be. With the death of his mother, he returned to Malden to teach after his graduation. He worked hard in the community, developing both night and day classes as well as Sunday school hours. He was a young and eager teacher, and he developed a number of local protégés who were eventually sent on to Hampton Institute. He did not charge if a student could not afford an individual lesson; he basically survived on a small fund raised by the town for him being the "public-school teacher" (76).

In 1877, which coincides with the ending of the Reconstruction Era, Washington witnessed the Ku Klux Klan (KKK) intimidating freedmen to not exercise their right to vote. Schoolhouses and churches were burned to the ground if it was known that meetings were taking place to mobilize community politics. Washington admits that these acts of violence made a deep impression on him as a young man. He recalls one encounter that can be deemed a "race riot" where up to a hundred African Americans faced the hatred of the KKK and its followers who had turned out in a similar number. He saw General Ruffner trying to defend the "colored people" against the mob and being seriously injured in the process (78). This kind of violence upset the young Washington, and he only brings it up in 1901, the time of his writing, because the KKK was disbanded by then. He viewed it as a bygone day of violence against African American communities. Sadly, he would be proved wrong, as there was a revival of the KKK in the 1920s and its members even marched down Pennsylvania Avenue and passed in front of the White House in August 1925.

Ku Klux Klan (KKK)

The Ku Klux Klan was a white supremacist organization formed in the aftermath of the Civil War in 1865/6. A former Confederate general, Nathan B. Forrest was elected the first Grand Wizard (overall leader) in 1868. The purpose of this group was to intimidate African Americans in the South and restore the power lost to white Southerners due to the abolition of enslavement. Their tactics were based on violence, arson, and lynching in order to drive fear into the hearts and minds of African American communities. They wore hoods to hide their identities, as many of the members were prominent citizens of towns and cities across the South. The KKK also targeted Jewish people, Catholics, and any liberal minded person who fought for social justice along racial lines. The organization waned for some years but there was a revival in the 1920s, culminating with a massive rally in Washington, D.C., in 1925. The aims and objectives remained the same: to maintain white supremacy over people of color and to end Jewish and Catholic impact in American society. There are many ironies, but a glaring one is that the KKK regarded itself as a Christian-based faith organization, conveniently forgetting that Jesus Christ was a Jew.

The Ku Klu Klan (KKK) was established in 1866 by a former Confederate General, Nathan B. Forrest (1821–1877). The main objective of the KKK was to terrorize African Americans and to disenfranchise them, in part by taking away their voting rights. KKK members wore hoods to hide their identities as they rode, mainly in nighttime, to bring violence to African American communities. (Library of Congress)

In the fall of 1878, Washington took up a course of study at Wayland Seminary in Washington, D.C. Though he benefited from the experience, he left after eight months. He spent time with middle-class African Americans in the city and did not think they were using their time or money in a manner that would enable a stronger economic base. There was no sense of planning for the future, no deferred gratification. Compared to Hampton Institute, for Washington, Wayland Seminary fell well short in his expectations in preparing the African American for the future. As he states, "They knew more about Latin and Greek when they left school, but they seemed to know less about life and its conditions as they would meet in their homes" (88). His training at Hampton Institute was in stark contrast to what he witnessed in Washington, D.C., at Wayland Seminary in 1878. It was basically a hedonistic lifestyle that was grounded on economic sand. Inevitably it would lead to personal disaster or long-term debt. He continues, "I saw young colored men who were not earning more than four dollars a week spend two dollars or more for a buggy ride up and down Pennsylvania Ave" (89). It was superficial to Washington and wasteful. His education and life experience had taught him to be thrifty and to save for a future that engendered a stable income and outgoings. Overall, his time at Wayland Seminary would rarely be alluded to in his later years, but it did have an immense impression on his values and attitude to how one should succeed in life. Certainly, if one was building an economic base, it was not through wasteful spending and extravagant luxuries that were unnecessary that one could sustain oneself and extinguish poverty.

In the spring of 1879, he received a letter from his mentor, General Armstrong, inviting him to perform the graduation address at Hampton Institute. He was thrilled to receive the invite and worked on his speech "The Force That Wins," practicing it over and over until he had perfected a delivery of promise. His address was warmly received by everyone on the day, and he regarded his return as a triumph. That same summer he was invited back by his mentor to teach and to further his studies. Apparently, it was the good work he was doing with the students he was teaching in his home area and sending them on to Hampton Institute that convinced Armstrong to offer him a teaching position. Washington takes pride in mentioning that one of the students he sent to Hampton Institute went on to be a successful physician and a member of the school board in the city of Boston, Dr. Samuel E. Courtney (96).

Undoubtedly, the twenty-three-year-old Booker T. Washington was proving himself to be a competent teacher with tangible results in the number of his successful students he was providing Hampton Institute. As he arrived in the summer of 1879, he was confronted by the news that Armstrong was about to embark on educating about seventy-five American Indians from various Western states. Armstrong wanted Washington to live in the same dormitory and act as a "house father" to them as they settled into a new environment and culture (97). Although he was apprehensive at the thought of teaching a group of American Indians, he was determined to succeed. He did not want to let down Armstrong due to the faith he had shown in him to take on this special duty. It is rather illuminating how Washington explains his thoughts about the American Indians. Firstly, he felt he may not succeed because the American Indians would never respect him; his thought was that they had not and would never submit to enslavement. Secondly, he was aware that some American Indian cultural groups had held African Americans in bondage. Yet this anxiety was unfounded, as not only would he be respected, but as his pedagogy developed there was a sense that he had gained their "love and respect." More importantly, he found in teaching the American Indians that they were like any other human being, "that they responded to kind treatment and resented ill-treatment" (98).

In addition, according to Washington, the American Indians did not like to have to cut their long hair and to ease up on their smoking and the wearing of their cultural mosaic blankets. This is a fascinating insight from Washington because he openly empowered the American Indians. He states something particularly profound in sharing his thoughts on the control of the white man and his philosophy: "No white American ever thinks that any other race is wholly civilized until he wears the white man's clothes, eats the white man's food, speaks the white man's language, and professes the white man's religion" (98). This is a powerful statement from a man like Washington, as he is slipping off his mask to share a deeper consciousness. He is noting the unfair control of the white man over other cultures. This is a critique of the treatment received by African Americans and American Indians. He concludes his assessment of teaching these so-called savages by stating how delighted he was to see the African American students at Hampton Institute helping the American Indians learn to master the curriculum. He wondered if this would be possible in a white institution, leaving the reader in little doubt that it would be very unlikely (99).

Later he recalls a situation in regard to traveling to Washington with a sick American Indian child to get permission from the secretary of the interior to have the child returned to his reservation. On board the steamboat Washington was not allowed to eat in the dining room, but the American Indian was, and when they reached the Washington, D.C., hotel, again the American Indian could be accommodated but not the senior, the teacher in charge, Booker T. Washington. He was disbelieving, and he regarded the entire experience an absurdity in racialized discrimination. A vanquished child who has had his ancestral land taken away from his people can secure food and lodgings, but not the African American who belongs to a people who labored under force for 250 years without pay and cannot eat on a steamboat or sleep in a hotel. Not only did Washington successfully teach the large group of American Indians at Hampton Institute, he was also asked to teach at a night school for students who could not afford to pay tuition. He found teaching the night class group of African Americans extremely keen to learn. They were earnest and so dedicated to learning that he called them "the Plucky Class." He gave each a certificate of merit with their name placed on it for providence (105).

Overall, his return to Hampton Institute as a member of the faculty proved highly successful for the young teacher. He had proved himself as a student, and now he had proved himself as an inspirational teacher. Armstrong was convinced there was a special future for Washington, and he would be proved right in due course. What can be measured at this stage in the life of Washington is a tremendously difficult journey for one so young. To have achieved what he did under such horrendous circumstances is quite remarkable, a genuine rags-to-riches tale. However, the insight provided by Washington in regard to the American Indians underlines his deeper thought regarding his dislike of discrimination. With distinct lack of bitterness he explained how the forced assimilation of the American Indians, who were as sensitive as any human being he had ever encountered, was rather despicable. Being of African American heritage, he knew firsthand the visceral experience of coercive domination. He disregarded the paternalism of Armstrong from what can be deemed the greater good of his deeds. Washington viewed him as a white man stepping up to help the development of African Americans. Who are we to judge whether he was wrong to admire a man who gave him solid opportunities to further himself in his goal to help his people?

For Washington, the most important issue facing African Americans was to lift themselves up from the dire poverty condition the masses found themselves in after the Civil War. For Washington education was the solution for this issue—an education that not only gave deeper cultural knowledge but also skills in trades that were required to build up their capacity to own property for the future economic security of their communities. In 1881, African Americans were only sixteen years beyond the close of the Civil War that ended with their physical freedom. How they would prosper in the coming decades depended on how well they received education and how well they reacted to the psychology of racism. Tuskegee Normal and Agricultural Institute now beckoned the twenty-five-year-old.

3

Tuskegee Institute and Family Matters

In May 1881, Booker T. Washington was completing his first year of teaching night school at Hampton Institute. By all measures he had made an exemplary impression as a young teacher. He was industrious and dedicated to the welfare of his learners. Indeed, no matter the age of his students, he gave his best attention and shared all he knew to aid them in their own journey to greater knowledge. There was something burning inside Washington that only needed an outlet for expression, and soon an opportunity arrived. General Armstrong received a letter asking if he could recommend a white principal to take charge of a newly developed school for African Americans in Tuskegee, Alabama. He knew that he could not recommend a white person, as there was no one available, but he immediately thought of Washington being the best candidate for the job. He ushered him into his office and shared the idea of recommending him for the principal position. In *Up from Slavery*, Washington recalls the incident in an interesting undertone of resentment in the fact that they asked for a white man to take charge. This is a strong theme in his life story, and he often referred to the fact that if he failed at anything he did, it would reflect negatively on his people as a whole. He was a man clearly emerging with a deep sense of pride and sense of self. His reply to his mentor was simple: "I would be willing to try" (107). To Armstrong's credit, he wrote back to the Tuskegee officials and stated unreservedly: "The only man I can suggest is one Booker Washington a graduate of this institution, a very competent capable mulatto, clear headed, modest, sensible, polite and a thorough teacher and superior man. The best man we ever had here" (Harlan 1972, 110).

Given the deeply paternalistic aspect of Armstrong's recommendation, the reference for Washington was laudatory. Armstrong may have viewed Washington as a perfect specimen of an African American who could inculcate his ideas and act them out with precision. There was something about Washington that was clearly special in how he disarmed white men of power and influence. Armstrong would not have written such a glowing recommendation if he had one iota of doubt in his mind that Washington would not be able to perform the "Hampton ideals" in practice.

His opportunity to be the first principal of an institution, based on very similar principles as Hampton Institute, taught him that whites took "for granted no colored suitable for the position could be secured . . . [and they] were expecting the General to recommend a white man for the place" (100–107). That is until a powerful white man, in Armstrong, recommended the man of color. This paternalism stuck with the young teacher, yet he did not change, because fundamentally Washington had all those human attributes by nature: he was cool, calm, and collected. Indeed, there is no record of him ever losing his temper erratically, even when provoked.

The Tuskegee officials wrote back: "Booker T. Washington will suit us. Send him at once" (107). On hearing the news, what followed at Hampton Institute was a moment of joy and celebration that one of their star students had secured a position as principal of a new school. Both students and teachers congratulated the anxious young man who would be entering a new world, a new community, and essentially a new life. All this was exciting yet overwhelming too. Washington would also have to say a temporary goodbye to his sweetheart, Fanny Smith, whom he had been openly courting while at Hampton Institute. She was from the same Malden community, and they had known each other as children. She was an attractive slender woman of African American heritage with a quiet disposition. She would come to be his first wife, but first he had to settle into his position as the new principal of Tuskegee Normal and Agricultural Institute.

Washington arrived in Tuskegee, Alabama, in the month of June 1881. The town was small with approximately two thousand inhabitants, with about half being of African American heritage. Since the Civil War there had been white flight from the town, and with the industrial North building economic empires on the back of coal and steel, Tuskegee was still largely farmland with the main commodity being cotton. There was much work to be done in terms of basic educational opportunity for the masses of African Americans struggling to eke out a living in the harshness of limited opportunities. Yet nothing would deter Washington; his energy

> ### FANNY NORTON SMITH WASHINGTON (1858–1884)
>
> Born in Malden, West Virginia, Fanny Washington was a student of Washington's but only two years his junior. He recommended her to attend Hampton Institute, and once she graduated she joined him at Tuskegee Institute. They married in August 1882 and their only child, Portia, was born in June 1883. Unfortunately Fanny died young from internal injuries after a fall from a wagon on the Tuskegee campus grounds; she was about thirty-one or thirty-two years old at the time of her death.

and desire to succeed were beyond reproach. To his chagrin, when he arrived he found that no school building was erected. The town was at least five miles from the closest railroad station. He was a keen observer and was pleased to find that it was an ideal place for a school for African Americans. All the ingredients were there for a successful educational enterprise. He also noted that the relations between whites and African Americans seemed "pleasant" with a degree of cooperation between the two dominant cultural groups.

There is in the development of Tuskegee Institute a rather hidden history. Most often the story begins and ends with Booker T. Washington having found the school and built it. However, he would not have had such an opportunity without the input of a former enslaved man, Lewis Adams. Adams was a skilled craftsman in shoemaking, harnessing, and other artisanship and had largely taught himself to read and write. Generally he had become a well-respected citizen within the Tuskegee community across the racial divide. In a sense, he was the personification of what Washington wanted to achieve: men and women who could read and write and possess practical skills for each to earn a living and grow in a cultured sense. Adams had struck a deal of sorts with an ex-slaveholder and a colonel in the Confederate Army, Wilbur F. Foster, who in 1881 wanted to get into politics. To secure his senate seat in the Alabama state legislature Foster needed the Black vote. The two men from opposite worlds came to an agreement that if he got the votes, Foster, and a political colleague, Arthur L. Brooks, would then help secure the African American community with state funds for teachers, which is what Lewis Adams ultimately desired. Briefly, what was secured was an annual $2,000 to pay the teachers' salaries. However, no funds from the state were set aside for the school building. Hence, a despondent Washington arrived in theory with authorization to secure teachers for a school where he would be the principal, but there were no prepared school buildings on his arrival.

> **LEWIS ADAMS (1842–1905)**
>
> Lewis Adams was born enslaved in Macon County, Alabama. A very intelligent man, he taught himself to read and write. Adams had numerous trade skills from tinsmithing, harnessing, shoemaking, in addition to being a storekeeper in the Tuskegee community. With his influence in the town he was able to help secure the young Booker T. Washington as principal of a newly founded school that would eventually become Tuskegee Institute. Adams is often overlooked in history because of Washington's personality becoming so prominent. But without Adams's input it is doubtful there would have been an opportunity for Washington to develop his famous institution. There are many "Lewis Adamses" who linger in the shadows when others take the limelight. It is important for new generations of scholars who write on the legacy of Tuskegee Institute to be sure to include Lewis Adams as a central figure in its history.

Yet through the collaboration of a former white slaveholder-Confederate-colonel and an African American formerly held in bondage, the Alabama legislature approved an act for "a Normal School for colored teachers at Tuskegee." This passed into law on February 12, 1881, and the grounding was set for Booker T. Washington to be hired (Mathews 1948, 63). The two men who would actually write the letter to General Armstrong requesting a potential principal were another ex-slaveholder, George W. Campbell, and Lewis Adams. Campbell was a merchant and a banker at the time based in Tuskegee. After the politics were concluded via Foster and Brooks at the state level, it was Campbell who partnered with Adams to put in place the school and principal. Again, this shows a degree of cooperation that local powerful Tuskegee whites offered their African American community. Yet it was always in both parties' interests, or so they thought, to have the institute in place. The fact remains that both Campbell and Adams on the ground level were indispensable to getting Washington's plans off the ground. Moreover, Washington turned frequently to his mentor, Armstrong at Hampton Institute for advice, assistance, and funds to get Tuskegee Institute up and running.

Much of this important aspect of history often gets lost in the origins of Tuskegee Institute. Without these men from polar opposite sides of the cultural spectrum forging an alliance, who knows how this institute to educate adult African Americans would have worked out. The annual $2,000 secured and set aside for teachers' salaries was an essential component in this venture. At the time, Washington was unaware that there was no actual school built, but support from the local community of African Americans and progressive whites was the key ingredient.

Lewis Adams is a man who should not be lost in the history of Tuskegee Institute. He was pivotal to the establishment of the school. Adams had the passion and foresight to push and cajole to have his community develop in terms of assessing the dire need for a type of educational establishment that could take the next generation of African Americans forward. The community was just sixteen years shy of the abolition of enslavement. The majority of the young Tuskegeans were illiterate and poverty-stricken. It was in this environment that Washington began some of his most important work. This was a challenge he relished because it was an opportunity to put all he had learned to the test. He was determined to succeed and prove to the world the varied competence of African American institutional building.

When Washington arrived, he set about getting to know the essence of what was required and how he would convince the locals that he was there to stay and to build a school fit for their needs. After getting feedback of where the best location would be, he settled on a rundown shanty near an African American Methodist Church. Both buildings were in desperate need of repair. Yet he recalls that the "colored people were overjoyed, and were constantly offering their services in any way . . . [in] assistance in getting the school started" (110). He would somehow get things up and running, and he did what was necessary to get some semblance of a classroom set up. After roaming the Tuskegee area and talking to the people, he gathered thirty students as his first class, and the Tuskegee Normal and Agricultural Institute was officially opened on July 4, 1881. The majority of the students came from Tuskegee, Macon County, and the class was equally balanced between male and female students. All were above the age of fifteen and had received some prior elementary education. Most of the students were designated "public school teachers," and one was over forty years of age (121). The shanty leaked when it rained, but this did not deter the ambitious young teacher; one of the students would offer to hold an umbrella over his head as he recited a lesson from one of his books to the eager students hungry for education. There was no denying the poverty that engulfed the start of this project, but as things developed slowly and surely, there was always progression in the force behind Washington's plans for Tuskegee Institute. In other words, things improved little by little until the buildings and campus looked like a proper college campus; all this took place from the 1880s to 1915. Washington was an energetic and serious-minded individual on a mission.

Today the National Council for Black Studies (NCBS) has a motto "Academic Excellence and Social Responsibility." This maxim drives the organization to promote in its young scholars the idea and practice of giving back to one's community—to not just receive your degree and leave the African American community but stay and build it up with skills received during your college or university experience. This philosophy, one could argue, is taken out of Booker T. Washington's handbook for education. It is something that is lost in the contemporary analysis of his life and work. He was an educator who sought primarily to link whatever was learned back to the local community and ultimately for the benefit of its economy and spiritual elevation. He was a practical and innovative thinker who lived to improve his students and their communities—the two were inextricably interwoven in his philosophy.

In getting to know the community, he actually slept and ate with the people he visited. He visited what were their schools, farms, and churches. His reputation filtering around the community was as a keen young teacher wanting to help them reach their full potential as students by giving them previously unavailable opportunities. Washington kept these experiences with him for life. He was a man of the people, drawn to the folklore of the South, comfortable and at ease with the farmers who eked out a living using their innate wisdom and skills they had developed over time. Washington developed great respect for the ordinary everyday masses of African Americans; using their idiom to express both the humor and wisdom was something he enjoyed deeply, particularly when giving speeches.

Along with getting to know the people of Tuskegee, he was a keen observer in how they lived, having spent a lot of time with them in various homes. What he noticed was the lack of basic organization and usefulness of the land they lived on. Families would be buying expensive food products that could be grown on their farmlands. He envisioned vegetable gardens yielding potatoes, corn, tomatoes, carrots, and other foods. Yet the majority simply grew cotton on their land. In his mind, he was developing agricultural classes that future students would embrace and spread across the community in order for his people to be self-sufficient.

He also encountered a lack of home economics, whereby he would enter a cabin and find a gaudy expensive clock but no utensils for eating. In one example of his experience visiting a home in need of basic cutlery and dishes, he exclaims, "One fork, and a sixty-dollar organ!" (113). These experiences in the homes of local families had a profound impact on the formulation of his ideas on what kind of education was necessary. He wanted to provide better ways for students and families to organize their lives because he saw squalor and misplaced ideas that produced a waste of their natural resources. A sociologist would deem Washington's observations as "being in the field" or of Washington himself as being a "participant observer" in that he was able to get a real life insight into the lives of the people who would ultimately be benefiting from Tuskegee Institute. Moreover, he was not patronizing these families, because he had endured a similar experience during his time in enslavement. Washington was not someone who looked down on people who happened to be mired in poverty. He fully comprehended that this was not their fault, that all they needed was a new way of life that would enhance and advantage them. The impact of enslavement and its aftermath was the true culprit of the social condition, and the sweltering heat of oppression that accompanied it.

He had also come to understand that most of the farmers were in debt and basically on a subsistence standard of living. It was a form of peonage whereby the farmer is effectively in debt to the plantation owner, bank, or local store that provided tools and seed. Another system that was common was sharecropping whereby the farmer worked the land for the landowner and at the end of the year took a "share" of the "crop" but most often would be out of pocket after all expenses were paid at the end-of-year cotton harvest. Effectively this was the form of systems that increased the hold whites had over African Americans after enslavement had been abolished. According to Washington, those African Americans who had no land ownership would not get beyond subsistence working in the current manner. They required a new way of developing broader crops and ways of saving that would bring about greater solvency, and eventual ownership of land if they worked hard, planned, and saved for a better future.

The young teacher also observed in the surrounding schools a dire lack of resources with five children usually having to share one book. Overall, there was work to be done in Tuskegee, and he went about it with a vigor and passion that surpassed the average human being. He was focused and determined in all that he did, though with a notable sense of humor. Washington was a great imitator of the dialect of the rural African Americans he met and greatly admired. He recalls one encounter with a man about sixty years old. He observed there being something very interesting about the "peculiar mental processes" of the country folk he encountered. He asked the man to tell him something about his history in order to understand his life experience more deeply. The man replied that he had been born in Virginia and sold in Alabama in 1845. Washington then asked him how many were sold at the same time, and the old man stated, "There were five of us: myself and brother, and three mules" (117). Washington often recalled and shared these kinds of stories when speaking to large crowds, and he would have the audience rolling about in laughter. Some of his critics found this practice demeaning, but Washington felt he was sharing the reality of many rural African American elders and their experiences during enslavement and afterward. There is also a degree of tragic comedy in the experiences that Washington shared. Yet, he never belittled his people, nor separated himself from them. He shared the psychological trauma inflicted on those who were once enslaved. The enormity of the task in moving beyond such a debilitating mental process was immense. What can be worse than to consider oneself akin to a mule? The manner in which Washington told that story had an element of humor in it that should also be understood more profoundly in terms of psychology. He was explaining the need to get his people literary "up from" not only enslavement but the mental scars it can leave on the mind.

When it came to the assessment of the colossal task in front of him, it was at times overwhelming for Washington. This was after considering his sojourn throughout the month of June, spending time with the people he would grow to depend on and vice versa. His mission was to turn around the dire situation of poverty and misdirected education to a more efficacious lifestyle that empowered the community. Although he received much support in the African American community for his efforts, there were some murmurs of discontent from the white section. They argued that giving education to African Americans would only increase their flight to the North and off the land; they also would not be in the right mind to continue as domestic servants. It could not have been easy navigating politically through the complex community relations at that time. One thing that is evident from a reading of this history is the nature and fear of violence perpetuated against African Americans. There was a real concern not to antagonize the whites who were against such an institution of learning. But those with power saw a basic need that would help the community in more ways than if there was no school for the education of locals. Indeed, any community, whatever the cultural make-up that is mired in poverty does not prosper the broader sense. In fact a poverty-riddled community most often becomes a hindrance to the overall economic development of the region. In the rural context this becomes even more evident. Washington surveyed the scene and knew what he had to do to improve the conditions.

Therefore the opposition that emerged was not enough to stifle the progress of the project. With men like Campbell and Adams on both sides of the color line, there was an umbrella of safety covering Washington's daily progress. Again, for the young teacher his observations were in line with *need*, what was the actual requirement in terms of education in the Tuskegee region is what haunted his mind day and night. A major critique of Washington that came down the historical pipeline was of his perspective on the child he witnessed in a dilapidated cabin, wearing sullied clothing. He put what he witnessed in this manner: "One of the saddest things I saw during the month of travel which I have described was a young man, who had attended some high school, sitting down in a one-room cabin, with grease on his clothing, filth all around him, and weeds in the yard and garden, engaged in studying a French grammar" (122). This caused much consternation later from his contemporary African American liberal arts critics based in the North who evidently took what he meant out of context. For Washington it was pretty obvious, given his extensive knowledge, that the study of French in the context of that child was not a worthwhile exercise. It was a fruitless endeavor if indeed he has not learned the art of personal hygiene, the need to have a clean home, and how to use his labor productively. The immediate need is often more important than an ideal or fantasy.

Yet, Washington's liberal arts critics, past and present, have condemned him for stifling the mind of a child who was extremely unlikely to make it to France in the socioeconomic condition he was currently in. It did not mean that Washington was against learning French at an appropriate stage in life. But when the need is for a good home and diet and clean bed and clothes, then what should come first? He speaks of a misplaced mentality whereby the child is studying the French language that could be a considered a luxury given the existing conditions of poverty and a dire need for immediate relief from it. Yet Washington has been criticized for being anti–liberal arts due to that passage in his autobiography. It is unfair and should not be taken out of the context of what his mission was, to alleviate the impoverished state of families in Tuskegee and its surrounding locality.

After teaching for a month, the first class rose from thirty to fifty students. Word of mouth spread, creating a real interest, but it was becoming too much to handle for Washington alone. Another stroke of fortune happened when Olivia A. Davidson turned up. She was of African American heritage and originally from Ohio. She had a preparatory public education. She also studied at Hampton Institute, and after graduation she took a further two years of education at Massachusetts State Normal School in Framingham. Although light skinned, and with a possibility of being able to "pass" for white, Washington reveals that she would never under any circumstances deny or deceive anyone in regard to her African American heritage (125). She was very proud and committed to the uplift of her people, just like Washington himself she too was drenched in the same kind of passion for social justice. With experience teaching and nursing in Mississippi and Memphis, helping the African Americans in the harshest of conditions, Davidson would become an ideal coteacher at Tuskegee Institute. What pleased Washington more than anything was that Olivia's education and philosophy mirrored his, and she brought much new and additional pedagogy to Tuskegee Institute. She was a breath of fresh air and would be indispensable in the coming years as she and he worked in tandem building the curriculum and scope of the school.

In these early weeks there was an emphasis on developing personal hygiene skills. Book learning was always part of the curriculum, but Booker and Olivia consulted to think about teaching the students the best way to bathe, to look after their teeth with a toothbrush, to have clean clothing, and to learn proper etiquette. These may sound like basic skills to a person in the twenty-first century, but not necessarily for students emerging from

> ### OLIVIA AMERICA DAVIDSON WASHINGTON (1854–1889)
>
> Olivia was born free in June 1854 in Mercer Count, Virginia. She was very intelligent and hardworking but suffered from health issues throughout her young life. She met Washington when she was a senior at Hampton Institute and he was visiting as a commencement address speaker. He asked her to join him as a coworker in the 1881 at Tuskegee Institute. She was extremely dedicated to the uplift of her people, and though light skinned and able to "pass" in the white community, she was proud of her African American heritage and would rather die than commit to what was deemed "race suicide." After Fanny's death, she comforted Washington in grief and they fell in love, marrying in the year 1885. They had two sons, Booker Jr. in 1887 and Ernest in 1889. Though she escaped the blaze, her health declined after a fire in their house. She caught a very bad cold that added to preexisting tuberculosis and died in May 1899.

the days of enslavement. It is not surprising that cleanliness and proper manners were often disregarded. In this sense, Olivia was a wonderful role model for her female students. Her focus was to help develop a sense of self-respect, particularly in regard to the female students. How to impart such skills without being condescending proved again the depth of empathy she had for her fellow African Americans.

Alongside personal hygiene classes, there was the push for students to acquire tangible skills that could help the local community. These services could take the shape of a trade or a profession. The emphasis was always for students to learn something beyond mere book learning. Washington was always thinking further than the classroom experience. He wanted his graduates to expand their lives into competent citizens who could use their skills to prosper themselves and their communities. In short, this was "academic excellence and social responsibility" in practice. Nothing more than tapping into the fundamental needs of the typical rural African American communities in the Black Belt South of the 1880s. How to grow food, take care of one's home, provide ways to enhance one's economic base were all part of a holistic pedagogy that was progressive and challenging.

In learning about the lives of the Tuskegee students, Washington came to the knowledge that about 85 percent of them were from agricultural backgrounds (127). They depended on agriculture for a livelihood, and therefore he simply devised a curriculum that met a substantial part of such life. The philosophy was basic: if students could learn the deeper elements of farming, then they would want to stay and not flee after their education to the cities. Mere book learning would be a disastrous method for the community at large, because what would form is an exodus of young educated African Americans who would leave the area and it would remain impoverished without their newfound abilities. Though this may sound like commonsense for the time, it was rather ingenuous to meld the student, along with her or his required skills necessary for community development, to the essence of what Tuskegee Institute hoped to produce and capsulate in the graduates. Another key element in the curriculum was the importance of Christian morality in order to give the students a foundation for solid character-building. Again, Washington was drawing from what he considered the best practice of Hampton Institute. Religious instruction therefore was an essential part of the life of the student. It was a rather puritanical version of Christianity that was imposed on all students. Washington was a strict taskmaster; he valued above all else the inculcation of hard work, individual discipline, and thrift. The Protestant Ethic meant deferred gratification, whereby one puts off hedonism in order to prosper later, and students learned how to be leaders through austere character shaping.

The role of fundraising went hand in hand with their teaching roles. Booker and Olivia worked tirelessly to raise the awareness of Tuskegee Institute and the good it was doing in the role of educating African Americans. Initially the need was to buy land for a permanent building. Olivia was out and about in the community raising whatever she could to boost the funding goal of $500. Booker was able to secure funds from the treasurer at Hampton Institute, General J. F. B. Marshall. He had a good relationship with Washington and loaned him $250 for a deposit required for land and property. The purchase was for a former plantation about a mile from the town of Tuskegee. The owner wanted $500 and would accept a $250 down payment. This was a good price, but Washington felt a sense of anxiety having such a heavy responsibility for such a lot of funds, especially being the private funds of General Marshall. With a sense of pride and anguish, the land was bought in the fall of 1881, and Tuskegee Institute would be officially built on the grounds of a former plantation. This fact is rarely mentioned in history books, and it represents an interesting twist in African American liberation history. Indeed, for a plantation to be turned into a renowned institution of learning is rather commendable and noteworthy.

In August 1882, Booker married his childhood sweetheart, Fanny N. Smith. She had graduated from Hampton Institute in May, and after their marriage she joined him and his work in Tuskegee. The house they lived in as a married couple was also the home of the Tuskegee Institute faculty, which numbered four in the autumn of 1882, but would rise to ten by the following year (Harlan 1972, 138). The first major brick building to be built on the newly acquired property was Porter Hall. The funds for this were mostly provided by a white philanthropist, Alfred Haynes Porter, a Brooklyn businessman who was a friend of General Armstrong at Hampton Institute. Indeed, the initial large funders of Tuskegee Institute came via Washington's relationship with Armstrong. Often the two institutions were linked in a twin-like fashion, rightly or wrongly. Porter Hall was largely made by the hands of the students at Tuskegee Institute. Students learned to make bricks in a kiln. This operation took at least four attempts before they could create the perfect brick. In time, Tuskegee Institute would become known for its brickmaking. But more than this, the trades learned were those that gave students skills for life that would be useful in the broader community. Porter Hall was a fine example of the philosophy and practice that was being instilled through the Tuskegee pedagogical method. Once classes were done for the day, students were marched over to the building site to get to work on the erection of Porter Hall. Washington himself took to an axe to show the students that he was just as committed to labor as they should be. He led by example and kept up this steady work rate for all to witness. Porter Hall would raise three stories. In the basement were the kitchen, dining facilities, and a laundry, with a room for selling food and supplies to students. The first floor held six classrooms for teaching, and the second floor held the library, chapel, and an area for reading and reflection. The top floor was the dormitory for students. Porter Hall was a magnificent achievement for the twenty-seven-year-old Washington. It opened for the 1883/4 academic year.

During the first years there were many sleepless nights when Washington tossed and turned unable to sleep due to the worry he had in meeting the costs of Tuskegee Institute, but he persevered, and with good fortune, kindness, and above all hard work, he managed to survive the first years of uncertainty. In these short years he had made himself known in a strange town; connected with local people by living with them and showing them his genuine interest; he had bought land and erected a fine building built partly by the hands of himself and students. It had all the ingredients that Washington would adhere to: work ethic, fundraising, grit, industrial training, liberal arts, religious ethos, and community participation. In a real sense, everything he tried to do had a holistic component in helping students get ahead in life, employing an individual and community paradigm.

In June 1883, Booker and Fanny Washington welcomed what would be their only child, Portia Marshall Washington. All of Washington's three children would eventually be born on the Tuskegee campus. Unfortunately, Fanny Washington had a fall from a farm wagon, received internal injuries, never fully recovered, and died in May 1884. Devastated, Washington had to carry on life alone with eleven-month-old Portia. There is not much in the historical record of Booker T. Washington in terms of how he handled grief. He was a very private man who tried not to let the disappointments in life stop him from moving ahead. He seems to have been a man who suffered in silence, not letting anyone know how he really felt in terms of his internal pain. He had lost his mother when he was a teenager; he had never known the man responsible for his birth. Maybe he learned to be emotionally detached due to the many struggles and disappointments life had put to him. Or maybe he just had no way of knowing how to express grief. Most men of his era were not nurtured to show too much emotional distress, and therefore it was usually suppressed.

Fortunately, he had at Tuskegee Institute a large group of supporters along with his brother, John, and his family, and Fanny's mother visited from Malden to help with baby Portia. But the most important person for him at this time was Olivia Davidson. She was his strength for many reasons, the main being her undeniable role in helping him establish Tuskegee Institute and Porter Hall into a viable institution of learning. Olivia was instrumental on every level of operation, whether it be curriculum formation, new forms of pedagogy, or in being a talented fundraiser. Inevitably, they grew closer after the death of Fanny, and in the late summer of 1885, they married. They continued the work of the institution, creating more complexity and more buildings on the campus with the help of donors and the tangible work of the students. They were a very skillful team, Olivia being more graceful and classy to Booker's earthy personality that pushed his energy to its limit. At times she would try to get him to slow down in his work activities, but he was such a man of action that he found it difficult to slow down in his work ethic. To be sure, both did not have the best of health throughout their lives. She was a frail woman who had been ill at various times even before she had arrived at Tuskegee Institute. She experienced bouts of exhaustion, just as he would at several points in his life. With the work they performed being so demanding and with the constant travel and fundraising, teaching, building the school, and taking care of the students' needs, it was a tremendous demand on both these young souls. Moreover, to teach well, with a degree of passion and interest, takes a great deal out of a person. Teaching is a profession that most cannot do because it takes a great deal of energy that is often not considered. Yet both of them had so much more to do on top of their teaching roles in keeping Tuskegee Institute on the right path to further success.

In 1886, their first son, Booker T. Washington Jr., was born. This brought joy to their hearts, and then in 1889 their second son, Earnest Davidson Washington, was born. Olivia sadly become weaker after her second child. To add to this, there was a fire in their home as a result of a defective chimney. Booker was at this time doing his fundraising in the North. Olivia and the children all escaped the burning home in the early hours of the morning. However, between having to stand in the cold and the trauma caused by the fire itself, Olivia's health deteriorated rapidly. This was an unfortunate incident that had a tremendous impact on her capacity to overcome illness—she simply no longer had the strength to withstand this new assault on her health.

On Washington's return from the North, with his wife seemingly not improving, he arranged for her to be taken to Massachusetts General Hospital in Boston. Unfortunately, regardless of the treatment she received, she passed away on May 9, 1889. At the relatively young age of thirty-three, Washington was once again confronted by profound grief and was now left to raise three young children: Portia was only six years old, Booker Jr. was three years old, and Ernest was just three months old. Washington was devastated by her loss and nearly went bankrupt in the period directly following Olivia's death. Somehow, he managed to survive, but he was shaken to his core with the loss of his beloved Olivia. If one was to guess the true soul mate of his, it would not be amiss to consider Olivia as his true love because they had so much in common. Both were teachers, curriculum innovators, institutional builders, and fund raisers. Olivia was a massive loss, and how he coped with it is difficult to imagine, but in true Washington spirit he kept moving ahead; he knew of no other way to handle grief other than to keep moving forward.

In the summer of 1890, Washington had to hire a nursemaid for his children, Mrs. Dora King (Stewart 1977, 22). He continued with his work as best he could while he grieved. Tuskegee Institute probably saved him from deep depression due to the work that involved his constant attention; in a positive sense, it was a diversion from the pain of loss he was enduring. How anyone deals with such loss and manages to keep going speaks volumes to his inner strength. From all accounts of his life, there is this salient feature of a calm temperament and positive outlook regardless of the forces set against him. Whether it was enduring the horrors of enslavement, struggling to gain an education, or bearing the loss of two wives he loved dearly at young ages, he somehow managed to survive. Washington was therefore emotionally and mentally an extremely strong man, though it is known that his nervous system suffered due to simply overworking his mind and body to the extent that it occasionally gave up on him (Harlan 1972, 1983). In October 1885, not long after he and Olivia were wed and before she passed away, he was confined in hospital for about ten days with sheer exhaustion, and she constantly worried more about *his* nervous condition while suffering her very own acute fatigue and other health issues. In the case of Washington, he was only twenty-nine years old when a bout of exhaustion laid him up (Harlan 1972, 151). Clearly it was a sign that the long hours of work would eventually take a toll on them both.

With Olivia gone, he was alone, but that innate inner strength of his kept him alive and focused on the future of Tuskegee Institute. In the

> **MARGARET MURRAY WASHINGTON (1865–1925)**
>
> Margaret (Maggie) Murray was a very talented student, who met Washington when he visited Fisk University on a speaking engagement. He was impressed by her manner and maturity as a speaker. She had been writing to him, and eventually she joined him at Tuskegee Institute in 1890. They would marry in the year 1892. Margaret was rapidly promoted due to her talents in administration and in teaching; her title was lady principal of Tuskegee Institute. Margaret—a very strong advocate for women's rights and anti-lynching—was instrumental in establishing a Tuskegee Women's Club. She also helped Washington refine his oratory skills. She was an extremely effective leader in Tuskegee Institute and the community.

spring of 1889, he was invited to give the commencement address at Fisk University in Nashville, Tennessee. Washington often hired graduates from Fisk to teach at Tuskegee Institute. While there he met a talented graduating senior at a dinner table, who let him know that she had written inquiring about a possible teaching position: Margaret Murray. She was originally from Macon Mississippi, from a poor background, and had overcome many obstacles to get to Fisk, where she developed into a stellar student. Washington was very impressed with her level of maturity for a twenty-four-year-old and hired her to teach English, but within a year he had promoted her to head the women's industries, and in 1890 she took the role left by Olivia to

Margaret Murray Washington (1865–1923) was an educator and advocate for the education of African Americans, women's rights, anti-lynching, and education in the Jim Crow south during the late nineteenth and early twentieth centuries. In 1892, while a teacher and administrator at the Tuskegee Institute, Margaret Murray married the institute's founder, Booker T. Washington. (Library of Congress)

become the new lady principal with a salary of $500 annually (Harlan 1972, 182).

Margaret excelled in administrative competence and was a reliable faculty colleague at Tuskegee Institute. She was also a tad conservative and puritanical as he, and with a sharp wit like Washington. Clearly, he was impressed with her vitality; there was a presence and a strong leadership demeanor in her that he greatly admired. Washington kept their relationship cordial and professional, but she began to write letters to him with stronger feelings that went beyond the professional. Once he began to return her admiration in kind, there was a reluctance on her behalf due to the unfavorable relationship she had developed with his young daughter, Portia. Apparently, she got along with young Ernest and Booker Jr., but the young daughter of seven years did not take to Murray. She had called her stepmother (Olivia) "Mama" and did not want another mother. Booker tried to play the role of mediator between the two, but it seemed to be a lost cause. In a letter to him, she wrote expressing that she "could not feel toward Portia the way she should" and it made her feel bad. His proposal to Murray in the fall of 1891 was not immediately answered in the affirmative (Harlan 1972, 184). Regardless of her apprehension toward Portia, in the fall of 1892, they married in Tuskegee. Their marriage had a hint of convenience for both parties.

Again, in reading the history of Booker T. Washington's wives, it appears that his "true love" was Olivia Davidson. It is evident too that he loved both Fanny and Margaret, but there was something about Olivia and the work she did to help him in the early years that stands out. Each wife had a place in his heart and created a warmer world for him, but Olivia Davidson stands out as a woman who was his definite soulmate, his true helpmate in the biblical sense. They worked in tandem in the early years, both to the point of physical and mental exhaustion. They lived for the very same cause, with the same intensity and passion. Finally, they both partnered in fundraising as comfortable as a hand-in-glove.

If Olivia was Washington's soulmate, then Margaret was his savvy political partner. Life certainly went on very well with his third wife, and she held the status of Tuskegee Institute in prestige as the lady principal. In addition, Margaret did a great deal for women and their empowerment causes. Among numerous roles from establishing kindergartens to programs to improve women's lives, she served as the secretary on the executive board of the National Association of Colored Women (NACW). Considering that women were still fighting for the right to vote, this was a progressive position to take, and it confirms that Washington himself wanted social justice for women to be just as important as racial uplift. Booker T. Washington was a man who empowered women in the workplace by giving them positions of power within Tuskegee Institute. He was never intimidated by the women in his life and work. Indeed, for his time and place he was a rather forward-thinking male who supported all of his wives in their pursuit of women's equality. For example, Ida B. Wells-Barnett, the crusader for women's rights and anti-lynching was very impressed with Washington and called him a "fellow crusader" (Harlan 1972, 196).

Too often, Washington himself has been confined to the label of "conservative," but this does not mean he was not progressive in pursing fundamental rights for both women and men. Margaret Murray was known as "Maggie" in private circles, and she was a strong force in taking her husband's fame to even greater heights. Indeed, from 1895 to 1910, his standing in the world as the leader in African American affairs was undisputed. She is known to have helped improve his speech writing and his delivery of addresses. She was in many ways the person behind his most formidable period in politics. She served on the executive board at Tuskegee Institute, making decisions with some of the most powerful white men at this period. For any woman to serve on such a board was progressive, but to have a woman of African American heritage in such a position speaks volumes of the confidence she exuded and more importantly the assurance her husband had in her. If Olivia had been his rock in establishing Tuskegee Institute, then Margaret was the one who expanded it into the realm of national and international renown. The outdated saying "Behind every powerful man is a good woman" finds new meaning here: Washington had three such women who stood *beside* him, not behind.

Margaret was a particularly good host to the many guests that came to visit her husband at The Oaks. Indeed, there was a constant stream of visitors, including President Theodore Roosevelt and other statesmen, giants in business like Andrew Carnegie and William Baldwin, and many in local politics and education related to the business end of the school. The main reason for all this hobnobbing was to extend the Tuskegee campus and by the outset of the new century there would be over sixty buildings and a thousand students benefiting from the work of the Tuskegee Institute leader. Apart from being an excellent leader for women and Tuskegee Institute, Margaret did play the role of the dutiful wife in these ascetic Victorian times.

Her relationship with Portia did not improve greatly; from the writings to her father, there is evidence that Portia was unhappy whenever he was away on fundraising trips and she had to endure the wrath of Mrs. Washington. There was a cold chill between the two that did not dissipate. Portia developed a love for music, and her skills would eventually take her to the level of a teacher in classical music. As an adult, she traveled to Europe and was helped by the famous Black British musician, Samuel Coleridge-Taylor. But prior to developing her musical talent, she first had to attend Tuskegee Institute, and she recalls detesting the dress making class that her father insisted upon. Her passion was for piano, and she lost herself in it (Stewart 1977, 25). Portia embraced the Negro Spirituals, and one of her favorites was "Sometimes I feel Like a Motherless Child," a fitting tune for a child who had lost her biological mother and her surrogate mother. It is noted that her father loved to hear her practice the piano at their home, and she would spend hours practicing (Stewart 1977, 26). Portia's discipline for the piano was as strong as her father's will power when he focused on a task—they were both determined characters.

The two boys were younger than Portia and were not adverse toward Mrs. Washington. Murray particularly enjoyed the company of Ernest and had a special place in her heart for him. She was very upfront about her general aversion to children. Margaret remained childless all her life, but they did adopt one of her nieces, named Laura—and Mr. Washington was very fond of her. His family clearly gave him comfort even though he had to spend such a long time on the road. In all measurements, he was good to his family and to his siblings. Washington's two sons grew to be educated at Tuskegee Institute and beyond. Both went on to be educated to a high level. Booker T. Washington Jr., however, would often irk his father's sensibilities because he did not have the same resolve for learning. He got by but never excelled in school work. Washington's youngest son was more like his mother, rather fragile, and quiet. Moreover, he was akin to his elder brother who did not enjoy the process of academic life. He enjoyed loafing around and being a prankster rather than doing steady work. It seems that the discipline was left to others, because their father was so busy away from home. Neither son lived up to their father's deeds and instead lived out rather undistinguished lives by comparison. To be fair, it could not have been easy being the son of such a famous man who was both loved and loathed during his lifetime. Overall, he was the best father he could be, and his children knew they were loved and they were cared for during and beyond their father's life. Historians appear to agree that Washington was a good family man, and his travels were punctuated with family time during holidays, like Thanksgiving and Christmas, when celebrations took place. That is not to suggest there was not the Victorian stiffness in the family household: there was, due to Margaret's strictness. She kept a rather disciplined home, and this was a good foil for her husband who often indulged in kindness toward his children.

As Margaret kept the home running competently, her husband continued to build a reputation for the school on a national level. An important acquisition to the Tuskegee Institute faculty occurred when George Washington Carver joined the school in 1896 as the chair of the Department of Agriculture. This was a major coup for Washington. Carver was a brilliant agricultural chemist, a renaissance man of sorts who liked to paint, fashioning colors from plant materials, and he played the piano. Among his passions were plant life, animals, and anything to do with soil and what could be grown in it. Carver became particularly famous for his peanut experiments, finding over one hundred ways to use the peanut. As did Washington, he had a deep love of nature and was a devout Christian. Moreover, they each had a passionate desire to help their people move up out of poverty and ignorance, having both struggled so hard to gain an education.

Carver was a very humble man, who had also suffered as a child with various illnesses, with whooping cough being near fatal. As with Washington, his early life was filled with heartache and family upheaval in Missouri. He and his mother were enslaved and then kidnapped by outlaws who raided the Carver plantation in 1861. This was a time when lawlessness was rife. Yet, somehow baby George Washington Carver survived through the trauma of his young life (Holt 1943). Developing a love of nature, specifically of plants in his early years, gave him the nickname "the plant doctor" because he was able to nurture and bring ailing plants back from dying to thriving. Before arriving at Tuskegee Institute, Carver had numerous other offers of faculty positions because of his unique abilities and knowledge of agricultural science. Carver was, not to use the word lightly, a genius. Having mastered the disciplines of botany, herbal medicine, mycology (the study of fungi), art, and music, he also had a profound interest in cooking and massage therapies. One of his noted inventions was a peanut oil that could help alleviate the effects of polio. His mind was full of ideas, and he was a perfect fit for Tuskegee Institute in so many ways. Firstly, the area offered a lush environment for his love of soil and nature. Secondly, the people he would be helping mostly would be African American farmers struggling to move beyond the commodity of cotton, and who needed the knowledge to diversify their crop yields. Thirdly, Tuskegee Institute was essentially an African American school led by African American faculty. Even Fisk could not boast to having African American leadership in their administration. Having never experienced the definite institutional empowerment of his people, this appealed to Carver. Though he was a man of love and compassion, he was also a man who had experienced prejudice, violence, and social injustice. He was not a naive man even if he was genial to all he encountered. The fact that he would remain at Tuskegee Institute for the rest of his career and life, amounting to a forty-seven-year record of service, is testimony to his unwavering dedication to Tuskegee Institute. Even though he was known to clash heads sometimes with the campus's leader on aspects of his role, he remained loyal and contributed so much to the evolution of the institution. Indeed, in his time he became good friends with Henry Ford and other key inventors of the day, who sought him out for his expertise and advice. Therefore,

Washington was very pleased to lure him to Tuskegee, as it gave a massive boost to the institution. He would go on to provide such a variety of agricultural innovations through his work on plants, peanuts, and potatoes that are universally employed today across the agricultural landscape.

Tuskegee Institute in the mid-1890s was essentially thriving through the unrelenting charisma and vision of Washington. Regardless of setbacks, he seemed to pick himself right back up and achieve another resounding success in the face of hardship. Whether it was a loss through death, or a lack of funds to fund Tuskegee Institute further, he just never gave up. Most often he would find a way to get over any grief, he was a man who never seemed perturbed or downcast for long; he seemed to always find a way past loneliness with the help of a "feminine hand" (Harlan 1972, 147). The key to this is in his philosophy and mindset. From what can be gleaned from a reading of his history in building Tuskegee Institute, he had a mind that would not ever be reduced to bitterness. He befriended rather than offended the people he met, whether they be white American, African American, or from abroad. Some commentators have viewed this as a personality weakness, stating that he was some sort of pushover. But he was simply a very positive man. His hunger to build an institution of learning that met the needs of the African American community was his priority. For him to delve into unnecessary feuds with those who were stronger financially or politically would have drowned his efforts completely. Why on earth would he jeopardize the welfare of his students, his faculty, and its administration by being bellicose or having misplaced bravado? It made no sense to antagonize when diplomacy and tact could win an argument for an increase in funds for his beloved Tuskegee Institute.

Washington endeavored to share his philosophy with the student body every Sunday evening. The institute would gather to hear his words of advice and wisdom. He would deliver the talks in a conversational tone designed to inspire students to head into the following week with gusto and renewed faith in what Tuskegee Institute was offering them—an opportunity for growth in character, in their community, and in their life chances. Washington was a very sincere man when it came to his philosophy of self-help. He believed in it because he was a product of it, and it does not mean one cannot gain aid or assistance as one adopts such an attitude. Self-help for him meant developing a character that went out into the world to seek success. Instead of wallowing in self-pity or rancor if life has treated you unkindly, he believed that if you worked very hard at any goal in life, then in some manner it could be achieved. This is the philosophy he would share with both the students and faculty during Sunday evening talks in the chapel.

A topic most dear to him was the notion of helping others. That when an individual steps up to help a weaker person in need of support it is the most empowering thing someone can do. To be of service to others is humanity at its best. He knew full well that the world was harsh and cruel in general to his people. Yet, he had also come to comprehend the foolishness that bitterness can do to the mind and body. It can dry out one's soul, damage the internal tissue, and draw one into the worst external binges, such as alcohol and drug use. It is vital for the human spirit to stay healthy, and one can achieve this through helping others and by always being grateful for one's overall health and physical strength. No matter how punitive life could be, one should never give in by adopting a negative attitude to life.

The Sunday evening talks allowed Washington to expand on his ideas, to reflect, and to pass on his nuggets of wisdom received through his many struggles to achieve success. A number of his talks were compiled into book form and published in 1903. The title of the book is in line with his key philosophical perspective: *Character Building*. He opens the book in the preface with the words "In these addresses I have attempted from week to week to speak straight to the hearts of our students and teachers and visitors concerning the problems and questions that confront them in their daily life here in the South" (Washington 1903, ix). He was a man of holistic thought, someone who knew instinctively that in order to build character in students, then one had to connect with their lives, to know something about how they lived and survived in the world. In understanding their hardships, their challenges, and the deep-seated racism that confronted the students, he would offer some of his worldly wisdom to calm their collective anxiety.

His language was also accessible to any listener; there was no esoteric verbal gymnastics in Washington's Sunday talks. He was there to share knowledge and wisdom to all without verbosity. In addition, he was a very humorous, engaging speaker. It must have been quite entertaining to listen to the anecdotal tales he weaved into his addresses. Historians speak of him having audiences rolling about in laughter. He was a man of great wit to be around. Yet he was very serious about his work too. The phrase "tragic comedy" is suitable in evaluating how Washington would get his audience's attention. If one is to be an effective speaker and keep listeners attentive, then bringing humor into the address is key, and he knew this well.

One of his Sunday evening talks was titled "The Highest Education," and it was designed to stress again his philosophy on what a proper education entailed. He emphasized by stating he was aware of his propensity to continually infer the notion of what is the most optimal education a student can receive; yet it was at the heart of what their role was—to empower each student to be the very best under the guidance of Tuskegee Institute. For Washington, the task at Tuskegee Institute was to prepare students to be the best through the acquisition of an education rooted in vocational and liberal arts studies. He was ardently against the simple regurgitation of facts and figures, of when or where an event in history took place. This was rather banal, and certainly not central to what a very good education should entail. Washington contended for the importance of having a well-organized mind that can recall facts and figures when required for a given task. Whatever is gleaned directly from textbooks or a variety of other references should have truth at its core, otherwise it is not an education that is worth receiving. As Washington contended, "Unless you have got truth, you have failed in your purpose to be educated" (Washington 1903, 113). At the heart of his theme regarding "truth" was the principle of developing honesty as one went out into the world. It could be argued that much history taught through textbooks was written with a distinct bias against African Americans or people of color generally. He was not a man who was naive about the danger of book learning, and in his own style he was alluding to being an honest critical thinker when one steps into the world to deal with folks generally.

Washington was big on the idea and practice of lifting up one's fellow man and woman. "Education in the broadest and truest sense will make an individual seek to help all people" (Washington 1903, 114), regardless of where they came from or what color they happened to inherit. He continues to explain the need to be "kind" to the downtrodden and not to look down on anyone less fortunate than yourself. To be an educated person is to have compassion, not just a head full of facts. Compassion for those who need assistance to get started in life, to give opportunity when necessary and possible. There is a passage on cleanliness in self and in one's habit. To be truly educated one should not live in a "dirty, miserable shanty," as this would not be true to what you have been taught (Washington 1903, 117). Personal hygiene for Washington was a key component to a person's success in life. There are few humans in the world who want to engage with another human who is unclean, ill-kept, and shabby. Even if a person is poor, he or she can find a way to get washed and get some clean used clothes and a pair of decent shoes. Even if poor, anyone has a chance of surviving and rising if he or she takes the time to adopt these basic principles.

Sunday evening addresses also talked about having a love of nature. In the world of today he would have been deemed an ecologist, one who believes in the beauty and importance of keeping the planet clean and healthy from carbon dioxide and other pollutions. In a sense, he was ahead of his time, he truly led by example when it came to sharing an affection for nature and animals; it was also something he had in common with George Washington Carver. Washington was always passing on nuggets of wisdom to help Tuskegee students raise themselves to a higher level of compassion and understanding. Moreover, he would emphasize the importance of forging good relations with whites. This philosophy he passed on was to ensure the safety of his students and to foster good relations in the surrounding community. He often drew from the Bible for his addresses, and one theme that was strong was "loving thy neighbor" as your friend. He often pointed out to white Southerners they could not go forward in prosperity across the South if one group of people was mired in poverty and ignorance. Some progressive white Southerners took heed of his wise words and agreed, but the majority continued to be racist. Tuskegee Institute was allowed to grow without interference from envious whites because it was "protected" by the philosophy and powerful friends of Booker T. Washington. He knew if he had boasted about how superior his students were intellectually to the average white in the area, his institution would have been attacked and burned to the ground—that was the reality of the milieu he operated in.

When Washington surveyed the wellness of the campus, he would do so riding on a horse. He would rise very early and do his inspection of the campus majestically, looking for anything that did not look right to his keen eyes. A broken fence, discarded litter, or a pathway that needed maintenance attention, he would readily note in his little book. He did not take well to those who slackened in his desire to have an educational institution that could be deemed the best in the South. Washington often surmised, and often lost sleep over it, that if he failed then it would be put down to the cultural group failure of African Americans, not individual incompetence—this was part of the psychological pressure he encountered. Hence, his daily inspection on horseback, to make sure all was in ship-shape on the campus grounds, was routine when at home. Nobody could deny that Tuskegee Institute was not in good shape in the middle part of the 1890s. Certainly it was onward and upward for the institution that confounded and astounded many onlookers. African American success was etched into the mortar of every brick, in every building erected—and it was only going to get bigger and better. His growing student and faculty body, one thousand and one hundred respectively, could attest to this fact. Therefore, with the comfort of his blended family, the Tuskegee Institute leader would now head into the limelight of national politics and international fame, having laid a firm foundation for continued success.

4

The Atlanta Compromise and Beyond

On May 26, 1892, to emphasize the growing status of Tuskegee Institute, the great Frederick Douglass gave the commencement address. He had earlier praised Booker T. Washington's efforts in establishing "this great and leading institution." Douglass was seventy-five years old when he spoke to the students at Tuskegee Institute, and the title of his speech was the "Self-Made Man." His message was for the students to develop "thrift and common sense" in their everyday lives in order to build an economic foundation for themselves. However, he stressed the need for the African American to be given a "fair chance" in life to succeed and prosper. He emphasized, "But be sure you *do* give us a fair chance" (Spencer 1955, 108). Douglass, who had spent his life fighting for the true liberation of his people, was very impressed with the work Washington was conducting at Tuskegee Institute. He had lived long enough to witness an institution in the Black Belt South that would empower and alleviate those mired in poverty and ignorance. Frederick Douglass passed away on February 20, 1895, twenty-one months after his inspiring address to the graduating students at Tuskegee Institute. Booker T. Washington was a great admirer of Frederick Douglass and regarded him as a noble man of his people. As fate would have it, he would come to be regarded as the successor to Douglass. Though far from the same in temperament and intellect, Washington simply found himself in the right place at the right time in history, as was often the case in his rise to fame.

Arguably, Washington's most enduring legacy by the turn of the twentieth century, apart from Tuskegee Institute, was his famous address given at the Cotton States and International Exposition, held in Atlanta, Georgia, on September 18, 1895. This occurred almost seven months to the day of Frederick Douglass's passing—a rather symbolic, or auspicious, coincidence in the development of the thirty-nine-year-old Washington. If the timing of the address was simply fortuitous, what followed is akin to the reaction of Dr. Martin Luther King Jr.'s "I Have A Dream" address at the Lincoln Memorial, Washington, D.C., on August 28, 1963. In other words, Washington's Atlanta address would go down as a speech to live in the annals of time. As with any noted speech, it also depends on one's reading of it on how it is accepted in historical terms. Often the analysis of orations is left to literary folks and historians, who can sometimes distort and take much of what was stated out of context.

Before taking a deeper examination into the address at the Cotton States International Exposition, it would be beneficial to consider Washington's approach in speaking to a predominantly white Southern audience in the 1890s. His first major address as a public speaker was in 1884 when invited to address the National Education Association (NEA) in Madison, Wisconsin. He was extremely nervous as this was an audience of four thousand strong and mostly white. Washington recalls white Southerners who had traveled from Alabama, some from Tuskegee, to hear the South being "abused" and being "pleasantly" surprised when there was not one word of abuse in his address. The human condition is a reality; no one enjoys being criticized, no matter how necessary the criticism is. If there is a social problem and an abused citizen is to address an audience of which the majority belong to the cultural group responsible for such abuse, then it is incumbent upon the public speaker to be aware of the sensitivity involved. That is, if he or she wants to be successful in reaching such a problematic audience.

Washington puts his argument for speaking about the racialized South in a more engaging manner, explaining how he "early learned that it is a hard matter to convert an individual by abusing him, and that this is more often accomplished by giving credit for all the praiseworthy actions performed than by calling attention alone to all the evil done" (Washington 1986, 200). In other words, when speaking to the white South, he would endeavor to express the good rather than the bad, and he would tread lightly on the areas that needed refinement. Fundamentally, he was aware that at that time and place African Americans were in a weaker position, socioeconomically and politically, to overstep the boundaries. Was this courageous? Not particularly. Was it efficacious in his pursuit of the objectives he was pursuing for the good of Tuskegee Institute and its need for economic stability? Yes. To otherwise chastise and criticize would only further entrench the racial animosity he knew they held, some deeply and some with the possibility of waning their racist views.

Washington was a social psychologist without the degree. He knew instinctively that it would harm his institution if he ran foul by bad-mouthing the white South, especially if he were in the West or North regions of the United States. Largely, his focus in his address in 1884 was the need for the white and African American communities to develop friendly relations. Cultivating this would no doubt be the task of the progressive and wealthy white Southerners, and the educators. It was their concern for increased harmony that he tried to foster. He played the mediator between two hostile cultural groups. Both held grievances toward each other based on a historical relationship, and one was more powerful than the other, which further perpetuated conflict and resentment. For the whites and African Americans in the South, Washington felt that it was necessary to ease tensions between the two. Moreover, there was a need to allow African Americans to develop a level of self-determination whereby they would be of use to the South and not a burden. This is how he fundamentally approached public speaking. In the North, to whites, his speaking tone was in order to raise funds; if speaking to whites in the South, it was in order to foster good relations, and to see the similarities rather than the differences between the two cultural groups. In addition, when addressing an African American group, he would emphasize the "importance of industrial and technical education in addition to academic and religious training" (206). This is a key theme that stayed with him throughout his career. Indeed, after this confidence-boosting experience Washington went on to become a renowned public speaker. Whatever the audience, he would usually win them over with his charm and stories from the Deep South that spoke to the character, desires, and humor of his people.

The buildup to the Cotton States International Exposition was two-fold: first, he was invited by a prominent group of Atlanta citizens to travel to Washington, D.C., to help in their case to raise funds for the exposition from Congress. He agreed to go and met with the twenty-five strong committee of Congress. His role was to speak about the progress African Americans were making since the abolition of enslavement in 1865 up to 1895. Although a little apprehensive due to never having experienced such a prestigious committee, he spoke for about fifteen minutes. Washington's main theme was a call for greater cooperation between the two cultures and that they were literally "next door neighbors" in the South. He stated, "I tried emphasize the fact while the [African American] should not be deprived by unfair means of the franchise, political agitation alone would not save him, and that back of the ballot he must have property, industry, skill, economy, intelligence, and character" in order to succeed (208). He spoke honestly and with a degree of diplomacy to the Congress committee. The Atlanta citizens were very pleased with his address, in part because he did not completely demand the right to vote for African Americans. However, he did *not* suggest disenfranchisement: his words were measured and carefully presented as to not antagonize the white power structure, both of Congress and of those he traveled with, to help secure funding for the Atlanta-based Cotton States International Exposition. The significant role that Washington played in obtaining federal funding for the exposition is rarely noted in historical volumes.

After returning to Tuskegee, Washington received notice that the Atlanta citizens expressed a desire to have a building that depicted the rise of the African American since enslavement displayed at the exposition. Moreover, the building would be erected by and designed by African Americans. They suggested he should be the man in charge of the exhibition that dealt with the African American experience, and he agreed in principle but stated that his role at Tuskegee Institute was too time-consuming. Instead he suggested that a Mr. I. Garland Penn be contacted in his place. However, Washington was asked to deliver the opening address, and he was thrilled and yet anxious at the thought. He accepted the responsibility and in doing so reflected in this manner: "I remembered that I had been a slave; that my early years have been spent in the lowest depths of poverty and ignorance, and that I have little opportunity to prepare me for such a responsibility as this" (210). The pressure he felt is understandable, given that he would be sharing a platform with Southern whites, men and women, and speaking largely to a wealthy group—the former masters of his people. There would also be a section in the audience reserved for African Americans.

Because of the enormity of the occasion, he paid great attention to the content and delivery. He practiced with his wife, Margaret, who aided him with judicious feedback, along with the Tuskegee faculty. They all approved, but he was still not fully convinced of his ability to pull it off. This was a different audience because it involved rich and poor white Southerners, rich Northerners, along with African Americans. He recalls a white farmer who was passing through Tuskegee jokingly regarding his dilemma, "I am afraid you have got yourself in a tight place" (213). He knew that there was a very thin line between success and failure. Washington then recalls an elder African American pointing him out and explaining to another, "Dat's de man of my race what's gwine to make a speech at de Exposition to-mor-row. I'se sho' gwine to hear him" (214). The dilemma was as an old one, with just an added ingredient of trying to bring all groups together for one cause: the good of American racial relations in the South.

Being a religious man, drenched in the word of God, he prayed hard the night before for guidance and strength. He had his family with him on the day; they took the train journey to Atlanta, Georgia. It was a swelteringly hot day, and by the time Washington reached the exposition, he was about to collapse, likely due to dehydration coupled with nervous tension. When one considers the time and place, it surely would have taken its toll on any average soul having to deal with such pressure. Yet he recovered his composure and met his date with destiny. The venue was large and imposing but excellent for public speaking. On the program, first to speak was the ex-governor of Georgia, Rufus Brown Bullock, who kindly, with maybe a tad apprehension, introduced Booker T. Washington as a representative of African American enterprise and civilization. When he stood to speak, he heard a thunder of cheers from the African Americans in the audience, who were segregated and confined to a specific space. The white listeners gave a mild applause of appreciation, no doubt wondering how his speech would advantage them.

Washington's daughter, in her memoir, recalls the day vividly. She was twelve years old at the time and sat in the gallery with her stepmother Margaret, along with her two brothers, Booker Jr. and Ernest, who were still rather young to take it all in. Portia recalls seeing a "white mob of rednecks formed up beside the stage waiting to set upon my Pa if he had said but one word against the South. By the time he had finished speaking, they were wildly applauding and slapping their thighs in approval of what the black man had said" (Stewart 1977, 28). This is from an eye witness, a child daughter, watching in anguish as her father speaks to a potentially hostile audience, or certainly those of the redneck variety. What exactly was it that Washington uttered that day that has both congratulated and confused, and most often the same person? Washington set out to explain the relationship between the white South and African Americans. He evaluated the way forward that could involve harmonious relations, again in keeping with his long-held belief that the only way forward would be through genuine cooperation. The title of his address was "Cast Down Your Bucket," but it is now informally known as the "Atlanta Compromise." The speech holds complexity and messages for both whites and African Americans in the South of the mid-1890s period. He set out by exclaiming the wonder of the exposition and how the exercise itself will do more to "cement the friendship of the two races" than anything else that has occurred since the outset of African American freedom. This was rather overblown praise, but it was always part of Washington's addresses to quickly disarm his white audience.

There then follows his emphasis on the need for African Americans to build up from the bottom to reach the top. He alludes to it being an error for his people to have taken seats in Congress during Reconstruction rather than seeking to build their foundation in real estate and industrial skills. In other words, they moved too fast, too hastily in the pursuit of progress. The dying need in the South was for African Americans to toil for their welfare, to be self-determined, while offering their skills to the white South who needed them; "cast down your bucket" was a metaphor taken from the novel *Moby Dick* by Herman Melville. This meant two things: the white South needed to have faith in their African American neighbors who once built their houses and toiled on their plantations, and that Washington was a faithful servant to the South. For African Americans, he was alluding to it being best to stay in the South, to "cast down your bucket" there where future optimal interests were bound up in prior centuries of their ancestors' toil and struggle. Washington also played down the idea of seeking refuge back in Africa, stating that here in the South is where African Americans belonged and would find their best hope for a better life. The South needed skilled workers in agriculture, mechanics, and technical work and in the various professions. The best chance for his people was in the very soil that was labored by their forebears: his people should "cast down [their] bucket" in the South.

During this period, thousands of African Americans were heading North for work in the industrialized cities, and because it was often dangerous for them to be in the South due to white mobs, lynching, and convict leasing that would trap any African American who violated the weakest of laws into prison. Freedom could be lost easily in this climate, and Washington did not address this fact in his speech. As for the white South, Washington made the case that they should allow the African American "a fair chance" just as Frederick Douglass had alluded to a few years earlier. This would entail allowing the African American the space to live in peace, to prosper, and be of significant use to the new South. He put forward his message of the loyal African American who took care of their households and made their fields blossom and that no foreign born could come close to the closeness that has been forged in their collective history.

It must be stated in hindsight that the address reads rather too kindly to the South, but again, Washington was a practical man. He was situated between the devil and deep blue sea that day. There was not much wriggle room for any notion of "pay us *now* for the unpaid labor you took from us!" Washington knew that had he uttered anything remotely radical, he might have been lynched, and that is coming from an eyewitness account. He had no real choice but to be humble in his approach, and so, to paraphrase, he argued, please allow my people to get property, build their lives productively, and get educated with skills that can be of benefit to both communities (219–220). In return, he vowed that his people would abstain from agitating for social equality, because this would only come when the world is put right and all are in good shape in terms of property ownership, personal wealth, and education throughout the South. He further contended, "In all things that are purely social we can be as separate as the fingers, yet one as the hand in all things essential to mutual progress" (222). These twenty-seven words have haunted many African American minds due to the implicit acceptance of segregation. Yet the context has been overblown for there was deeply embedded social segregation all over the South at this time. Washington knew this, and it was not for him a concession. After all he ran Tuskegee Institute for African Americans and knew segregation like Americans knew apple pie. Those who have lambasted Washington down the corridors of history have never really accepted the fact that he alone could never have opened up the South, or stopped the lynching of thousands of African Americans because most of them took place *outside* of the law. Too much has been put on his shoulders for this five-minute address; this is sometimes the negative aspect of African American history when it comes to Washington, and it is erroneously unfair.

Washington is often left on the scrapbook of African American history for having given a speech that basically stated, "Hey Mr. White Man of the South, let us be friends. Allow my people to live in peace and prosperity and to build our communities without interference or hassle from you. We in turn shall offer our skills when paid a decent dollar for our labor, and we will keep to our communities, as you will keep to yours—peacefully." However, again paraphrased, he also stated, "We expect a fair chance, and no violence from law enforcement, no unfair judicial system, and no disparity in jail sentences compared to our white counterparts." This is his basic message, and the idea that he abstained from politics is not quite right, as he stipulated, "It is important and right that all privileges of the law be ours" (224).

To be sure, Washington operated in *very* dangerous times. No African American could feel safe in proximity to a group of white men in the South—even if well educated. Did he come over as naive and overly optimistic in Atlanta? Yes, he did. But what else could he do in an environment that did not allow African Americans to prosper in any small way without giving them hell on earth? The culture of Black codes that curtailed the movement, labor, and prosperity of African Americans was still evident in the South. Therefore, Washington had to offer some form of negotiation toward the white South; and for those who criticized, he could refer to Matthew 7:1: "Judge not, that ye be not judged." There is an irony in the criticism that would follow this speech way beyond Washington's lifetime, mainly due to one of his biggest historical critics: the renowned scholar W. E. B. Du Bois. However, immediately following the address, Du Bois praised him and wrote to congratulate Washington:

Dear Mr. Washington,
    Let me heartily congratulate you upon our phenomenal success at Atlanta—it was a word fitly spoken.
    Sincerely yours,
    W.E.B. Du Bois.
(Aptheker 1973, 39)

Du Bois and others would later change their minds and become very anti-Washington in the following years (chapter 5 covers Washington's critics in greater detail). Yet just after the address, he received adulation from near and far, and the press reported the address as a triumph for the South going forward. One could argue that he leaned more toward the power of white supremacy, but in hindsight the reality of the suppression of African Americans had been well under way since 1877 and the close of the Reconstruction Era. To lay at his feet, as many historians have done, the blame for African American subjugation because of one speech is quite myopic in scope. Nonetheless, history textbooks published on African American experience, since the 1895 address in Atlanta, encapsulate or fossilize Washington as the great "accommodationist" or the "compromiser" to white supremacy.

Washington was an extremely perceptive individual, and he knew the hatred that was being fed to the average white Southerner through popular culture. The whites who resided in the rural areas, and small towns of the South were largely ignorant and unworldly. They were fed disgusting racist images of African Americans daily via popular newspapers and magazines that basically depicted them negatively. As Robert Norrell writes, "uncivilized animals and sexual fiends who hated whites and would attack them when least expected—a dangerous enemy in their midst" (Norrell 2009, 119). If a people are consistently disparaged and maligned by popular cultural images and it is passed on through generations, then it will adversely impact the way they are treated and viewed. This is not rocket science; all one has to do is examine the history of World War II and the attack by the Nazis on Jewish people. They were viciously attacked in popular German culture from 1933 when Hitler gained power, at first when basic rights of citizenship were taken, and then when their lives were taken through mass extermination. In hindsight, the attack on African American humanity had been going on much longer, and it depended upon the considerable psychological manipulation of ignorant whites. Magazine and newspaper editors from the South specifically had much responsibility for the animosity they collectively created against the African American population in the nineteenth century and early twentieth century.

Washington knew full well that the people he was addressing in Atlanta were not particularly enlightened to racial equality. Even the citizenship of the African American was not yet respected; he knew this fully, and he had to tread very carefully in a culture that despised the very fact that an articulate African American, formerly enslaved, was standing before them at a prestigious event in the Deep South and holding court confidently. That in itself was a dangerous undertaking that few historians have contemplated. His address has since been largely taken out of context, and the twenty-seven words suggesting that the cultures can remain socially "separate as the fingers" have been etched in stone as a tacit sanction of segregation as a new reality. In fact, segregation had been sweeping through the South since the 1880s; in 1887 Florida would enact a segregation law on railroad travel, and Mississippi, Louisiana, Texas, and other Southern states would soon follow suit.

Almost two decades before Washington spoke at the Cotton States International Exposition, African Americans were continuously assaulted and denied their right to the pursuit of happiness. It is folly to suggest he was responsible entirely for African American disenfranchisement. This had long been going on and was getting increasingly worse. The fact that he was able to get Tuskegee Institute up and running was a miracle in itself. If one thinks of the "art of war," then African Americans really had no choice but to be careful in the way they moved upward. This is why, in many ways, Washington was a genius tactician. His message of "friendly relations" being fostered was sensible in order to tap into the goodwill of the few progressive wealthy whites. The intelligent racist white Southerners also knew there had to be some compromise; they needed African Americans, and they knew it. The ignorant racist did not know much, other than to despise African Americans because they were fed lies daily and images in horrific caricature forms (Gates 2019).

Too often, again unfairly, the great and fiery Frederick Douglass and the patiently humble Booker T. Washington are pitted against each other, Douglass being the firebrand intellect of no compromise and the vote is sacred, while Washington being meek, willing to compromise, and undecided on the vote being as necessary to goodwill and partnership. Both men had different struggles and lived in different time periods with some overlap. Douglass was an intellect-activist, whereas Washington was an institutional builder-activist, a job provider, a businessman, and an instigator of local economic prosperity. Overall, Douglass and Washington cannot be lumped together as "either/or," because their lives were in many aspects entirely different. Yes, they were both African American males in a viciously racist society—they each had much in common. But one man stayed and fought most of his life in the North, and the other stayed and fought most of his life in the South.

Washington had nothing but great respect for Douglass and even wrote a biography of his life with the aid of a ghost writer. The biography of Douglass by Washington was first published in 1906, and it is rarely cited, or even known today. It is a worthy biographical portrait of the exemplary life Douglass lived. On the issue of Douglass abstaining from residing in the South and largely refraining from Southern politics, Washington stated, "Frederick Douglass was wholly right in his determination not to take up his residence in one of the Southern states for political purposes. Had he followed the advice of some of his friends, his career would have been considerably marred by the exigencies of party and sectional politics, and his character as a natural leader of his people would, in all probability, have shrunken to that of a state politician" (Washington 2003, 273). There is something very informative in how Washington explains the dilemma faced by Douglass had he operated in the South doing his laudatory work in African American liberation. Clearly he knew the potential pitfalls encountered by a deeply racist culture. Of course there were good white men and women in the South who disliked the racial antagonism and prejudice, but they were by and large in a small minority. Without being too facetious and cynical, it is probable too that when faced with the choice between the empowerment of an African American or a white Southerner they would lean toward the latter.

Much of the Southern character of racism and prejudice is found in the work of Thomas Pearce Bailey (1867–1949), a noted scholar in the fields of education and psychology. One of his more popular publications is *Race Orthodoxy in the South, and Other Aspects of the Negro Question*, which was published in 1914 while Washington was still alive. It included many deeply flawed notions regarding "race" as a science. The book is profoundly racist, and the author espouses the salient racism that was prevalent in the South at the time and prior to its publication. What is both insightful and concerning is the fact that during his career Bailey spent time all across the United States spreading his overtly racialized pseudoscientific ideas. He was once at the University of California, the University of Chicago, and the University of Mississippi: quite a list of well-known universities. His work was well received throughout the South and beyond because he also took positions as the superintendent of schools of Memphis and was an investigator for the New York Bureau of Municipal Research.

Bailey was well placed, and the popularity of his work serves of an example of why Washington had to maneuver with great caution. Briefly, Bailey provided a fifteen-point summary of his ideas that were disseminated across the South and broader nation, five of which were as follows:

1) Blood will tell; this is a white man's country and domination of the white race will remain.
2) Teutonic people stand for racial purity, and there will be no social or political equality.
3) If there is to be education, it will be crumbs from the white man's table; let African Americans have Industrial education as to only serve the white man.
4) Any civil or legal rights will always be subordinate to the white race.
5) Only Southerners know the African American, so let the South settle the African American problem; only peasantry is the social status they can hope for if there is to be peaceful co-existence; the lowest white man counts more than the highest African American (Bailey 1914, 93).

Bailey (1914) sealed his "Southern Credo" with the idea that it was "God's Providence" that assigned the African American to a lower social position. If his espousal of racialized hierarchy was coming from a marginalized corner of society, then it would make more sense, but this was articulated by a leading scholar who had literally been endorsed across the nation as an academic of repute. Yet if these ideas were floating around in 1914 at the time of the book's publication, then what can be said for the ideas' dissemination in 1895 when Booker T. Washington gave his Atlanta address? Any reading of this time period emanating a white perspective, from the 1890s to 1915, is largely devoid of providing a "fair chance" in society for African Americans. Thomas Pearce Bailey's intellectually dishonest work served to disseminate racialized lies and stereotypes which still have life today. If an avowed racist thinker like Bailey is given kudos in the academic world of his day, then it is understandable that those outside of academia would take it as worthwhile knowledge.

The fact that the *Plessy v. Ferguson* decision of the Supreme Court came about in 1896 that essentially sanctioned in law the separation of whites and African Americans as long as it was "separate but equal" was mere coincidence, because the case had been in the courts since 1892, working its way up to the Supreme Court. It is incorrect to put this decision in relation to Washington's Atlanta Address, because it was well underway. In fact, the South had been discriminating against African Americans in public amenities systematically since the end of the Reconstruction Era (Logan 1997). Nevertheless, the *Plessy v. Ferguson* ruling put in law segregation, and this would last well into the 1960s; one could argue it still exists today in de facto terms in many schools and public amenities across the South and in the North (Hacker 2003).

> ### HOMER PLESSY (1862–1925)
>
> The U.S. Supreme Court decision in the case of *Plessy v. Ferguson* of May 1896 led to almost sixty years of de jure segregation. It ruled that equal but separate accommodation for whites and African Americans was legal, if all is equal. Homer Plessy had paid for a first class train journey in New Orleans, Louisiana on June 7, 1892, and was arrested for not moving to the "colored section" of the train. His case went right up to the Supreme Court and it ruled in favor of the train company, leaving the doctrine of "Separate but Equal" in place until *Brown v. Board of Education* made the idea and practice of separate but equal unconstitutional. Segregation was ratified and sanctioned throughout the Southern states. What is significant for the life of Booker T. Washington is that this case unfolded three years before his Atlanta Address in 1895. The South was disenfranchising and segregating African Americans since the post–Civil War era and it would be unfair to suggest that Washington was responsible for segregation and discrimination. He fought behind the scenes in a number of cases involving railroad transport discrimination. Ironically, Homer Plessy was a man of just one-eighth of African blood, the rest being of white European. Again, this emphasized the profound absurdity of racism.

The average white Southerner fed from the racist popular culture without having much opportunity to learn more in a critical sense. However, if education was imbued with the ideas of Bailey, and other racist thinkers, then inevitably there were few places where one could find the African American depicted in a human light (Woodward 1971, 352). This leads to the difficulty faced when evaluating Washington and his Atlanta address at the exposition. He walked a very fine line between success and failure that hot and sunny September day in 1895. Some would argue that it was a pyrrhic victory, that the loss was greater than the gain. Yet he walked away from that stage a praised man, by both whites and African Americans, as someone who was trying to find a positive way forward for the South.

There was a specific type of white men who had power in the South during this period and who had a deep antipathy toward African Americans and their progress in society. These white men had been disenfranchising African Americans long before Washington took to the stage. Benjamin R. Tillman (1867–1918), for example, was a viciously racist white Southern planter who was situated in South Carolina and was known for whipping his African American field hands in the post-enslavement era. Apart from his open hostility toward African Americans in his speeches and everyday life, he would also endorse lynching and violence against African Americans. His aim was to disenfranchise African Americans by any means necessary. He was governor of South Carolina (1890–1894) and then elected to Congress as senator from 1895 till his death in 1918. He never diminished his hatred, though his anger may have inadvertently been from the tumor that impacted him so badly his left eye was removed. Although there was no real explanation for his cruelty against African Americans, Tillman was able to support and induce his hatred and white supremacist views in the highest levels of government for nearly thirty years, both in the South and at the federal level (Kantrowitz 2000). As with Thomas Pearce Bailey, Tillman had a very powerful position of influence in society during the Booker T. Washington era.

Another well-known figure and white supremacist active during this time was Thomas Dixon Jr. (1864–1946), who wrote a number of novels glorifying the Ku Klux Klan (KKK). One novel published in 1905, called *The Clansman* that would later be adapted for a movie, *Birth of a Nation* (1915), which both glorified the KKK and then helped revive the rise of the hate organization in the 1920s. Dixon came from a family of Klansman and inculcated the ideas of white supremacy. He grew to be a clergyman, a lawyer, a politician, and had a career as a writer. His father had joined the KKK during Reconstruction and did all he could to intimidate African Americans from exercising their right to vote. His son, Thomas Dixon Jr., ran with the ideas of nineteenth-century racism right into the twentieth century. Indeed, the film *Birth of a Nation* was praised highly by President Woodrow Wilson who premiered it at the White House. The height of Dixon's fame and influence came during the lifetime of Booker T. Washington.

James K. Vardaman (1861–1930) was an outspoken white supremacist and the Governor of Mississippi from 1904 to 1908. He was highly responsible for creating fear and mistrust of African Americans and inciting hatred for them. (Library of Congress)

James Kimble Vardaman (1861–1930) was another viciously racist white supremacist and only five years younger than Washington. He was a Mississippi lawyer and newspaperman who turned his hand to politics. He served in the Mississippi House of Representatives between 1890 and 1896; much of his work was in denigrating African Americans and suppressing their rights to vote. He was known for his overt racist language in speech and for putting down any hope for African American empowerment in Mississippi. An avowed white supremacist, he did not want any form of educational uplift for African Americans. Vardaman went on to be the governor of Mississippi from 1904 to 1908 and later was elected to Congress as a senator from 1912, serving till 1919. Throughout his adult life he thought to keep the whites in the South empowered and the African American disempowered. He was another contemporary of Booker T. Washington and someone who detested his work at Tuskegee Institute. Had Vardaman won his way throughout the South, then African Americans would not have been allowed any form of education. African Americans were to be used only as a form of labor for whites and be confined to illiteracy had Vardaman gained his outlook on the South and racialized relations.

The final example of the typical white supremacist based in the South during the Washington era is John Sharp Williams (1854–1932), but note

JAMES K. VARDAMAN (1861–1930)

James K. Vardaman was a Southern politician who represented the typical white supremacist who did nothing to hide his racism. He was a Democrat who styled himself as "the Great White Chief" of white supremacist ideology. His rhetoric was shaped to attract a populist following among the poor whites of the South. As such the assault of African American empowerment was unrelenting and intimidating. He was elected to the Mississippi House of Representatives between 1890 and 1896, and later in his career he served as the governor of Mississippi (1904–1908). In one of his speeches relating to the Mississippi Constitution in 1890 he stated, "There is no use to equivocate or lie about the matter. . . . Mississippi's constitutional convention of 1890 was held for no other purpose than to eliminate the nigger from politics. Not the 'ignorant and vicious,' as some of the apologists would have you believe, but the nigger. . . . Let the world know it just as it is. . . . In Mississippi we have in our constitution legislated against the racial peculiarities of the Negro. . . . When that device fails, we will resort to something else" (McMillen, 1990, 41). Vardaman was a passionate racist who exemplifies the times from the 1890s through to the 1950s in the Southern states. Other Southern politicians were just as vehement toward African Americans, and this is the milieu in which Booker T. Washington operated.

there could be an ongoing list of hundreds of empowered white supremacists. The point here is to show the reader a handful of very powerful Southern racist politicians who were 100 percent against the positive work that Washington was providing his people in Tuskegee, Alabama. Williams was one such who displayed and acted out his antipathy toward African Americans at every opportunity. Born in Memphis, Tennessee, but raised in Yazoo County, Mississippi, Williams was educated at the Kentucky Military Institute in 1870. He was apparently short of some science credits to gain a bachelor's degree from the University of Virginia at Charlottesville. After spending about two years in Europe at the University of Heidelberg, he returned to the University of Virginia and graduated with a degree in law in 1876. He would return to Yazoo County to run a family plantation and law practice. After about five years, he ran for political office and was elected to the Congress and the House of Representatives in 1893. Therefore, by the mid-1890s, he was apparently an educated and global traveler, with experience of business and in federal political office representing the Democratic Party and Mississippi. In the winter of 1898, he declared, "You could ship-wreck 10, 000 illiterate white Americans on a desert island, and in three weeks they would have a fairly good government, conceived and administered upon fairly democratic lines. You could ship-wreck 10, 000 [African Americans], every one of whom was a graduate of Harvard University, and in less than three years, they would have retrograded governmentally; half of the men would have been killed, and the other half would have two wives apiece" (Logan 1997, 90). Williams was another white man who did all he could to keep African Americans disempowered in the South; he was the minority leader in the House of Representatives and would eventually move into the Senate. He spent about twenty years in politics and eventually returned to Mississippi and his family plantation to live out his last decade. What is significant is the fact that these racist white men yielded great political and/or cultural power and influence across the South and in Congress.

Crucially, Booker T. Washington had a powerful group of white racist Southern politicians against him who were both educated and ruthless in the pursuit of white supremacy. If John Sharp Williams was disparaging of the Harvard African American graduates, like W. E. B. Du Bois, then you can imagine how negatively he thought of African Americans based in the South. However, regardless of these vicious forces held against his efforts, Washington would not be deterred. His mind was set on creating at least an economic and educational foothold that African Americans could employ to uplift themselves. It appears that Tuskegee Institute was a "shining light" on a hill where all below were efforts to dim the sparkle and bring it down. The year 1895 was not the best of times for African Americans; that is obvious, but it was a time when Washington seized whatever he could to stifle the enemies who fervently opposed them. He did it with the political skills that were natural to him; his character was not that of an angry man. He was a calm soul; regardless of the problems he confronted, his personality did not dim. He kept his deeply felt feelings and sorrows rather private. Yes, there was upset and exhaustion in struggling, but it was not in his nature to give up on his cause in empowering his people in the best way he could, and in a time when so many were against it. If he had acted without having a forthright vision for success, then failure would easily have knocked on his door. Washington was above all a practical man in a rather insensitive and injurious world.

Regardless of the white racists and skeptical African Americans, the immediate aftermath of his Atlanta address was largely successful. The press was very praiseworthy in the response to Washington. In *Up from Slavery* he cites a number of the press releases covering his speech. One from the Boston *Transcript* editorial page in part stated, "The speech of Booker T. Washington at the Atlanta Exposition . . . seems to have dwarfed all the other proceedings and the Exposition itself. The sensation that it has caused in the press has never been equalled" (226). Irrespective of the profound racism, it appears that Washington's view was an acceptable "compromise" for the middle of the road Southern racists. The diehard racists depicted earlier would never be won over and this should be understood.

Appearance and reality can be two different aspects of the same phenomena. The press gave Washington a boost, and it catapulted him into national and international fame. With this came more prestige but also more envy and enmity. Something historians and biographers have failed to capture is the immense resentment Washington drew from his newfound fame. They simply point to this address as if it is the beginning and the end, at least when it comes to the essence of the man. This is partly to do with the hysteria created from the press, and the adulation he received as a consequence. Sometimes adoration can take over the actual substance. After all, he was simply asking for the viciousness of white Southern racism to calm down so that African Americans can be given the space to develop themselves—to get some form of educational and economic base. In doing so, the social segregation that was *already* imposed upon African Americans could continue *if* his people were allowed to build a community infrastructure that could sustain itself without interference, particularly in the exercise of intimidation and violence against them.

After the address he struck up a good relationship with President Grover Cleveland, and when you mix with the high end of society, this inevitably creates more success. Yet, what many do not know is that Washington sent a copy of the speech to him right afterward, striking while the iron was hot in order to use the press coverage to gain the president's attention. It worked because President Cleveland replied in letter form, and part of his reply reads, "Your words cannot fail to delight and encourage all who wish well for your race; and if our colored fellow-citizens do not from your utterances gather new hope and form new determinations to gain every valuable advantage offered them by their citizenship, it will be strange indeed" (227). This message coming from the president of the United States in 1895 is rather instructive. It reveals potential "new hope" for African Americans in the South. That may also indicate the depth of racism that they were up against, and something that President Cleveland was fully aware of.

Taken in this context the speech was not a blow-out for African Americans, and those present that day in large number cheered on Washington. Nevertheless the history books have not been kind and have simply labeled it a "compromise" that gave away too much. A response to such a narrow perspective is "How can you give away what you do not have?" Another way to view this is to argue "What if Booker T. Washington had not spoken that day? Would the white South suddenly have halted their racist violence and racism in popular culture?" What if, in fact, Washington's words actually saved hundreds of African Americans from being lynched, even though lynching was still a part of the growing racist culture? Basically, it is difficult to pin on Washington the disenfranchisement label that was already in full swing. Moreover, Washington in private contested voting and other discriminations against African Americans (Harlan 1972, 1983). He quietly resisted the forces that endeavored to stifle African American progress in the South—he could not do this overtly; it had to be done covertly.

There is no doubt that the Atlanta address reverberated around the nation as a new dawn for the South, but this was largely "press talk" and hopeful wishing. The Tillmans, Vardamans, Dixons, and others would continue to spill out racist bile and encourage the white masses of the South to hate their African American neighbors. Washington could not put a stop to the racist ideology being disseminated against himself and his people. The racism in the South was simply too ingrained, and much of the bitterness came from the loss of the Civil War to the North. All this profound resentment could not be washed away with a speech requesting greater harmony and collaborative coexistence between, according to many, two incompatible cultures.

One wonders why historically Washington has taken so much heat for endeavoring to find a way toward reconciling and abating such a hostile environment. He should no longer be the reason why African Americans encountered such violence and mistreatment in the early part of the twentieth century. There should be a continued revision, reevaluation, of the historical record. An interesting study on the illicit sex between white Southern women and African American males illuminates the resentment and explains the depths of white insecurities that led to such violence after the Civil War. One of the major myths to come out of the South was the notion of the "pure white innocent female," particularly prior to the Civil War. Martha Hodes in her fascinating book *White Women, Black Men: Illicit Sex in the 19th Century South* gives an explanation to white violence: "White concerns about the preservation of slave property could . . . check violent reactions to a sexual transgression between a white woman and a black man. The end of slavery also meant the end of property concerns and thus helps to explain . . . the shift toward extreme white violence in the decades following emancipation" (Hodes 1997, 5).

Martha Hodes goes on to explain that once the value of their property, in terms of African Americans in bondage, diminished then it was open season on violence and intimidation. White women had always "crossed the line" in sexual relations with African American males. Yet, history only accounts for the rape of African American women by the slaveholder and any white male in the vicinity. Hodes (1997) brings out into the open the deep-seated insecurity white male Southerners had toward African American males, particularly with the phallic symbolism and stereotyping of such in the white imagination. The fear of sexual prowess and interaction of African American males and white women were always reasons or causes for lynching after the Civil War.

Therefore, the loss of property value that white Southern plantation owners suffered and their fear of African American males encroaching on white women were major sources of the enmity. The South lost the Civil War, which ended enslavement, and white Southerners found ways to get back at those who benefited from it most: African Americans. This is a way to comprehend the level of strong resentment in many white thinkers, politicians, and businessmen toward African American advancement. Washington could not have overcome such deeply entrenched psychological fears in white Southerners in one speech. Nor could he have been expected to save the South from its sickness that had started in the 1600s and endured through the centuries. Enslavement was a curse on the South in the 1800s, and by the end as time ticked toward the twentieth century, the disease of racism had not abated; it had simply festered and manifested in ways that appalled the very notion of humanity. Washington, having experienced bondage and having fought hard to be where he stood in 1895, went forward with a greater sense of self. He had a perfect wife for his celebrity status in the form of Margaret Washington, who was in every sense of the word a supporter and an advocate for women's rights. He was fortunate to have her counsel in a time when he stood up against virulent racism in a clandestine manner. Washington was never a "showy" person. He did not take kindly to braggadocios persons who had pretentious manners. It is fair to describe him as a "salt of the earth" man who wanted the best for humanity—he was not a man who sought conflict when peace could be attained.

On racial prejudice, his perspective was direct: "No man whose vision is bounded by color can come into contact with what is highest and best in the world. In meeting men, in many places, I have found that the happiest people are those who do the most for others; the most miserable are those who do the least" (229). This was an important aspect of Washington; there is no detection of animosity between himself and whites, be it from the South or North. He genuinely was not a man to harbor resentment toward any man. This has often been characterized as a form of weakness, especially by his critics in the African American community, who often felt one should be in a constant mood of agitation. Frederick Douglass appeared to be this kind of personality, always combative and ready to take on the world. But Washington did not have that kind of demeanor; he was born with great patience and developed a way to see the best in everything, no matter how awful things were. For Washington, there was always a silver lining, a rainbow of hope that would get him over a tricky spot.

More importantly, there was no bitterness in him, and the best psychologists will always express the notion that anger and rancor in the body only brings on more disease and discomfort. In evaluating his motives, one must also consider his personality type; he was a man who did not enjoy confrontation. This does not mean he was a pushover; it simply expresses how he communicated with people regardless of race or gender, and certainly class. If anything he was content in his own skin, and unapologetic about being a man of African American heritage. Indeed, he celebrated the African American culture and its rich heritage with all who visited the school. He was a very proud "race man" who delighted in comprehending the cultural heritage of African Americans in the South particularly—he loved his people.

One of his greatest hopes was to have a president of the United States visit Tuskegee Institute, as it would bring prestige to the institution, its student, and faculty body. With his success in Atlanta, he was able to attract more funders for Tuskegee Institute. Eventually President McKinley accepted an invite and made a visit to the institution in December 1898. Everything Washington did had an ultimate aim in improving the image of his people and pushing through his agenda. Washington walked through life like a fox on ice; he was extremely cautious. He was very careful with his words; especially with regard to demands for betterment and progressivism, he pitched his arguments cautiously. One of his key strategies was to make friends in high places, and for an African American of his generation, there was no one who could come near to his ability to disarm white men with power. He was particularly popular with self-made white men based in the North, particularly Andrew Carnegie and William H. Baldwin.

Having President McKinley visit Tuskegee Institute was a real coup, and it gave him great satisfaction, but not in a pompous way. Always the target was growth and development, onward and upward, with the hope also of lessening the tension between the white South and African Americans. When word got out that he had secured President McKinley's visit to the town of Tuskegee and Tuskegee Institute, everyone got excited. Washington recalls, "The white people of the town, including both men and women, began arranging to decorate the town.... I think I never realized before this how much the white people of Tuskegee and vicinity thought of our institution" (306). It was literally a one-off occasion when all people, of all classes, came together for the president's visit. It was a grand occasion with floats passing by with various aspects of the school's work on display.

In his speech, President McKinley praised the institution for its renowned contribution to African Americans. He stated that Tuskegee Institute was known across the country and even around the world. He paid special tribute to Washington, stating that without "Booker T. Washington's genius and perseverance [this] would not be impossible. The inception of this noble enterprise was his, and he deserves high credit for it. His was the enthusiasm and enterprise which made its steady progress possible and established in the institution its present high standard of accomplishment" (308). High praise indeed from the president of the United States who paid tribute to a forty-two-year-old Washington who had risen out of enslavement, and with drive and support built an institution of learning that could attract a president to visit it, and who, in turn, would shower its leader with praise and honor—quite an incredulous tale.

The ease with which Washington could hobnob with white men who had made fortunes was in part because of his down-to-earth attitude to life. He did not seek to be a wealthy man; he merely sought to establish Tuskegee Institute and for it to be successful. The majority of the wealthy patrons of the institution who supported Washington's vision with tangible funding came from the North, particularly Boston and New York. In order to get an insight into the relationships, he developed it would be useful to have a snapshot of a few. Most often when Washington was critiqued by his own people, it was due to his "reliance on white men" for funds. Yet, this was a rather superficial view, because those who did help in this manner were philanthropic and at best wanted to help Washington in his quest to provide educational opportunities for his people. Those on the board of trustees would be there most often for support of *his* ideas and methods. Even if some of them held notions of inferior/superior human beings, one could ask, "Who did not in the early twentieth century?" Eugenics and the measuring of men and women's attributes was then a "pseudoscience," and it had an impact on everyone, from immigration officials, scholars, teachers, to everyday people. So it is a rather weak argument to suggest that there were whites that were free of all forms of racialized prejudice. Just as it would be difficult for any male of that era to recognize a woman as a coequal, though Washington was a rather progressive soul when it came to empowering the women in his life.

That stated, after General Armstrong, and a few others based at Hampton Institute, a number of key white men were in Washington's favor for quite a few years in the early development of Tuskegee Institute. There were also a number of women, particularly two sisters, Olivia Phelps Stokes (1847–1927) and Caroline Phelps Stokes (1854–1909) who after learning about the Tuskegee Institute enterprise funded a permanent scholarship of $2,000 to help students who were developing a religious propriety. They were committed philanthropists and donated toward the construction of buildings at Tuskegee Institute; Phelps Hall was one of the buildings they donated. They worked with the African American architect Robert R. Taylor (1868–1942), who was responsible for a number of key buildings on the campus. The affluent sisters were based in New York City, and they funded other African American educational institutions as well, including Hampton Institute and Berea College in Kentucky. There was nothing superficial or racist about these women. They only wanted to help young and impoverished African American men and women. Booker T. Washington was one of their benefactors because they were impressed with his work. He was also very transparent with whatever funds he received and would invite donors to see the outcome of their charity.

There were quite a number of key philanthropists who aided Washington's school. It would be fair to state that he actually attracted funding with good publicity and with the number of speaking engagements he undertook in the North to raise awareness. Washington was a genius in raising funds, and this seems to be underplayed in the existing biographies. All that can be given here is a snapshot, but enough to get a good understanding of the breadth of his interaction with the wealthy of his day and age who were based in the North. Although he had raised lots of funds from ordinary folk who were not rich, his major contributors, like the Stokes sisters, were a great boon. Two benefactors in particular worked with Washington for years and were also on the board of trustees, Robert C. Ogden (1836–1913), and William H. Baldwin Jr. (1863–1905). Ogden was a businessman based primarily in New York, who after visiting the South during the Civil War became good friends with General Armstrong. In assessing his relationship with Washington, it probably relates to both men being in contact with General Armstrong. Ogden had known Washington from his days at Hampton Institute, using his philanthropic contacts to gain more funding he helped Tuskegee Institute get established. Ogden loaned Washington funds whenever he was struggling to keep a cash flow going in the early years. He was interested in Southern education issues and was drawn to the African American experience via Armstrong. He would become close to Washington as an adviser during the establishment of Tuskegee Institute and remained involved till his death in 1913. Ogden was particularly prominent in the organization of the twenty-fifth anniversary of Tuskegee Institute in 1906.

William H. Baldwin Jr. was a benefactor and friend who was too nervous to be in the audience when Booker T. Washington spoke in Atlanta, Georgia, on that hot September day in 1895. Apparently, he spent the time outside the venue hoping that Washington was able to do a good job in his address. Baldwin and his liberal colleague Ogden were prominent in strategizing business for Tuskegee Institute and in identifying funding opportunities as trustees. Baldwin could be deemed a very close confidante to Washington. He had made his fortune in the railroad industry, and in getting to know the South for business purposes, he realized it was in the nation's interest to develop an industrial education system. Baldwin therefore contributed to Tuskegee Institute until his life was relatively cut short by intestinal cancer at the age of forty-one. Washington spoke at his funeral in New York in January 1905, and this is an indication of the depth of friendship that had developed between the two men. Among the mourners were the New York City elite such as Andrew Carnegie and William Vanderbilt (*New York Times* 1905). Baldwin was close enough to Washington to have kept a rent-free house available for Washington and his wife whenever they stayed in the New York region. Overall, his main advice to Washington involved the running of the institution in terms of keeping it on a solvent footing. To be fair, Tuskegee Institute was run very stringently by Washington, and he had learned much from the administrators at Hampton Institute on how to manage financial responsibility.

Washington was proud to not have any debt on Tuskegee Institute; the former plantation property was by the early twentieth century a thriving enterprise. He was wise and fortuitous to use wealthy white men of the North for the expertise they offered, and most notably, their social contacts to other wealthy donors. Philanthropy was a popular pastime for the rich who had developed an interest in the uplift of African Americans after the Civil War, particularly in the realm of education. Along with the obvious influence of Armstrong, Ogden, and Baldwin who were pivotal in the early rise of Tuskegee Institute, others would follow their lead. It could be argued that there was a degree of paternalism involved in the relationship, but Washington's ideas were never compromised because he sincerely believed that the best way forward was in taking careful steps toward African American prosperity: hard work, thrift, common sense, and moral character. He had learned these lessons studying his mentor at Hampton Institute. Armstrong, his teaching methods, and his Christian faith, all impacted how Washington would build Tuskegee Institute. Yet, again to be fair to Washington, his drive and his intelligence drove the institution up from a shanty to a splendid "educational village" full of student life and innovation. It was his drive and tenacity that brought success to Tuskegee Institute, and many of the rich and wealthy were glad to be associated with its ideals.

The Protestant Ethic was Washington's credo, and the white Christian patrons knew he was a sincere man in his goal to help the broader African American community. No one was being fooled, especially Washington. He knew how to meander through the labyrinth of patronizing and entitled white folks. Moreover, he knew fundamentally that "no man is an island," and without the assistance of rich patrons from the North he would not have got Tuskegee Institute to where it was by 1900—a thriving center of industrial and academic learning. His motto of the "hands and the head" was a basic building block in his educational philosophy. All students should leave Tuskegee Institute armed with a trade skill and enough academic abilities to thrive in the surrounding areas of the South. Therefore there was no need for him to hide too much from rich white patrons, other than his belief that racism was absurd.

Though Washington's fame was secured after the Atlanta speech, with it came more responsibility and contact with the broader world. Washington's major autobiography, *Up from Slavery*, was published in 1901 to wide acclaim at home and abroad. Sections of the book were first serialized in a popular magazine titled the *Outlook*. Andrew Carnegie (1835–1919) would come to read the account of his life and be impressed by the struggle he had overcome to succeed and how he wanted to help his people. Yet, Washington recalls it taking a long time to get Carnegie's attention as he had tried to make contact in the early 1890s, but Carnegie had shown little interest in Tuskegee Institute at the time. But by 1900 things had changed at Tuskegee Institute to the degree that most people of wealth were impressed by the work Washington was leading. The two men would eventually meet in the early years of the twentieth century and stay in touch as friends, so much so that Carnegie invited Washington to stay at his Skibo Castle in Scotland when he was on a speaking tour of Europe in 1910 (Harlan 1983, 290). It is rarely emphasized by biographers or historians just how admired Washington was by self-made white men such as Carnegie. Once Carnegie had read Washington's autobiography there was an affinity due to their life stories of hardship. He admitted that Washington had clearly met the greatest battle, having not been born free and with little hope as a child. Both men shared a keen interest in helping their fellow man. Carnegie had come to North America as an immigrant and achieved the American Dream with his hard work and good fortune in building an empire of steel and industrial manufacturing. Washington had been born during the era of enslavement, yet he had built Tuskegee Institute in order to free his people from poverty and ignorance. Each wanted to help improve society for the masses. Carnegie proved this by giving the vast majority of his wealth to charity before he died. He created over three thousand public libraries in order to allow poor children an opportunity to learn as he was once given such from a kind man when he was young. Carnegie never forgot how using a library in his youth changed his life and gave him a love for education.

Washington was from the dawn of the twentieth century a benefactor of Carnegie's vast wealth and charity due to his work at Tuskegee Institute. He received $600,000 to build a library and to fund other projects that would enhance Tuskegee Institute, including other interests that Washington was involved developing. One such idea was the establishment of the National Negro Business League (NNBL) that he set up in 1900. The idea was first created by W. E. B. Du Bois, but he never got it fully off the ground due to having less wherewithal and contacts across the nation as did Booker T. Washington. Whether right or wrong, Washington picked up the idea and ran with it because he was in a position to do so. Many ideas have been taken and further advanced by those with greater skills and resources, it is the nature of business. One could argue, it is the "survival of the fittest" that get to win in life. This was also the doctrine being espoused by Herbert Spencer (1820–1903), who was a good friend of Carnegie.

The NNBL idea was initially financed and supported by Carnegie; indeed anything that matched his ideas with that of Washington's would be supported by Carnegie. This was not racism or paternalism; it was simply mutual interest. The man came to admire Washington, and this should not be brushed under the carpet. Not everything is racially determined and discrimination; there is no way Andrew Carnegie would have supported Washington had he been a racist. If one reads his "Gospel of Wealth" philosophy, it was evil not to help your fellow humankind, especially those mired in poverty. Therefore, if any idea that Washington brought to Carnegie fit his philosophical grounding then it would be supported. The NNBL was supported under his foundation because it was about aiding the organization of African American small to large businesses that could compete more effectively in society. It was about giving African Americans an opportunity to build and improve their existing business ventures.

Washington believed that most things important to the uplift of African Americans were derived from an economic base, and if this could be nurtured and improved, then all other relevant things associated to community uplift would naturally emerge. Therefore the NNBL set out primarily to improve the commercial and economic viability and effectiveness of African American businesses. This would be achieved by creating a national network of the organization. NNBL chapters emerged in most of the big cities across the nation, along with annual conferences dealing with contemporary issues directly impacting the development of business among African Americans. It was a very successful enterprise and was supported by Carnegie annually, along with other key philanthropists. There were no demands put on Washington other than a hope that the funds would improve opportunity in business. To be fair, it was Washington who took care of his business first and foremost. What he did with the funds was always based on transparency. No scandal with money ever followed Washington; he was rather careful not to lose the faith of those who could provide philanthropy.

By the early 1900s, Washington's influence was felt across the African American experience and beyond. Had he not given that speech in Atlanta some years previous and completed his autobiography, then it is likely that his fame may not have reached so far. This again comes down to his skills in making his ideas known to the world. He kept records and was a copious letter writer to those philanthropists who were willing to support his work. His trip to Europe in 1900 had further cemented his relationship with Carnegie. And while in London, he was invited to a tea party at Windsor Castle to have tea with Queen Victoria. To the average American, this was the "big time" to mix with British royalty. It probably did not impress someone like Carnegie, who was at heart a freedom-loving Scotsman who was proud of his Scottish roots, and part of that was rivalry with the English!

Nevertheless, Carnegie's admiration for Washington was on a human level, he knew that this African American man had climbed so far in life with little or no support. It is no surprise that a renewed Washington felt empowered to use his fame to further boost his aims and objectives. With this increased power some critics of the man, mainly Du Bois, began to call his work the "Tuskegee Machine" that controlled all aspects of important hiring and firing of African Americans for key employment positions. This perspective has been overblown, being based in the South Washington primarily kept his focus on Southern matters. African Americans based in the North were largely another entity who had their own organizations. Washington's influence was within the confines of Tuskegee Institute, the NNBL, and in advising presidents, Theodore Roosevelt and later Howard Taft. But advice does not always lead to outcomes that the adviser wants, nor expects. Washington's critics tended to place him too closely related to white power, when in reality it merely amounted to gaining funds for Tuskegee Institute and schooling within the rural South.

Obviously, it could be argued that the NNBL was influential in bringing African Americans together in business. Could it be beneficial for a person to have a recommendation from Washington for a position, and could he do likewise and recommend someone for a position? Of course he could. This happens in every organization and in every walk of life. The phrase "It is who you know" applies today as it did in his day. Washington's critics have drunk the Kool-Aid because it is in full supply, most history books do not give nuance to the depth of his relationships; he is merely deemed a puppet for white folks. This is erroneous, if he had a "Tuskegee Machine" it was because he had influence in the ideas he believed in. Rarely is it explained why Washington went to the African American liberal arts institutions, such as Fisk, so often to hire teachers? In addition, few historians, if any, explain why he tried his best to assist many who did not agree with his philosophy. He was a puritan, a man who believed in deferred gratification and in making sure the people he worked with had a sense of his philosophy. Yet he was not inflexible and would balance between industrial and academic curricula at Tuskegee Institute.

However, is it not normal practice in any business to develop a brand? Would it be wise, for example, for a business person in sports clothing to hire a person who has expertise in mechanical engineering? Surely not, most business people endeavor to build a brand that speaks to what it is they sell in the marketplace. Washington had a brand, a philosophy on education that linked the hand with the head. Many African Americans had the idea that labor with hands was below their dignity. They felt that education would free them from working with their hands. These individuals were not perfect for the Washington brand, but he often accommodated them (to use a pun). The bottom line is Washington has been too easily condemned as a puppet and weak-willed man who gave in to white supremacy. Those who led the charge were safely far away, or had locked themselves in, from harm. Moreover, had not Washington walked daily like a fox on ice, his work would have been made moribund by the forces of white supremacy. Instead, he chose to do business in a manner that allowed him to hobnob with the rich and powerful. This gave him some cover from those who wanted him destroyed for numerous reasons, but ultimately for finding a way to uplift his people.

If the "Tuskegee Machine" was a brand that pushed for a certain philosophical perspective, then that was his right; anyone disparaging of his approach in defending his lot, and rightly so, seems profoundly blinkered. Yet the annals of historical interpretation have accounted for Washington's power over his endeavors as sleazy, undemocratic, and underhand. What business enterprise does not have those types of characteristics? Is it not a common phrase that you have to be ruthless to get ahead, and even more ruthless to stay in business? This may not be the popular note to strike in defense of Washington, but it seems fair to him only in hindsight. For too long his legacy has been usurped and put into simple clichés as "accommodationist" when in fact he was just dealing with the ruthlessness of his times. His enemies in the African American community spoke of a "Tuskegee Machine" simply to articulate and undermine the influence he was having in society. On reflection, these labels speak more of envy and jealousy rather than logical critique.

In considering his essential role, one should remember that he was an educator first and foremost and, secondly, a businessman who had to find ways to defend the institution, his students, and faculty from harm, those very persons who relied on him for their futures and livelihoods. Education and business come to mind in relation to Washington's book *The Negro in Business*. This volume was first published in 1907 and explains the origins of the NNBL and what it hoped to achieve. Moreover, it covered numerous and diversified examples of good practice in business for the era; among them were agriculture, banking, catering, manufacturing invention, and undertaking. In short, Washington offers a self-help book on African American business acumen and development.

What is particularly useful in *The Negro in Business* is in the explaining how the history of enslavement kept the African American from reading and writing, and the learning of science. Regardless of this dire situation, African Americans still developed skills, and often the very intelligent and forthright men and women in bondage taught themselves how to read and write, sometimes with the aid of a kindly white person. He explains the scenario that encountered the freed African Americans after 1865: "At the close of the Civil War the South was, from one point of view, an extremely unfavorable field for [African American] trade. The whole section was in a condition of extreme poverty. The [African American] was in a condition of extreme poverty" (Washington 1992, 11). They were left to face the world penniless and often homeless. This being only forty-odd years from when Washington was explaining this history, and only thirty years prior to when he spoke in Atlanta in 1895. In other words, he was endeavoring to explain that after almost 250 years of enslavement, it was astonishing to realize just how far African Americans had come as a people in such a short space of time by the early twentieth century. Washington always viewed the glass as half full, rather than half empty.

There are many examples of poor white Southerners taking the land or successful business from an African American family. The law did not protect them from being terrorized as it protected the average white man and woman. If a critique of Washington could be had, it was in his sanguinity; he did not consider that successful African Americans posed a great threat to the white South. Especially from those too ignorant to comprehend that it was in the best interest of all to have a prosperous South. Washington offered a view that denied the envy and enmity one could find easily in the South. In a section on how well the African American is doing in the South, he writes, "I have been repeatedly informed by [African American] merchants in the South that they have as many white patrons as black; and the cordial business relations which are almost universal between the races in the South prove, as I have elsewhere said, that there is little race prejudice in the American dollar" (13).

There is truth in the saying that the only color that matters is green when it comes to business. There is much to be contended about whether or not this was the right attitude, but really other than outright despair and melancholy, it was the one taken most by Washington. That is what can be gleaned if one reads his utterances carefully and follows the evidence of his actions. There was never a sign of failure in Washington's outlook; his vision was that of success through toil. If the goal was to get a building built, he was there with hand and shovel to show the way, to gain the respect of those involved in the project. Yes, the man led by example, in education and in business. Never did he ask of anyone what he did not engage in himself. It was a pioneering spirit, the ideal of the "self-made man" in line with many of his wealthy white friends; it is fair to suggest that they were actually for the most part admiring friends—it is folly to suggest otherwise.

On this theme of having a pioneering spirit in business, he stated, "The very conditions under which we are compelled to do business demands that we show the energy and initiative of pioneers. The task of the [African American] businessman is not merely to develop the latent wealth in the soil and in the mountains but still more the latent capacity of the [African American] people" (15). Here again he is very positive explaining that, yes, these are difficult times, but if we tap into our latent skills, there is nothing we cannot achieve. Always encouraging, always positive, never viewing the world around him in unspeakably negative terms. Indeed, as with all his business acumen, Washington was a pioneer who led the NNBL for fifteen years as its president, and during his tenure he left many examples of long-term success.

Another area of his life rarely fully acknowledged is in the partnership he developed with the president of Sears, Julius Rosenwald (1862–1932). Rosenwald had dealt with hardship in his early life. He too understood the value of education and admired the work Washington was doing. He wanted to help in a way that was tangible and lasting; developing education opportunities for young African Americans in the South was his target. Both men partnered to build elementary schools in the rural South. Washington had gained a substantial amount of funds from a white philanthropist, a Quaker woman from Philadelphia, Anna T. Jeanes (1822–1907). Through her philanthropic organization, the Anna T. Jeanes Foundation, Washington was granted a million-dollar donation in 1907 to specifically improve the dreadful condition concerning a lack of basic education throughout the South for African Americans. Following the wishes of Ms. Jeanes, he and Hollis B. Frissell from Hampton Institute were asked to put together a board of trustees to develop an independent agency for African American rural schools. The eventual board was mirrored on the Tuskegee Institute model, and on it among the white members were Robert C. Ogden, Andrew Carnegie, and William Howard Taft. Among the African American board members were Robert R. Moton of Hampton Institute and A. M. E. Bishop Abraham Grant. Before she passed away Ms. Jeanes created a pension fund for teachers with the help of the Carnegie Foundation. She passed away in September 1907, but she lasted long enough to have an organization set up with prominent sponsors to aid in the education of African American children of the South.

Therefore, they began the task of setting up small schools in the rural South. Washington was smart enough to work with any philanthropic organization that would aid the development of African American education. These schools would provide basic reading and arithmetic knowledge and act as feeders to the more adult institutions such as Tuskegee Institute and Hampton Institute. What many historians assessing Washington tend to limit is his impact on the development of education beyond the realm of Tuskegee Institute. When the phrase is suggested that he has been "fossilized" as merely an accommodator to white supremacy, it is not factual on the ground. Yet, he was always aware of the danger in going about the work because white supremacists tended to be very vicious, unrelenting in their intimidation, and profoundly insecure when it came to African Americans progressing in society.

Washington was introduced to Rosenwald through the high society in New York City and the Goldman Sachs enterprise. At first Washington invited him onto the Tuskegee Institute Board of Trustees, always a wily move because it meant Rosenwald would ultimately also look after the needs of the institution. Initially, Rosenwald gave "small grants" to help build elementary schools in the Macon County area, those closely connected to the Tuskegee Institute project. Once Rosenwald was satisfied with the way these schools were developing, he expanded his investment. The broad way Washington worked as the "educational statesman" of his time was by not merely looking after his institution's welfare, which was obviously a priority, but by sharing his contacts and spreading the wealth shared by philanthropists. This action puts to rest the stereotype of him being a mere "accommodationist" and "self-seeker." The fact is that Washington was passionately always wanting to help African Americans based across the South and North progress at all levels of education, but particularly industrial. As Harlan states, "In a skillful and broad-gauged way he brought the money of the philanthropists into conjunction with the areas of need at every level of black education" (Harlan 1983, 199). This is rather illuminating given the common view that he was only for industrial or vocational education. Of course, he felt strongly that the needs of both, his immediate community and their welfare, rested in trades that would be of benefit holistically. Not to be facetious, but what good is learning Latin and Greek if you will need to earn a living mainly in the surrounding rural community? Only a few of the thousands of students left their families and the South, even though there was a rising tide toward migration to the Northern cities for employment. What Washington tried hard to do is to get communities to adopt education at an early age, hence the Rosenwald Schools sprung up across the South with the aid of other enlightened philanthropy that emanated from the North.

Washington was on the cutting edge of what was needed on the ground level in the South. He had not only witnessed the poverty and ignorance but lived among it for long periods, he interacted with the common people. He knew both the white and the African American psyche and as a visionary he had no compulsion to harm the progress of any form of education—though he preferred to support industrial and vocational because of its practical necessity. Using his fame since 1895 onward, he sought to push his energy and knowledge in the direction of educational opportunity from elementary through to higher education. When the rural school projects were taking hold, he was careful not to antagonize the whites. Washington, in a letter to a supervisor of the Alabama rural schools buildings project, stated, be sure "not to put so much money into a building that it will bring about a feeling of jealousy on the part of the white people who may have a schoolhouse that is much poorer" (198). He knew the environment and how dangerous it would be to antagonize the wrath of the white neighbor who would inevitably develop a reason to exercise envy, usually by burning down a church or a school. Was this cowardly or intelligent on behalf of Washington? What does one do if outnumbered by a callous enemy hell-bent on finding ways to stifle progress? A man like Washington did not lack courage, he simply understood in his day the psychology of the white Southerner. He had to find ways to cooperate and to live in peace with his neighbors. There being gaudy buildings erected to educate African American children, buildings that would dwarf anything offered to the white community, could only cause grief for African Americans due to the animosity of white Southerners.

Some would argue that it is an insult to be limited in expression, but Washington never viewed keeping a schoolhouse basic and functional as limiting. What was necessary was a decent room that allowed children warmth and cover from the elements in order to enjoy their classroom learning experience. The Rosenwald Schools, under the guidance of Washington, were neatly put together and unpretentious in style. There was more effort put into providing the teacher with adequate materials so that the children would be taught with up-to-date textbooks and materials. The key was to have substance in the education offered, more than comfort in the building environment. Yet what it really reveals about him is his quiet way of dealing with those ignorant whites who would harbor resentment. Those who call his strategies a sellout simply do not have a handle on the depth of danger he encountered, and the peril that followed every advancing step in African American socioeconomic progress.

What some historians and commentators tend to overlook too easily is that Julius Rosenwald was introduced to Washington by his fellow philanthropists. After reading *Up from Slavery*, he became a firm admirer of Washington, and once they got to know each other, they remained steady friends. This aspect of friendship was human, not racialized. There were some rich Northerners wanted to aid the plight of African Americans in the early twentieth century and Booker T. Washington was a man who could navigate such charity to the right places. The reason this is important is due to the fact that it allows one to gauge the actual agency of Washington. He attracted persons of goodwill to him because he was a good soul, and they wanted to help him in any way they could. Philanthropists were not foolish people; they were simply very rich and wanted their legacies to live on with good causes that they believed in. To aid the African American was a human cause if one accepted their humanity. Those who did not recognize their humanity represented the racism that was embedded in society. To be sure, there were millions who did not recognize or accept the humanity of the African American.

In considering the address that Booker T. Washington made at the Cotton States and International Exposition in September 1895, it is clear that it ushered in a new phase in his life. Whatever is stated about it, there is palpable evidence that his star rose higher and shined like a beacon of hope for many African Americans who believed in his message. Those who supported him realized there was something special about the man. He did not have a high opinion of himself, nor did he consider himself inferior to any other human being. He pitied those who put racialized thoughts ahead of getting to know a person for what he or she offered in character. He resented stereotyped images of African Americans; he resented the negative depictions of them too. Washington lived with this but never let it stop him in his quest for excellence.

After the publication of his most celebrated autobiography, *Up from Slavery*, he found greater fame and honor—and with it came larger responsibility. As the symbolic and designated leader of African Americans after the passing of Frederick Douglass there followed trips to Europe and tea with Queen Victoria, which again cemented his rise and fame. After the assassination of President McKinley in 1901 when Teddy Roosevelt took over the presidency, he thought Washington would be useful for his political ambitions. Roosevelt was an imperialist and in many ways an outward white supremacist. However, like many others before him, he admired Washington as a man and as someone who had overcome adversity and risen to help his people in their need. Roosevelt was a man of action, someone who would take African safaris and happily kill a young lion in its prime just to demonstrate his manliness. The irony is that Roosevelt was an avid conservationist and naturalist who saved many green areas from the encroachment of urbanism. This was an impressive aspect of Roosevelt's all-action style of personality, saving parts of land from being gobbled up by property developers.

Roosevelt wanted to be seen as giving African Americans a fair chance and requested Washington to be his adviser in such affairs. This was cemented by inviting him to dinner at the White House in October 1901. The occasion rubberstamped Washington's standing as an African American leader, but it also indicated that his speech in Atlanta was not actually etched in stone. After all, this was a man who had uttered those infamous twenty-seven words alluding to being as separate as fingers in all things social and here he was dining at the White House with Roosevelt, his wife, and another guest. The fact that he was the first African American to have been invited for dinner at the president's abode gave the event more intrigue. Nonetheless, Washington by this time was a distinguished educator and leader of the renowned Tuskegee Institute along with his newly established NNBL. He was truly at the top of his game. The dinner was rather uneventful; the two men discussed the affairs of the day and the hope for a better future. They left each other on cordial terms and promised to work hard together for the betterment of the African American experience (Davis 2012).

However, the next morning the press had a field day with this unprecedented moment in American history. It particularly provoked hatred in the South. Both men were accused of disturbing the social order. The controversy shook Roosevelt, and he had to backpedal on his progressive attitude toward trying to improve racial relations. Both men were relatively young: Roosevelt was forty-two and Washington forty-five; had things been taken in a positive light, maybe the occasion would have put prejudice and racism on a downward trajectory. Unfortunately, it backfired as an event; Roosevelt was lampooned in the Southern newspapers with ridiculous caricature cartoons depicted with grotesque features, making him look more like a gorilla than a human being. It is rather instructive to gauge how such a benign event would become something akin to a cultural earthquake.

Hardcore white supremacists, like Benjamin Tillman, stated, "The action of President Roosevelt in entertaining that nigger will necessitate our killing a thousand niggers in the South before they learn their place again." Governor Vardaman of Mississippi expounded, "President Roosevelt takes this nigger bastard in his home, introduces him to his family and entertains him on terms of absolute social equality" (Norrell 2003, 66). This gives an indication of the racism Washington encountered back in the South. Washington was accused by a female white supremacist suffragist, Rebecca Felton, from Georgia of taking off his "mask" after he was "supposed to be a level-headed, educated colored" (66). She went on to warn him to take his Tuskegee Institute back to the North after dining in the White House. If this appears incredulous, it was merely the tip of the iceberg when it came to white Southern enmity toward African Americans in 1901. The racialized sentiments are deep rooted and alive presently, though it could be deemed less overt in how it is articulated (Feagin 2014). Regardless of the negative response, these two men were a yin and yang team who complemented each other with their personalities. Washington being a naturally cautious man of patience and methodical planning. Roosevelt, on the other hand, was gung-ho and rash in personality, often getting involved in the wrong subject at the wrong time. The public forgave his attempt at forging harmonious relations, and he kept Washington as his adviser. Roosevelt did not always support Washington's advice and ignored some important racist issues involving African Americans. Given that Roosevelt was basically an avid imperialist—and an unashamed believer in superior/inferior races—it was no real surprise. Nevertheless, Washington continued to offer his best advice and would gain some concessions and political appointments from the Roosevelt administration.

The highlight in their uneasy alliance was getting the president to pay a visit to Tuskegee in October 1905. Again, symbolically it told the racists of the South that a man born in bondage had risen to the top of society—regardless of the intense racism. His interactions with President Roosevelt also gave him indirect kudos. That is the strange thing with being a "celebrity" as other successes often follow by virtue of being in the company of celebrities and government officials. Washington carried on building his institution as usual, extending his network of "rich white folks" with big hearts and bank accounts. Many other patrons of his beloved Tuskegee Institute were pleased to help Washington in his cause of African American uplift as he had created a formula for success. *Up from Slavery* was his calling card to the rich and famous, and most of the philanthropic minded would be charmed by Washington's charisma and forthright perspective on the need to improve the poverty and ignorance that plagued the Southern region. Men like Henry H. Rogers of the Standard Oil Company, banker John D. Rockefeller, and the camera manufacturer George Eastman all added dollars to the work that Washington had put his faith in. It would take up too much space to cover all those who aided, but there were many prominent figures who contributed to the cause in improving African American education.

With fame came a lot of envy, as has been discussed, from many white Southerners and a small number of elite African American intellectuals based mainly in the North who felt Washington had sold them out in Atlanta. Due to the importance of this being a key aspect in unpacking the fossilized depiction of Washington, there will be a deeper look at the debate between W. E. B. Du Bois and others in the following chapter. What has been revealed so far is the rise of an exceptional human example of inner strength and determination. To suggest that Washington lacked courage in his manner and deportment is not to understand him. For a man born with so many social handicaps he had a resilience that is unparalleled. His was the strength of character that was so admired by other "self-made" men. This phrase, as you would have gauged, is never completely correct. All men and women need help in their lives to get ahead and Washington took full advantage of any morsel of kindness offered to him. He developed a philosophy of self-help but it was based on a brilliant strategy in fundraising. Without this skill and energy, coupled with a penchant for gifted oration in convincing potential wealthy donors, he may not have broken into that group of philanthropists with his cause. His writings too, with the help of a stenographer and editorial staff, were extremely important. He wrote letters incessantly, and kept records of almost every person who corresponded with him. He was organized with the assistance of his secretary Emmett Scott, and used this talent to develop broader support, a larger campus, and create greater influence. Everything was built upon doing the work what he set out to do in building a learning institution that was modeled on Hampton Institute. Yet it grew bigger, his project expanded, and he touched thousands with his speeches, with his philosophy of conciliation and of peace between the white South and the African American. However, there were those who at times viewed his style as ingratiating, this cannot be fully denied. But the man was extremely perceptive; there was no chance of success without playing the role of a negotiator between these seemingly mismatched, complex, and interrelated cultural heritages. There was a need for someone to find a way to calm down the antipathy and to bring the South to some kind of sanity. Indeed the psychosis of white racism was an insuperable disease that few men of African American heritage could overcome—but he tried. On reflection, it is difficult to deny that Booker T. Washington did not do his best to bring together the two main cultures of the South during his lifetime. If anyone deserved a Noble Peace Prize for work *within* nations during his lifetime, it was Booker T. Washington who would have been a deserving recipient.

5

Of Dr. W. E. B. Du Bois and Others

Arguably, a major key to understanding the life and times of Booker T. Washington is by thoroughly comprehending his complex relationship with W. E. B. Du Bois (1868–1963). This chapter aims to examine the critics of Washington mainly through the lens of Du Bois; this is not to undermine other critics, most notably William Monroe Trotter (1872–1934). However, due to the debate between Washington and Du Bois being so prominent in the sphere of education, particularly higher education and liberal arts, there is a definite need to unpack some of the background to this debate in order to "un-fossilize" the generalized perspective that proliferates studies concerned with Washington.

What is particularly problematic about this aspect of Washington's life is that most critiques begin and end with W. E. B. Du Bois's noted 1903 essay "Of Mr. Booker T. Washington and Others" from *The Souls of Black Folk* (2004). Indeed, it is the essay that most scholars go to in order to assess the critique of Washington's overall perspective on politics and life. It cannot be emphasized enough that this is rather unfair and quite erroneous in a scholarly sense. Nevertheless, because it is so widely employed as the barometer for examining his role in African American life, it has to be looked at closely here. Before that is attempted, it is important to place both men in context to each other.

Too often both men are simply put together as "peers," but this is incorrect. First, Washington was born in April 1856 and Du Bois in February

> ### W. E. B. Du Bois (1868–1963)
>
> Du Bois was born in Great Barrington, Massachusetts, three years after the end of the Civil War. He lived a relatively stable life for an African American child, though he grew up largely without a father. His mother's love secured his emotional wellbeing, and he was able to experience school in an integrated environment. Because he was so strong in intellect, he never suffered from an inferiority complex that many African Americans and people of color have to shake off, if fortunate, due to the pervasiveness of white supremacy. Du Bois went on to achieve remarkable accolades as a student: the first African American to gain a PhD at Harvard, study abroad in Germany, and produce the first urban sociological study. Though he wrote many books, his *The Souls of Black Folk* is a classic American book of essays that still capture the minds of scholars, young and old. His activism in civil and human rights was unshakeable, and he is regarded as a beacon of scholarly righteousness in many circles. However, he was human and susceptible to the foibles of envy and insecurity. His relationship with Booker T. Washington is largely misunderstood to this day.

1868. That makes the former almost twelve years older than the latter. The age gap is only the start of significant differences in comparing their lives. Second, Washington was born in the South in bondage and remained in it up to the age of nine years, while Du Bois was born free in the North and never endured anything but mild racism compared to what his counterpart experienced. Third, Washington struggled under poverty and harsh conditions, and there is not one photograph of him prior to the age of about sixteen that exists; yet there exists photography of a well-groomed and well-fed toddler Du Bois—indicating a life of at least relative warmth and care. Fourth, Washington never knew his father, other than probably him being a local white man from a neighboring plantation, whereas Du Bois did not grow up with this father but knew of him. Du Bois also had a well-to-do grandfather whom he could draw confidence from. These are the only four key salient points: age difference, family background, location of birth, and one's parental line on the paternal side.

The two men both had loving mothers, whom they adored, but Washington's mother endured enslavement, while Du Bois's experienced freedom. The preceding differences need to be alluded to just as if it was an analysis of Martin Luther King Jr. and Malcolm X from the 1960s. The fact remains that each individual has a particular history and biography that determines, most often, how each will progress in life. It is important to note these differences between Washington and Du Bois because, quite frankly, they are quite profound. Another aspect of difference that is crucial in understanding these two men relates to their specific education. Washington, as has been discussed in earlier chapters, struggled to attain a rudimentary level of education. He arrived at Hampton Institute disheveled, hungry, and penniless. He was sixteen years of age with what can be regarded as merely basic educational skills, though fortified with a spirit that has a special place, it seems, in few souls. He arrived with hope in a hopeless situation. He found what can be deemed an educational haven that broke his poverty, built his academic prowess, and gave him confidence to forge ahead. Although his knowledge was not profound, he left with a love of the Bible and a knowledge of the Protestant ethic, something the renowned sociologist Max Weber deemed was the spirit of capitalism (Weber 1992).

W. E. B. Du Bois (1868–1963) was a pioneering sociologist, historian, and African American activist. He is renowned for his opposition to Booker T. Washington. (Library of Congress)

Washington soaked up many life lessons, but he did not receive cultural capital. His diploma was from a newly established African American institute, set up to aid the freedmen and women after the Civil War. It was run in missionary fashion with a degree of paternalism. Washington was grateful because they had saved him from a life of poverty—he was humble because he remembered being hungry and poor. The paternalism he endured went over his head because at the bottom of his heart, he viewed the teachers and principal as saviors of his people. That is deeply laudatory, yet imagine being ragged and hungry, having trekked nearly five hundred miles, and the doors of Hampton Institute were opened for you. Maybe you too would feel grateful and have a good disposition toward those in whom you found genuine kindness.

On the other hand, at sixteen years of age, Du Bois *finished* his education at Great Barrington High School. He was a precocious child, no different than Washington, and was encouraged to exploit his academic talent—unlike his counterpart. In 1884, he went on to higher education at Fisk University in Nashville, Tennessee, an institution set up after the Civil War, again to aid in the education of freedmen and women. This was Du Bois's first experience of being in the company of African American students; until then he had competed and very often outsmarted his white peers. Du Bois was a confident man because as a young boy he knew how good he was—his talent was reinforced. His experience of being smarter than his white counterparts gave him an edge over his African American peers. While at Fisk, he had the experience of teaching during the summers and had come face to face with the dire poverty among rural African Americans. Du Bois graduated in 1888, aged twenty years, with his BA degree. He decided to go to Harvard but was only given two year's credit for his bachelor's degree from Fisk. So he gained his Harvard bachelor of arts, cum laude, in 1890. Du Bois then entered the master's program in history at Harvard and gained his master of arts degree in 1891.

From 1892 to 1894 he was able to secure a scholarship to study at the University of Berlin. While there he felt more "human" and was never treated with racism and discrimination. As his posthumously published autobiography states, "As a student in Germany, I built great castles in Spain and lived therein. I dreamed and loved and wandered and sang." These pretty words explain his freedom of thought and his ability to explore the life of the mind without hindrance. This is how he continues in explaining his return to America: "[T]hen after two long years I dropped suddenly back into 'nigger'—hating America!" (Du Bois 1968, 183). Although he wanted to stay at the University of Berlin, his funding had come to an end and would not be renewed. In 1894, he settled for an offer at Wilberforce University in Ohio and took up a position as professor of classics, while continuing with his doctorate studies in history at Harvard. He graduated as the first African American to gain a PhD in 1895. To top this, in 1896, he would publish his thesis, the first in Harvard University's Historical Series, *The Suppression of the African Slave-Trade to the United States of America, 1638–1870*. By 1896, Du Bois was an academic star, and still at the outset of his career. He was only twenty-eight years old, a person who had clearly been gifted with opportunity, the good life, and had a profound sense of individual empowerment.

To return to Washington, for perspective, once he had graduated from Hampton Institute in 1875, he would spend a couple of years teaching in Malden, spend some months at Wayland Seminary in D.C., and eventually return to Hampton Institute to be part of the faculty. In 1881, at the age of twenty-five years, after proving himself a competent teacher, he gained the opportunity to be the first principal at Tuskegee Institute. It was here that he built up an educational institution that mirrored his major influence, Hampton Institute. To fast-forward fourteen years from 1881 to 1895, both men were at very different stages in their lives.

Washington was now a thirty-nine-year-old well-established principal of a successful educational institution; he had built Tuskegee Institute from a shanty building with thirty students into a fully functional campus with many imposing buildings. There were over one thousand students and one hundred faculty members. He had built not only an institute of learning but also a community that created wealth for the town of Tuskegee. By 1895, he was a tremendously successful African American leader in the field of education in the South. Though he had learned the essence of tapping into the available philanthropy, which allowed him to extend the breadth of Tuskegee Institute, without his drive and enthusiasm, there would not have been such progress.

Du Bois, however, was a very talented scholar with the acclaim of being the first African American to gain a PhD from Harvard University. Nevertheless, in essence, he was a glorified and privileged bookworm. Up to this point in life, he had never suffered any length of poverty or hunger, had never experienced heavy-handed racism, and was rather fortunate for an African American male in 1895. Du Bois had a position at Wilberforce University but was increasingly unhappy there; apparently he found it too rigid and stifling. Ironically, and rarely noted, Du Bois had refused an offer to teach at Tuskegee Institute. It came not long after he had accepted an offer from Wilberforce, so he felt obliged to refuse Washington's offer. Yet he stated, "It would be interesting to speculate just what would have happened if I had received the offer of Tuskegee first, instead of that of Wilberforce" (Du Bois 1968, 185). What is significant to note is that Du Bois had written to Washington inquiring about a possible appointment as a professor. This is something that is rather incongruous with the core of Du Bois's philosophy that denied the efficacy of Tuskegee Institute being able to accommodate a scholar of liberal arts. It proves to some extent that he was a tad disingenuous in regard to explaining the essence of what Washington offered as an educator. To be sure, Washington often used the phrase "hands and head" when it came to developing the student for the world: to have a skill that would allow one to survive in a world where you had to earn a living and to have a mind that was cultured and able to develop him- or herself for a good, healthy, enjoyable life.

Whenever Du Bois wrote about Tuskegee Institute, he did not fully explain that the curriculum offered lessons in mathematics, rhetoric, religion, and a host of other academic disciplines, including African American history. Instead, Du Bois would merely focus on the industrial/vocational aspect, with the implication that this was not "manly" or that it was limited in scope. When one juxtaposes Du Bois's critique alongside him writing for a potential position and him being offered a position initially to teach mathematics at Tuskegee Institute, it belittles his perspective on Washington greatly—at least in regard to his negativity toward Washington's philosophy on education. Moreover, this is crucial when it comes to critics who labeled Washington as anti–higher education and called him a purveyor of industrial education as the only way for African Americans to prosper. This is arguably the most erroneous point of view, and if one reads Du Bois more closely, there are more myths than truths about his views. It could be asked why the following citation from Harlan has rarely, if ever, been cited: "In his role as an educational statesman, Washington challenged the broad-gauged stereotype of mere accommodation and self-seeking. . . . He also helped to channel philanthropy into a great number and variety of black higher educational institutions" (Harlan 1983, 199). Rarely is this aspect mentioned by Washington's critics because it would not fit in with the narrative they have created. Crucially, if he was specifically against higher education and liberal arts, why would he channel funds into universities such as Fisk and Howard? It does not make sense, at least in regard to the narrative that has come down through the decades against the man who built Tuskegee Institute.

Yet there is more to this, Harlan points out: "As a trustee of both Fisk University and Howard University, he showed himself to be a friend rather than an enemy of black higher education" (199). Again, one wonders why such an important point in the analysis of Washington's life is overlooked and dismissed other than to allow the counter-narrative to prevail. Whatever faults Washington had, and he had them just as Du Bois did, he was not against the higher education pursuits of African Americans. Indeed, the lives of his own children exemplify this point. His daughter, Portia, in particular, had a life devoted to music and the teaching of it at Tuskegee Institute and beyond. More importantly, it is a fact that Washington was a supporter of African American scholars coming out of the universities in the North and South seeking employment in a racist society. There was no chance of them being employed in white universities. Much of Washington's support for African Americans in higher education is lost to the fossilized version of him being an "industrial/vocationalist" who despised the classics and the study of dead languages. The fact is that he simply felt that education should reflect the needs of the people where they were at. He was a practical man on a mission to build institutions that would last for generations. Du Bois and other critics knew better than what they put in essays condemning the man basically as a traitor to his "race," and it was deeply unfair.

By 1896, Du Bois was so fed up with his life in Ohio at the historically Black Wilberforce University that he took up a position as an assistant instructor of sociology at the University of Pennsylvania. It should be explained that he was a man with a PhD from Harvard and had spent two years as an assistant professor at Wilberforce. This is significant in the sense that he took a lower rank, far lower, to be at a white higher educational institution. In short, generally today, one requires a doctorate in order to take the title "Assistant Professor," and one works through a probationary period of about six to seven years before he or she tries for promotion to gain tenure. Promotion criteria may have been different back in 1896, but that does not matter, as Du Bois took the lowest title as an "Assistant Instructor" with a doctorate. One could be an instructor with just a bachelor's degree, and certainly with a master's degree. Du Bois had two bachelor's degrees, a master's, and a doctorate, and his terminal degrees were from one of the best universities in the United States.

One could argue he would have done anything to get out of Wilberforce, but in relation to his critique of Washington, it reeks of a man running to "whitey" for any position available. There was nothing relating to "manliness" in this decision, no action of self-worth, no standing up for his people. What was the cost to his "manhood" to be so devalued by a white institution in this manner intellectually? Of course, he made the best of it as he went on to produce the first sociological study of an urban community in Philadelphia. His book, while he was at the University of Pennsylvania, is the classic *The Philadelphia Negro*, published in 1899. Little, if anything, is written that disparages Du Bois's decisions to kowtow to white superiority in this manner. Yet he was able to peddle the same argument against Washington over and over again. Du Bois, at worst, was a hypocrite. He was a brilliant scholar who would have survived in any institutional setting, but this "unmanly" approach to his standing as an African American intellectual has gone unnoticed, until now.

Washington never chastised Du Bois in public or in his writings, as did Du Bois to him. Obviously, like any person with a degree of dignity and self-worth would, he did what he could behind the scenes to limit Du Bois's assaults, as they would be rather vicious in tone and substance. When the light is turned back on Du Bois critically, there are many reasons to feel a degree of doubt in his "love of African Americans." In fairness, Du Bois did the best for his people, but he also regarded at least 90 percent of them below his stature. Whereas Washington was deeply rooted in the 90 percent experience of African Americans, he lived up close and personal, regardless of his fame and success in later years. He was consistently pushing the need for self-determination, and this could be deemed somewhat naive at times, especially in not considering the aversion and envy of many white Southerners. But he never wanted to be white, so to speak. In a sense, Washington was saying "leave us alone" and "allow us to develop," and we will be fine. His message was "live and let live" and let hatred between us dissipate.

There is something curious about Du Bois that few commentators consider, and that is in his love of European culture, particularly the German Romanticism he picked up while studying in Germany. He wanted to stay there too but had to return due to a lack of funds. In regard to his respect for German austerity and regularity, Charisse Stelly-Burden and Gerald Horne state, "He became a devotee of a German culture he had come to appreciate, as embodied by the works of writers such as Johann Wolfgang von Goethe and Heinrich Heine; he imbibed a form of German Romanticism that was to be espied—by some analysts—in his coming fascination with Pan-Africanism" (Stelly-Burden and Horne 2019, 15). There is something incongruent to put Du Bois in the realm of Pan Africanism juxtaposed with German Romanticism, but this is something that one finds when one peels away the layers of Du Bois. His love of German culture extended to his dress style too. He would adopt a rather dandy style with a goatee that resembled the average German aristocrat of the age. Not to disparage the brilliant Du Bois, but this was somewhat of a contradiction when it came to his assaults on Washington for supposedly leaning too heavily toward whites.

Washington was a trustee of both Fisk University and Howard University, and he often recruited teachers from both institutions for Tuskegee Institute. Why would he do such if he did not want anything to do with higher education? Moreover, his third wife, Margaret, was a graduate from Fisk and would become extremely important as the first lady principal of Tuskegee Institute. This narrative does *not* speak to a man who was devoid of attention to higher education. Indeed, he inculcated it into his curriculum model and tried to balance the life of the student between vocational and academic skills. In addition, he wanted the community to be connected to the campus and vice versa. Washington was a pioneer in Black Studies philosophy and has not been given the credit.

Apart from his brilliant writings on the African American experience and his activism in politics, where did Du Bois ever link strongly to a place of higher learning beyond Atlanta University? What did he do to build an institution of higher learning? His role at Atlanta was crucial, but after that his career in direct educational issues goes blurry. Washington, however, stayed with his project because he had a tremendous responsibility for a community of students, scholars, and staff. The Tuskegee community relied upon him heavily for their livelihoods. Did Du Bois ever speak to this in his critiques of Washington? No, certainly nothing of substance relates to Tuskegee Institute, which would become the key employer in the town by 1900.

If one reads between the lines, and minus the letter "n" in "lines," there is something very odd about Du Bois in his relationship with Washington. There is something beyond mere ideological differences; there are so many incongruities. Washington tends to be viewed as his peer when, in fact, he was elder and far more established than Du Bois. Indeed, Washington was in a position of African American academic and political national leadership. Did Du Bois harbor a hidden resentment toward Washington beyond differences in political strategy? There is a strong indication that he did, and this is something commentators have generally not explored, especially the Du Boisian scholars who tend to see him through rose-tinted glasses. It is almost blasphemy to critique Du Bois in Africana Studies circles—especially in regard to the leftist scholars who view him as a Pan African/Socialist doyen.

The historical evidence points to Washington being the one always reaching out in the affirmative and Du Bois ever saying no to his offers. Washington's letter to Du Bois in October 1899 is revealing in its forthright respect to him and his admiration for the skills he possesses as a scholar. He put to Du Bois a substantial offer of employment: "I write to renew the proposition that you connect yourself permanently with this institution. What I wish you to do is to make your home here and to conduct sociological studies that will prove helpful to our people. . . . I am especially anxious that some systemic and painstaking work be done with the country districts in the Black Belt. . . . All the work of course would be done in your own name and over your own signature" (Aiello 2016, 86). Du Bois was offered a decent salary for the time ($1,400) and a home, along with printing facilities for his papers and books. All Washington required in return was the exposure of Tuskegee Institute on each publication—which is standard practice of any university press.

Now, if only to add insult to injury, Du Bois did not reply to this offer until April of 1900, that is, six months later. This is absurd in the realm of job-seeking academics. Very few scholars would have the temerity to reply to such a decent offer six months later, and very few administrations would wait that long. Washington was a very patient man; he withstood the incessant insults Du Bois egregiously slung as an arrogant thirty-two-year-old man not long out of graduate school. Du Bois, after the long delay in replying to Washington, rejected the offer of being an independent researcher, who would only be expected to teach only one course a year. Du Bois stated, "I think I ought not keep you any longer in uncertainty as to my coming to Tuskegee. I have given the matter long and earnest thought and have finally decided not to accept your very generous offer. . . . I thank you very much for the offer and for other kindnesses and I need not assure that you will always have in your work my sympathy & cooperation" (99–100). Well there it is, at the very least, the disingenuous Du Bois stating privately to Washington that he thanks him for the "generous offer" and the "other kindnesses" that he has shown him. Moreover, and this is crucial, he assured Washington that he would always have his "sympathy

& cooperation" in relation to the work he did at Tuskegee Institute and beyond. This was April 1900, five years after the Atlanta speech at the Cotton States International Exposition. Either Du Bois is simply disrespectful, or he is a liar, but one thing we know is that the history books have him largely interpreted as a man of integrity—this may be a stretch too far in praise. Du Bois was then a young and arrogant scholar, a man who regarded Washington below his intellect and status. He most probably envied Washington's position as the de facto heir to the great Frederick Douglass. This of course is speculation, but if one considers the number of times Washington reached out to him, and stayed silent in public against his insults, he should be given credit for being a class act in this sense. Du Bois, in turn, was rather classless, and he was insincere in his dealings with Washington. What is particularly disagreeable about Du Bois is his disregard for anyone other than himself; he wrote brilliantly but walked and acted like a fop.

Given that overview of the early relationship between Washington and Du Bois, it would be efficacious to consider the essay "Of Mr. Booker T. Washington and Others" from 1903. This is the piece already alluded to earlier that comes from the acclaimed *The Souls of Black Folk*. It is the essay that has fossilized Washington, and the biographical side-by-side synopses presented earlier regarding both men that have been largely overlooked by generations of scholars—who endeavor to comprehend these two brilliant African American souls. What is the essence of Du Bois's point of view in his essay on Washington? Briefly, to answer this question, Du Bois argues selectively that Washington asks African Americans to give up "at least for the present" three things: political power, insistence on civil rights, and higher education for African Americans. Each of these charges is actually rather selective. Du Bois refers to the twenty-seven words from the Atlanta speech of 1895 (a speech he initially praised; see chapter 4), where Washington stated to white Southerners, "In all things purely social we can be as separate as the five fingers, and yet one as the hand in all things essential to mutual progress" (Washington 1986, 221–222). Du Bois regards the speech "the most notable thing in Mr. Washington's career," and one can gauge there is a tad amount of factitiousness in that statement. There were many things in Washington's career that were more notable, and the most notable was clearly his building and administering of Tuskegee Institute—a mammoth achievement.

Anyhow, let us consider the three points of criticism. First, African Americans were being systematically disenfranchised well before 1895, as discussed in the previous chapter. It is rather overly critical to suggest that Washington had the power to stop or start the ability of African Americans to exercise their vote. The fact is that Harlan (1972, 1983) has provided ample evidence that Washington worked behind the scenes, conducting clandestine assaults on white Southern attempts to suppress the African American vote. He did what he could in an extremely volatile and dangerous environment for an African American male in a leadership role. Indeed, and Du Bois knew this, had Washington spoken openly and aggressively for voting rights, he probably would have been assassinated. Even in this hostile environment, he did not give up the vote; he argued for "fairness" in all matters pertaining to voting rights. Du Bois is tricky with his language and selective in his critique. It is very easy to knock down an African American in the midst of white supremacy, especially from a far safer place in society—the North.

On not insisting on civil rights, this is rather ridiculous because Washington always stipulated "You do your thing. We'll do ours" and please let us work together for peace and reconciliation between whites and African Americans. Yes, he was certainly a man employing an olive branch to a rather vicious culture, but what *really* was the alternative? Should Washington have been belligerent and bellicose he would have been killed, given this was the dangerous South of the 1890s where any African American could be lynched at will? There is a rather slippery way Du Bois puts Washington in a theoretical bind; clearly the man was between the devil and the deep blue sea, and he chose to navigate cautiously. Moreover, African Americans in the audience cheered him on that day in Atlanta. Keep in mind that Du Bois's essay was also published a significant eight years after the event; it is therefore easy to critique a speech from a distance. What if all had gone swimmingly well in the following eight years? What we now know is that Du Bois was economical with the truth in regard to his personal relationship with Washington. Du Bois would praise him in private correspondence, as cited earlier, yet lambast him in public and in publications. In spite of this Washington said nothing in public to disparage Du Bois and tried to stifle the assaults on him in private, as he did with his white enemies.

The third critique is the weakest when he states that Washington does not advocate higher education for African American youth. Then why does Washington shepherd funds to Fisk and Howard and sit on the board of trustees of both schools? This is a rather facile critique by Du Bois. It does not deserve much attention because there is more than enough evidence to defend Washington in this regard. Yes, he believed in vocational education coupled with academic skills. That is his prerogative as it is Du Bois's to promote liberal arts and social science. It does not make either right or wrong, but it does make Du Bois disingenuous in his selective critique of Washington (Du Bois 2004, 24–28).

It is wise to have had the biographical backdrop earlier because it gives an insight into the how each thinker developed. Nonetheless, the historical narrative of these two men has been unduly unfair on Washington, since he was never able to respond to perspectives beyond his lifetime. Du Bois, however, was able to shape the debate, having lived almost fifty years beyond Washington's death in 1915. Moreover, left of center higher education scholars further shaped the historical view of Washington after Du Bois passed away in August of 1963. One of the key scholars who continued to fossilize Washington's legacy was Herbert Aptheker, who acted like a watchman over Du Bois's legacy. Continuing with Du Bois's essay, he has this repetitive theme of "manhood" and "manliness" that somehow has been given away with Washington's political stance on how African Americans can advance slowly and surely up the economic ladder. Yet, as stated earlier, there are examples, if one wishes to interpret, where Du Bois could be deemed having given in to the notion of white supremacy. It is wise to know that if there is a stronger opponent, whether in sport or in life, there are many ways to elude and cajole a victory. One way is to let the opponent think they are stronger, and while the adversary is dealing with delusions of grandeur, one can gain or steal a victory. This is life; the example is often said in husband and wife relationships—often the wife simply lets her husband think he is the head of the house, but in reality she is making decisions that are best for herself in a supposedly unequal relationship in terms of a power dynamic. Washington was wily, a self-taught social psychologist who instinctively knew when to pass or move in the game of life. Indeed, the man had more victories than losses in a time of overt white supremacy and the violence that accompanied it.

What is particularly irritating with the arrogance of Du Bois was his notion of the Talented Tenth who would lead the poorly educated, misdirected 90 percent of African Americans out of the wilderness and into the Promised Land. The Talented Tenth are men with higher education who supposedly possess a superior breeding and knowledge. These men then take up the notion of instilling "manliness" and "manhood" into the ignorant 90 percent. With no concern for innate intelligence, one had to have experienced the culture of the classics, that is, the European canons of knowledge, before one could actually rise out of poverty and ignorance. Du Bois also assumed that power belonged ultimately in higher education. Yet, one may question, Did he suggest that the 90 percent can only find manhood by experiencing learning from the Talented Tenth? Of course, this concept or theory was evidently irritating to a man like Washington who had learned life the hard way—the hard knock life way.

A reading of each personality, Washington and Du Bois, has left for history basic impressions that come from men and women who knew them. Washington was very amiable; he was not a man who sought conflict, but he did want to control his world as best as he could, like any man usually does. He could get along easily with the ordinary folk; he frequently used the idiom of his people to express the wisdom and humor in African

American Southern life. Du Bois, however, was arrogant and aloof, and he even admits as much in his final autobiography. He openly states that while at Harvard as a student, he did not take the time to get to know his classmates, another indication of his aloofness. In summing up his time there, he wrote, "For the most part I do not doubt that I was voted a somewhat selfish and self-centered 'grind' with a chip on my shoulder and a sharp tongue" (Du Bois 1968, 139). It is informative to note that these words from Du Bois were composed when he was in his nineties. It is expected that at that age one slips down guards and does not care to be untruthful. In his own words he lets the readers know that he was a difficult, selfish, and conceited person who felt he was too good for those around him.

The main issue one tends to read about Washington and his character is that he did not like disorder on his campus. He was a little uptight about having things done correctly and in an orderly fashion. He controlled Tuskegee Institute quite tightly largely because there was much pressure on him to be a success. He did not want litter strewn and fences broken and would do inspections on his horse across the campus—this was a man determined to run his institution properly organized. The objective was to show the world, particularly the white world, that a man of color could efficiently run an institution of learning in his time. With due respect, what he achieved in that time and place was a phenomenal accomplishment.

Yet outward arrogance and selfishness were not characteristics of Washington. His feet were firmly on the ground in a humble and respectful manner. On reflection, it is not surprising that these two men did not get along, as they were definitely opposites in many ways. What is known about Washington is that he wanted the best for Tuskegee Institute. In this sense, Du Bois was the best academic around, even if his personality was clearly prickly, and Washington would have been elated to have had him at Tuskegee Institute. Du Bois was a genius in terms of his production of scholarship and theoretical thought, but in his practical thought he was no match for Washington. One could argue that Du Bois's love of European culture, particularly German, was at odds with his later interest in Pan African liberation. Du Bois was not comfortable around lay people, and even many professionals; maybe he was a shy man at heart, but unlike Washington he was not an easy socializer. The downside was in his haughty nature, and in his underlying envy of Booker T. Washington and the success he had achieved. This is something that is fundamental in Du Bois, because he espoused such a negative perspective on Washington that was a tad exaggerated. When he wrote about Washington, he often left out all the good aspects of him, while extending anything remotely negative. Du Bois was not fully candid about his early relationship with Washington and in how often the man reached out to him to request his talent to be part of Tuskegee Institute. Maybe Du Bois simply did not want to be "underneath" the power of Washington, even if he offered Du Bois a free reign in his studies and publications. The example of Washington hiring the eccentric genius George Washington Carver to be among his faculty is testament to the idea that he wanted only the best and brightest at Tuskegee Institute. Washington was intelligent enough to know as an administrator that to be the best you recruit the best, regardless of differences in temperament or personality. Unfortunately, maybe it was asking too much to have the dandy Du Bois at Tuskegee Institute, for in his self-important mind he was the top man who did not desire playing second fiddle to the most famous African American in the world at that time.

Ironically, Du Bois admits in his essay of 1903 that the "ignorant Southerner hates the [African African]," and at this time they also feared competition from African Americans (Du Bois 2004, 31). Therefore, he did acknowledge implicitly the complexity faced by Washington because in the South the vast majority of African Americans were mired in rural poverty. They were simply not ready for the pursuit of higher education, the reading of Shakespeare and the classics, which was the staple diet of education in historically Black colleges and universities (Woodson 1990). African Americans required basic literacy and schooling, which could lead to further education, and then higher education for anyone suited to it. Washington *knew* the terrain from birth, circumstance, and experience deeply rooted in the South. He was intimately cognizant of the depth of antipathy white ignorant Southerners had toward African Americans. In a real sense, Du Bois knew it too, but he was interested only in breaking down the leadership of Washington by placing the dire conditions for all African American ills on his shoulders. It was cowardly and unbecoming of a man so profoundly intelligent to try to topple Washington, who at bottom was a man of his people, for his people, and who loved his people.

Another criticism of Washington from Du Bois was in him being too indebted to white philanthropy. This is a very shallow critique given his own attempts to receive the very same dollars that were being offered. Let it be known here that Washington was a brilliant fundraiser for his institution and causes. He was relentless in going after the philanthropic dollars that were often available from genuine donors, who gave the funds to aid African American uplift. Most often a building was named in the donor's honor, but the benefactor did not interfere with the day-to-day education. A specific request, for example, for a library from the [Andrew] Carnegie Foundation yielded a brilliant one for Tuskegee Institute, allowing thousands of students to benefit from a wonderful structure. Carnegie never stipulated anything to Washington other than to build and use the library for his students.

This Carnegie example is employed here to illustrate the shallowness of Du Bois's critique that Washington was beholden to white philanthropy—however, there is more to this that rarely is exposed. If one researches deeper other than the essay that has fossilized Washington, one will find evidence of Du Bois trying to raise funds from white philanthropy in the very same manner as Washington but not being as successful at it. Fundraising is a skill in itself; very few can pull it off. Often it is gained through a genuine cause, results, and reputation. If one has definite examples of success and can prove to some degree that the monies put forward are going to the very cause they were asked for, then this again improves the repute of the fundraiser. The point is simple: Washington would invite those who gave donations to come and see the fruits of their donations. Tuskegee Institute rose from debris to become a magnificent beacon of hope for African Americans in Alabama and eventually around the world. These funds came from ordinary folks and mainly from rich white Northerners. Du Bois did not put his heart and soul into fundraising but looked on Washington with a degree of resentment because he was so successful. Du Bois came up with brilliant theoretical and empirical studies but failed to follow through because his personality was not in tune with what is required when one interacts with humans who can help get something up and running with funds. He was successful with the establishment of the National Association for the Advancement of Colored People (NAACP), which grew out the Niagara Movement. When the NAACP was set up it also involved the input of white philanthropy. So was Du Bois indebted to those white folks? The answer is beyond the scope of this biography, but it raises the hypocrisy offered by Du Bois's criticism of Washington being in the pocket of white philanthropists.

In May 1906, Du Bois wrote a short report to Andrew Carnegie, asking for funds. Carnegie by this time was a very good friend of Washington, so it is difficult to know why Du Bois would even attempt such a thing. Human nature operates on the principle "If you hurt my friend, you hurt me"—that is usually the practice in life. However, Du Bois requested funds from one of Washington's key donors, and this was the very thing he criticized him for. Du Bois wrote to Carnegie, "I beg leave to bring to your attention the work of the Atlanta Conference with the view of securing if possible financial support for this work" (Aptheker 1973, 121). In his letter to Carnegie, Du Bois continues to give a long list of the sociological studies he had pursued on African Americans while at Atlanta University; research that Washington had hoped he would have conducted at Tuskegee Institute. In hindsight, given Du Bois knowing the close relationship Carnegie had with Washington it seems as if he was taunting his rival rather than expecting funding. For such an intelligent scholar it is odd, but he was forthright in his request for funds from the rich white philanthropist whom he scolded

Washington for working with. Du Bois continued with his request to Carnegie: "I have made bold therefore appeal directly to you and to ask if you would be enough interested to look into the merits & needs of this work. If you are I should be glad to lay before you (a) a complete set of our publications (b) our programs for future study & (c) Press notices & commendations of our work" (122).

There is no immediate evidence in the correspondence book that Du Bois received a reply from the Carnegie Foundation, but it is probably unlikely. What is important to note here is that he was doing exactly what Washington did to improve his institution: fishing for funds. Yet he criticized Washington heavily for being a "puppet of white philanthropy" and unable to act independently for the benefit of African Americans. It was both selective and hypocritical of Du Bois to lay this at the feet of Washington, especially when he too was trying to do the very same thing. What is also relevant is that even today in the 2020s, African American organizations rely heavily on white philanthropic organizations for funds. The Carnegie Foundation and the Ford Foundation, among others, have provided funds to support the National Council for Black Studies (NCBS) for decades. Washington, however, was quite brilliant in raising funds because he not only wrote letters; he actually met with the funders themselves and built long-standing relationships. Moreover, he would become genuine friends with a number of them, including Carnegie, superseding the fact of "race" and cultural differences. Washington was an amiable fellow; Du Bois was aloof and arrogant. This difference was vital in their success in the area of raising funds or organizing events on a national level, which often meant many months of travel, speaking engagements, and appealing for sponsorship of this or that specific project.

Since a very early stage in Washington's career, he had no alternative but to appeal to the better angels of rich philanthropists. Most often they heeded to his entreaties because they believed his philosophy and practice in the uplift of African Americans and Tuskegee Institute. What historians and biographers have not fully grasped is Washington's appealing personality and charm. Why is this part of his nature summarily described as being ingratiating? The logic that is followed in this sense is to be affable and pleasant in manner toward one's fellow human beings is to be a weak person. This is a ridiculous proposition. In reading the life of Washington it is quite palpable that the man had a wit, a calm demeanor, and an aversion to conflict among humanity—the kind of personality which won him friends, support, and funding. He would be a magnet for funding that aided African American development, particularly in the sphere of education.

Du Bois has been rather fortunate that scholars have not dug deeper into his personality type and how he was as a person on a day-to-day level with peers and potential business associates. Evidently, from reading his autobiographies, he selectively framed Washington as a weak man when it came to "manhood" or "manliness," and it is an erroneous standpoint. In the 1903 essay, "Of Mr. Booker T. Washington and Others," he concludes by lamenting, "Mr. Washington apologizes for injustice, North or South, does not rightly value the privilege and duty of voting, belittles the emasculating effects of caste distinctions, and opposes the higher training and ambition of bright minds" (Du Bois 2004, 32). His conclusions are sadly rather economical on truth and do not explain the real extent to which Washington worked to prevent lynching, voting suppression, and other social atrocities facing African Americans.

Washington worked behind the scenes rather than in public simply because he had no choice, unless he sought to get Tuskegee Institute burned to the ground and himself lynched. A sample of his clandestine work comes from the early 1890s. Thomas Harris, an openly confident man who had become involved in local politics, was a middle-aged African American lawyer who had settled in the town of Tuskegee. Like Washington, Harris was born into enslavement, and after the Civil War he pushed for greater political empowerment. He strived to obtain better conditions for African Americans, and this brought more attention to him. Local whites who were against Tuskegee Institute and any form of African American empowerment worked hard to stifle Harris. In brief, he was warned to get out of town for being "too uppity" or too pushy in wanting rights for his people. Washington was guarded by his friends in high places and by his ability to navigate around the evils of white racism. As he built his institute he was always calm and careful with his words. When Thomas Harris opened up his law practice in the town the ignorant whites in Tuskegee viewed him as a troublemaking African American. An African American lawyer was an unwelcome entity in 1890s Tuskegee. Again, this should indicate the depth of racism that surrounded Washington. On June 8, 1895, Harris welcomed an itinerant white minister to stay at this home, further enraging the white rowdies of the town. Integration was not something they could stand for, not to mention a lawyer of African American heritage. One could work in education for African Americans but moving up into politics and law was frowned upon. With growing tension the whites bullied Harris to get out of town; nonetheless he stayed, and in a scuffle outside his home, he was shot at. He was fortunate to dodge one bullet, which hit one of his assailants, but a second one hit him in the leg. While the white mob were distracted by their fallen member, Harris was able to scurry away. With the help of his family, he fled to the home of Booker T. Washington. The next morning the official story in the newspaper reported that he was rejected by the Washington household and told to leave because it would be harmful to Washington's students, faculty, and

Tuskegee Institute itself. This is the story that went down in the annals of history until it was revealed by a biographer that Washington had actually shepherded Harris to a "safe home" to get his wound addressed and then helped him and his family to escape town. Harlan regards Washington as being "clever" and an "artful dodger," for he maneuvered in a very dangerous environment. Yet he took good care of Harris, and this was acknowledged by the man himself in writing (Harlan 1972, 171–175). Washington was certainly no coward; he was a clever man who kept a cool head as he went about his business raising educational opportunities for his people. From a safe distance Du Bois and other critics could critique anything he did, yet it would rarely be a fair assessment of the facts. Manliness is something that needs in-depth debating—especially during this era of outright violence and intimidation. Who would have had the courage to work in the middle of white rage as Washington did? If one considers the surroundings he was more than a man to deal with so much stress and with so few resources at his disposal. He saved the life of Thomas Harris in a clandestine manner, which was the best way to deal with the situation against an angry, ignorant lynch mob.

Overall, Du Bois's essay disparaging his assumed rival in *The Souls of Black Folk* is still *the* source to go to when assessing the essence of Washington. It is apparent that a revision of the existing historical interpretation of Washington is more than appropriate. Appreciatively, this work is gradually taking place with scholars reassessing his life (Brundage 2003; Norrell 2009; Wright 2015). However, there needs to be further investigation, and hopefully this biography will give a younger generation of scholars' greater holistic insight into Washington. When juxtaposed with Du Bois, there has been an unfair balance in the essence of each man. Indeed, Du Bois in a 1940 semi-biographical work, *The Dusk of Dawn*, returns to his debate with Washington. It is pertinent to keep in mind that this work was published almost forty years since his initial essay, and twenty-five years since the death of Washington. Du Bois was again able to impose his ideas onto a new generation of scholars and readers, who ran with this perspective for another two generations. Washington could not respond beyond the grave, and there was no one who knew him intimately left to defend his legacy. Today, more than four generations have passed since Washington's passing, and thankfully, as it has been a long time coming, there are signs of a revision taking hold.

In the *Dusk of Dawn*, Du Bois adds more insult to Washington than was previously in the historical record, stating that he had met with Washington face-to-face over possible job positions, and with nothing settled the issue continued in writing. This does not make much sense if one considers Du Bois's evaluation of the in-person meetings between the two men. He argues that he was encouraged to go to Tuskegee Institute by William H.

Baldwin, a trustee, donor, and friend to the institution and its leader. Both Washington and Baldwin wanted the best for the students at Tuskegee Institute, and as stated earlier, Washington was trying hard to convince Du Bois to join the faculty. Yet, Du Bois appears to be suffering from selective amnesia when he writes, after supposedly having two in-person interviews (there is no evidence of this in the Booker T. Washington papers),

> I was elated at the opportunity and we met twice in New York City. The results to me were disappointing. Booker T. Washington was not an easy person to know. He was wary and silent. He never expressed himself frankly or clearly until he knew exactly to whom he was talking and just what their wishes and desires were. He did not know me, and I think he was suspicious. On the one hand, I was quick, fast-speaking, and voluble. I found at the end of the first interview that I had done practically all the talking and that no clear and definite offer or explanation of my proposed work at Tuskegee had been made. In fact, Mr. Washington had said about as near nothing as was possible. (Du Bois, *Dusk*, 1992, 78–79)

Fortunately for Washington, his letter to Du Bois refutes all of the above. But that correspondence did not come to light until Booker T. Washington's papers were published over three decades later. Du Bois could actually overtly tell lies, and there was no one to respond because all parties besides him were no longer alive. What we do know is that Washington wrote an extensive offer to Du Bois on October 26, 1899, and in it he outlined all the particulars of employment to him. Du Bois would have been an independent faculty member, teach one course a year, and have all his publications in his name. As noted earlier, the only thing Washington requested, which is routine in academia, is to have noted that Tuskegee Institute was the press for his publications and the place of his scholarly residence.

Du Bois also takes liberty with his supposedly in-person interviews for employment. He paints Washington's personality as antithetical to what is known of him. Washington was very amiable and a man of wit, and of course everyone is somewhat cagey when in an interview discussion. But he was nothing like how Du Bois describes. Moreover, Du Bois sets himself up as "quick," "fast-talking," and "voluble" when he "met" with Washington about a possible position at Tuskegee Institute. A critical thinker may ask why Du Bois would take the time to even have one in-person meeting with a man he clearly did not agree with in principle. In addition, after the first meeting went so badly, why would he have met Washington for a second time? It appears to be a poorly fabricated lie by Du Bois. He was in his early seventies when he wrote *The Dusk of Dawn*; maybe his memory was failing him. Yet he went on to live till the age of ninety-five, and in his final autobiography he reveals more about himself as a person. He was "aloof and arrogant," nothing like the character he claims to be in the interview with Washington. It is very disappointing to unpack the character of Du Bois as it relates to Washington. There seems to be an implicit envy that went deep into his soul, and he manipulated the interaction with Washington to have the man invented as far more nefarious than what he actually was in real life—because by all accounts the person Du Bois depicts is not the Washington more widely known.

Now, it is only fair to explain Washington's character flaws as well and to put them in the context of the times. It is widely accepted that he did build on Du Bois's idea for the National Negro Business League (NNBL). The idea came from Du Bois's theoretical work at Atlanta University. Washington took the idea about African American businesses further and made it a very successful organization. Maybe this is why Du Bois disliked him; though he kept it to political differences, it seems to have had become more personal after 1900. In addition, when Du Bois sought the job of superintendent of schools in Washington, D.C., he actually asked Washington for a recommendation. Again, why would ask for a reference if he clearly disliked the man and his politics? Washington obliged the arrogant Du Bois in his request; however in the end the position went to another African American candidate for the role. Du Bois blamed Washington for this outcome, yet it is well known that a recommendation does not necessarily mean one gets a position. In reading the correspondence in regard to this position, it is not clear if Washington had the power to demand that Du Bois got it or not get it. Nevertheless, Du Bois held this against him as part of his Tuskegee Machine operation, which again was just a useful degree of mendacity on Du Bois's part because it suited his narrative. It is very possible that Du Bois did not get the position because he was not suited for it as far as the search committee was concerned. To put this rejection solely at the feet of Washington appears merely convenient in finding an excuse for Du Bois's own failure in not securing the position. The so-called Tuskegee Machine is a derogatory term to run down the fact that Washington had a strong influence in the African American experience and was able to get some of his like-mined thinkers into positions of power. This, again, is something that is part and parcel of a brand. Powerful persons in society do what they can to improve their brand. But because Washington was an African American, and played his cards in life cautiously, he was not popular with those who did not benefit from his brand. Those critics, led by Du Bois, were a growing but small number after 1903—mainly due to Du Bois's disparaging essay in *The Souls of Black Folk.*

Another major critic of Washington would be William Monroe Trotter. He was part of a small group of Northern-based "African American Intellectual Radicals" who had graduated from Harvard and other higher education institutions, mainly within the Boston region. A number of them had been Du Bois's classmates when he was at Harvard. It is understandable that they would desire higher aspirations, but it is selective criticism to suggest that Washington stood in the way of such. In fact, he recruited his teachers mainly from higher education establishments. What is significant about this group is that they were trained in the European classics; they wanted to be respected as an elite group of highly educated men, singled out from the masses of African Americans. The brand of Tuskegee Institute did not suit their aspirations. But it is not as if Washington stifled their progress in business, education, or anything else. They were, in essence, the Talented Tenth that Du Bois alluded to in reference to them leading the masses of African Americans.

There was a meeting scheduled by NNBL's Boston chapter on July 30, 1903. William Monroe Trotter and a few of his followers tried to disrupt Washington from speaking and a commotion broke out. In short, the police intervened, and Trotter was arrested. This catapulted him to national fame on the notoriety of "violently" trying to disrupt a meeting where Booker T. Washington was speaking. Keep in mind that the crowd was two thousand strong that evening in Boston, and there were only a handful of agitators. Du Bois was not there, but it is assumed that he knew about it. Trotter was passionate in his assault on Washington's program and focus on industrial education, conveniently forgetting all the things Washington was doing besides. Again, it was the drum call of "accommodationist," "conservative," and "anti–higher education" nomenclature that was designed to bring Washington down. This has been alluded to in

---

WILLIAM MONROE TROTTER (1872–1934)

William Trotter was born in Ohio, but raised in Hyde Park, Massachusetts. His family was a middle-class African American family, and he never suffered the sting of poverty during his lifetime. He was educated at Harvard and could be deemed a very privileged person compared to the vast majority of African Americans. He would become the editor of a popular African American newspaper in Boston named the *Guardian*, and much of its focus was on the criticism of Booker T. Washington's ideas and practice in education and politics. Trotter experienced a month in jail for disturbing a meeting in Boston at a chapter of the National Negro Business League that took place in July 1903. His main aim was to embarrass the keynote speaker, Washington. Trotter passionately advocated for the rights of African Americans through his writings, the Niagara Movement and the National Association for the Advancement of Colored People (NAACP), but found it hard to compromise with anyone. Although there is some mystery to his death in 1934, it does point to an apparent suicide.

chapter 3, but it should be emphasized that Washington's children all experienced both Tuskegee Institute *and* higher education institutions. Portia spent two years in Europe studying piano in Berlin under the renowned Martin Krause and even met with the noted Black British musician Samuel Coleridge-Taylor in London (Stewart 1977, 61–63). Booker Jr. studied at Fisk University, while his younger brother Ernest attended Talladega College and then Shaw University in North Carolina. Moreover, Washington, after Booker Jr. had passed through, was on the board of trustees at both Fisk and Howard Universities. Collectively, this is not the action of a man who did not respect higher education; Washington was intimately connected to it through his work and family.

Returning to July 30, 1903, apparently from witness accounts Washington was cool and calm during the commotion, and once order was restored he carried on as if nothing had happened. What he primarily wanted to get across to the audience that night was for African Americans to focus on self-improvement and self-determination and to build an economic base for the next generation that would form the bedrock to gain a much stronger foothold in the broader society. In addition, and in a clandestine fashion, Washington continued his fight for the vote and attack lynching in the South (Harlan 1983, 33). In sum, the "Boston Riot" coupled with Du Bois's essay in the same year created a "them and us" scenario. It gave rise to two camps, one for Washington, who were clearly in the majority, and a small group of radicals led by Trotter and Du Bois. The members of the latter group were all about in the same age group. One man who belonged historically in both camps was William H. Lewis (1868–1949). He was an extremely talented athlete, lawyer, and orator. Educated at Harvard in law, he would later become an assistant attorney general under the Taft administration. Initially he was against Washington, like the other so-called radicals, but after meeting him and discussing his career ambitions, he changed his mind. He eventually prospered as a top-level legislator. Washington actually did what he could to help any young talented African American professional.

Lewis presided over the meeting the night of Boston commotion with Trotter. He condemned the actions and sided with Washington, and yes, he probably went on to benefit because of his contacts with the Tuskegee Institute leader. Did that make him less than useful to African Americans? Absolutely not. He went on to have a wonderful career, breaking through numerous barriers as an African American male. As assistant attorney general in the U.S. government, he was the first African American to occupy this seat. Washington recommended him to Taft, but he still had to be confirmed and be proven as the skilled attorney that he was. This had nothing to do with industrial education, it was simply a case of Washington being in a position to help a talented African American young man. He tried to do the same with Du Bois too but was rejected by him and then misrepresented profoundly by the erudite scholar.

Whatever can be stated about Washington, the one truth about him was that he never criticized the younger generation in public. Of course, like anyone with business sense, he did what he could behind the scenes to limit the assaults on Tuskegee Institute, the NNLB, and his brand. For that he has been deemed a type of "mob boss" who had "agents" and "spies" here, there, and everywhere. The fact remains that with his broad coalition of activities, he met many individuals across the nation, for example, African American newspaper editors and business men, whom either wanted his assistance or who could help him in his cause. He operated with those whom he did business with for a common cause—the progression of African Americans in society. What seems to have been his Achilles heel is the thought that he gave up some form of *demand* for social equality. On reflection, and in contemporary times, that impression is very much in debate in regard to the idea that egalitarianism could have been secured in Washington's era. Indeed, this notion of fighting for social equality had been with African Americans since the 1600s. Washington simply wanted space for his people to build up wealth and property unhindered; therefore he articulated his strategies in a manner that was certainly coded not to rattle the cage of white rage and its monster. On the other hand, African American elites who had experienced some level of privilege and comfort did not understand this; they were at a social level that was way beyond the basic living standard needs that 90 percent of African Americans based in the South required. So radicals like Trotter and Du Bois, educated mainly in the North and having never experienced enslavement, were obviously coming from a different point of view. Also, being much younger than Washington, these fresher highly educated men had expectations of getting social equality *immediately*. If they could return, it would be interesting to consider what they would think of the 2020s. After all, hindsight is a wonderful thing that few get the opportunity to experience.

The younger group of African American intellectuals were sometimes supported by elders who opposed Washington. Henry McNeal Turner (1834–1915) and Alexander Crummell (1819–1898) were prominent in their disapproval of the Washington brand that promoted "dignity in labor" and property ownership. They too felt that in Washington's words there was a message expounding acceptance to social inequality. Again, most things can be interpreted way out of context, and without comprehending the place from which the criticism is derived it can be misleading and self-serving criticism, as we have noted with the brilliant scholar and wordsmith W. E. B. Du Bois.

Bishop Turner was an interesting and cultured character. Born free in South Carolina, he had learned to read and write. He became a minister in the African Methodist Episcopal (AME) Church and later promoted the idea of going back to Africa. During his time, the American Colonization Society (ACS) was initially created in 1816 to encourage free African Americans to return to Africa and specifically to Liberia. Maybe it would have been received better if *all* African Americans would have been guaranteed freedom by repatriation. Unfortunately this was not the case and enslavement would continue for almost fifty more years. Nevertheless, the ACS idea was intensely revitalized after the Civil War and as the scheme of repatriation was always voluntary, only a small number of African Americans took up the opportunity. It must be noted that the ACS was created by a white man, Robert Finlay (1772–1817), and there was strong opposition to its premise. A notable opponent of this society was Frederick Douglass, and his argument was simple: African Americans had labored, enduring intolerable conditions for almost two hundred and fifty years for free and deserved more than a stake in America. Douglass was emphatically against the ACS and the repatriation idea, but others like Bishop Turner took up the option. In the mid-1890s, Bishop Turner organized two ships to take about five hundred African Americans to Liberia. Unfortunately, there was wide publicity that the emigrants were in poor condition and unable to acclimatize to the African conditions. Liberia at the time was still primarily rural with little infrastructure. In addition, the fact is that it was a poorly resourced region, and terribly underfunded by the U.S. Government.

However, Bishop Turner was a strong voice for African American empowerment and it clashed with Washington's call to "cast down your bucket" where you are. As had Frederick Douglass, Washington believed that the home for African Americans was where they had toiled and sweated in the South. The South was the land they knew best after centuries and generations of being there. Bishop Turner offered a different kind of self-determination than Washington's in that he claimed that the best option for future generations was to return to their homeland. The counter argument was that no living African American knew Africa as their homeland. The "return to Africa" theme would be taken up by others and a small group of African Americans did settle in Liberia, but the number was only ever in the hundreds, never in the millions.

Alexander Crummell was also a brilliant man, and like Bishop Turner he had been educated in the European classics and was gifted in an intellectual capacity way beyond the average. He was born in New York City in 1819 and raised in a "free" African American household. His father had come directly from Africa enslaved but in his adulthood he had gained his freedom, and his mother was also free, remarkable as that was for the time period. To give some context, Alexander was only a year younger than Frederick Douglass. It is clear that his life would be special after such an auspicious beginning. After he spoke at a meeting for the antislavery convention in New York, he became a preacher, and studied for a bachelor's degree in philosophy at Cambridge University in England. Continuing his work in the antislavery community, he later went on to be a professor at Liberia College in Africa, teaching English and Philosophy. Crummell was a brilliant young man, and eventually returned to America at the end of the Civil War. From that time onward he got involved with writing and publishing his ideas on African issues at home and abroad. He published a book in his early seventies titled *Africa and America*, and it covered the key issues of the day facing the continent and the African American experience. He was very religious and intent on linking and helping African Americans know the depth of their motherland. He was also influential with younger scholars like Du Bois.

As with Bishop Turner, Martin Delany (1812–1885), and other African American intellectuals, Crummell sought to link the African continent with the broader African Diaspora—this was something that impressed some of the younger scholars like Du Bois. What the younger radicals had in common with the elders like Bishop Turner and Crummell was their affiliation to higher education in the European classical canon context. They were all dripping in the philosophy of European canons and sought to empower Africans in an elitist context. This is the irony of many African Diaspora intellectuals who often went to the African continent tinged with the biases of Western thought, even if they did not consciously seek to do so. The consequence most often was to see Indigenous Africans as heathen and in need of "civilization" that the West apparently offered—especially through the Christian religion.

At least Washington did not consider himself better than anyone, unlike Du Bois who espoused the concept of the Talented Tenth. Washington was primarily concerned with the plight of the 90 percent of African Americans and to meet their needs head-on through their local experiences in the South. Du Bois devotes a chapter in *The Souls of Black Folk* to Alexander Crummell, who was an ardent believer in African American advancement through the AME Church, and that belief would be exported to Africa. If this had taken hold, it would have been a better form of the missionary zeal that was being meted out by European missionaries in Africa. On his meeting with Crummell in the mid-1890s at Wilberforce, Du Bois writes, "Instinctively I bowed before this man, as one who bows before the prophets of the world" (Du Bois 2004, 115). High praise indeed and an indication of how respected Crummell was among the younger generation of the radical Harvard elite scholars.

As a response to Washington's brand of industrial education, which again was only a front to enable Washington to gain funds for Tuskegee Institute, though there was always the "head and the hands" philosophy being inculcated into the minds of students, Crummell at seventy-eight years of age set up the American Negro Academy (ANA) in March 1897. The objective of ANA was to gather elite, college and university educated African American intellectuals to produce writings and responses to the contemporary socioeconomic, political, and cultural conditions their people were encountering. There was a strong advocacy for higher education and liberal arts, enthused in order to counter the Washington brand. At the outset the originators requested Washington to be a founding member, but knowing that Crummell, Du Bois, and others were critical of his educational model, he politely refused, stating he would be at another engagement. Unfortunately for ANA, Crummell passed away the following year of its inception and Du Bois was unanimously voted in as the new president. This gave him a platform but few members joined because there were not many among the African American experience that had the required credentials and academic background. Among the intellectuals that joined ANA was the brilliant scholar from Howard University, Kelly Miller. Other noted African Americans who would become associated with ANA were Carter G. Woodson and James Weldon Johnson. The symbolic importance, if anything, of ANA was the acknowledgment that those purely noted for their elite education could have a home in a world that quite frankly was not friendly to the African American intellectual. The ANA was significant, but it never harmed Washington's overall strength as the de facto key leader of African Americans.

With all due respect to Du Bois, in a fiscal sense he was never good at keeping an organization sufficiently strong. As the president of ANA, there was nothing significant to note under his leadership, only sporadic publications. The annual meetings never gained great support due to its rather small-scale focus on supporting the work of African American intellectuals and their careers. It was a worthy cause because white universities would not employ them, Du Bois had the "unmanly" experience of being humiliated at the University of Pennsylvania during his period as the president of ANA, his position as assistant instructor was incredulously inappropriate to his credentials, and it underscored institutional racism in mainstream (white) education.

Washington was a very savvy man, and he knew how to maneuver in the white world. He understood the vicious violence and vituperative nature of those white Southerners who held deeply rooted animosity toward African Americans. Moreover, he knew too well that his paternalistic and non-paternalistic white funders would not be at ease in funding an organization that preferred full and unequivocal rights for African Americans. Washington was just too shrewd—that is the best and unpretentious way to explain him. White people of his era tended to be extremely fragile when it came to African Americans exercising their fullest humanity.

Both Washington and Du Bois knew this well. This is not an indictment on ANA, but it is a fact that the price to be paid for outward defiance in that time period was further exclusion and indifference. The ANA was an African American organization that was necessary, but without the skillful leadership that would attract more membership and much-needed resources, it inevitably suffered from fiscal problems. Du Bois cannot be blamed entirely, but he should be noted as not having taken ANA further into the twentieth century than only to the mid-1920s. Nevertheless, whatever its impact, it made no major difference to Washington and his agenda. The key aspect of ANA that is worth noting is its acknowledgment of the elite African American intellectuals as a force in society. Future generations could stand on their shoulders and find a foundation of intellectual discourse favoring African American empowerment and creative expression.

Incongruously, and not well known to history is that a mentee of Washington, Alain Locke, would later become a member of ANA. It is contradictory only because it defends Washington in a number of ways. First, Locke was one of the intellectual elites who graduated from Harvard with degrees in English and philosophy in 1907. Locke would later go on to be one of the key architects of the Harlem Renaissance, a movement largely of literature and art that honored the cultural aspect of African and American heritages in 1920s New York City. However, what is not known to many is Locke's connection to Booker T. Washington and Tuskegee Institute. Evidence of this and more is from a letter Locke wrote to Washington in September 1912. In it he writes, marked Personal: "My dear Doctor Washington, I was just on the point of writing you when I received your letter of 12th [September]. . . . Saturday, the 14th I was elected an assistant Professor at Howard, in English and Philosophy, upon the recommendation of Dean Moore. . . . I was about to write you news of this, and to thank you for your valuable and timely help in the Howard matter, when your letter with its still greater willingness to assist me in getting placed arrived to put me still more in your debt" (Locke 1982).

What is significant about this letter from Alain Locke to Booker T. Washington is that historically they were supposed to be in completely opposite camps. The letter is clandestine in tone; he thanks Washington for his input and willingness to help him further in getting placed at Howard University. Reading between the lines it seems that Locke had been at Tuskegee Institute in a teaching role and transferred to Howard University with Washington's blessing. But more than this it is clear that as an influential trustee, Washington was able to put Locke forward for a faculty position. It is a phenomenal primary document because it proves without doubt that Washington was a man who helped and encouraged all African American scholars. Locke would become a major philosopher; it is highly unlikely that he would have been involved in anything remotely "industrial" at Tuskegee Institute as a teacher. Locke continues in his letter to Washington, "I shall see to it that I myself and certain of the Howard authorities appreciate the fine disinterestedness of your willingness to assist me in locating at Howard when you were yourself able to use me at Tuskegee. I shall hope and expect to serve your very best interests at Howard and elsewhere, until I more than repay you for your deep and personal interest" (Locke 1912). Through this letter there is now a historical link between Alain Locke and Booker T. Washington, and it blows out of the water any idea that Washington was anti–higher education or anti–liberal arts. Harlan (1972, 1983) does not mention this correspondence. With due respect he may not have even understood the significance of this letter from a young African American scholar who would go on to be a major Harlem Renaissance figure. Locke edited and published a book *The New Negro* in 1925, and it is still read to this day. The book covers the essence of the writers, artists, and thinkers during the height of the Harlem Renaissance. The irony again is that twenty-five years earlier, in 1900, Washington's portrait was featured on a book cover with the title *A New Negro for a New Century*. This is actually another key twist in the historical record of African American history because it shows that the notion of the "New Negro" did not appear in 1925 as most writers and thinkers believe, but it actually appeared a generation earlier with Booker T. Washington (Gates 2019, 236).

Those who criticized Washington were often self-righteous and self-serving. Du Bois, Trotter, and Crummell and others had good reason to stand up for higher education and the life of the mind, but really the fight that Booker T. Washington was waging had him between the devil and the deep blue sea. He had to navigate choppy waters in endeavoring to find space for the lowest African American to rise up and prosper. The Black radical intellectuals were fighting a cause too, and it is important to understand that both groups, the Bookerites and the Du Boisians were in some way always right, and always wrong. The nature of a white supremacist world created these fissures and dichotomies that are still alive and kicking today.

Washington had to deal with the African American radicals more as they focused on him for the ills faced by their people. He was the successful accommodationist who ran the Tuskegee Machine, and in real terms he simply endeavored to limit the attacks on him and his organization. A number of organizations grew in response to his rise in power and fame. The Niagara Movement was established in 1905, led initially by the likes of Trotter and Du Bois to stem the tide of Washington's philosophy and practice. They were a group designed to curb Washington's influence as he was politically very strong as an advisor to President Roosevelt and was running a successful Tuskegee Institute and NNBL. Though the struggle continued overall for African Americans, poverty in South was rife, and disenfranchisement of communities continued to plague the environment.

The Niagara Movement was a powerful group of African Americans, who met on the Canadian side of the border at Niagara Falls in July 1905, simply because no hotel in Buffalo, New York, would accommodate them. Although the aims and objectives were largely the same as Washington's, the Niagara Movement demanded rather than maneuvered, rallied rather than rendered genuine outcomes. The group fizzled out due to a lack of funds and in-fighting. It eventually morphed into the National Association for the Advancement of Colored People (NAACP) in 1909. However, the NAACP was integrated with paternalistic white liberals who could offer the resources required to keep the organization afloat. W. E. B. Du Bois, though a founding member, would be hired as the editor for the new institution's publication, *The Crisis*. The NAACP was an organization that could effectively challenge the so-called Tuskegee Machine that due to Washington's overwhelming authority tended to dominate the African American political landscape. Along with Trotter's newspaper, the *Guardian*, published in Boston, there was a rather vicious assault on Washington's leadership and his focus on the presumed accommodation to white supremacy. Much of the criticism was hypocrisy given the fact that the NAACP was "controlled" financially by white donors, and if it was, then the likes of Du Bois should not have criticized Washington for his white philanthropic donors. Again, much of the criticism from Du Bois and others was self-serving. The bottom line is that both camps were fighting the same enemy, white supremacy, and they took different routes to achieving their aims and objectives. That fight for equal justice, economic opportunity, decent housing, non-voter-suppression, political representation, an end to police brutality and criminalization, and the overall dignity for the humanity of African Americans continues to the present day—even as the reader turns the pages of this biography.

Another important man who moved between Washington and Du Bois, but ultimately stayed in the Tuskegee man's corner was T. Thomas Fortune (1856–1928). Born into enslavement the same year as Washington, he grew to have an important role in African American journalism and civil rights issues. He also helped Ida B. Wells-Barnett with her career as a budding journalist writing on lynching and other issues impacting the African American experience. Fortune had a patchy education and was largely self-taught, but he rose to be a brilliant editor/writer and journalist with his paper, the *New York Age*. His role with Washington was as an adviser for his work and publications as they expanded after 1900. Fortune was a very light-skinned African American with wavy hair; in fact he could have passed but was a fervent "race man" in philosophy and practice.

> ### T. THOMAS FORTUNE (1856–1928)
>
> Thomas Fortune was born enslaved in Marianna, Florida. After the Civil War ended and freedom emerged, the family moved to Jacksonville, where Fortune went to elementary school. His education was sporadic, but he gained some experience with local newspapers and became a proficient writer. Later he spent some time at Howard University and began working for a newspaper called the *Peoples Advocate*; he dropped out of school to become a journalist. He settled in New York and established first the *Globe*, which changed to the *New York Freeman*, before finally settling with the *New York Age*. This newspaper developed into the most popular African American paper of its day. Fortune was a man who would work with both Washington and Du Bois. But for many years he was a confidante of the former, advising him on strategy for the North because Washington was primarily based in the South. Fortune was a powerful voice in the African American experience, and later worked with Marcus Garvey and the Universal Negro Improvement Association (UNIA).

Harlan regards Washington and Fortune as opposites in thinking and manner. Fortune was more of a passionate militant and was less able to be affable with whites. He was more in tune with the radical intellectuals though he had more in common with Washington's early life than any of the younger radicals coming out of the North and Harvard. Harlan writes, "Fortune was a leader of civil rights, inclined to fling down the gauntlet to whites rather than to conciliate them in Washington's fashion. Fortune took barbers and restauranteurs who would not serve him into court. Fortune's closeness to Washington is something of a mystery, but perhaps the best explanation is that they needed each other, that each had some quality or insight that the other lacked" (Harlan 1972, 192). This is a pretty good way to explain most men and women of business—there is always some form of give and take in any private or business relationship.

Fortune was very charismatic, tall and very articulate in manner, and he wore round-rimmed glasses (in the John Lennon style). He was based in New York and had access to African Americans that Washington may not have had. Fortune was instrumental in sharing insights into African American elites because for the most part Washington interacted with "the people" and later with rich white philanthropists. Before 1900, Washington rarely interacted with the middle-class elites of the African American experience. Harlan continues, "Such an adviser could be a sure guide through the unfamiliar paths of black leadership. Fortune, a high-strung, erratic personality, on the other hand, depended on Washington's steadiness and his ability to pull Fortune out of the difficulties his neuralgic illnesses and alcoholism caused" (193). Washington and Fortune would work together, mostly surreptitiously, in order to sway African American opinion through the press. Washington was always promoting Tuskegee Institute while keeping his political work for voting rights, anti-lynching, and anti-segregation undercover, lest he lose favor with white philanthropists and important politicians. In this regard, Fortune would often direct Washington's opinion through the African American press. Critics also label this form of business a part of the Tuskegee Machine, but it really is the natural occurrence of a man wanting to achieve his goals in the world he operated in. He was, at bottom, a businessman with aims and objectives to secure and the press was a means to get his message across to the people.

Yet, which brand does not try to win favor through the press and politics? This in contemporary language is called lobbying. Washington worked constantly with lobbyists to push forward his brand that was successful for him at Tuskegee Institute and the NNBL. In this capacity Fortune proved invaluable, but there was always an underlying distrust between the two men because they were of vastly different temperaments. This actually encapsulates the broader issue of Washington's relationship with Du Bois. Many commentators fail to take into account their different personalities *and* stations in life. Washington was very well established when Du Bois emerged on the national scene and though a brilliant fellow, like Fortune, he was not as well known like Washington. Yet the history books ordinarily put these men in context as "equals," and this particularly gives the wrong impression of Washington. They were not equals in education or in life experience. However, Fortune and Washington were more like peers and established men, but Du Bois was neither in their age group nor as yet nowhere close to being as established. It is only because the narrative seems to put greater emphasis on the educational credentials of Du Bois that it has carried much weight in the debate between him and Washington. The bottom line is that the understanding of both men has been very one sided due to the framing of their interaction and ideas only within the narrative of Du Bois—Washington has never been able to respond to the ideas laid forth by the manipulative Du Boisian brand.

Analyzing personality types is essential for comprehending the era Washington lived in, and this will prove a useful exercise in future assessments of these two important African Americans. Both of these men faced assaults on their manhood and had to find ways to deal with the extremities of white supremacy. What was the best way to live out a life with the crushing insuperable reality of hatred and violence meted out toward African Americans? On reflection, it seems rather insensitive and judgmental to point a finger at Washington for the ills his people suffered at the hands of an unutterably cruel system. It is interesting too how the most successful

African American of this era, who left the strongest viable legacy in Tuskegee Institute, is the one who is dismissed so easily.

There is another interesting issue raised in the writings of Du Bois and scholars who have studied Du Bois in relation to Washington; rarely, if at all, has it been recognized that he never discussed the published contributions of Washington. The accusation that Washington used ghost writers is most often expressed in a derogatory manner. Washington often had a stenographer with him to record his words. His correspondence was voluminous and thankfully most of it is recorded in the Booker T. Washington Papers for the historical record. That stated, reading his books one can "hear" his voice in the text. He was a man who had a unique style and there is evidence that suggests that the books he published had his indelible imprint on them, even if a ghost writer would polish up the product for publication. There are at least two volumes with *both* Du Bois and Washington in collaboration. *The Negro Problem*, published in 1903, is a volume that Booker T. Washington edited, and Du Bois and Fortune both contributed essays. This is a clear indication of Washington's importance as a thinker who wanted to be associated with other thinkers, regardless of the differences in the approaches to African American liberation. Other contributors to Washington's book are Charles W. Chesnutt and Paul Laurence Dunbar, who were important African American voices in literature and poetry. What is curious is that there is little mention to such an important book. One has to be a rather tenacious scholar to find this material and to give it proper context. The Washington book was published the same year as Du Bois's *The Souls of Black Folk*. Yet, rarely is Washington's book referred to as a valid response to the Du Bois essay that has fossilized Washington for generations.

Interestingly, both men put forward in *The Negro Problem* their views on what were the key issues facing African Americans at the dawn of the twentieth century. The opening paragraph of Washington's essay in this volume actually summarizes his views on education for the African American in the South. It is important to note how he relates to the Southern part of the United States because the majority of African Americans resided there, and it is where the greatest need in social uplift was. Washington put his perspective this way: "The necessity for the race's learning the difference between being worked and working. He would not confine the [African American] to industrial life, but believes that the very best service which any one can render to what is called the 'higher education' is to teach the present generation to work and save. This will create wealth from which alone can come leisure and the opportunity for higher education" (Washington 2020, 2). This is as clear and concise as it can get in regard to his view of higher education, which was basically an education in European classical thought. He was firm in the belief that he would not confine African Americans to industrial education, but currently he felt that as a people they did not have the bedrock of a large middle class.

The collective economic base had to be built in order to provide the wherewithal for mass higher education. It was foolish to think solely of higher education as a primary need because almost 50 percent of African Americans were illiterate. Washington understood higher education as an important aspect of African American life, but there was a need for his people to buildup to such privilege. What gets lost in this argument is the fact that he was trying to state the importance of building an economic foundation for a generation and have that wealth and property in families to compensate the next generation. His was a long-term goal for mass higher education, because in the present conditions of dire poverty and ignorance, there was a greater need for basic literacy and vocational skills. Keep in mind that this was also the condition of millions of poor whites in the South. But these whites were filled with delusions of grandeur with a popular culture daily caricaturing African Americans in a demeaning manner. The racism ran deep in the psyche of poor white Southerners. The manifestation of this enmity came out in the culture of lynching that had spread throughout the South. Washington, Du Bois, Fortune, and others were working to find solutions to a problem of such magnitude; sometimes they each failed in their endeavors. Yet it is difficult to reduce Washington's institution building to a mere achievement. His effort in creating a highly relevant institution was a phenomenal accomplishment and he was adamant about Tuskegee Institute being a model for the further education of African Americans across the South.

Du Bois put forward an alternative model in *The Negro Problem* that made sense theoretically, but it was not practical in the real world of the South. There were already a number of higher education institutions in the South, most notably Fisk University, and Washington had a very strong relationship with them. Indeed, Fisk is where his wife, Margaret, had graduated, and where his son, Booker Jr., attended as a student. But in terms of the masses of African Americans in the South there was more required than merely studying European canons of knowledge, which was the staple education in historically Black colleges and universities.

Du Bois's perspective was understandable even though it was both impracticable and not holistic in its approach to the problem in the South. His essay in the edited volume is titled "The Talented Tenth," and it is introduced by Washington in a very insightful manner: "A strong plea for the higher education of the [African American], which those who are interested in the future of the freedmen cannot afford to ignore. Prof. Du Bois produces ample evidence *to prove conclusively the truth* of his statement that to attempt to establish any sort of a system of common and industrial school training, without first providing for the higher training of the very best teachers, is simply throwing your money to the winds" (Washington 2020, 13; italics added for emphasis). Washington's introduction to Du Bois's essay clearly agrees with the premise that institutions like Tuskegee Institute need to have the very best teachers in the skills and education that they provide to their students. Washington recruited teachers from Fisk, Howard, and those who had been educated at Harvard. The manner in which he tried hard to recruit Du Bois to conduct sociological studies, exactly the type Du Bois produced at Atlanta University, and to teach at Tuskegee Institute is again an example of Washington's desire to have the best teachers for his students. As noted earlier, Du Bois refused the "very generous" offer that Washington offered him to join the Tuskegee Institute faculty.

The point here is that future generations of scholars were not aware of these nuances, such as Washington's agreement on many issues with Du Bois. *The Negro Problem* proves that there was unison in the basic premise put forward by Du Bois that there need to be top class teachers in African American schools and institutions of vocational and further education. This was an established concept between the two men and yet it has been lost in the historical record, or at the very least, misplaced. Du Bois, however, puts forward a very narrow conception of what the Talented Tenth actually meant. He forgot, or conveniently overlooked, the fact that many brilliant minds that emerged from the African American experience were largely self-taught; Frederick Douglass, arguably the greatest intellect of the nineteenth century, did not experience elementary school, high school, or higher education. He learned to read and write primarily by his own wit and intelligence and rose to be a brilliant writer, journalist, orator, editor, strategist and activist for African American liberation. One can run up the centuries and find men and women of African heritage who had no formal schooling, from Sojourner Truth to Fannie Lou Hamer, and from William Wells Brown to Malcolm X. Not to belittle Du Bois, but being formally educated in a higher education establishment does not necessarily impart knowledge that is practical for liberation purposes (Woodson 1990).

Being lofty and overly righteous was Du Bois's personality and his prose was flowery and often a tad pretentious. With due respect, the rank and file African American in 1903 would find it difficult to read parts of *The Souls of Black Folk*. Why? Because the prose is often complicated and inaccessible to an average reader. This is not to suggest Du Bois had no place in society to peddle his haughty prose; in fact, his brilliant social scientific studies were useful to policymakers. But to manipulate and rearrange Washington's practical approach was rather misleading. The concept of the Talented Tenth was ultimately elitist in its scope, and demeaning to any African American who had not had the privilege or good fortune to have gained a higher education diploma. Thousands of African Americans had skills that were not sanctioned with a diploma.

Indeed, the man, Lewis Adams, without whom there would have been no Tuskegee Institute was an extremely gifted artisan with no formal education. He was self-taught, yet talented way beyond his peers. Harlan puts his significance this way: "If there was a heroic history-maker, it was the black tinsmith Lewis Adams. As a slave artisan in Tuskegee he had learned tinsmithing, shoemaking, and harnessing, and during the years of freedom he built a substantial business in tin. He made kitchen utensils for the housewives of Tuskegee, roofed the business buildings, and moved into hardware and leather making. . . . Lewis Adams never attended school a day in his life, but somehow had learned to read and write" (Harlan 1972, 113). The fact is that there were thousands of men and women like Lewis Adams who lived, loved, and prospered under the worst of times. Talented, unknown, unappreciated, yet unbowed by enslavement, segregation, and the ever-specter of violence. Though Du Bois had the right intentions from the perspective of his experience, the masses of African Americans were not in a position to appropriate the values of higher education.

Du Bois mentions Frederick Douglass passingly as "self-trained but yet trained liberally" (Du Bois 2020, 17). It is assumed that what Du Bois means by "liberally" is that he taught himself via liberal arts. It is a fundamentally self-serving statement. The fact is that Frederick Douglass and many others rose from the ashes because they were exceptional, and exceptions to the rule, men and women. Du Bois is unabashed about his conception of a Talented Tenth as he asks two pointed questions: "Can the masses of the [African American] be in any possible way more quickly raised than by the effort and example of this aristocracy of talent and character? Was there ever a nation on God's fair earth civilized from the bottom up?" He answers, "Never; it is, ever was and ever will be from the top downward that culture filters" (18).

Washington published Du Bois's perspective even though it did not agree with his philosophy. He was man enough to allow Du Bois to express himself openly and probably because he thought it would not make much impact; mainly due to Du Bois's inherent implication that without having a higher education elite leadership, one cannot expect to uplift the masses of African Americans. In short, the masses are ignorant and without direction; therefore they require the cultured direction of the Talented Tenth. Indirectly, to put it mildly, Du Bois was disrespecting Washington's pedigree as an educated teacher-scholar—along with their mutual colleague T. Thomas Fortune who had only received a sporadic formal education.

Du Bois would not find his perspective or statements on the Talented Tenth out of place because he viewed most men and women below his intellect. If one considers his envy toward Washington, who had received an honorary master's degree from Harvard in 1896 and an honorary doctorate from Dartmouth College in 1901, there are few who would disagree that Washington fully deserved both honorary degrees, and lived up to both levels in terms of his achievements in education and business acumen. Actually, and this is rather nuanced, after 1901, the Tuskegee Institute leader was most often addressed as "Dr. Washington," yet Du Bois in his essay from *The Souls of Black Folk* in 1903 is sure to let the reader know him as "Mr. Booker T. Washington." Knowing the nature of Du Bois's ego it is unlikely he was unaware of Dr. Washington's elevated status after receiving his honorary doctorate. This may seem a rather trivial matter but it does reveal the depth of Du Bois's need to separate himself from Washington in terms of his "superior" education in European classics. Overall, Washington edited and published *The Negro Problem* in 1903 to give voice to various perspectives and approaches to how best tackle the current needs of African Americans residing in the South, in regard to their educational needs. He was fair to different writers and gave Du Bois in particular an important platform for his ideas. In 1903, Washington was the most famous African American on earth, and to allow Du Bois to be part of his book was in itself an olive branch and another show of his respect for the first African American to gain a degree at Harvard University. Given the personality type of Du Bois, it is of no small interest to consider how he would have acted if the tables were turned and he had the required power to include or exclude Washington from airing his ideas on a similar platform.

There is no similar publication that Du Bois ever originated that brought his ideas up against Washington's. However, there is one that was initiated by the Philadelphia Divinity School's Christian lecture series, likely to have taken place in late 1906 and early 1907. Two lectures were published from Washington and two from Du Bois in one volume; and they came not long after the September 1906 anti-African American riot that took place in Atlanta, the city where the lectures were delivered. The publication is titled *The Negro in the South*. The Divinity School had a proviso that the only restriction placed on the lecturer would be "He shall be a believer in the moral teachings and principles of the Christian Religion as the true solvent of our Social, Industrial, and Economic problems" (Washington and Du Bois 1970, xxii). This is significant because the scholar who edited the 1970 reissue of the book, Herbert Aptheker, displayed his bias for Du Bois and his implicit disdain for Washington. Aptheker was one of the radical left white scholars who interpreted the scholarship of Du Bois for over a generation, from the 1950s onward. What is concerning about Aptheker's introduction to this new edition of the volume is the manner in which he shaped the debate and carefully left out the previous publications of Washington. Here he writes at the outset of his introduction, "The book now in the reader's hands is quite unique; it is the only work which consists of the writings of Washington and Du Bois, the two giants of post-Reconstruction Afro-American history" (iii). It is difficult to imagine that a scholar of Aptheker's ability could fail to know about Washington's edited volume, *The Negro Problem* that was published only four years before *The Negro in the South*. In effect, Aptheker consigns Washington's book to the scrapheap of historical scholarship because any neophyte scholar wanting to learn about these two men would have trusted his insight. Frankly, it is astounding to learn how this type of scholarly manipulation unfolded—it was underhand, unsavory, and unscholarly of Aptheker to have overlooked *The Negro Problem* edited by Booker T. Washington in his introduction of *The Negro in the South*.

Washington deserves a tad better than this, and what is more confounding is another glaring oddity emanating from Aptheker's introduction. This time he derides Washington for expressing his belief that the best way forward for African Americans was in developing a habit for self-determination through hard work, thrift, and a love of God. Again, this was the Protestant ethic model in embracing capitalism in the age of progressivism. This was a lecture series promoted by a Christian divinity school from Philadelphia, and the only insistence on the speakers was that they believe in the word of God, the Bible. So why disparage Washington for speaking in a way that fits with his beliefs and that of the sponsors? It makes no sense unless Aptheker, writing in 1970, was doing all he could to show Washington in a bad light with the present Civil Rights generation that were moving toward Black Power, and with the revival of *The Souls of Black Folk* showcase Du Bois as a "radical" savior of Black pride. What is profoundly odd as well is that Du Bois was also a believer, of sorts, otherwise he should not have been giving lectures under the auspices of the divinity school—maybe he was once again being economical with the truth to the organizers.

Without a critical reading, the average reader may miss such nuance, but an editor as skilled as Aptheker skillfully depicted Washington in a bad light, and on the contrary, he portrayed Du Bois as a redeemer for African Americans. Aptheker's introduction to *The Negro in the South* is replete with erroneous facts, contradictory statements, and a fair degree of hypocrisy. Keep in mind that Aptheker was a Marxist historian, and a key shaper in the Du Bois scholarly legacy. The fact that Du Bois joined the Communist Party in 1961 before departing for Ghana to live out the last two years of his life gave Aptheker good cover to assault Washington's open advocacy for capitalism. But, again to be fair, Washington simply worked with the system as it was, he was not a fan of the unions because they were overtly racist toward African American labor. If anything, Washington was nonaligned and did the best he could with what was available for him to use to improve the conditions of Tuskegee Institute and beyond.

That is key to understanding the man. Washington surveyed the scene, realized his options were limited, and made the best of what was on offer. Capitalism was the system, and he worked it to the benefit of Tuskegee Institute and the NNBL. To suggest that this was somehow detrimental to African Americans is like stating to a starving man, "Don't eat this food. Just wait until we can get you something more palatable." Well, the social fact remains, African Americans made Soul Food out of the inedible diet the enslavers allowed the enslaved. As such, and in line with their inherent genius they went into the woods and created spices, and served greens with corn bread. They made the best of what little was available. The same can be stated with Washington, the road to his success involved using the model of philanthropic funds, his concomitant knowledge of Hampton Institute and its philanthropic contacts to build his mini empire.

Herbert Aptheker wrote many books on African American history. He was a white progressive Marxist, who influenced an array of young African American scholars in the 1960s and 1970s. Therefore, he should take a lot of the responsibility for the fossilization of Washington, and for the future generations who did not bother to learn anything beyond Du Bois's perspective and the so-called Atlanta Compromise speech. This is grossly unfair and terribly misleading because the man offered far more than what the Marxist scholars have espoused. Washington was a brilliant institution builder, who actually built with his own hands, and used his head to make it happen. He taught his students to be self-sufficient, to believe in thrift, in having a bank account, and how to erect a habitable clean home for one's family. He never emphasized avarice or to pursue money for money's sake—always the emphasis was to build an economic based that would sustain a man and woman with their children. He was a family man who believed in hard work, deferred gratification, and generational wealth accruement.

One other misleading interpretation of Washington coming from Marxist scholars is the very fact of them not interpreting Karl Marx very well. For Marx, at the heart of his critique of the system of capitalism was the exploitation of the laborer who worked for the exploiter who owned the means of production. Marx wanted the worker to be free to enjoy his or her work, to wake in the morning with joy at building something for oneself rather than being alienated from the product that one ordinarily produced. This in turn would allow for more leisure time and enjoyment with one's family. Well, this is exactly what Washington was inculcating, the idea of working for oneself, in order to have a life that could lead to more leisure. Yes, it could take some years to develop your prosperity, but with determination and a stick-to-it attitude, it would emerge. Washington was living proof of his mantra, he did not play with his brand—unfortunately those who interpreted it did so with impunity.

When one reads the Introduction to the 1970 edition of *The Negro in the South*, there is a distinct bias toward Du Bois that takes into account his scholarship, while not only disregarding Washington's but eliminating it from the historical record. There is not a balanced account of both men and their ideas. Again, there is an overly dismissal of anything good and the legacy of self-determination that Washington left behind. Du Bois is the victor in the debate without a discussion taking place; also, Aptheker leans Du Bois over to the left when in fact he was bourgeois in his lifestyle and manner. He was not a Marxist in the fullest sense, but Aptheker manipulated his legacy to look like he was a man of the people. Du Bois was a man to himself, a flawed genius with an ego the size of the moon. According to him no one should dare fault his Talented Tenth concept, and conveniently Aptheker does not allude to it because it would mess up his Marxist applecart and show Du Bois as merely a de facto member of the "Politburo"—just another elite making policies for the ignorant masses of uninformed African Americans who needed direction and guidance to an indistinct Promise Land of European canons and classical education, dead languages, and the acquiring of dubious philosophy when it came to African humanity.

In addition, Aptheker cites Du Bois criticizing how the United States should not be regarded as a Christian nation due to its treatment of African Americans, and rightly so. But that is not a condemnation of Christianity itself, as a Marxist would have it. Du Bois stated, "It is absurd to call the practical religion of this nation Christian. We are not humble, we are impudently proud; we are not merciful, we are unmerciful toward friend and foe; we are not peaceful nor peacefully inclined as our armies and battleships declare; we do not want to be martyrs, we would rather be thieves and liars so long as we can be rich" (Washington and Du Bois 1970, 186). The words from Du Bois are eloquently written, yet some of them could speak on a micro level about his personality. He was not a humble man; he was impudently proud; he was most often unmerciful toward Washington, and he could be economical with the truth in regard to their relationship. For all of Du Bois's undoubted brilliance, there were undoubted flaws in him as there are in all human beings.

Another theme that comes out of the past writings on Washington is regarding him "not being an intellectual," and quite frankly this should also be a stereotype that becomes moribund. Somewhere in time a philosopher stated "we are all philosophers," and therefore it is rather elitist to label Washington as unintellectual. This is an easy shot to take due to him not having gone through higher education like Du Bois and some of his other critics. Yet, it is a narrow criticism given his record as a brilliant orator and a man who could speak comfortably with any man, particularly the rich and powerful white men of the day who actually sought out *his* company. It has been argued that intelligence is not easy to define. But one aspect of human intelligence that can be accounted for is a person's ability to adapt to any given situation. If this be a yardstick for measuring intellect then Washington was a genius. How many individuals could have survived what he did in his life and still prosper? Why did Andrew Carnegie admire him so much? Because Carnegie could at least relate to Washington's struggles in early childhood and they had the same hunger for education. Carnegie knew Washington had the added burden of enslavement and racialized prejudice to deal with on top of all the other hardships.

There is an interesting part to Washington's relationship with Carnegie that is recalled by his daughter, Portia. She states that in 1903 the tycoon offered Washington a staggering $600,000 to take care of himself and his family. Apparently, Carnegie called him the "Moses of your race," and Washington refused to take the money for himself. He asked Carnegie to donate it to Tuskegee Institute to help the "boys and girls down there get an education." They did work something out where he received a monthly stipend from the interest but the bulk of it went to the institution. Portia goes on to state that when her father died he was "poor as Job's turkey and even the interest didn't go to us" (Stewart 1977, 66). That gives an insight into the man that few are aware of; he died relatively poor personally, but the institution he built was rich with no debt incurred for future generations.

Carnegie and others like William Baldwin were good friends with Washington, and this is hard to grasp from a racial standpoint, especially if one considers the racism that prevailed. There had to be a degree of paternalism but there is no evidence of such on the personal level. Rich men do not need African American friends. Washington spoke at Baldwin's funeral in 1905. That would not have been possible without the request of the man being interred. The point is this: Washington was a bright, perceptive, cautious man, who had an outgoing and friendly manner. He attracted warmth yet ran his institute extremely carefully with the help of his loyal secretary Emmett Scott. Little of Washington's personal life and interactions is detailed by many scholars, other than Harlan (1972, 1983). It is a crudely conceptualized "Black and White" affair. Washington was extremely intelligent; he may not have been book smart and yielded prose like Du Bois, but there were many skills that Du Bois could not do that Washington could. That is why comparison of these two men is important. If one is to comprehend the two men fairly then it has to be done in a manner of fairness and in an evaluation of both their backgrounds, personal obstacles to success, and overall achievement while on earth. Washington wrote these words in summing up one of his lectures from *The Negro in the South*: "I believe that it is possible for a race, as it is for an individual, to learn to live up to such a high atmosphere that there is no human law that can prevail against it. There is no man who can pass a law to affect the [African American] in relation to his singing, his peace, and his self-control" (Washington and Du Bois 1970, 41).

Washington loved his people, and to protect those around him he was a very vigilant man, and rightly so. He lived among the worst elements of humanity and yet strove to bring all together. Historians have too easily cast him as weak, ingratiating and servile—as such it could be argued that they do not know him well enough. Aptheker, for example, derided Washington's use of the idiom that rural African Americans employed. Yet, literature folks like Paul Laurence Dunbar, Zora Neale Hurston, and Langston Hughes would be praised for using the dialect of African Americans from the South. In doing so, Washington was not putting down his people; he was elevating their humanity and wisdom. A white historian dripping in the mores and values of elite academia would probably not comprehend this. In *The Negro in the South*, Washington shares a story of an African American cotton grower, who was illiterate but smarter than all around when it came to growing several cotton bolls on one stem. Each year at Tuskegee Institute there would be a conference for farmers to share their best techniques for using the soil for their products. An elderly farmer took the stage and stated, "I'se had no chance to study science, but I'se been making some science for myself," and he went on to show how his technique of growing cotton had yielded from a stalk having two bolls to one having fourteen bolls of cotton. He was applying a scientific method to the soil and yet he was supposedly "uneducated." Washington finishes the story by stating that someone in the crowd was amazed by what he had witnessed and wanted to know the man's name. He replied, "When I didn't own no home and was in debt, they used to call me old Jim Hill, but now that I own a home and am out of debt, they call me 'Mr. James Hill'" (Washington and Du Bois 1970, 53–54). Washington often used these types of stories, some very humorous, to show the depth of wisdom in the African American rural experience. He even stated, "I have gotten more material in this way than I have by reading books" (52).

Much wisdom is found beyond books and formal education, and the idea that a Talented Tenth can somehow fill in the minds of the 90 percent the necessary knowledge for civilization and culture is deeply patronizing—especially when that knowledge, as Du Bois experienced, is derived from reading almost exclusively European male thinkers. The concept of the Talented Tenth was deeply flawed, and Washington understood the needs of his people more than most, having experienced the worst of life and the best of life with them. The impression he gave to the white world was essentially a cover, for anyone who witnessed Tuskegee Institute up close and personal could see clearly that the young men and women were cultured, disciplined, and proud African Americans, and that the curriculum offered both crafts and knowledge combined with a respect for self and community.

Du Bois and others who criticized him had their agenda, and they felt Washington had "too much power" and sought to limit it through protest and the NAACP. Yet it was never uniform or total because Washington was in support of all that they stood for as well, he just could not openly state as much. This is not making excuses, for some aspects of his decision-making did appear to be rather ingratiating and servile in retrospect. Yet one must consider the fox that walks on ice does so with careful comprehension of the wolves that sit waiting for him to slip and fall. In reflection, however one interprets history one cannot put the ills of white supremacy at Booker T. Washington's door—that would be grossly unfair. Du Bois, twenty-five years after Washington's passing, had full control of the interpretation in considering their interaction. In *Dusk of Dawn* published in 1940, he provided a metaphorical "nails in the coffin" analysis on Washington's fossilized legacy. With the correspondence between the two men not being available, and with Washington unable to defend himself, the titan of African American scholarship had full reign in establishing himself as the righteous overlord of African American history. Though an exceptional scholar, in reading the life and times of Washington, Du Bois had mendacious propensities when it came to interpreting his relationship with the Tuskegee Institute leader. Above all, Du Bois writes, " I resented the Tuskegee Machine" (Du Bois, *Dusk,* 1992, 80). Washington's "machine" was simply the power he had accumulated to make good his brand. He was a powerful African American, and sadly envy is the concomitant reality when a man of color reaches the heights of success Washington experienced.

Yes, he had influence, but it was not as omniscient as is claimed by Du Bois and others. He worked very hard behind the scenes to defend voting, and he worked hard in public view to support higher education, particularly with his roles as a trustee on the boards of Fisk and Howard universities where he ushered philanthropic funds. Du Bois's claim that Washington disliked colleges and universities is simply erroneous. There is too much proof to the contrary; though he may well have preferred the Tuskegee Institute model in education, that should be considered in his realm a prerogative and personal preference. After all, Tuskegee Institute and its success is what made Washington famous. Why on earth would he have steered away from an educational model that had proved successful, efficient, and useful to the broader community is a ludicrous proposition. In *Dusk of Dawn*, Du Bois returns to his famous essay "Of Mr. Booker T. Washington and Others" and contends he is "satisfied with it" as a historical reference. Well, it should be brought to present and future generations that there is much more to Washington than offered by Du Bois, it is hoped here that some of the omissions in that essay have been adequately highlighted. Historians like Aptheker, and later Manning Marable, who was close to him, continued the Du Bois legacy in largely undermining Washington as a "power hungry" man who sought to destroy his enemies, and so forth. Well, this is a tad beyond the reality; Washington was too humble, too focused, and bereft of pettiness to publically harm young men like Du Bois, whom he wanted at Tuskegee Institute to help establish a sociological investigative academic department, one like what he headed at Atlanta University.

What Du Bois fought for was "full manhood" for the African American. A noble and righteous cause that no one would disagree with, certainly not Washington. Therefore, dear reader, keep in mind that there is nothing but respect for Du Bois's sentiments and undaunted spirit in the fight for African American rights. It is the manner in which he aided in the fossilization of Washington and his legacy that is a problem to be rectified by future historians. There is a greater need for balance and fairness in the assessment. Both men were brilliant and beyond the realm of the average human faculties. One was much younger than the other, more privileged than the other, and more talented in prose than the other. Yet this does not make Du Bois a better man than the other. Washington had skills and abilities of persuasion that outshined Du Bois by a mile. Had the two sets of skills been melded and energies focused entirely on the real enemy then history would have been written differently.

Manning Marable, an African American scholar who emerged in the 1970s and could be deemed a Du Boisian scholar, was someone who learned much from Aptheker, and who leaned heavily toward Du Bois, his philosophical mentor, when writing on Washington. He did provide a useful analysis that put the time and place they operated in proper context. According to Marable, in 1901 there was a dearth of funds going into Southern white colleges and institutions of higher learning. Moreover, he explained that this would have a knock-on effect for African American education. He wrote, "Given the poverty in white higher education, it is not surprising that black colleges and industrial schools fared poorly during the flood of white supremacy. White critics complained that college and technical training had made blacks 'uppish' and 'bumptious' and prompted them to 'despise' work" (Marable 1999, 36). As such, state legislatures began to cut budgets for African Americans that received state support. This is the reality of the times in which Washington operated.

Another key issue that historians have overlooked is the immense pressure on Washington's shoulders for the livelihoods of his faculty and administrators. There were over one thousand students, and one hundred faculty on the Tuskegee Institute campus at the turn of the twentieth century. He had the responsibility for a great many lives, something Du Bois, Trotter, and others did not take fully into account. Instead, it was all about his supposed dislike of higher education and African American "manhood," which was humbug. The evidence that few consider is that most of the attacks on higher education came from the parsimonious white world and its continued assault on any form of African American development. Washington found a way around this by working exclusively with the Northern philanthropists. To suggest that Washington's public announcements of appeasing social distancing from whites, while allowing African Americans the space to breathe economically and educationally, gave them the authority to disenfranchise is putting him way ahead of his importance. Those white Southern lawmakers who had enmity for African Americans were never going to hold back on their stifling tactics because of what Washington stated or did not state. White supremacists detested Washington and everything he stood for, and this is noted by the reaction to his dinner at the White House with President Roosevelt in October 1901 (Davis 2012). Historians have given Washington far too much power than what he could wield, and the "Tuskegee Machine" is a myth in terms of how it was blown way out of proportion.

Overall, there needs to be a revision of the relationship between Washington, Du Bois, and his critics. There has been mendacity put forward by the brilliant Du Bois that has gone undetected for too long. With the Booker T. Washington papers now available to be mined and more comparison taking place (Aiello 2016), more will be revealed that should de-fossilize the relationship he had with Du Bois. Too many historians start with "Of Mr. Booker T. Washington and Others" without context. Du Bois was an upstart when he first came into contact with the Tuskegee Institute leader. Age, experience, and career status should be taken into account. Washington was by far the established man, while Du Bois saw him as the man to topple—by any means necessary. Why? Because his ego would settle for nothing less. He was a manipulator of facts and that has been proved above. Washington was no innocent bystander, and he did what he had to do to keep his brand successful. Crucially, he wanted Du Bois to be part of the Tuskegee Institute success just as he had recruited the great George Washington Carver, but Du Bois could never accept being less than the top man and the sole focus of attention.

6

Africa in His Mind and Practice

In terms of human history, all roads lead back to ancient Africa, and its civilizations attest to the greatness of humanity. Indeed, the brilliance of the African past before the onset of Arab and European conquest is not a romantic notion (Asante 2007, 9; Davidson 1987). Even Booker T. Washington would come to know of its great and vital history—he would eventually usher in the importance of having a text, *The Story of the Negro*, first published in 1909, for his history students that spoke to African and African American history (Washington 2007). Yet Washington's contact with Africa during the era he existed as the leader of Tuskegee Institute is rarely acknowledged (Wright 2015; Zimmerman 2010). Therefore it is important to flesh out some of this hidden history regarding Washington's interest and contact with Africa and related affairs. Keep in mind that he is not regarded ordinarily as a Pan Africanist historical figure in the African Diaspora as, say, W. E. B. Du Bois, that is, someone who fought for African liberation from European control and to link Africa with Africans in the Diaspora. As the de facto African American leader (1895–1915), Washington lived during arguably the worst period of European conquest and colonialization of Africa. Nevertheless, he still did what he could under severe restrictions to support African advancement at the turn of the twentieth century, as will be evidenced in the following chapter.

However, at the outset it is important to note that there has been a long history of African American and other leaders in the African Diaspora who endeavored to develop tangible links with the African continent. Yet, ironically, most often in the eighteenth to early twentieth centuries, those persons of African heritage raised in the African Diaspora had usually developed subconscious Europeanized biases and stereotypes toward Africa. Even though they always had good intentions, there was a tendency to look upon the African continent as needing Western knowledge, religion, and culture. Indeed, this could be deemed a warped and inverted paternalism emanating from African heritage leaders born outside the continent. We cannot openly lay blame for this on the likes of Henry McNeal Turner, Alexander Crummell, W. E. B. Du Bois, or even Marcus Garvey for harboring such subconscious notions of African continental inferiority. This was something the Europeans fed minds in the West from the day born through pseudoscientific racism and a misplaced education system that denied African agency (Woodson 1990). Sadly miseducation of Africa was interwoven into the minds of early African Diaspora travelers to the continent, especially in the early stages of forging social and cultural connections during the eras of European enslavement and colonialism. Moreover, when European conquest directly took over the African continent (late 1800s), things got even worse. In short, Africans in the Diaspora have had to overcome varied psychological impediments and inner conflicts toward the African continent caused by miseducation via both Arab and European predatory invasions going back centuries (Asante 2007, 209–221). Booker T. Washington was someone like many before him who was proud of his African heritage, yet he also had to learn how to strip away the psychological racism brought on by years of miseducation via European-derived education to finally embrace Africa's historical depth, positive cultural offerings, and immense significance to world civilization (Asante 2007; Davidson 1987).

One such respected African American who exemplifies this conundrum is Alexander Crummell, who was born in 1819 and lived until 1898. As noted in the previous chapter, he was a scholar and a pretty good one too, but his education was forged largely through European Christianity and therefore tinged with the psychological malaise that infected most persons of note who traveled to Africa and were of African heritage from the West. In an address given at the American Geographical Society in New York on May 22, 1877, and extolling the virtues of Christianity, Crummell wrote, "We stand at the commencement of a grand endeavor of Christendom to wipe the blood from the bruised brow of Africa, to lift up its vast populations to enlightenment, and to rescue a great continent from the dominion of superstition and barbarism" (Crummell 1891, 30). The ingrained ideological and cultural superiority was a product of being educated or rather miseducated in European notions of white superiority. Crummell and contemporaries like Henry Highland Garnet were free

African Americans. Crummell and Garnet both spent many years in Liberia, Africa, but they each had a zealousness for missionary work. With them being of African heritage, it was not the usual European missionary style tinged with racism; nonetheless it was strongly related to European subjugation of African Indigenous religions in favor of the "superior" Christianity that they had each embraced as African Americans.

When Crummell spoke to the geographical group, it was about eight years before the Berlin Conference of 1884/5 that would carve Africa up into the political and colonial pieces to be devoured by the "enlightened" European nations led by Britain, France, Germany, Portugal and others. Maybe Crummell would not have been so optimistic had he knew the devastation that European conquest would bestow on many African generations to come. Crummell, Garnet, and others who sought links with Africa were very intelligent men, but they misunderstood what enlightenment meant for those outside of its European cultural hegemony. Africans, American Indians, and other peoples of color were not part of the positive aspects of European advances into Africa and other parts of the world. Crummell did speak the truth, and he loved Africa in many ways, but unfortunately in the wrong ways. In that talk in May 1877, Crummell spoke to would-be exploiters, stating, "Africa is a land of most magnificent resources. It abounds everywhere in its tropical regions with woods and dyes, and gums and minerals and oils" (310). He would know as he spent almost twenty years in Liberia from 1853 to 1872, only to return to America to head up St. Luke's Episcopal Church in Washington, D.C.

The American Colonization Society (ACS) was an organization set up to provide repatriation for African Americans to return to Africa. But this was also to get rid of the growing number of the "free" or "freed" from enslavement in the North American borders. Some African Americans took advantage of this, and later even Abraham Lincoln supported the ACS as a way to solve the problem of racialized conflict. Frederick Douglass and later leaders like T. Thomas Fortune were adamantly against emigration schemes due to the longevity of African American presence and the stake that they had in the economic growth of North America. Fortune also reported that those emigrants who did go would often experience disillusionment and regret due to the harsh realities of resettlement in Liberia, Africa (Thornbrough 1972, 141–143).

The above gives a brief indication that the generation before Booker T. Washington had forged a strong connection with the African continent, and not only in Liberia. There has been slight insight into Washington's contacts with Africa and the role he played in endeavoring to empower Africans through his educational model at Tuskegee Institute. The majority of biographers employ the fossilized version of Washington with the usual the "conservative capitalist" and "accommodationist to white

> **AMERICAN COLONIZATION SOCIETY (ACS)**
>
> The American Colonization Society (ACS) organization was established in 1816; it was initially called the Society for the Colonization of Free People of Color of America by its founder Robert Finlay (1772–1817). Finlay was a clergyman who was based in New Jersey and wanted to help the free African Americans find an escape from the racism in America. However, some viewed this as simply a way to rid the African American population of its abolitionists who were fighting to free their enslaved brothers and sisters. Abraham Lincoln, for example, saw the ACS as a way to solve the problem of racialized relations in the United States by repatriating African Americans back to Africa. Abolitionist Frederick Douglass was opposed to the ACS, and others like Booker T. Washington felt the same way. But men like Bishop McNeal Turner and Alexander Crummell felt that it was a good thing to have a way to get "back home" to Africa. Liberia in West Africa was set up by the ACS as a colony for free African Americans who would, supposedly, have better prospects unrestricted by white racism. Liberia declared independence in 1847 and was recognized as such by the U.S. government in 1862. Thousands of African Americans settled in Liberia but faced a lack of support in resources; many died of disease and struggled to survive in the climate. Nevertheless, it continued to be a site for the "Back to Africa" African American liberation movement right up to the 1920s.

supremacy" labels. Yet, ironically, the likes of Crummell, Garnet, and others drenched in European Christianity and values deeming Africans being in need of saving from heathenism is not exactly the height of self-determination and having pride in African Indigenous cultures. Yet most writers on African American history cite them as Pan African pioneers in the early migration to Africa movements.

By 1900, the continent of Africa was inundated with European missionaries and conquests. The renowned anti-imperialist American writer Mark Twain and the Tuskegee Institute leader would become friends, each enjoying their wry humor. Few historians note this friendship; it may be too much to consider an intellect of the deadpan Mark Twain variety wanting to spend his time with Booker T. Washington or anyone who did not inspire some likewise interest. Clearly, they shared interests in defeating the inhumane realities that were juxtaposed with the European conquest of Africa. According to Norrell (2009, 154), Washington and Twain were actually "chums," and this is important to note because it indicates they shared intellectual interests, apart from considering the onslaught of imperialism. Particularly, in regard to the atrocities that were taking place under King Leopold II of Belgium. Both men took a stand on the inhumanity taking place, with children having their limbs hacked off for not bringing enough rubber to the colonists, or women being raped, and men being killed or maimed. These were daily occurrences in the Belgian Congo and Washington had first heard about this while on a tour in Europe in 1899. He also met with the British explorer Sir Henry Stanley who discussed his African experiences. Washington soon wrote articles for the Congo Reform Association protesting the inhumanity, and Mark Twain would publish the satirical *King Leopold's Soliloquy* that would become a template for anti-imperialist literature. Both Washington and Twain lobbied President Teddy Roosevelt to pressure Belgium to intervene on the torture taking place in Africa. Twain is said to have concluded in his deliberation that Leopold was a "Bloody monster whose mate is not findable in human history anywhere" (Twain 1905, vii).

Washington was proud of his people and was an ardent "race man" who did not want to be anything other than what he was: African American. He fully understood the evils of enslavement and the torturous reality that had brought his people to the shores of North America. There was no animosity in his heart for the malicious treatment of his people at the hands of the white structural plantation system. Washington instinctively knew that bitterness would only destroy his soul. Instead his aim was to build himself up first and then spread the lessons he had learned to his people through education. His love of his African heritage was openly stated, and regardless of his European genes that emanated from his mother's interaction with a local white man, whether consensual or not, he knew the prevailing social order did not regard that aspect of his heritage—he was an African American and proud of it.

This aspect of Washington has been vastly underplayed mainly by white biographers and historians because, to be frank, it was not in their comprehension to bring it directly out. Instead they tended to focus on his ideas in education, politics, and business. What made Washington tick as a human being has been grossly under-researched to date. What made him so comfortable in his own skin too has been missed in the analysis of the man. For Harlan (1972, 1983), at bottom, Washington was an enigma, someone who ultimately he could not fully comprehend. Almost forty years of study and the liberal white Southerner could not get to the essence of Washington. He put far too much emphasis on his dealings with his critics, emphasizing the so-called Tuskegee Machine, the label that came from the frustrated and disgruntled Du Bois. Crucially, what Harlan and others have misunderstood is Washington's deep admiration of his African heritage, his respect of their collective strength and humanity to overcome such cruel, inhumane, and unhealthy conditions and yet still rise up. In one of Washington's many books that have been consigned to obscurity, *The Story of the Negro*, if read carefully one can hear *his* voice and not that of the ghost writer (Robert E. Park), as he states, "The feelings that divided my mind and confused my purpose when I was a young man, have also divided the members of my race. The continual adverse criticism had led some of us to disavow our racial identity, to seek rest and try our successes as members of another race than that to which we were born" (Washington 2007, 19). What he alludes to are the many African Americans who tried to "pass" into the white world due to their lightness of skin or ambiguous ethnicity. Those who did this usually had an internal life of pain and psychological anguish. Washington continues, "It has led others of us to seek to get away as far as possible from association with our own race, and to keep as far away from Africa, from its history and from its traditions as it was possible for us to do" (19). As stated, Washington published *The Story of the Negro* in 1909, and it is a study of over four hundred pages that covers the origins of the forced migration of Africans and how those Africans born in North America would be turned off their culture by the myriad forces of white supremacy. By all accounts it is a powerful book because it reveals some of Washington's deepest thoughts—yet it has largely been ignored. The first chapter is aptly named "First Notions of Africa" and covers how negativity of the African continent seeped into his life in America. Yet it never impacted him enough for it to destroy his implicit fondness for the rhythms of Africa. For example, he relates to having listened to the Black British composer Samuel Coleridge-Taylor's working of European classical music with respect and admiration. However, for him "I would rather hear the jubilee or plantation songs of my race than the finest chorus from the works of Handel or any other of the great [European] composers." Washington was an admirer of European classical music, but for him it did not reach the visceral depth that he received in listening to his people's music. As he states, "This music is the form in which the sorrows and aspirations of the [African American] people, all that they suffered, loved, and hoped for, in short their whole spiritual life, found its first adequate and satisfying expression. For that reason, if for no other, it should be preserved" (20). There it is, a clear statement from a man who had by now traveled through Europe and found no better place than at home with his people and their cultural foundations that emanated from the harshness of enslavement but traced back to Africa. Out of this experience came the work songs, and the spirituals, that led to gospel *and* the blues, and finally to the nascent ragtime and jazz melodies. Washington could feel the soul of his people in the "songs of the plantation," and he felt connected to this most as his African origins, and not in listening to European classical music.

He ends this chapter by recalling a time he visited Harvard and met with a group of young African American scholars. Washington is stunned by how much they prided themselves in knowing so much about European knowledge and languages such as French and German, yet they knew nothing about the history and culture of their African American heritage. This experience was part of the reason why he wrote *The Story of the Negro*; ultimately he wanted his students and future generations to be inspired by *their* history and culture. Booker T. Washington's words are important here because they have been lost to a barrage of disparaging clichés that have fossilized a great thinker into something he was not. Washington deserves to be heard, and his own words are the best testimony because few, if any, biographers up to the twentieth century fully gave them space. Again, on his pursuit of African-centered knowledge, Washington writes, "All this helped to increase, as time went on, my desire to know what was back of me, where I came from, and what, if anything, there was in the life of my people in Africa and America to which I might point with pride and think about with satisfaction. . . . What I learned in his way only served, however, to increase my desire to go farther and deeper into the life of my people, and to find out for myself what they had been in Africa as well as in America" (16). In short, Washington should be regarded as a pioneer in Africana/Black Studies. There is no denying his importance now to the field and future scholars need to start reading his books, those that have been discarded, maligned, or denied by scholars like Du Bois, Aptheker, and Marable even up to the present day. Washington had a deeper interest in Africa than what is portrayed. Indeed, he is rarely mentioned as a Pan Africanist thinker, one who connects all African experiences globally, and someone who did groundbreaking work to connect Tuskegee Institute to Africa. Yet he did seek out his African roots, and what he did in practical terms simply complemented the theoretical work he did in producing *The Story of the Negro*.

A pioneering study that is optimal in placing Washington in the realm of Pan Africanist history is by Tyrene Wright (2015). Her study situates Washington squarely as a man who linked Africa and the African Diaspora. She rightly notes that Washington was in correspondence with Henry Sylvester Williams, who organized the first Pan African Conference in London in July 1900 (Wright 2015, 13). He invited Washington to participate in the conference, but he could not make the trip due to recovering from a bout of fatigue. He also had numerous commitments at Tuskegee Institute with the newly establishment of National Negro Business League (NNBL). Had Washington participated in this conference, his presence would have comfortably overshadowed that of Du Bois's and Pan African history would have probably been shaped differently and involved Washington as one of the pioneers. The fact is Washington wholeheartedly supported the gathering of intellectuals and activists of African descent from all over the world. As Wright notes in her study, Washington was very enthusiastic about it and made sure to advertise the conference in the African American newspapers he was associated with (14).

The reason why this aspect of Washington's life has been underplayed is basically down to biographers not wanting to highlight it or finding it unimportant to his domestic relevance in the African American experience. For whatever reason, it is a massive omission to have him not regarded as part of Pan African history. Wright puts this issue into perspective: "African intellectuals . . . have the very lofty responsibility of qualifying historical facts and offering a more centered account of the lives of African leadership" (xv). This means, in the context of Washington, it is paramount for African-centered scholarship to holistically embrace that which has often been ignored by European interpretations of African American leadership. Too often, great leaders are undermined by those who have the power to publish and interpret history and the lives of persons not as powerful. However, it is not only writers of a certain hue, it can be writers from a different ideological perspective than Washington's who have also fossilized his contribution and limited his impact for future scholars; there was a time when this very author drank from the same cup of those who have undermined Booker T. Washington. It is difficult to confess, but much has been learned from Washington that was once not known about this courageous fellow.

Indeed, most of the writers shaping the life and legacy of Washington were on the left of center or even far-left in terms of scholarship (Foster 1954). By the 1950s Washington was consigned to academic oblivion and labeled disparagingly by white leftists such as Aptheker (1970), and later African American leftists in academia. One of the young African American scholars in the 1970s, Manning Marable, who would grow to be a full-fledged Du Boisian with the encouragement of a mentor in Herbert Aptheker, was an early writer to point out Washington's links with African Nationalism. Yet he conceptualized Washington in a very negative way in relation to Africa. The opening sentences of his article reveal his bias against Washington: "Early Twentieth Century South African black nationalists owe much to Booker T. Washington. Washington's pro-capitalist and pro-Colonialist attitudes markedly influenced his direct activities in Africa, and especially Togo" (Marable 1974, 398). This is a rather damaging second sentence that has substance only in the fact that Washington embraced the idea of hard work, thrift, and property ownership. He was aware of the exploitation of capitalism and did all he could to teach his people how to acquire it for themselves. He knew that it was unlikely that the United States would endure yet another revolution over the mode of production.

Marable is therefore rather harsh and myopic and has little understanding of Washington's anti-imperialist assault on King Leopold II and the rabid European invasion into Africa. Instead, he props Washington up as a conservative-capitalist and runs away with it, just as his mentor Aptheker had taught him. To suggest Washington was a full on capitalist out to exploit his people is folly; he worked within a system that kept his people firmly at the bottom, and he endeavored to help as many as he could to gain the skills that would allow them to move up the social ladder. One of the many hypocrisies encountered when observing the leftist scholars is how hard they work to get into the higher echelon of academia, the Ivy League. Then they pontificate about a man like Washington who spent his life giving back to his people and aiding some of the Harvard, Fisk, and Howard graduates to get ahead in life. Washington did this to help his people holistically, he fully understood the importance of higher education, but he was not a hypocrite. One must consider why so many "Black radical academics" can be found in the most prestigious universities in the United States; because they are very unlikely to meet many working-class revolutionaries in such surroundings—the hypocrisy is incredulous.

When it came to linking Tuskegee Institute to Africa, it was about teaching Indigenous Africans to become better farmers and therefore to have a stronger impact in their communities. There is an irony here in that it took a white supremacist to understand Washington's real work and focus on Tuskegee Institute. Thomas Dixon Jr., the writer of a number of racist novels that were lauded in his day, one of which was based on the film *Birth of a Nation* (1915), premiered in the White House by President Woodrow Wilson, another white supremacist. In 1905, Dixon wrote an article for Philadelphia's *Saturday Evening Post* where he stated, "Mr. Washington is not training Negroes to take their place in any industrial system in the south which the white man directs or controls him. He is not training his students to be servants and come at the beck and call of any man. He is training them all to be masters of men, to be independent, to own and operate their own industries, to plant their own fields, buy and sell their own goods and in every shape and form destroy the last vestige of dependence on the white man for anything" (cited in Wright 2015, 35).

In thirty and more years of writing and publishing in Africana Studies, it is the first time this author has been fully in agreement with a white supremacist. Dixon was correct in everything he wrote regarding the manner in which Washington taught and espoused the role of Tuskegee Institute. The heart of the curriculum was to develop African American empowerment in agricultural and related skills. There was also an array of liberal arts and social science classes. Moreover, students from Africa and the Caribbean were also being taught at Tuskegee Institute. Now, one should ask, Why and how did Du Bois and others overlook something that a white supremacist easily surmised? It is rather incredulous and unutterably sad that Washington has never been given the credit for his work in empowering so many persons of African heritage to be self-reliant and useful to *themselves* and *their* communities. Dixon could see that Washington was teaching his students to be self-determined and to be separated from the white man as the fingers on the hand.

Africans on the continent read and learned about the great man of Tuskegee Institute, and the Africans in South Africa who read his articles were inspired because they too were living under similar conditions that were strangling the life out of their humanity. White South Africans were just as vicious and vehement against Indigenous Africans as white Southerners were to African Americans. Washington was more than aware of such atrocities in his homeland and in the motherland. The fact that Marable and other left of center scholars could not bring themselves to give Washington any credit, as the white supremacist Dixon revealed, says more about them having either poor perception or scholarly skills. Washington has been fossilized by the Du Boisian scholars simply because he was someone who worked within the system to get what he could. No more than what the Marxists deem a "war of position" whereby the less powerful make what strides they can, with what resources they have. African Americans did not have much to work with and made the best of a bad situation. Africans on the continent were also being stripped of their collective power as the Europeans encroached slowly but surely across the beautiful and resourceful African continent.

Wright (2015) explains that the Tuskegee Institute model was exported to Africa by sending students there and having Africans come back to Tuskegee to learn as well. Why was the exchange of African American students going to Africa and African students coming to Tuskegee Institute to study not cited by Du Bois in any meaningful way? Is this not a major Pan African event that is both tangible and efficacious to his story of genuine empowerment of Africans at home and abroad? These questions lean to the fact that such knowledge of Washington would only empower his legacy, and those who diminished this aspect of his work wanted him on the scrapheap of history. The fact that scholars agree with the words of the white supremacist, Dixon, to gain the essence of Washington's real work is difficult to accept. Another white supremacist, President Roosevelt, helped Washington with his plea to aid Liberia in its hour of need as it was being threatened by a tripartite of colonizers: Germany, France, and Britain were involved in a tug of colonial exploitation. Roosevelt admired Washington, and connected with him beyond the realm of racialization. The fact that he invited Washington to the White House and worked with him on various projects is indicative of his admiration. However, and this is often missed too by historians, Washington could have declined Roosevelt's dinner invitation at the White in October 1900 as this was going against his "separate as the fingers" promise.

This again allows a perceptive mind to learn that at bottom Washington did not take white supremacy too seriously. As long as he gained space to empower his people he did not give too much attention to ignorant white racists. His foray into Africa among the white supremacist Europeans was no different from this interaction with their American white cousins in the Southern states. What was at the front and center of his mind related to one thing only: "what can I do to empower my people in this situation?" Africa presented an opportunity to grow Tuskegee Institute, to expand it beyond the boundary of Alabama to become an institution of international renown. At the dawn of the twentieth century, the world was experiencing a tremendous change with the invention of the automobile taking great significance, the expansion of science in all areas of life, and the strangulation of the African continent by European colonizers. This is the entry into Africa that Washington tread. Always operating in the worst of times yet producing something tangible for those whom he fundamentally endeavored to empower: peoples of African heritage.

As mentioned, Washington's major biographer up to, arguably, Norrell (2009) was Louis Harlan, who wrote two biographical volumes reaching almost one thousand pages in small print, along with fourteen edited volumes of papers, and numerous journal essays over a period of almost forty years. Harlan could be deemed a liberal white Southerner who had a stranglehold on how scholars and commentators interpreted Washington. Norrell (2009) has succinctly described Harlan as creating a vision of Washington as a man of "dirty tricks" with a propensity to lean toward his major critics, Du Bois and Trotter. Norrell is another white biographer, but at least he seems to be balanced in his assessment of how Washington has been undermined by Harlan. Norrell explains this nuance well: "The positive symbolism of Tuskegee Institute got hardly a note. . . . Harlan shaped virtually all the writing on post-Reconstruction race relations published after 1972, including the interpretation purveyed in college textbooks of American history" (Norrell 2009, 437). This is noted due to the disparity between what Washington writes in *The Story of the Negro* as opposed to how Harlan interprets his African connections. Washington is very positive in his overall writing toward Africa and Africans. Harlan actually does not say many positive things about Washington, and if he does it is shrouded in a negativity that gives the reader the impression that there was underhandedness in all things. This is just not the case when one reads Washington's letters and follows his actions. Harlan never put Washington's critics to the sword. Actually, it is rather disconcerting as a scholar to find such misinterpretations and selective analysis having been employed by a major biographer.

In an essay, which is not part of his two-volume biography, Harlan writes extensively in regard to Washington's connections with Africa. He sets up Washington as a man who disparages Africa as "uncivilized" and this takes the reader away from anything good in Washington's active relationship with Africa. One has to read between the lines, as expressed at the outset of this chapter that there is not one leading African Diaspora or Pan Africanist of note who did not have elements of Western ethnocentric leanings when it came to Africa: Crummell, Delany, Turner, Du Bois, Garvey, and others had some form of superiority complex over the peoples on the African continent during their lifetimes—these men are *the* known Africanists, and they could not escape the influence of Western conditioning. So to turn this onto Washington, as Harlan does deftly, is rather disingenuous. At bottom, Washington was a man who did not reject his African roots and who wrote very positively about it, as proved earlier. Harlan and others conveniently left out so many positive aspects. The essay from Harlan was originally published in 1966 in the *American Historical Review*. The title is revealing, "Booker T. Washington and the White Man's Burden," as it juxtaposes Washington with the negative racism of Rudyard Kipling's racist poem that was lauding the European colonization of Africa, Asia, and the so-called New World. Therefore to put Washington in that group is rather undermining and it reveals Harlan's deeply implicit prejudice toward his forty-year biographical subject. But even Harlan could not deny Washington's fingerprints across the African continent: "Washington and other Tuskegeans were actively involved in Togo, Sudan, South Africa, Congo Free State, and Liberia. These activities and his many contacts with African [students], teachers, missionaries, and nationalist intellectuals shaped a view of Africa resembling that of the more enlightened European colonialists" (Harlan 1988, 69). Harlan could not stop himself from implicitly demeaning Washington, adding that he was interacting with Africans who could be deemed "enlightened" European colonists, which must be the missionaries. It cannot be the "African national intellectuals" because they are not related to Europeans. Indeed, they were the group that would create the foundation for Africa's eventual liberation from colonialism. If one does not read Washington's books, nor reads his correspondence independently, then it is too easy to get the wrong impression of the man. It is important to read widely and not take any writer for granted because this can lead to a narrow conception of a subject matter.

Marable is also selective in negativity toward Washington's perspective on Africa in his article, stating, "Unlike African Methodist Episcopal Bishop Henry McNeal Turner that a return to Africa for the Negro is out of the question." And further, "Tuskegee's self-help programs run by white liberals could be a very proper modern education for Africans" (Marable 1974, 399–400). What Marable conveniently overlooks is that even the great Frederick Douglass was opposed to African repatriation for all African Americans. Moreover, after two failed expeditions to Liberia, Bishop Turner later spent most of his time in the United States with the AME church and is buried in Atlanta. If these facts were not added to counter

Marable, Washington would be left looking like a weak man who despised Africa, when he was the opposite; of course, he had to work with African diplomatic officials from the European colonies to get a foothold into African affairs. In addition, to follow Marable's degradation of Washington, why was it that Marcus Garvey followers on route to settle were not allowed into Liberia in 1924? It was simply because Garvey represented the radical Black Nationalism that Marable is alluding to that Washington did not possess; he should know that had Washington challenged the hegemony of the European colonial powers openly he would never have succeeded in having students from Tuskegee Institute travel to Africa and vice versa. The critique by Marable is self-serving and does little to fully explain the dynamics and political domination Washington encountered. But the underlying issue was in the fact that Marable being a Du Boisian scholar who could never allow Washington to have his day in the sun.

Marcus Garvey (1887–1940) was inspired to improve the lives of peoples of African heritage after reading Booker T. Washington's biography, *Up from Slavery*. Originally from Jamaica, Garvey led the largest Black Nationalist movement that the world has known in the 1920s, based on racial pride and self-determination. (Library of Congress)

Togo opened up as an opportunity for Tuskegee Institute to fully explore their model of education. An expedition set out in 1900 from Alabama to Togo in Africa, which was under German colonial rule. The objective was to help Africans learn the art of agricultural methods employed by Tuskegee Institute. However, there were a lot of problems with acclimation to the African soil and the diseases with up to four of the Tuskegee students passing away from various accidents or illnesses while in Africa. This is similar to the scenario Bishop Turner faced with his expeditions to Liberia. The fact remains that malaria and other infections were the enemy of those who were not born in Africa. It was a dangerous trek to make in the early twentieth century. But Washington's critics never explain the failure in broad terms because the ultimate conclusion was to see him fail due to his philosophy and practice of hard work, thrift, and character development, coupled with self-help and property ownership. This to a leftist scholar like Marable is like a red flag to a bull. The same criticism befell Marcus Garvey in the 1920s because he too worked within the capitalist economic framework to promote Africans around the world to benefit from wealth creation and self-determination.

This perspective is not about deriding the left in scholarship, it is about explaining why Washington has been so maligned since his death in 1915. During his lifetime he faced tremendous discrimination and hatred and historians and biographers have underplayed this fact (Norrell, 2009). Given the knowledge that is known about Washington's links with Africa and the first exhibition into Togo to set up agricultural techniques for African farmers it is an indication of his determination to make a positive impact (Zimmerman 2010). Of course he had to maneuver politically through the European colonizers, but what else could he do? Marable offers no solutions, and only undermines Washington's endeavors to link with his African brothers and sisters on the continent. The irony is that employing the words of an overtly white supremacist like Thomas Dixon Jr. is more efficacious in defending the work of Washington. Dixon worried about the covert manner in which Tuskegee Institute was producing real men and women, empowered in character, to enter the world with their backs straight and focused on building self-help practices in the African American experience. This model of education was being transported, as best as it could be, to Togo.

Of course, as Wright (2015) explains, Tuskegee Institute's model would be exploited by white supremacists in some form or another simply because it was successful. Dixon wanted, for example, to have all ten million African Americans transported to Liberia to "solve the race problem." But many millions of African Americans being transported back to Africa were unrealistic and illusory. Frederick Douglass was a vocal protestor to such an idea, even though other prominent thinkers of his generation like Martin Delany felt it was a good proposition due to the atrocious conditions many African Americans faced. This was understandable considering the violence, but impracticable to think that ten million African Americans at the dawn of the twentieth century could repatriate to Africa after twelve or more generations of presence in North America. The idea was quite ridiculous in practical terms, but there was always a group who would endeavor to return, small in number but passionate in advancing the idea.

Washington was a man of the Southern states; he would not want to return permanently to the homeland of his African roots, but this does not mean he was not interested in Africa's development. His strategy for dealing with the white man in Africa was no different than his approach in America. As Harlan writes more maturely, almost twenty years beyond his belittling 1966 essay on Washington and Africa, "In African colonies as in America, Washington cooperated openly with white authorities and business promoters, while he sought through industrial education to encourage back self-reliance and the work-ethic, and privately gave encouragement to black nationalist movements, particularly in his effort to help independent Liberia survive in a colonized continent through an American protectorate" (Harlan 1983, 267). Harlan admits that Washington was doing all he could *privately* to do what was possible to help Black African nationalist movements on the continent. This is a very important point missed by Marable (1974) because he was fixated on Washington and his embracement of capitalism as an economic system. Again, to be fair to Washington, very few would had read Karl Marx in 1900 and knew anything about capitalism having the seeds of its own destruction embedded. Rather, Washington was concentrating on getting his people educated and out of poverty conditions. Tuskegee Institute students and faculty, Du Bois, and others were not reading Marxist theory. Indeed, Du Bois didn't come close to such a theory until the publication of his *Reconstruction* in 1935, a long twenty years after Washington had passed.

Whether or not the economic system favored African Americans was at the forefront of Washington's mind, but he was not an ideological revolutionary and nor was Du Bois. Therefore it is unfair to analyze Washington within an anti-capitalist framework. The objective of his work was always to improve the education and economic base of the Africans and African Americans he came into contact with. Even if the white ghost of racism hovered over everything he tried to do and watched his every move, Washington did the best he could under extremely difficult circumstances. Between 1901 and 1909, nine students from Tuskegee Institute spent time in Togo, with tragic drownings and illness taking the lives of four, giving an indication again of just how difficult it could be in Africa for African Americans to acclimatize and navigate the terrain safely. One of the most zealous settlers from Tuskegee Institute was John W. Robinson who remained from 1903 till his accidental death in a drowning while crossing a river (Harlan 1983, 268). The longevity of Tuskegee Institute's relationship with Africa in the first decade of the twentieth century is testimony to Washington's impact, and during this period he secured scholarships for African students to study at Tuskegee Institute.

Washington used his influence with President Roosevelt on a number of occasions to aid Africans in the Congo, Liberia, and South Africa. It was not an easy task dealing with white Europeans who ultimately wanted to exploit Africa. Washington did what he could to empower Africans against the marauding European assault on their lands. It is easy to accuse Washington of "cooperating" with the colonizers, but that is a rather myopic approach to take. If one covers his entire interactions that benefited Africans, then he should be regarded as a bona fide Pan Africanist (Wright 2015). Yet he is denied this due to the overwhelming scholarship ignoring and/or undermining his achievements while highlighting any weak parts in his efforts. For Liberia, Washington lobbied President Roosevelt to block the foreign encroachments on the nation that was free from European exploitation. History can only guess what would have happened if Washington had not intervened, it was his influence with Roosevelt that allowed Liberia to continue its development unrestricted by the British and German colonizers. One wonders why Du Bois never commented on this aspect of Washington's efforts, but he also failed to truly depict him broadly. There is never a mention of Washington's African connections and no mention of the African students who benefited from studying at Tuskegee. In fact, the faculty member who accompanied Tuskegee Students to Togo in 1901 was James Nathan Calloway, a former Fisk University graduate. It is surprising Du Bois would not know of this fellow Fisk man, but it would not have fitted his narrow portrayal of Washington, who he fictionalized as not being partial to graduates of higher education. The appearance Washington gave to the world was not the reality, as he recruited often from Fisk University because he wanted the best available faculty for the students at Tuskegee Institute.

In reflecting on Washington and Africa, he should be considered a pioneer in study abroad experiences for African Americans and in having international students from African nations study in a Southern institution solely for African Americans. It is difficult to deny his tremendous groundbreaking feats as an African American leader in education. However, denied he has been of such achievements, particularly his African connections. Wright writes, "Washington and the Tuskegee model were one of the most solid and successful. . . . [He] coupled it with his developing Pan African consciousness and it became a method of addressing the conditions of African people seeking independence from economic exploitation and domination" (Wright 2015, 48–49). It should be noted Washington had links with not only Henry Sylvester Williams, but also Duse Mohamed Ali, who would later mentor Marcus Garvey on Pan African affairs. Though he derived from Egypt, Ali was the editor of the *African Times and Orient Review* and was based in London. In other words, Washington was corresponding with leading Pan African thinkers and this too is something not given enough attention. He was a man who supported Pan African causes but was cautious in his articulation of African liberation movements because of his interaction with those who held power. Any overt notification of his plans to aid African nationalism would have brought him to the negative attention of the Roosevelt and later Taft administrations. Washington was too savvy to be caught providing overt support for anti-colonial Africans and their pursuit of freedom from colonial rule.

Zimmerman (2010) comprehends the legacy of Washington as being somewhat tainted or undervalued in relation to his African connections. Moreover, that his interactions with European colonialism and imperialism on the African continent was in fact an uneasy and seemingly contradictory relationship. Zimmerman also argues that the historical dichotomy between Washington and Du Bois occurred gradually over time, but reading the historical legacy one would not think as much. The same can be stated about his relationship with African affairs, it developed due to his travels to Europe and his meetings with various different experiences from leading persons of African heritage. This was from 1899 onward as Washington's rise from obscurity to world renown took place after the publication of his second autobiography, *Up from Slavery* in 1901.

Once Washington's star rose in international circles and he attracted, ironically, both Pan Africans and European colonialists. The Pan Africanists wanted Washington as part of their groups, and the European colonialists wanted to learn his agricultural skills. Washington, as shrewd as ever, used the resources of the European colonizers to enhance his model, while quietly helping African nationalists. It was not a perfect partnership with the European colonists, but when did Washington ever have an ideal partnership with whites who always had the lion's share of power in the relationship? Never, but like a true politician he worked between the gaps making sure Tuskegee Institute benefited from whatever scheme whites were offering.

In terms of the Pan Africanists, who ultimately wanted a continent free from European rule, it would take another two generations and two world wars before the shackles of colonialism would be broken. In the early 1900s, European colonization of Africa was in its early stages and the extent of the exploitation could best be measured by the whites of South Africa who derived from both Dutch/Afrikaans and British settlers, though there were some French and German settlers mixed in with the Dutch. The second Boer War (1899–1902) in South Africa was part of the internal wars between the European settlers, the Afrikaans wanted independence from the British Empire. The Black inhabitants of Southern Africa, the Indigenous Africans, were caught in the middle and suffered much like the Southern African American. Washington understand the dynamics well and eventually, though they lost the Boer War, the Afrikaans would gain their independence from Britain in 1931 and introduce an apartheid system of social segregation from the Africans and the so-called coloreds (mixed heritage African and European persons). The Afrikaans based their system largely off the American segregation version of apartheid.

African students were reading Washington's *Up from Slavery* and being inspired by his rise from the depths of despair and building Tuskegee Institute from a dilapidated shanty into a campus to be admired by all who had a chance to witness it. They were inspired by the model of industrial education and its social philosophy that gave a strong tilt toward independence of mind and spirit for Africans. John Langalibalele Dube, a Zulu from South Africa received some education at Oberlin College and also touched base with Washington in New York and in visiting Tuskegee Institute. He eventually returned to South Africa to model an industrial school based on Tuskegee Institute, it was called the Zulu Christian Industrial School. Dube struggled between his knowledge of European Christianity from the West and his African traditional culture. He navigated both worlds to become a leader in South African/Black politics. His major inspiration was Booker T. Washington, and much of what he achieved was by imitating the Tuskegee Institute leader. He even set up the Bantu Business League, which was again an imitation of the National Negro Business League, founded by Washington in 1900. If this is not Pan Africanism in practice then it is difficult to know exactly what else it would be.

In reflection, is it most probable that Black South Africans like Dube found in Washington someone who had survived the onslaught of white supremacy and risen to the top by his wit and determination? Because the treatment in South Africa at the hands of the white settlers was akin to what African Americans were experiencing. Harlan (1988, 83) notes that Dube earned the title "the Booker T. Washington of South Africa." Dube also built his school in South Africa largely with finance of white American philanthropists.

More significantly, John Langalibalele Dube in January 1912 founded the African National Congress in South Africa. Therefore a Black South African of the Zulus who was inspired by the life and works of Booker T. Washington founded the organization that would eventually go on to free South Africa from apartheid. This fact is hardly known by the African American and broader African world. Indeed, in reading a book titled *Pan-African History: Political Figures from Africa and the Diaspora since 1787* by Hakim Adi and Marika Sherwood, there is a list of prominent Pan Africans, but there is neither Dube nor Washington on the list; there is Frederick Douglass and Martin Luther King Jr., but no Booker T. Washington. The fact that Dr. King is on the list may surprise some readers, but in fact he should be there, and although Douglass did work in Haiti, his main focus was on the plight of Africans in America. Not having Washington and Dube on the list is astonishing given what each man did for the history of Pan African thought and practice. Of course, Du Bois is on the list as a key theoretician of Pan Africanism, but one should ask, "What *practical* work did he do in Africa itself? What school did he found or support?

What institution did he build?" Should such criteria be the litmus test for being a prominent Pan Africanist? Not really, but what actually is it to be one? Surely, Washington had done enough in his life and times to have made such a list, and the reason he did not was due, it seems, to the fossilization of his life by scholars who misinterpreted a lot of his political strategies and failed to measure his African connections and outcomes. It could be assumed that John Langalibalele Dube failed to make the list because he was nicknamed the "Booker T. Washington of South Africa" and therefore to be shunned by the "radical" Pan Africans. It is a rather miserable thing to destroy a man's reputation as this has effectively been done to Washington via Du Bois; and other scholars who were economical with the truth about Washington and diminished his Pan African credits that he had earned with grit, determination, and political savvy.

What can be revealed with certainty is the unassailable evidence of Tuskegee Institute's influence across the African continent at a time when African peoples were being subjugated and exploited. Washington offered tremendous hope, and this is forgotten in the story of his life. To attach disenfranchisement to him is spurious, as that was happening regardless of his speech in Atlanta in 1895. Ten years previous, the Europeans were carving up Africa like it was a birthday cake to devour and cut up as they pleased. White South Africans would learn to segregate and dehumanize the Black South Africans from watching their white cousins in the Southern states. This is a social fact not fiction, and it is shocking to realize how Washington has been made such a scapegoat while doing so much good. As Norrell (2009) has provided an alternative

---

African National Congress (ANC)

The African National Congress (ANC) was founded by John Langalibalele Dube in January 1912 in South Africa. It would form the political organization that would eventually defeat apartheid in 1994, and has been the ruling political party since. Dube was highly influenced by Booker T. Washington and modeled a school based on Tuskegee Institute in South Africa. Historians have largely failed to acknowledge the importance Washington had in the life of Dube, who found his inspiration for African self-determination through Washington's example. Like Washington, he had to be very careful while articulating the suffering of Indigenous Africans perpetrated by South African white Afrikaners. The ANC demanded better conditions and eventually found leaders who would dismantle the hold of white supremacy on the majority Black South Africans. Nelson Mandela is arguably the best-known ANC leader, but the roots of the organization lead to Dube, and in an indirect sense to Washington.

to Harlan, or at least recalibrated some of the insidiousness held in that biography, there needs to be more studies conducted by future generations on how Washington impacted Africa, because from a cursory insight it looks like the Tuskegee Institute model was employed in a number of African nations.

Another interesting omission of Washington and his African connections comes from one of the top African American scholars, arguably the most productive, Molefi K. Asante, in his book published in 2007, *The History of Africa: The Quest for Eternal Harmony*. Chapter 13 is titled "Africa Regains Consciousness in a Pan-African Explosion," and it looks at the development of African nationalism in relation to key Pan African thinkers. A number of names are again listed, but there is no John L. Dube or Booker T. Washington. Keep in mind there would be no African National Congress without Dube, and there would be no Dube without the inspiration he received from Booker T. Washington. This is nuance in the development of Pan Africanist thought. Most of the thinkers in some way had to shed the mental incarceration of European thought, some of the Pan Africanist thinkers given the most kudos were deeply drenched in European canons like Du Bois who was taught what the best the West could offer in education.

Why is it that Du Bois is given the benefit of doubt in African-centered circles but not Washington? Because Du Bois was able to set the framework for analyzing Washington and he left out all his influences on the African continent. Indeed there could be a quiz in an Africana Studies class with the question "Find out what Du Bois says about Washington's impact in Africa and its peoples via Tuskegee Institute?" It is a question that no student could adequately answer because Du Bois never shared this information. It is extremely unlikely that he did not know about Tuskegee Institute's expedition to Togo in West Africa. This was only a few years before he wrote his derogatory essay "Of Mr. Booker T. Washington and Others" in *The Souls of Black Folk*. There is no mention of Tuskegee Institute's strong connections with the African continent; nor is there any mention of Washington's public denouncement of the atrocities taking place in the Congo with King Leopold II's regime maiming and exploiting Africans.

What future Africana scholars need to consider is the manner in which Washington has been interpreted in a very limited manner, there needs to be more focus on the outcomes, not the method, of his works. He was a man who inspired many young Africans to develop their local communities because white European colonizers would not. Of course, Washington was not able to fully change the social order, not in the South in the United States or on the African continent. But he did drop seeds that were cultivated further in the younger minds of persons like John L. Dube of South

Africa and a young Marcus Garvey from Jamaica. This is a historical fact and cannot be denied, but what is deprived to present scholars is *this* very knowledge. One has to possess a very critical mind to wade through the mendacity of Du Bois, and his protégé Herbert Aptheker, and Manning Marable, who, in turn, was Aptheker's protégé, and the many who have followed them all. Thankfully, there is now a nascent response to Washington's broader impact and his political impact, which is more than useful (Hamilton 2017; Norrell 2009; Wright 2015; Zimmerman 2010).

Though Washington was not an "African centered scholar activist" and a person who boldly took white supremacy head-on like a Marcus Garvey, one could state the same about most others who worked to liberate Africans globally. As stated earlier, there is no African American or African on the continent or in the Caribbean that was not in some manner impacted by European cultural hegemony in the last five hundred years. It is too easy to criticize a man or woman who navigates the terrain of white supremacy in a manner that does not look as strong as another who may have been bold and fierce in encountering the domination. It is more useful to compare his or her social conditions, the milieu, before one judges how well or badly someone has fought the good fight. A reading of the "art of war" contends that it is intelligent to weigh up the adversary, its strength and its weaknesses, before one attempts any form of counter-resistance. Anyone can run into a burning fire, but it is wise to know the possibility of surviving its heat, otherwise it is an act of insanity to venture into something that will inevitably take one's life.

Pan Africans ordinarily in Africana Studies are regarded as those warriors who wanted unity and pride among all persons of African heritage. They pushed for the downfall of European rule over Africans on the continent and in the Caribbean region with courage, vigor, and at times martyrdom. This may give a degree of cultural pride, and there is a time and place for such, but the essence of struggle is to improve the time and space one occupies so that the future generation builds upon the foundation that has been placed. Having the best minds of African Americans being assassinated has caused great loss to generations the that followed. Consider how life may have been had Malcolm X and Martin Luther King Jr.'s lives had not been cut short at the age of thirty-nine years? Both these men were connecting the lives of peoples of African heritage, and inspiring the lives of progressive whites to refuse the ideology of racism and discrimination.

Washington spent most of his life, in biblical terms, in the lion's den. His personality was extremely cognizant of those who held power around him. Moreover, as with many other African Americans learning to escape from the confines of physical and mental enslavement, he had developed a way to survive that is regarded as "wearing the mask" in order to live without encountering the wrath of the white man with greater power.

Nevertheless, his mind was perceptive enough to know that the oppressor was actually oppressing himself when shackling the life of another human being. Washington's insights are either caricatured or ignored by writers on Pan African history. Asante (2007) elevates Du Bois as the "key organizer" and leader of the first Pan African Congress in Paris in 1900, but the most significant meeting for African solidarity was actually the Pan African Conference held in London in July 1900, which was led by Henry Sylvester Williams. More importantly, Williams was in correspondence with Washington in regard to his participation, but unfortunately he was tied up that summer with work at Tuskegee Institute and in preparation for the onset of the National Negro Business League. Nonetheless, as mentioned earlier, Washington spent a great deal of time promoting the Pan African Conference in the African American media that would take place in London.

When Washington organized the Togo expedition in early 1900 he did so with a degree of not fully comprehending the extent of German colonization; in fact, all European domination was an oppressive affront on Africans. But it was a new adventure, to expand the work at Tuskegee Institute and that work was about empowering Africans and African Americans. To suggest anything else is to not understand him or his passion to improve the lives of his people. Wright (2015) is clear on the Pan Africanist aspect of his thinking: "As the 20th Century approached Booker T. Washington already had a Pan African sentiment, but lacked actual experience in the African context." Wright is right and goes on to explain that the Togo expedition was a learning curve for Washington and Tuskegee Institute. A transferal of the agricultural teaching was easier said than done; there were failures on his behalf, and tragedy with the drowning of a number of Tuskegee graduates on swift-moving African rivers. Yet, what should be not forgotten is that his efforts were noble in the sense of providing opportunity for his graduates and to engage with the motherland in a tangible manner. Wright continues, "When confronted with the opportunity to send Tuskegee graduates to the Togo upon invitation from German colonists, Washington failed to see or ignored that imperialists in Africa were in fact oppressive forces" (Wright 2015, 79–80). Wright again is right, Washington underestimated the extent of European oppression on the African continent, and he also failed to consider the difficult terrain encountered by his students and their faculty leader. However, should he be consigned to historical oblivion for trying to connect to Africa in ways that were beyond his power? It may not have been as successful as one had hoped, but as the saying goes, "If we fail, get up, dust off, and try again." Washington was always a man with the least power doing the most extraordinarily powerful things. He managed to get Tuskegee graduates into Africa, to work with Africans on their land, and this was Pan

Africanism in practice. Yes, the ghost of white supremacy hovered over them like a cold and impenetrable cloud, but it was a start in Pan African relations. One cannot dismiss this man because he found a way to work within the confines of the most extreme racism to get a foothold on the African continent for future Pan Africanists to benefit; Washington should be applauded for his ingenuity and political courage.

Andrew Zimmerman, the latest white liberal scholar to chip away at Washington, has put forward a disparaging term to describe Washington's Togo experiment in sharing his institution's graduates and skills. He states, "The type of colonial Pan-Africanism advocated by Booker T. Washington" was supported by the U.S. government (Zimmerman 2010, 63). Indeed, the very term "colonial Pan-Africanism" is itself incongruous with what Pan African thought and practice stood by, which was the unity and empowerment of African peoples globally. It did not associate with itself with "colonization" as that was for European history and culture. What Zimmerman (2010) tries to do is deride Washington's historical record using the playbook from previous narrow scholarship. The fact that Tuskegee Institute had a student exchange system in taking African Americans to Africa, and Africans to Tuskegee Institute is a testimony of success not failure. Remember that the reality of an African American educator navigating the transfer of persons of African heritage back and forth from the African continent during the late 1890s to about 1914 is rather remarkable. Moreover, if this is not an active micro Pan African experience, then what is? Nor should the major role he played in the lobbying the U.S. government over King Leopold II's atrocities in the Congo and his advocacy for Liberia be forgotten. These are tangible examples of Washington's deep and practical interest in African affairs that do not relate to "colonizing Pan Africanism" as Zimmerman (2010) would suggest.

Du Bois gets far too much credit for his Pan Africanist reputation, but this is largely due to his friendship with Nkrumah and his resting place being in Ghana. One could be facetious and ask why did it take Du Bois so long to move to Africa? He was ninety-three years old when he migrated to Ghana in 1961. So writers in Pan Africanist history deem him the "father of Pan Africanism" and other laudable epithets associate him with Africa. Yet he did nothing compared to Washington's practical work in linking palpable projects in human interaction. Du Bois was all about the writing and Pan African Congress organizing, and maybe that was enough to cement him into Pan African history. The point is that Washington operated under far greater scrutiny and in far greater animosity worked his skills combining his philosophy and practice to Africa. In his book *The Story of the Negro*, Washington states, "[In early 1900] a group of our best students was selected for this mission. They went to Togoland, West Africa, and began to establish stations in different points . . . and they started to grow cotton . . . doing a large part of the work themselves" (Washington 2007, 33). The point is they worked with the local Africans and did a large part of the work themselves—that was partnership, not exploitation. They did meet with various problems in terms of the cotton seed from America not suiting African soil and other complications, but they persevered working with local Africans in partnership.

There was also the usual Western ethnocentrism that *all* African Americans held implicitly toward Africans. Washington was no different than Du Bois, and before him Crummell and Bishop Turner who each held notions of cultural superiority over the Africans on the continent. In retrospection, this kind of thinking was merely an offshoot of their North American conditioning that emanated from the education they had received. But at least with Washington's Tuskegee Institute the graduates worked alongside Africans in the development of cotton fields. Washington goes on to state, "Native Africans have been sent from Africa to Tuskegee. Our Tuskegee students have returned from time to time and made their reports of successes" (35). This is the evidence that links Tuskegee Institute with Africa, employing a book published by Washington in 1909—*The Story of the Negro*.

One wonders why Washington's impact on the African continent has largely been ignored for over a century, especially by the Pan Africanist and Du Boisian scholars. The only logical reason could be that because Washington worked through the German Embassy in North America and this meant it was not a bona fide Pan African project. Again this is ludicrous because any African project involving African Diaspora connections was vetted and sanctioned by the colonial powers. Washington was famous and had the ear of President Roosevelt during his presidency between 1901 and 1909—the high point of Tuskegee Institute's connections with African affairs. Keep in mind that Pan Africanism has most often been an idea rather than a movement. Africans have never fully progressed in full unity, and that maybe due to both internal cultural differences on the continent and in the African Diaspora. However, the overriding impediment to African unity across the globe has been the ability of European and North American politics to divide and conquer any attempt at such. Theoretically there have been small strides but nothing concrete even to the present-day has ever emerged that has brought on a United States of Africa that embraces its African Diaspora.

Back in the early 1900s, Booker T. Washington was attempting to make links with Africa, and quite frankly he did far better than most. Yet he has been dismissed as someone not regarded with Pan African status, even though his fingerprints are connected in a practical sense to a number of African nations and African nationalists. Du Bois took the credit in being a superior academic writer, but in applied terms he did little other than "head up" Pan African Congresses. Washington quietly influenced Liberia affairs, inspired African leaders, and created an exchange between African American students and Africans. The problem for him, in the analysis of Pan African history, is that he did it with the aid and sanction of European and North American power, yet even the great Kwame Nkrumah needed the cooperation of the British and U.S. governments to gain Ghana's independence over fifty years later in 1957. In short, Pan African historians tend not to comprehend the nuances of Washington, yet the likes of white supremacists such as Thomas Dixon Jr. were able to work out Washington's skillful manipulation of white power to the benefit of African heritage peoples. This is quite disappointing but future writers and thinkers will surely explore these deeper aspects of Washington—and his subtle ways that produced practical ends in empowering Africans and African Americans (Wright 2015).

One of the negatives for Washington was his own power built up within the Tuskegee Institute model, for it appears that writers tend to view African American leaders more favorably if they show a definite defiance to the white power structure of the day. This is a rather narrow conception in analyzing Washington, because he was a brilliant communicator and a friendly person to be around, attributes that disarmed his enemies. For example, most who understand his relationship with President Teddy Roosevelt note that it was one of convenience, yet they got along well too in each other's company. Roosevelt was fundamentally a racist, a man who believed in the superiority of white European derived cultures over any other human cultures. This is a known fact, but in his interaction with Washington, there was an element of curiosity and friendship that went beyond racism. Roosevelt visited Tuskegee Institute at Washington's request and aided his effort to stop Liberia being encroached by the Germans and British.

However, it was not all good relations between the two men. Roosevelt did not listen to Washington over the Brownsville Affair in August 1906; whereby African American soldiers based at a barracks were accused of shooting a white man. There was significant evidence of a frame-up, and even the white commanders revealed the African American soldiers were in fact in the barracks at the time of the incident. In short, Washington quietly advocated for the African Americans of the 25th Infantry, but Roosevelt ignored his plea and had the one hundred and sixty-seven men discharged without rights to their pensions. It took almost seventy years, but the 25th Infantry would be exonerated in the early 1970s after another investigation. Roosevelt made a terrible decision in ignoring Washington in 1906, but that is the nature of a white supremacist taking advice from a man of color.

This is not digression, it is an example of a white supremacist president doing bad things to African Americans, yet he is still willing to visit

Tuskegee Institute under the auspices of an African American educator and institution builder. Washington knew he had to either work with these white supremacists or his institute would flounder. The methods he used were always subtle, and clandestine, but an African American male based in the South with his power had to be cautious, savvy, and conscious of potential threats to his life and world on a daily basis. Now, in terms of Du Bois, he was able to be granted the "great one" in Pan Africanist history. However, he supported arguably one of the worst white supremacist presidents in Woodrow Wilson. President Wilson was a staunch segregationist and once he got into the White House from March 1913 to 1921 he was openly racist in his overall policies in segregating the official duties and accommodation inside the White House. He even had a premier of the white supremacist movie by D. W. Griffith, *Birth of a Nation*—based on Thomas Dixon Jr.'s *The Clansman*. The movie was overtly praised by President Wilson, who was a former classmate of Dixon, as being a true depiction of the South, and he was particularly pleased with the glorification of the Ku Klux Klan. Wilson was no true friend to African Americans, nor was Roosevelt, they were both white supremacists in essence—yet Du Bois saw past this.

The endorsement of Woodrow Wilson by Du Bois, and his support for African Americans to fight in World War I was a tragic mistake on his behalf. Yet it is largely forgotten or overlooked when Pan Africanists write favorably about Du Bois's legacy. What is important to note is that both Washington and Du Bois had no choice but to interact with white supremacists in endeavoring to move African Americans forward. It appears in the historical context of this experience that Washington has come off rather badly in terms of reputation, yet he made the greatest strides in planting seeds for future generations to reap from his work. It is too easy to reject him because he does not have the flamboyant lyricism of a Du Bois in prose, nor was he alive to defend himself against the various assaults on his life and works. In a 1980 study of Pan Africanism, the author writes, "Despite the flood of books and articles on Pan-Africanism in recent years, the study of the phenomenon is still in its infancy," and later adds, "Not surprisingly, there is still no agreement on what it is all about" (Esedebe 1994, 3). This is a fair assessment, Pan African history and practice is still relatively young in scope. Many African Diaspora thinkers who have contributed to this area of Africana history did not fully comprehend how best to connect, and under what conditions (Christian 2008). There was the key idea of Africa requiring its independence from the clutches of European dominance. But how to do that from the early twentieth century appeared to be an insurmountable task. The fact that Washington did what he could to make contact and to develop communication with Africans is rather impressive, especially while maneuvering between the ever present ghost of white supremacy and its far-reaching tentacles.

Later, in the early 1920s, Marcus Garvey tried to set up a settlement in Liberia of African Diaspora men and women but was thwarted by the forces of political white supremacy and most probably with some help from Du Bois (Martin 1976, 262, 302). Garvey's message was simply too powerful, too honest, and too obvious for the North American and European hegemony to accept. Importantly, Garvey was impressed with Washington and his message of self-determination, and wrote to him to tell him of his plans for African liberation in his homeland Jamaica. He was encouraged by Washington through correspondence, and they would have met in person had Garvey arrived before the death of the Tuskegee Institute leader. Garvey arrived in New York in March 1916, four months after Washington had passed. Undeterred, Garvey went on to establish arguably the strongest Black Nationalist movement the world had known with his organizations, the Universal Negro Improvement Association (UNIA) and African Communities League (ACL). Garvey owed much to the ideas of Booker T. Washington, but Pan African historians have largely overlooked this fact (Wright 2015).

Harlan (1983, 274) also notes that Washington was in correspondence with a number of renowned Pan Africans, among them: J. E. Casely Hayford, Duse Mohamed, and Henry Sylvester Williams. All very much involved in Pan African ideas, organization, and aspirations. Unfortunately, Washington was not able to attend the noted Pan African meetings, but this does not mean he was not a supporter of the overall aims and objectives. He was a man who had endured enslavement and prospered in freedom, and this is something he shared in private about the continent of Africa. In his daughter's memoir, Portia recalls spending an evening, while in Paris in 1905, as a guest of the great Edward Wilmot Blyden who was then a minister in the Liberian government and in his seventies. She wrote to her father, "It was a glorious evening! I was especially glad to see Dr. Blyden. . . . He seems a like a dear old man. He is going to take us sight-seeing Saturday afternoon. He sails for America next month and says he is coming South—mainly to see Tuskegee" (Stewart 1977, 61). One cannot read anything on Pan African history without coming across the name of Edward Wilmot Blyden.

Washington was in touch with Blyden via his connections with Liberia, and if Blyden could take Washington's daughter sightseeing in Paris, then one can assume he was close to the family. Again, all this is missing from the average history book on Washington or on Pan African history. But if one follows carefully all the correspondence in the Booker T. Washington Papers it is clear that the man was a Pan Africanist who kept his work and politics secretive due to the reality of white supremacy haunting the lives of Africans and persons of African heritage in the Diaspora. Washington was not a coward; he was a very brave man who should be given his due for all he accomplished under the most difficult of circumstances. Africa was a particularly difficult prospect to achieve lasting success because of the political stranglehold Europeans had over the territory. Yet it is evident in numerous ways that he did make a positive impact during his lifetime, and inspiring future Pan Africanists to take up the struggle further. For men like Marcus Garvey, who took a number of ideas from Washington, he strove to unite Africa against colonial rule and to unite Africans in the Diaspora who were experiencing virulent racism. It will not surprise to learn that one of his greatest opponents would be Du Bois (Martin 1976). Whenever a man challenged Du Bois's de facto leadership of African Americans they would suffer under his analytical gaze. Washington had to deal with it for over a decade, but was able to survive simply because he was always, in real terms, politically and financially stronger than Du Bois. With Garvey, Du Bois had the upper hand being almost twenty years his senior. Also, with Du Bois having been born and raised in North America, he had much on Garvey in terms of local knowledge and in terms of the African American experience. This was not the case with Washington, Du Bois could never outdo him on the enslavement experience, knowledge of the South, nor on the mental strength to overcome and prosper. Nor could he outdo Washington in public speaking in the early days of their conflicting opinions.

The only area where Du Bois and his acolytes have been stronger is in the realm of higher education. Fortunately for Du Bois, he was able to overshadow Washington's African affairs and deceive future generations into believing Washington had done nothing to empower Africa. Moreover, Du Bois scholars conveniently tend to leave out the many flaws in Du Bois's legacy. For example, the Talented Tenth is a patronizing and rather insulting model that has dismissed the innate intelligence of the many thousands of brilliant African minds who overcame the assaults on them by sheer determination of talent, mind, body, and spirit. What university did Frederick Douglass attend, or what university did Malcolm X go to? The answer is that these brilliant souls did not ever attend formal university, nor receive a diploma for such studies, but each would prove to be of the greatest minds to emerge out the African American experience. This is merely to critique the shallowness of the Talented Tenth proposition put forward by the aloof and arrogant W. E .B. Du Bois.

Washington in his *The Story of the Negro* discusses the innate love an African has for his mother. He then explains the same can be stated about African Americans and their mothers. This is an extremely poignant passage because Washington had a deep affection for his own mother, who was enslaved and exploited from birth to death. Africans on the continent and Africans in the Diaspora, similar to Washington, shared a love for their mothers. Washington then juxtaposes the legacy of skills that

Africans on the continent had mastered with those common to the African American in his experience. For example, the blacksmith was common in Africa and common in the African American experience. Washington writes, "Just as everywhere in the Southern states today, especially in the country districts, at the crossroads, or near the country store, one finds an [African American] blacksmith, so, in some of the remote regions in Africa, every village has, according to its size, from one to three blacksmiths" (Washington 2007, 39). There is no doubt that Washington was a keen student of Africa, and more than this he put it in practice by using Tuskegee Institute as a living example of Pan Africanism—exchanging students, faculty, and skills and delivering tangible hope from African America to Africa and vice versa.

A relevant trait about Washington was his comfort with African heritage; this is exemplified through the visit of a group led by Julius Rosenwald, the man who provided funds to build elementary schools throughout the South for African Americans. Rosenwald greatly admired the work of Washington and what he had built at Tuskegee Institute. They visited in October 1911 and experienced the students singing the spirituals "God Down, Moses," "Swing Low, Sweet Chariot," "Steal Away," and "My Lord, What a Morning." Deutsch writes, "Washington encouraged students to remember the songs they had grown up with and to share them at chapel time, a reminder that God had sustained their people and would continue to do so. He called spirituals 'these old, sweet, slave songs' and said he hoped to make them 'a source of pride and pleasure' to the students" (Deutsch 2011, 105). At bottom, Washington admired African American culture more than anything else; he believed in his people, the masses, those who had survived the worst that white Southern brutality could throw at them. They came up with songs at a time when all seemed lost. Washington instinctively connected with Africa, and it is this fact that should be acknowledged. His style of combat was not in an embittered adversarial tone. He had a cool charm about him, was easy in speech, humorous, and basically good company to be around. His African affairs were due to the success of Tuskegee Institute and his fame as a gifted orator. This does not mean he was not exploited by those who simply wanted to take his methods and use them for other means than to empower his people. There was not much he could do about that in real terms, but whatever he set up was to benefit ultimately his people, whether that was in Africa or African America.

Arguably, the closest associate Washington had during his tenure as the leader of Tuskegee Institute was Emmett J. Scott. He acted as Washington's trusted secretary from 1897 up to 1915. Scott was very loyal but not in a sycophantic manner. He was simply quite brilliant at his job. Indeed the fact that the Booker T. Washington Papers exist is largely due to his organization and administrative skills. Of all persons who can assess the personality of Washington it would be Scott due to his longevity, and a man of his talent would not need to stay in an environment if indeed he was not in a place that nourished his own sensibilities. In writing on personality type, "Although intensely human and consumingly interested in humanity—both in the mass and as individuals, whether of his race or any other—Booker Washington thought and acted to an uncommon degree on the impersonal plane." Scott was relating to how Washington dealt on a day-to-day basis with racism in a detached manner. He recalls the incident when Washington was traveling with an Indian when he was working with a class at Hampton Institute, and on boats and hotels the Indian was allowed to eat and stay at the hotel, but Washington as the teacher was denied. Scott states that he never harbored bitterness or anger in regard to racialized discrimination. Scott continues, "He regarded these experiences as interesting illustrations of the illogical nature of race prejudice" (Scott and Stowe 2009, 76).

For Washington, the experience of Africans from the time they were taken forcibly from the African continent to the time they spent in North America involved barbarity and not civilization. Washington was big on noting that the oppressor who metes out such cruelty can only hurt himself more than the oppressed because it is ultimately inhumane. Washington was a voice of compassion and peace, and when he could not see it in the eyes of his oppressor, he simply felt pity for that person. He had no time for resentment toward any cultural group or any individual, yet he received much the same vitriol as Dr. Martin Luther King Jr. suffered some forty years later in the same state. Washington looked for the best in humanity always. What is interesting when looking at Washington, in relation to the experience of Dr. King, is the fact that the latter attended in 1957 the inauguration of the first president of Ghana, Kwame Nkrumah, in the fight for African Independence era. Both Washington and Dr. King were in a sense Africanists who have never really been given such credit. When one reads the life of Washington critically it is too often rather narrowly focused, and his admiration for the humanity he served is often lost under the erroneous and supposedly rejection of voting rights and higher education. In terms of Africa and African America, his message was sometimes lost but ultimately the evidence of his hard work to help African nations gain greater self-determination is irrefutable. As Harlan reminds, "Washington frequently explained that industrial education was for black self-reliance and was not exclusive of higher education, but this was frequently misunderstood in Africa as in America" (Harlan 1983, 276). Washington found a formula to raise funds while keeping white supremacy at bay. Never once did he undermine higher education aspirations and this has been proved throughout this biography.

Due to the immense caricaturing of Washington it has been necessary to constantly find his words, and those of others, that refute the manner in which he has been misunderstood, especially when it relates to his connection to Africa. To summarize, he had a strong influence on issues relating to South Africa, Togo, and Liberia in the early twentieth century. Washington worked within the system, and the confines of European colonialism and there is not much he could do about that other than his usual clandestine behind the scenes work. The fact that his student exchanges have largely been hidden from historical view is rather illuminating. He was also rather quiet in publicizing his efforts in African affairs. One thing certain is that he largely attracted attention through the success of Tuskegee Institute because the model of education gave an apparent example to European colonizers how to develop an agricultural method that could suit the Togo colony of the Germans. This is not the full story though because what was created did not disempower the Africans whom Tuskegee Institute interacted with, but it did prove a step too far, or too soon in terms of endeavoring to settle the land. There was too much in climate difference, soil substance, and other problems that made life for the Tuskegee expedition difficult.

Also, what is not carefully considered is the fact that Washington internationalized his institutional success, regardless of the circumstances not being perfect. He broke through barriers and linked Africa to Alabama in the first decade of the twentieth century (Zimmerman 2010). This is a remarkable effort considering the time he was operating in. Future historians will certainly need to revise the Pan African history that currently eliminates Washington from its curriculum. Pan Africanism was in the very early stages, merely an idea, and today that notion is yet to fully find its foothold in genuine exchange and unity among Africans on the continent and in the African Diaspora. There needs to be more knowledge of Washington's legacy in Africa. For example, very few know about his deep connections with Liberia. So much so that today there is a Booker T. Washington Institute in Kakata, Margibi County, in Liberia. This first agricultural vocational school founded in Liberia through the influence of Washington and Tuskegee Institute was discussed as a possibility during his lifetime but not initiated until 1929. Again, this is rather significant for Pan African history, and it should no longer be a debatable issue whether Washington should be a part of it. Neither should his reluctance to shout from the rooftops his avowal of Pan Africanism during the height of European colonialism need to be explained; it was not his style to do so for the superficial nomenclature of being a "radical agitator" in history.

To confirm Washington's profound interest in African affairs Tuskegee Institute held an International Conference from April 17 to 19, 1912, to address the needs of Africans in certain parts of the world. Washington sent out a call for participants in Africa, the Caribbean region, along with North and South America. His aim was to consider how the model of Tuskegee and Hampton institutes could be of use to other regions of the world, particularly Africa. He asked for missionaries to attend because they were having an influence on African affairs, and if Washington could persuade his perspective of learning then the damage done to Indigenous Africans would be less severe. Marable is correct, but incorrect when he says it was "oriented toward missionary and colonial guidelines" (Marable 1974, 400). This conference was groundbreaking in its conception for a leading African American institution of learning in the South to hold an international gathering. Washington gathered important government officials together in order to get Tuskegee Institute in the mix and between the African and the European colonizer in order to do what he did best, empower his people against the odds.

Wright explains that this conference should be deemed Washington's major impact on Pan Africanism because there were delegates representing all the areas outlined above. In his address to the conference delegates he explained in his humble style that he did not claim Tuskegee Institute to be superior but it may be of use to them who represent the peoples of African heritage who want to improve their conditions. Tuskegee Institute provided tours of the campus and facilities so that the delegates could take some ideas of the studies they provided. Moreover, he stated something crucial for Pan African historians to ponder: "For a number of years, we have had on our grounds a number of students from countries outside the United States. From year to year, we have from 100 to 150 students representing foreign countries and we are anxious that these students be fitted to go back to their homes and render the highest and best service" (Wright 2015, 141). Again, the influence of Tuskegee Institute is brought to light, and it has not been mentioned in Pan African terms, until the research of Wright (2015) emerged to set the record straight.

A large part of Washington's enigma was in the manner he did things under the "cover" of white power. He was a master of political strategy. For example, in requesting missionaries to attend the International Conference it gave him cover to have the delegates from Africa and the Caribbean to come without hindrance. Had he publicized the conference as purely Pan African to "free Africa from Colonial rule" he would not have succeeded in gaining the funds for such an event. Indeed, he would have been castigated. He more than anyone knew how to "get over" the white power structure in order to get his people empowered, and it could never be done overtly. The likes of Du Bois could be more bombastic because they had less to lose, and were not responsible for the welfare of a campus with over one thousand students, one hundred faculty, and numerous staff. Du Bois could write openly about the racism that was afflicting his people, but

Washington did his writing in far more subtle terms. What should be analyzed with Washington more is not what he stated but what he achieved. If one follows his words and not his deeds one will be lost in an avalanche of under-spoken phrases and innuendo. The idea of self-help, self-determination, and self-love in regard to African Americans was paramount—but not overtly pushed in the faces of whites who would seize upon any form of rebellion. Had Washington not gone undercover with his real ideas of self-determination then it would have been a lost cause and Tuskegee Institute would have disintegrated or have been burned to the ground by a mob of white haters.

Another major reason for Pan Africanists to acknowledge Washington's advocacy for Africa and its peoples is in his fight against an Immigration Bill from 1915 that proposed to exclude peoples of African heritage from entering the United States. His public fight against it was forthright, and he felt it was extremely unfair in the sense that it would do more harm than good. He was also concerned that this legislation, if passed, would harm Tuskegee University's growing body of foreign students from Africa and the Caribbean. He wrote an open letter to the editor of the *New York World*, and it was published on January 2, 1915. Part of it states, "For a number of years some of the brightest young people from Africa and elsewhere have been coming to this country to receive training [at Tuskegee Institute] to fit them to go back and help their people, and this they have done in an effective manner. All this, I understand will be stopped by the passing of this law" (Harlan 1972, Vol. 13, 209). Fortunately, Washington's lobbying prevented the Bill from passing through Congress, and the African and Caribbean students continued to study at Tuskegee Institute. This again validates all that Washington did to help aid the origins and development of Pan Africanism (Wright 2015).

In addition, in a letter from Marcus Garvey to Washington dated September 8, 1914, he explains the history of Jamaica and its struggling Black population. Garvey requests a donation from Washington for the work he intends to do. He writes, "Throughout the country we have abundance of evidence of the backwardness of our people, hence we have determined to do our best to raise them by education and industry, to a higher status among the civilized peoples of the world" (Hill 1983, 68). What is significant about this letter from Garvey to Washington is its open admittance to Jamaica having "evidence of backwardness of our people" and the need to "raise them by education and industry" to a "higher status among civilized peoples of the world"; this was the language of the day. Yet it is coming from a celebrated Pan Africanist; had those words come from Washington scholars and commentators would have lambasted him. The fact is that all the writers and thinkers of Washington's day spoke of there being "backward peoples" in need of "civilization" and most referred not only to

Jamaicans, but Africans as well. Washington spoke as all thinkers on progress thought, and this has also been misunderstood by Pan African historians. If Garvey can speak in this tone, and Du Bois can speak in this tone, and both be regarded as Pan African giants, then why not Washington? The answer is because he was fossilized and not given the breadth of analysis due to Du Bois, and later scholars continuing to downplay his contribution as the "accommodationist" who gave away the African American vote, which is a spurious and flawed assessment to lay at the feet of one man and one speech in Atlanta in 1895.

Moreover, Washington was acutely aware of the poor and downtrodden millions who resided in Europe. In 1912, Washington published *The Man Farthest Down: A Record of Observation and Study in Europe* that covered the plight of poor white European communities. He was a clever man because many of the poorest European immigrants were at this time entering the United States at a fast rate and would be the new competitors to African Americans. The first chapter is titled "Hunting the Man Farthest Down," and he reveals his objective: "I determined to carry out a plan I had long had in mind of making myself acquainted with the condition of the poorer working classes of Europe, particularly in those regions from which an ever-increasing number of immigrants are coming to our country each year" (Washington 2015, 3). He disembarked in Liverpool, England, from New York and went on to travel to London and on to other parts of Europe, visiting Italy, Hungry, Poland, and Denmark. This is the European tour in which he visited Andrew Carnegie at his home in Skibo Castle, Scotland; by this time they had known each other for over a decade. Carnegie too was a man from humble working class origins, and that is how the two men bonded.

Crucially, Washington was a canny soul, a very smart man who knew instinctively that racialized discrimination was a farce. He understood what lay behind one man or woman being able to succeed in life was a simple matter of opportunity and good fortune. Washington knew he was more advanced and experienced than the Indian American he had once chaperoned, yet the Indian could gain access to food and lodgings and Washington could not. He knew he was more advanced than the African Americans he met in the rural communities and sat, ate, and slept overnight in their homes, and he knew he was more advanced than the poor Europeans he met throughout his visits across the Atlantic Ocean. Washington did not hold onto bitterness because he knew also that such mentality was a disease to the spirit. Instead, he smiled inside, and joked a lot, and pitied those who could not see his humanity and the humanity of his people.

It is very odd, even to this day, to find scholars who misunderstand Washington completely. The study by Zimmerman (2010) is a perfect example of just how incorrect one can be about Washington, but also how easy it is to be wrong. He sets up Washington as an elitist who worked hand-in-hand with the German elites to exploit Africans in Togo. Nothing could be further from the truth, in fact one of the Tuskegee graduates married an African/Togolese woman during his time there. Moreover, Zimmerman goes on to suggest the Tuskegee Institute model was something that benefited the Southern whites, and that the transfer of this model to Togo was simply a matter of using the same exploitation there. How wrong could he be, Tuskegee Institute benefited African Americans solely. Zimmerman should have read the white supremacist Thomas Dixon Jr.'s piece on "Booker T. Washington and the Negro: Some Aspects of the Work of Tuskegee" from 1905, written at the same time as Tuskegee Institute's sojourn into West Africa. Zimmerman would then come to *really* comprehend Washington's outcomes; it seems that the fossilization of him is still working for some scholars (Zimmerman 2010, 249).

Washington's most trusted secretary knew him best, and Scott writes this about his boss, "Booker Washington was that kind of idealist. He kept in constant and intimate touch with the masses of his people, particularly those on the soil.... [He seemed] to renew his strength every time he came in contact with the plain people of his race" (Scott and Stowe 2009, 96). Indeed, Washington was a man of the people, and how anyone could mistake him for an elite is incredulous. Yes, he worked with white Northern elites but only in the service of aiding his people, never to exploit them. To comprehend Washington is to be riddled with complexity, coupled with the historical literature emanating from Du Bois and others, and it is rather easy for scholars to get confused. Yet he can be simple to understand if one's feet are planted in the soil. Washington was a man who loved nature and he truly admired farmers—men like this are not designed to be elitist. Once connected to the earth, to the rural life of the African American, and to those who had risen from the ashes of enslavement, there is no such thinking of exploiting another human being.

In America, he was limited, in Africa he was limited, but in his outcomes he was limitless. Hundreds of ordinary Africans passed through Tuskegee Institute under his wing, some stayed, many returned to help build their communities. They did what they could under the oppressive reality of European colonialism. Just as Washington did what he could in the sweltering heat of the South under Jim Crow and white supremacy. In hindsight, the writers of Pan African history have made a fatal flaw in omitting Booker T. Washington from his rightful place in the history books of that genre. Indeed, it is scandalous and hopefully future academics will rise up to follow the lead of scholars like Wright (2015) and provide a deeper critical inspection of the existing literature and studies.

To conclude, Washington states in *The Story of the Negro*, "The African slave trade was not the source of that was evil in the native life of the West

Coast [of Africa]. . . . It substituted the cheap machine-made European goods for the more artistic native manufactures, which take a great deal more time and energy to produce" (Washington 2007, 45). Africa was not only raped by Europe; it was subjugated by cheap European goods, by missionaries who lacked the humanity to recognize African humanity and its multitude of cultures, and by internal warfare that raged with the aid of European divide and conquer tactics. Booker T. Washington waded through the muddy waters to gain a foothold on the continent he adored from afar, though his home was ultimately, given his family roots and beloved Tuskegee Institute, in the South where he fought another valiant effort to secure African American and African liberation.

Why Booker T. Washington Matters

It is curious to consider the legacy of an African American historical figure who has been so maligned, misunderstood, and misinterpreted since his passing on November 14, 1915. Booker T. Washington requires revision, revitalization, and restitution by the historical community because he has been judged and fossilized by many unfairly. This is not hyperbole because the author too came looking at the life of this man with a skeptical mind. Yet when delving into the time period, the milieu, his start in life, one comes away embarrassed of ever having harbored scholarly resentment toward a truly good hearted and well-meaning African American man who wanted only the best for his people.

Washington possessed a number of salient attributes that require unpacking more profoundly and put into the context of his life and times. After all, his was "a life in American history" that will stand the test of time, the fact that his main autobiographical account is still in print more than six score years after its first publication is astounding in itself. Yet what riles the spirit as a biographer is the manner in which he has been fossilized—cemented into a caricature and simply associated with "accommodationist" and the architect of the "disenfranchisement" of the African American during his lifetime. This is both spurious and flawed, and it reminds one of the way Dr. Martin Luther King Jr. was also characterized as a cardboard "I have a Dream" figure in American history. Washington, just like Dr. King, was multidimensional in character and a force for the

Booker T. Washington speaks to a large audience in Pine Bluff, Arkansas, in the early 1900s. (Library of Congress)

practical advancement of African Americans in an insidiously racist and nefarious social and cultural environment.

The courage of Washington is underplayed by his detractors because it would not fit the narrative that has been established of him being obsequious and fawning toward white supremacy. It is rather too easy to assault Washington because he was a man who did not seek conflict, especially with his people—whether located in the South or North. The so-called "Tuskegee Machine" label, conceptualized by Du Bois, or so he recalls (Du Bois 1992, 73), was a way to belittle the influence of Washington. Yet, he was consulted by presidents and other leaders wielding considerable power and authority but mainly for the benefit of his people in the South. Washington lobbied for African Americans to get political positions, such as William H.

MARTIN LUTHER KING JR. (1929–1968)

Dr. King was born in Atlanta, Georgia, and raised in a loving African American middle-class home. His father and grandfather were preachers, and he would take up the profession from the age of nineteen years. He attended Booker T. Washington High School and Morehouse College, where he gained a BA in Sociology. He then went on to Crozier Seminary and then to Boston University, where he gained a doctorate in Theology at the age of twenty-six years. He was a brilliant orator and writer, who led the modern Civil Rights Movement with his charisma and team of organizers. His style was moral persuasion and consistent with Booker T. Washington's demeanor in having no bitterness toward his enemies, only pity. Dr. King was a man of the South, and he was a fighter like Washington. His life was ended in assassination on April 4, 1968, but his legacy lives on very strongly.

Lewis for U.S. assistant attorney from 1907 to 1911 under the President Teddy Roosevelt administration, but he was not always successful. In the case of Lewis, the Harvard man, keep in mind that he was only advanced by Washington because he had the talent to aid the broader African American experience. Later under President Taft, Lewis was appointed assistant attorney general from 1911 to 1913. Again, this was in part due to Washington pushing for him to get the position. A Harvard man like Lewis, in the narrative of Washington's critics, does not fit the supposed anti–higher education ideals of the Tuskegee Institute leader. But the truth is he helped empower many African Americans who came out of the Ivy League or other institutions of higher learning to get appointments. This is an important revision as we consider the legacy of Washington. The myths are more prevalent than the reality, and this needs to be reshaped in order for the real Washington to breathe holistically in future discourses.

Whatever the essence of Du Bois's envy toward Washington, because no matter how he has endeavored to disguise it in his flowery language, there is something about the "ghost of Washington" that lingered in the mind of Du Bois, whether in the *Dusk of Dawn*, published first in 1940, or his later posthumous autobiography, *A Soliloquy on Viewing My Life from the Last Decade of Its First Century*, published in 1968, he continued to put the proverbial nails in Washington's coffin. Attempting always to secure his own legacy over that of the Tuskegee Institute builder, Du Bois's efforts succeeded throughout the twentieth century. However, there are now more sophisticated ways to attain broader knowledge: the correspondence between Washington and Du Bois, and other primary documents that shed light on both of them are now readily available (Aiello 2016). Scholars can juxtapose more easily the exchanges and delineate the nuance between the two men that was largely established unfairly by Du Bois himself and his acolytes who look at *The Souls of Black Folk* master with rose-tinted glasses. To be sure, Du Bois was a magnificent scholar, but also an arrogant man, and he admits to being such (Du Bois 1968, 139). Ultimately, nowadays with there being greater opportunity in the digital age to access primary documents that confirm who said what, when, and how, it is a boon for a scholar of biography and history.

Chapter 5 has covered in-depth the origins of both men, and their differences in style and opinion. No need to repeat it here, other than to explain an example of an event that outlines Washington's effort to make peace with his critics in order to bring African American leadership more closely aligned for the benefit of all parties. This was in January 1904 when Washington tried to bring Du Bois and others together at a conference held at Carnegie Hall in New York. Briefly, the history books tend to describe Washington as a manipulator who schemed and planned it to be for his benefit only. On one level, given the fossilized narrative, this fits well with the Tuskegee Machine label. But on a more nuanced level one must consider why he would have the need to bring African American leaders together if indeed he was so powerful and ubiquitous in all areas of political life? To answer, the fact is that he was a man wanting the best for his people and it would be better if all prominent leaders worked toward the goals that could aid the multitude of African Americans suffering from poverty and ignorance at this time.

The typical view of Washington deemed his white philanthropic friends as pleased with him for his supposed suppression of African American rights (Aiello 2016, 201). But this is way off the mark and it distorts Washington's legacy profoundly. As discussed in previous chapters, Washington had relationships with white Northern philanthropists that went way beyond basic working relationships. Racists do not enjoy the company, especially personal, of African Americans. So it is important not to dichotomize every relationship between an African American and a white person as simply "Black and White" because it distorts genuine friendships that do not involve "race" and racism. Washington could cultivate solid friendships with *anyone* due to his personality being grounded, unsullied by bitterness, and openly appealing in nature. This is hard for scholars to comprehend from white experience because they tend to be less concerned about personal interactions and the development of personality. Historians in particular focus on "power relations" and the outcomes of such interaction. Well, if that alone is the case, Washington certainly came out more favorably in his dealings with rich white men.

Aiello (2016) puts forward a notion that the New York conference in January 1904 was bankrolled by Andrew Carnegie; yes this is true. But ultimately it was Washington who wanted to make peace between Du Bois and the others who were against Washington's perspective and approach. Aiello admits, "Du Bois prepared his faction for deviousness by the Washington faction, which essentially made the meeting a clash between two mistrustful groups. Washington was not devious, but the conference was controlled by his people and it would not solve the problems between factions" (Aiello 2016, 201). This again is true, but Aiello misses an important point: why would Washington even make the effort to set up a meeting if he did not want an outcome that was beneficial to all parties? The real issue, as expressed, is that Du Bois *arrived* at the meeting distrustful and expecting deviousness. If so, why did he even bother in the first place if indeed Washington was not being honest? Was it in the hope that they could have found common ground? The answer is, frankly, that Du Bois never wanted common ground with Washington because he envied his position as the de facto leader among African Americans. He coveted the powerful position he held and the friendliness he had with rich philanthropists.

In chapter 5, there is evidence of Du Bois requesting funds from Carnegie, which was no different than what Washington did. The problem with Du Bois was that he was not a good fundraiser like Washington. He was not amiable like Washington; instead Du Bois came off as aloof, supercilious, and haughty. Moreover, he was self-righteous in his prose; even though it was lyrical, it had the air of a man who had absorbed too much European thought and had not spent enough time with the masses as Washington had in his life, and continued throughout his life. At bottom, Washington was a peacemaker, there is no doubt he wanted an end to the hostility created by Du Bois, William Monroe Trotter, and others. There is too much evidence of Washington reaching out and trying to do the right thing, while receiving rather disdainful and disingenuous utterings from Du Bois in return. There is no way that the New York conference in January 1904 could have been successful because Du Bois did not want it to be so. Washington should be lauded for his attempt to reach out, to find ways to improve how they could work in harmony to offer the best of what they could do together for their people. Both men offered so much and it is unutterably sad that each could not find the formula to right the differences. With Du Bois, it was near impossible to find a way for him to lead within the realm of a stronger and more established African American leader. This though was a problem for Du Bois, not for Washington and his legacy in endeavoring to make peace and create goodwill.

While discussing the origin of the New York conference, Aiello (2016) provides indirect information regarding Washington's legacy that provides a useful synopsis in relation to his fundraising skills. He writes, "Andrew Carnegie built 29 buildings on the campuses of historically black colleges because of Washington, Julius Rosenwald, the head of Sears, Roebuck, built a series of more than 5,300 black secondary schools across the South, with Washington's guidance, at a cost of more than 28 million dollars. Carnegie, meanwhile, also built a new library at Tuskegee and became one of Washington's principal benefactors" (Aiello 2016, 201). Now, depending on how one considers philanthropy, the above is all about Washington guiding dollars to good deeds and to the benefit of African Americans gaining an education. That is, providing the possibility of literacy and competence that would in turn empower the communities and allow for a myriad of economic growth. Where in the above scenario is "accommodation"? It does not exist; you do not provide education to African Americans and expect them to be docile. It is only a matter of time before an education provides knowledge for greater freedom and prosperity. Washington engaged with white philanthropy for one thing only: the empowerment of African Americans. Certainly not for subjugation, and this ought to be comprehended more openly by future scholars. Moreover, if one carefully reads what Aiello (2016) states above, there were twenty-nine historically

Black colleges and universities that benefited directly from Washington's lobbying so the likes of Carnegie could direct his millions toward African American institutions of higher education. Therefore, why has Washington been fossilized as a person who "defunded higher education"—as Du Bois dubiously expounded in *The Souls of Black Folk* and to anyone who would listen? It is a false narrative that has stained Washington's legacy and this should have no place in future scholarship.

Washington's legacy should also refer to his immense contribution not only to the infrastructure of education, but his input to pedagogy coupled with practical skill trades training. Washington wanted his students to have a trade skill and mindset equipped for the outside world. The basic need for all persons, and that relates to the present day, is to be able to earn a living that allows for a life well lived. Washington envisioned students being able to own their homes and have savings in a bank account. He was a practical educator, instilling home economics, personal hygiene, and other positive living habits. His time as a student at Hampton Institute informed his pedagogy, but he took it further by producing individuals with flexible abilities that could adapt to the competition faced in the larger world. For Washington, it was also imperative for his students to leave Tuskegee Institute with the ability to contribute constructively to their community. There was so much required of them because of the state of affairs they encountered as African Americans—poverty and racism was a common factor for the rural communities. Washington described the essence of his pedagogy: "At Tuskegee, for example, when a student is trained to the point of efficiency where he can construct a first-class wagon, we do not keep him there to build more vehicles, but send him out in the world to exert his trained influence and capabilities in lifting others to his level, and we begin our work with the raw material all over again" (Washington 1904, vi). It is necessary to point out too that students were not only given trade skills, as Washington explained, "Mere hand training without thorough moral, religious, and mental education, counts for very little" (v). There was always in his pedagogy the "hands and the head," meaning a thorough education; for him this was holistic education, designed to create a man or woman who could firmly stand on his or her feet in life.

Another emphasis on teaching was to instill the idea of personal hygiene in the young men and women. The importance of cleanliness was put to them via the "toothbrush philosophy" whereby each student would be sure to take care of one's teeth with regular cleaning. It was an ascetic form of discipline rooted in the development of a Protestant Christian Ethic. The Bible was an important part of the education to impart merely the virtues of good living and healthy morals. For Washington, a good education revolved around healthy habits of living. Much of this he had learned from

Hampton Institute as a student, he found a lot of this useful in developing strong bodies and healthy minds at Tuskegee Institute.

As with pedagogy, his oratorical skills need to be acknowledged when assessing his legacy. Something that has been used *against* him but lauded by others was his use of African American idioms and the expression of humor and wisdom that emanated from rural folks. White scholars have tended to view this as a put down, but it could not be further from the truth. Washington was most at home with farmers and rural African Americans in general. He admired their love for the land as he too felt at home in the soil and surrounded by nature. Additionally, the use of idiom while giving a talk also enthused the crowd, whether it be African American, white Southerners, or Northern-based audiences. In point of fact, the African American writers, Paul Laurence Dunbar, Zora Neal Hurston, and Langston Hughes, won great praise for including such idioms in their writings and poetry. Washington even dubbed Dunbar the "Poet Laureate of African Americans." Hence, Washington admired the use of idioms, and part of his legacy is in the fact that he could arouse a crowd with humor and dialect that came from sharing his many stories of "life in the Black Belt" and in his experiences of the masses. He would actually display the depth of wisdom and merriment one could find while specifically in the company of rural African Americans. Washington lived by the African word *Ubuntu*: "I am because we are, and because we are, therefore I am," essentially meaning humanity toward all others, especially those within one's cultural group.

The oratorical skills he possessed also disarmed his potential enemies, and therefore he would gain more support for his work. Washington spent at least half of the calendar year on the road raising funds, and he did this largely through speaking engagements and correspondence with philanthropic organizations. His speaking skills coupled with fundraising acumen again attracted more philanthropic support, which was poured into Tuskegee Institute. Moreover, he insisted on having those who gave their money come to the institution to inspect how the funds had been spent. More often than not, the philanthropist was more than pleased, and the word of his good work and prudent use of the funds carried even further afield.

Washington worked tirelessly in order not to fail. He felt that if Tuskegee Institute floundered it would be a reflection of the entire African American cultural group, and he could not face such a predicament. The downside of this determination is that he never knew when to take a break, to recuperate his mind and body. According to Harlan (1972, 1983), Washington suffered at least two breakdowns from exhaustion. He never complained or shared his deepest emotions in public, because he was extremely private. He was always focused and driven to succeed in his objective to create a first class educational institution. Therefore one should consider this too as part of his legacy, his ability to work to one's capacity and beyond for the success desired. What this reveals is Washington's capacity to build an institution from the ground upward. Literary brick by brick he built Tuskegee Institute. Building by building was erected with a combination of philanthropic funds, student labor, and skilled local artisans gaining employment. Washington was a master at applying the principals he was teaching into practical work projects that benefited the expansion of Tuskegee Institute. Everything he did was for the uplift of the institution, which would then propel him to deliver another equally good or better building on the campus. All the time he would be thinking of new ways to build, build, build. The man was driven by an internal force most mere mortals do not possess. This has something to do with his humble, incredibly difficult, beginnings in enslavement that all but diminished his childhood. Having experienced the long night of poverty, the indignity of bondage, there was only one way for Washington to travel: forward and never to look back. In advancing his institutional building skills he found it expedient not to rest on his laurels but to keep striving onward and upward. To be sure, one can only imagine the feelings of hope and pride he must have felt watching Tuskegee Institute being built with the input of his students.

One of the biggest myths about Tuskegee Institute and Washington's legacy that has been rebuffed consistently within this biography is in the notion that he did not respect education beyond industrial training. That is why evidence in his own words is required to defend his memory. In Chapter VII of his book *Working with the Hands*, he explains the efficacy of both vocational and academic education. Washington wrote, "It is well to remember that Tuskegee Institute stands for education as well as training, for men and women as well as for bricks and mortar" (82). This is important to note because the fossilization of Washington in regard to him only endorsing industrial training is pervasive and dominant in scholarly debate. As such there is an unbalanced view of his philosophy and pedagogical model. Washington continued, "Tuskegee has always maintained an Academic Department, at present [1904] being housed mainly in four buildings" (84). This is something that is not mentioned in the debates surrounding Washington's views on education. Too often he is juxtaposed as merely a vocational advocate alongside the liberal arts education promoter Du Bois. This is not an accurate portrait of Washington and does not provide a fair assessment of his legacy.

In essence, he strove for balance and practical survival skills. For example, he was criticized heavily by Du Bois and others for chastising the young boy learning French while living in a hovel in rural Alabama. But what is overlooked is the real-world aspect of the boy's life and what his family required to live better. In the short term this student would not have an opportunity to study in France, nor employ the French language in his community. Washington was rather adamant in bringing education to the direct service of the community; otherwise it was not a practical or personal investment. However, he never dismissed the importance of liberal arts education, and again, to use his words, he stated, "On the faculty of the Academic Department are twenty-eight men and women of [African American] blood with degrees from Michigan, Nebraska, Oberlin, Amherst, Cornell, Columbia, and Harvard" (85). Washington goes on to explain the types of disciplines taught in liberal arts with a heavy emphasis on English, rhetoric, elocution, literature, geography, and history. In terms of history the areas covered were American history and its colonization, using African American history as a key component. With Tuskegee being located in Alabama there was a focus on the local history in relation to the African American experience. Students also covered mathematics, animal life, plant life and minerals. In short, one cannot state that Washington's legacy did not leave in place a holistic model for Tuskegee Institute. But there are rarely, if any, accounts of his critics considering the actual curricula offered; even the books left behind to evaluate Tuskegee Institute under Washington's leadership are rarely cited—Du Bois never once cited the books published by Booker T. Washington.

Another much overlooked aspect of Washington was his admiration of nature. He was very much at home in the fields growing vegetables, and his favorite pastime was to get his hands dirty in the soil. There was an emphasis on this form of exercise at Tuskegee Institute, and with the brilliant George Washington Carver there as a faculty member, it is pretty obvious how important the study of plants and nature in general were at the institution. Washington wrote, "The object of the work in Nature Study, as taught in the Academic Department, is to train the faculty of observation, create an interest in and love of nature, gain knowledge which will be of service in the future, and to cultivate a practical interest in Agriculture" (92). Here is the legacy of learning about nature that he so admired and ingrained in the institution's knowledge base—an emphasis ultimately on agriculture simply because Tuskegee Institute resided in the heart of rural Alabama.

The critics of Washington tend to hide the ideological perspectives they hold, and it impacts how one reads his legacy. Chapter 5 considers rather closely his contemporary critic, Du Bois, who is the key scholar responsible for Washington's fossilization. Other prominent scholars also stained his contribution to African American leadership; one being Oliver Cromwell Cox (1901–1974), a Caribbean Marxist theorist who emigrated to the United States as a young man. He critiqued Washington as a "collaborator" to white supremacists and the ruling class in an essay titled "The

Leadership of Booker T. Washington" and published in the sociological journal *Social Forces* in 1951. What Cox failed to disclose was his analysis being essentially a Marxist examination of the ruling class, in which Washington was a collaborator in the oppression of the African American masses. Cox gives him far too much power stating that Washington's role was basically to suppress the masses and play the role of "intercessor" or a go-between for the dominant ruling class and the masses. In other words, he acted as an agent for the powerful to foil the aspirations of the masses of African Americans. The problem with this analysis is it fails to come to terms with the many maneuvers Washington did behind the scenes to assail the efforts of the Southern racist powerbrokers. Cox did not have access to Washington's papers, his voluminous correspondence, nor have knowledge of his clandestine work in law cases to impede the segregation and disenfranchisement efforts put forward by white supremacists.

The problem for Washington, however, is that Cox's essay influences those who read about his life. There is something curious too about Cox's critique in the sense that he apparently spent time at Tuskegee Institute in the 1944, so maybe he had a bad time there and responded with his rather harsh critique. This of course is conjecture with a tad of perception, because when one peels away the layers of those who have critiqued Washington, there appear many dubious shenanigans in the process. Washington was not a "collaborator" keeping down the masses; he was a man who found a successful method to help pull poverty-stricken African Americans out of the dire social conditions to eke out a better life. He tapped into philanthropy as a means to gain funds to build better classrooms for his students, and to help those involved in education in the South. Now, was it perfect? No. Was there a degree of racism meted out to him? Yes. Was he possibly exploited? Maybe, but it seems that he got the lion's share of the exploitative relations in order to help as many African Americans get a foothold in education as was possible.

Another prominent African American sociologist, E. Franklin Frazier (1894–1962) critiqued Washington in his noted book *The Black Bourgeois*, which was published in 1957. Frazier was not a Marxist, maybe a Weberian or a reformist, but he argued that Washington did not actually train African Americans in the industrial skills that were required for the modern industrialism that was occurring particularly in the North. This may be a valid point in terms of harnessing and other trades taught, but the likes of bricklaying, carpentry, dressmaking, and other skills were as relevant then as they are today. It seems that the critics took one point of weakness in Washington and blew it up out of proportion. Frazier got his facts wrong in relation to the Julius Rosenwald Fund, he states it was established in 1917 to help build over five thousand schools (Frazier 1962, 61). The fund may have been established then but the friendship between Washington and Rosenwald was in play as far back as 1911. Rosenwald became good friends with Washington and visited Tuskegee on two occasions, and in turn, the Washington's visited Chicago to stay with the Rosenwalds at their home. Rosenwald was funding Washington endorsed projects from 1912 up to the Tuskegee leader's death in 1915 (Deutsch 2011, 103–120). Basically, Frazier upsets the entire discussion by simply not fully understanding the relationships Washington had, many of which were genuine friendships, beyond the realm of racialization and exploitation.

In terms of the industrial education offered at Tuskegee Institute being outdated, Frazier also knew as a sociologist that work culture is ever evolving just as society and culture, and with this comes changes in skill sets. In this sense, Washington was cognizant enough to have both sets of knowledge taught at Tuskegee Institute, trades and liberal arts. So new additions to the curriculum would inevitably come and go like in any institution of learning. Frazier takes liberties with Washington and leans on the fossilized stereotype started by Du Bois and built upon by Herbert Aptheker and others. Washington was a very easy target, a sitting duck for any scholar to take on and malign his impaired image. He was not alive to respond to the criticisms so it was easy for any critic to jump on the bandwagon of detractors, especially those with Marxist or leftist leanings.

After all, Washington was in as sense a capitalist, or at least someone who worked in the system to create opportunities within the context of property ownership, profit and loss. He was not a revolutionary, but neither were Du Bois and his other critics who largely represented the elite among African Americans. The Marxist critiques tend to be the writers who existed within academia and could not psychologically work out the legacy of Washington other than to place him as an agent of the ruling class. Unfortunately, this does not add up under close scrutiny as he was too organically connected to the masses. Anybody who studies Washington's outcomes in philanthropic relationships will find no malfeasance in his business. Washington was always transparent with any donor who contributed to Tuskegee Institute, and all monies went to efforts to improve the campus and the surrounding community of Tuskegee. In terms of his National Negro Business League venture, that was supported by Andrew Carnegie only to improve the networking and positive development of African American business. The main problem, it seems, the Marxists and other leftist scholars had with Washington was in his open connection with the politics of capitalism—in that sense he was guilty. Yet in regard to white supremacy, Washington did his fighting surreptitiously without fanfare, and to suggest that he did not fight racism would not be in line with the various evidence (Harlan 1972, 1983; Norrell 2009; Wright 2015). Moreover, according to his daughter, Portia, her father died relatively penniless, having given all accumulated wealth to the Tuskegee Institute endowment (Stewart 1977).

Maulana Karenga (2010) is very balanced in his assessment of Washington's overall legacy. He maintains that there are four key areas to focus on when assessing his contribution to the African American experience. First, his experience in enslavement and how he learned to cope with the "viciousness, violence and power" of white Southerners. Yet his experience at Hampton Institute taught him that one could be conciliatory toward them in order to gain resources. Moreover, he was clever enough to gauge that their power could be overwhelming in the South and therefore African Americans had to be wily to move among its perilous reality. Second, Washington advanced the notion of social separation during his Atlanta address in 1895 simply to hand them something that could be viewed in terms of mutual progress. In other words, he implied, "Leave us be, allow us to build our homes, communities, and economic base, and you do your thing without harming us." Third, he suggested that there should be fairness in the voting system; he expected the best of both groups to be allowed to exercise their right to vote, but agitation would not be efficacious. Finally, fourth, African Americans would comply with getting on with their lives in a cooperative relationship, but they would expect fairness in return for such compliance. Karenga goes on to explain that Washington worked within a system of white supremacy that was ugly and hateful and he operated as a cautious man while building his empire at Tuskegee Institute (Karenga 2010, 137–138). The fact is quite straightforward: Washington was a very skilled operator who was able to gain resources from rich white philanthropists to build an institution in the heart of the Black Belt. It was a remarkable feat by Washington, but with such success there often follows envy, deceit, and disruptive trickeries from those who wanted to limit this growing prestige.

Another scholar known for his forthright analysis and iconoclasm is Harold Cruse (1916–2005). In his best-known work, *The Crisis of the Negro Intellectual*, published in 1967, he explains how Washington's perspective was actually the most practical, and that Du Bois was fundamentally incorrect in the debate between the two men. Cruse explains Washington's main ideas as pushing African Americans to first gain education, property, and strong character, then the issue of civil rights would be settled naturally in due course. Cruse put it this way: "As far back as 1900, Booker T. Washington counseled the [African American] to seek economic self-sufficiency; to soft-pedal civil rights and social equality until he was on the road to achieving his own 'economic' base for survival." He further explains, "Although the ordinary [African American] has always understood the fundamental wisdom of his advice, his middle-class civil rights leadership (both Left and Reform) has chosen not to" (Cruse 1984,

175). This is a crucial intervention by Cruse for so many had drank the "Kool Aid" criticism of Washington because it was led by the erudite Du Bois. In a sense, Du Bois was deemed "untouchable" due to his reputation as such a good scholar; as such Washington's legacy was low-hanging fruit for critics.

Even respected scholars like John Henrik Clarke avoided the issues in critiquing Du Bois in regard to Washington. Indeed, Clarke (1991) writes a rather critical essay in *The Crisis of the Negro Intellectual*, and it appears to the reader that he is systematically addressing the entire book, but Clarke overlooks Cruse's perspective on Du Bois in relation to Washington. It is interesting because though Clarke was a Marcus Garvey admirer, he could not see the efficacy of Washington's philosophy and opinions in relation to Du Bois's critique of him because he fails to address Cruse on the topic. This could be related to the "untouchable" aspect of the doyen scholar Du Bois, as there have rarely been profound assessments of him (Clarke 1991, 365–381). Cruse was one of those few bold writers whom younger scholars admire, for he pulled no punches with his overtly refreshing writings. On Du Bois he was pleasingly correct: "Ever since the 1930s, both radical and reform [African American and white] intellectuals have refused to admit that despite Du Bois's brilliance and scholarly achievements, he has, several times, been grievously wrong" (Cruse 1984, 176). Yes, Du Bois was wrong and flawed like most other thinkers. Du Bois's support for the overtly racist President Woodrow Wilson may count as one of his profound errors. Yet, most often Du Bois comes across as sanctimonious and overly blameless in his statements on Washington. Moreover, for too long Du Bois has gone by without systemic critique in regard to his notion of a Talented Tenth leading the supposedly ignorant and maligned masses of African Americans. It was rather instructive of him to think that all culture and civilization comes from the top down, when in fact it is the bottom up that tends to create wealth, fight wars, which then often allows the freedom for those in the Tenth to pontificate ideas. Grassroots educators and their philosophy in mobilization and struggle have always propelled African American liberation, not the top down Ivy League, or Talented Tenth, academics. For example, it was the grassroots men and women in the Church who propelled the civil rights movement of the 1950s and 1960s.

Unlike Du Bois, Washington was a bottom-up man; he never displayed pomposity in his demeanor, especially toward his people. When his humor employed the idiom of the rural African American farmer, it was to share fundamentally their wisdom and not to denigrate. But this has been used against him when the left and reformist scholars, as Cruse explained, took to their typewriters or computers. The legacy of Washington should be released from this fossilization and set free for future generations to learn

> ### Marcus Garvey (1887–1940)
>
> Garvey was born in St. Anne's, Jamaica, and was raised by a strict father who had a love for books. He learnt the trade of printing and fought for the rights of workers. He traveled to Europe and South America between 1910 and 1912 where he met Duse Mohammed Ali (1866–1945) in London who ran the *African Times and Orient Review*, a newspaper that covered Pan African affairs. Garvey also read Booker T. Washington's *Up from Slavery* and was highly impressed with the idea of self-help and self-determination along with the idea of industrial education and the acquisition of property to aid African Americans. Garvey felt that the ideas offered by Washington could be expanded to the African Diaspora and the African continent. By 1920, Garvey's Universal Negro Improvement Association (UNIA) and the African Communities League (ACL) were the largest Black nationalist movement the world had every known, offering, with the help of his paper *The Negro World*, much-needed inspiration to his followers in the United States and around the world. Booker T. Washington was a major influence on some of his key ideas.

the holistic side of a wonderful human being who internally laughed at white supremacy. What has ordinarily been expressed in reference to Washington and his broad participation in African American life has been too narrow and rather myopic in scope.

Writing in 1967, Dr. Martin Luther King Jr. conveyed his thoughts on Washington, at probably one of the worst periods to assess him because this was the Black Power era. The more militant younger generation of the African American civil and human rights movement were not in tune with figuring out the many nuances to Washington who had literally and figuratively been dead and buried for over fifty years. Dr. King wrote, "Booker T. Washington tried his path to patient persuasion. I do not share the notion that he was an Uncle Tom who compromised for the sake of keeping the peace. Washington sincerely believed that if the South was not pushed too hard, that if the South was not forced to do something that it did not for the moment want to do, it would voluntarily rally to the [African American's] cause" (King 1968, 129). If anyone could comprehend Washington's life it was Dr. King, who also came out of the South, and who had made his commitment to dismantling segregation in the 1950s in Montgomery, Alabama. The seemingly insuperable racism was still prevalent in Dr. King's era. He continues to explain why Washington failed in his conceptualizing the intractability of racism in the South: "Washington's error was that he underestimated the structures of evil; as a consequence his philosophy of pressureless persuasion only served as a springboard for racist Southerners to dive into deeper and more ruthless oppression of the [African American]" (129). There is something rather poignant about having Dr. King assess Washington's legacy some fifty-plus years after the passing of the Tuskegee Institute leader. Because in 1967 Dr. King was also often disparagingly regarded as an "Uncle Tom," and it could not be further from the reality. Like Washington he hoped for reconciliation instead of continuous conflict with the diehard racists of the Deep South, and the liberal racists of the Shallow North. Dr. King was fundamentally a man of peace who could relate to Washington who was similar in personality: calm, cool, and collected. Neither of them raised their voices in anger but quietly and efficiently did what they could to improve the liberation prospects of all African Americans. It was a tall order, anyone who tries to confront institutional racism head-on receives an inevitable white backlash. Dr. King understood Washington's legacy probably more than anyone else in the 1960s, because he was actually, in many ways filling his shoes, attempting to find solutions to the roots of racism and its solutions just as Washington had been some sixty years previously.

Martin Luther King Jr. (1929–1968) was the moral leader of the twentieth-century Civil Rights Movement. He advocated nonviolence in the pursuit of an end to racism, poverty, and militarism. He won the Nobel Peace Prize in 1964. He was assassinated in Memphis, Tennessee, on April 4, 1968. (Library of Congress)

Too often "Uncle Tom" has been a denigrative term, and it needs to be unpacked. Especially when this phrase is largely misunderstood when associated with individuals like Washington and Dr. King. Only a fool would use such a spurious term against these men, but then there are many fools. Specifically, referring to Washington, Rebecca Carroll edited a volume of essays titled *Uncle Tom or New Negro?* The title itself deserves a mark of mean-spiritedness, as it actually implies the possibility of the negative without any thought. For example, if an African American woman marries a white man, is she simply an exotic foil for the white man? In other words, if one puts forward a negative, even if it is only a question, it can leave a sour feeling. That stated, the book revolves around considering Washington's *Up from Slavery* after one hundred years in publication. A number of writers have considered the either/or question about Washington's personality and demeanor, which in itself is a tall order given the fact that the man was extremely cautious with his feelings—and rightly so, given the times in which he lived and led.

The etymology of an Uncle Tom derives from the novel by Harriet Beecher Stowe, *Uncle Tom's Cabin* (1852), and the key character is Uncle Tom, an enslaved middle-aged African American male. The novel had an antislavery sentiment and was a major bestseller in the mid-nineteenth century. The Uncle Tom character, however, is a man who is obsequious and always trying to win the approval of whites. He is a willing cooperator and bent-backed in manner, excessively obedient toward white people. When one attaches such a character definition to an African American or person of color, it is deemed contemptuous and offensive. To attach the term to African American leaders who try to work within the mainstream of society to improve racialized relations is rather belittling.

The question remains, Was Booker T. Washington an Uncle Tom? The short answer is no, but one can comprehend why in some of his utterances there are those who would disagree. Avon Kirkland is a filmmaker and he considers Washington as both a triumphant and tragic figure in the sense of his life. It is a Jekyll and Hyde portrait of the man, but is this point not true of most men and women? Is there not the good and the bad in all persons? In an essay Kirkland asked, "I've been looking for somebody in academe to give me a theory of his [Washington's] personality" (Kirkland 2006, 63). Well, this biography has endeavored to answer his request throughout these pages. In short, Washington was a private man, a cautious man, and one who harbored no bitterness toward anyone, regardless of the evil that has been bestowed on him. He was a man with a calm temperament. He was also very grateful to those who displayed kindness to him, whether African American or white. It is understandable that those who cannot work out his personality would find him weak toward whites, and ingratiating. He did at times give the wrong impression, but if you follow his work behind the scenes, as Harlan (1972, 1983) has alluded, he was a man who did not bow down to white supremacy. Kirkland, it should be pointed out, writes about staying in Harlan's home as he prepared the final chapter of his two-volume, almost one thousand pages, biography. He recalls Harlan being confused about how to end his story in the second volume, and that all he could come up with was to conclude "Washington was an enigma" or a mystery.

Of course, Washington was a mystery in one sense; he was a man who had come out of enslavement, who had his psychological wellbeing attacked from a very young age. He rose to become an extremely hardworking man in part, it seems, to make up for lost time and to prove to the world that if given an opportunity African Americans would not only succeed but excel. Kirkland, when criticizing Washington, falls into the fossilized version, citing Du Bois and clichés that lock into place any hope of redeeming his rightful place as a brilliant African American historical figure. Even though Kirkland himself is from the South, and knows too well the social forces that pinned African Americans against the wall, he cites Du Bois as the top dog who never gave up on the humanity of his people. Kirkland forgets how Du Bois regarded 90 percent of African Americans unfit for civilization and in need of the Talented Tenth to save them. Kirkland overlooks the fact that Washington had the lives of others to care for at Tuskegee Institute where over one hundred faculty members and over one thousand students were under his leadership. How could an African American male with so much responsibility be overtly outspoken without putting their lives in jeopardy? It is ludicrous to contend that Washington had the space to openly shout down white supremacy; the best way for him was to *prove* them wrong by graduating hundreds of talented, cultured, young African Americans from his institution.

Kirkland also makes the unfound accusation that Washington merely used the National Negro Business League to suppress his critics. Clearly he did not read any of the minutes of the sessions that were all about expanding African American businesses and providing best practices in order to be successful. This is not Uncle Tomism, but Kirkland is among those critics who take Washington apart employing his good friend, Harlan, and his untouchable hero Du Bois. Washington *himself* has no opportunity to respond back; his life is shaped therefore by those who follow the line of the fossilized version (Kirkland 2006, 57–67). Crucially, if Washington was an enigma—and that is something one could apply to many historical figures—he still had a life that defied logic, and his achievements far outweigh any human inadequacies.

Kirkland does not mention Washington's wives, each rather powerful women in their own right. His third wife, Margaret, was not a woman who would put up with an Uncle Tom. She was too strong in character, and she did much to improve Washington's oratorical skills; she assisted him in crafting the famous Atlanta address (Harlan 1983). Washington's legacy should note how much he supported, and was supported by, all three wives. He was a good father and a good husband, who did all he could to provide for them and his extended family members. These are not the actions of an unmanly individual, but that of a man committed to his institution and his family. Kirkland and others use the stereotype that Washington did not care for higher education, but most of his teachers were recruited from higher education institutions. The point that needs to be emphasized is that future readers need to take a broader look, and not focus so much on the few words he employed to keep racist white folks confused.

The power of the fossilized version of Washington is rather ubiquitous. Even the great writer Ralph Ellison, in his acclaimed novel, *Invisible Man*, apparently employs a character based on the stereotyped version of Washington. Ellison actually spent three years at Tuskegee Institute from 1933 to 1936 in the music department, but left without receiving his diploma. Washington was gone some twenty years, so how he managed to characterize him must have been based on his thoughts and experiences at Tuskegee Institute. For any artist in the liberal arts, like Ellison, who was fundamentally a writer and musician, it would not have been a good fit. Tuskegee Institute had rather strict rules, and was puritanical in culture, focusing on personal discipline, because it was based on Christian ascetic values. Therefore his parody of Washington may have come from a more bitter experience of not having fit into the culture of Tuskegee Institute and puritan self-control. Most writers and cultural artists have hedonistic, racy, lifestyles that would probably find asceticism rather stifling. This is speculative but Ralph Ellison did leave Tuskegee Institute without receiving his diploma, even after applying on a number of occasions to gain entry, which in itself appears incongruous.

Again, this is conjecture, with a pinch of realism, but Dr. Bledsoe in the *Invisible Man* appears to be a caricature of the fossilized Washington created by Du Bois and others. Ellison's novel was published in 1952, so it was in line with the Du Bois/Aptheker anti-Washington rhetoric. Could it be that Ellison was influenced by Du Bois's writings on Washington, along with his bitter experience as a student at Tuskegee Institute? The upshot of it all is that the Dr. Bledsoe character in *Invisible Man* is another extension of the Washington caricature. Therefore the question of him being an Uncle Tom has been rather salient, but the fact is Washington was far more complex than such a simple character. As Dr. King stated, he did not regard that term suitable to Washington. But he did state that Washington underestimated the viciousness of the Southern racists when he expected conciliation and an end to violence. Furthermore, what he did not consider was the extent of envy those poor white Southerners harbored toward African Americans who had gained prosperity. The attacks on the African American communities in Greenwood-Tulsa, Oklahoma, in 1921 and Rosewood in Florida in 1923 exemplify the dangers faced by African Americans in the South. Both communities were burned to the ground by white mobs. It was Booker T. Washington who dubbed Greenwood in

Tulsa, an extremely affluent African American community, as the Black Wall Street. In an attack on the stores, banks, and homes that lasted just over a day from May 31 to June 1, 1921, all the stores were looted and burned to the ground with approximately three hundred African American souls murdered. Countless atrocities took place in the South and lynching was a favorite pastime for the virulent racists (Allen 2004; Ginzburg 1988).

In January 1923, Rosewood in Florida was burned to the ground, and African American women and children were killed, all because a white woman *alleged* that she had been assaulted by an African American male. Usually that is all it took to have anyone murdered or maimed. Lynching became a pastime in the South, and a form of social control that instilled fear in the African American population. Evil and envy was at the heart of most of the attacks on African Americans, and this is what Dr. King stated Washington failed to comprehend when he sought conciliation between whites and African Americans. Bullies do not give up unless there is a power bigger than them. Washington used his skill to navigate the power of the white liberal rich, and with trustees on the Tuskegee Institute board it was a form of security for the all–African American faculty and students. He was a clever man, rather courageous, and he found racialized prejudice rather absurd. Keep in mind, Washington, just a few years after stating "we can be as separate as the fingers in all things social," was dining at the White House with the most powerful white man on earth. He was despised for that, and he knew he would be, so it shows how much he really thought about social segregation. The absurdity of racism was not something he considered to be intellectually sound. His travels in Europe taught him about the poor Europeans and how they too most often only required the chance to live and breathe the fresh air of opportunity to access their potential. This is something he always knew about humans, no matter how downtrodden they have the capacity to rise up from poverty and ignorance. In comprehending the poor of Europe it allowed him to assess more thoroughly the poor whites of the South (Washington 2015).

What is certain in assessing the legacy of Washington is the fact that he did not invent his life in enslavement, but he had to find a way to survive it and its aftermath. The notion and idea of white supremacy had been around a very long time, but its systemic practice found a life in the so-called New World (Christian 2002a). That world was occupied for thousands of years by people of color, and added to the Indigenous peoples were Africans involuntarily from the continent. The story of the African American was captured by a keen observer in Washington (2007), and when one looks deeply at both European and African history in the manner that he did, these are not the actions of an ignorant man who felt, in any way, inferior to another people, because he knew through study the good and the bad of both cultural groupings. Washington was a profound observer of human behavior, and he found white supremacy rather incredulous and absurd. It is merely a method in maintaining social power over an oppressed and disempowered people—usually based on unfair and inhumane means.

This is overlooked by many, if not all, commentators when examining his life. Because he was an "enigma" to one biographer does not mean he was to all. To be frank, a white biographer who has never had to deal with life within the veil of "otherness" will find it difficult to comprehend the mind of any person of color, male or female. White experience is one of overall privilege in Western societies, and this should be taken into consideration when assessing the life of an African American being examined by a white biographer. Put another way, can a man ever fully understand the life of a female? He may have a good attempt, but at bottom there is nuance to womanhood that only a woman can explain. A woman has to deal with sexism and patriarchy; some cope with aplomb, some fight it with gusto, and some resign themselves to "this is the way of the world" and therefore get on with it. A man can never fully understand the life of a woman, period. Well, the same could be stated about the role of a white biographer examining the life of a person of color. Without visceral understanding there is something missing in the experience of comprehending such a life.

On the topic of women, Washington is rarely noted as a man who enjoyed being with competent and strong women in his life. His legacy should involve the fact that he embraced powerful women. In his book *Working with the Hands*, published in 1904, there are chapters specifically dedicated to women and their obvious importance in the uplift of African American communities. This may be obvious to the reader in the 2020s but in the late 1800s and early 1900s women's rights were not secured, nor could they vote until 1920. So to be empowering women as Washington did was something progressive in the Victorian age. When he started a Farmer's Conference in 1892, there was a need to involve women in the development of this local community enterprise in Tuskegee and beyond. Washington wrote, "Perhaps they did not dream that they [women] would someday have a vital part in the uplifting of our people.... What can these poor farmers do with the new ideas, new hopes, new aspirations, unless the women can be equally inspired and interested in conferences of their own?" And through the work of his third wife, Margaret, organizations were established that catered to the needs and aspirations of women. Margaret was a powerhouse and her work in the empowerment of women has yet to be fully explored. She was involved in many areas, particularly the health and well-being of women, and in anti-lynching protest. A highly educated and sophisticated graduate from Fisk University, who knew Du Bois personally from her time there, she complemented Washington's down to earth style with a refined charisma. Washington was a man who encouraged his women to be copartners in his life, and this is an important facet of his personality that is overlooked. He would support Margaret in her development of women's rights, hopes, and aspirations unlike many men of his era (Washington, *Working*, 2007, 119–134).

In addition, Washington was keen to develop working opportunities for women, and this again was rather innovative during the Victorian era. After a trip to England where Washington observed middle-class young women in an agricultural college (in Swanley, England) doing all kinds of subjects from botany to horticulture he was inspired to bring a similar opportunity to women at Tuskegee Institute. Therefore without looking deeper into the actions of Washington and seeking the actual implementation of his pedagogy this could be lost to history. He was an innovative and progressive man in terms of the empowerment of women in an age when it was not popular to be so. With the assistance and support of Margaret, women at Tuskegee Institute broke off the stereotypes and found new skills to ensure opportunity for growth in their talents (107–118). Although he was a private man, if one examines his motives carefully it can be gauged that he was sincere in his love and hopes for women in general. Often the man of color who has suffered the slings and arrows of discrimination finds it natural to side with the rights of women to be empowered. Washington, along with Frederick Douglass before him, did what they could to empower women because they knew it was the right thing to do—even Du Bois was noted for his support of women's rights.

In an excellent study, Dagbovie (2007) covers a century of scholarship that has assessed Washington. Most, if not all, however, has been framed within the Du Boisian framework that basically fossilized the man. No study, before this, has reached to integrate Washington's words from his numerous publications and correspondence, apart from *Up from Slavery*. Harlan has framed Washington as an enigma, a man obsessed with power, and quite frankly this is offbeat. Marable, a Du Bois and Aptheker scholar, continued the tradition in blaming Washington for all things that Du Bois put forward: accommodationist, disenfranchisement, declined to support higher education, and sundry—all within the anti-Washington Du Bois frame of reference. Dagbovie (2007) is adept at putting together the key elements of criticism, but he fails to follow through on exactly *why* and *how* the Du Bois perspective was so prominent and prevalent throughout the twentieth century. There is no fact-checking by Dagbovie on the ideology of the scholars, who tended to be anti-capitalist, anti-Black nationalist, and anti-Cultural nationalist. Washington straddles all three, plus the integrationist model because, at bottom, he was nonaligned. He was, as Du Bois stated, a man between the Southern whites, the African American elites, and the Northern whites; yet what is left out, maybe conveniently, is his fundamental aim to empower the rural African American masses whom he predominantly served via Tuskegee Institute—he not only served them, but was of them, and admired them. More importantly, those who knew him best were rarely cited by Du Bois, Cox, Franklin, Aptheker, Marable, and others. Emmett Scott, arguably his most trusted secretarial assistant, is not cited by any of those who wrote on Washington, other than Harlan (1972, 1983), who implicitly portrays Scott as a central figure in Washington's subterfuge and maintenance of his power. It is rather disconcerting because any African American leader would need to be careful, cautious, and clandestine if he were working to improve the entire culture. What has been tragically missed in the dumbing down of Washington's legacy is what he was actually *doing* to help anyone who came in his orbit of contact—even Du Bois himself had to acknowledge in writing the fine offer Washington had made him to come to Tuskegee Institute, though Du Bois never made this offer public knowledge (Aiello 2016, 87–88).

Dagbovie (2007, 255) explains how Harlan downplayed the intellectual capacity of Washington, especially in comparing him to Du Bois. What he did not continue to delve into is the damage that has been done to Washington's legacy, especially with Harlan, a white liberal Southerner, holding the "key" to his life via his long-winded tenure as both biographer and editor of Washington's papers. The word in academic circles is that there are still literary boxes of Washington's correspondence yet to be compiled. So, in fact, there is still only a partial understanding of the enigma of Washington. What has been gleaned to date in terms of his overall profile does not fit with the holistic man that he was. He saw through racialized discrimination and did what he could to secure the resources available through philanthropy. He learned those skills first at Hampton Institute under his mentor, the white Christian liberal General Armstrong. His having a mentor who was basically a white missionary is problematic for many, but again one must analyze the outcomes. Tuskegee Institute surpassed Hampton Institute in terms of campus offerings, and Washington made sure the curriculum covered both "hands and head" instead of purely industrial training. None of his critics really deal with any of the internal workings of Tuskegee Institute, only to portray Washington facetiously as the "Master of the Tuskegee Plantation" (Harlan 1972, 272–287).

Harlan's work needs an overseer (pardon the pun) to carefully go through all that he has covered, and this would take at least a ten-year study, only cut short by the digital world making life easier for scholars. Clearly there are some problematic aspects to Harlan that have been overlooked. He never seems to award Washington any kudos; it is evident that he could not comprehend the man he studied for almost forty years. For example, Harlan constantly disparages Washington's scholarly output, mentioning ghostwriters to let the reader know that he had assistance writing his books. First, in all the books he published, he gave credit where credit was due. As for editing and ghostwriting, Harlan should have known that many academics employ them on a regular basis. But what is obvious in reading the books by Washington is that his "voice" is clear and pragmatic. This point can best be explained by considering the autobiography of Malcolm X (1992a). It was Alex Haley who wrote the book as Malcolm X dictated his life story to him, but one can unmistakably hear the voice of Malcolm X within the pages of the autobiography. The same can be stated for Washington; he had a distinctive message/voice, and it comes out in all the books published under his name. Therefore, in terms of his legacy, in the future there needs to be more emphasis put on *his* published works. Too much focus has been on what his critics thought and not on what the man himself thought. Much of his ideas are in writings published by him in book form, or in the correspondence between persons in his papers.

Dagbovie (2017, 255–266) rightly points out that "very few scholars deal with Washington's 'Sunday Evening Talks' which were full of wisdom and philosophical thought." He lists many other books of his that have been overlooked. More importantly, indirectly he refers to what this biography has endeavored to explain in this manner: *Booker T. Washington has been fossilized.* Once scholars come to terms with this reality, there will be other

---

MALCOLM X (1925–1965)

Malcolm X was born Malcolm Little in Omaha, Nebraska. His parents were activists for the Marcus Garvey movement in the 1920s and 1930s. The family home was attacked by the Ku Klux Klan (KKK), and later his father was killed by them. The family disintegrated after the killing of his father and his mother had a nervous breakdown and spent most of her life in an asylum. Malcolm was a gifted scholar in school but was put off by a white teacher who discouraged his ambition to become a lawyer. He drifted into petty crime before being caught and jailed for ten years. In prison at first he would not cooperate, but in time he met a Black Muslim member of the Nation of Islam (NOI) who, in addition to the information on Islam being sent by his two brothers, was instrumental in his conversion. Malcolm rose to become a powerful spokesperson for the NOI, and even more so after he left them in 1964. Malcolm X offers another example in the legacy of Booker T. Washington in terms of his perseverance to overcome adversity. Also, the legacy of Marcus Garvey could be traced back to Washington. Malcolm was dedicated to the uplift of his people, just as Washington was in his day. Malcolm X was assassinated in February 1965 by a group of NOI followers from a New Jersey mosque. His legacy continues to inspire many who follow his advice of getting educated to help one's community.

scholars besides Norrell (2009) and Wright (2015) who are pointing younger scholars to a more varied and holistic analysis of Washington. Again, Dagbovie (2007, 256) is correct when he points out that the two main sources to explain Washington's legacy start with his Atlanta Exposition address in September 1895 and end with *Up from Slavery* (1901). There are at least twelve other books relating directly to his work at Tuskegee Institute and to those who knew him well that should be consulted to attain a broader insight into the man. Any future studies on Booker T. Washington should start with a reading of Dagbovie's insightful 2007 essay on one hundred years of Washington scholarship.

One of those books alluded to by Dagbovie is Washington's *My Larger Education* published in 1911. In this book his voice is clear, definite, and resolute in relation to his ideas and in response to those of his critics. Washington answers questions on his perspective of the Atlanta Exposition address; this is sixteen years later. On reflection, he stated, "I felt that we needed a policy, not of destruction, but of construction; not of defense, but of aggression; a policy, not of hostility or surrender, but of friendship and advance. I stated, as vigorously as I was able, that usefulness in the community where we resided was our surest and most potent protection" (Washington 2013, 59). This makes sense in relation to what can be gleaned about his personality. He felt that the best thing for the South was to get past the conflict to reach a conciliatory relationship. To be sure, this was a somewhat optimistic approach but Washington was in essence a sanguine soul who did what he could to improve any situation. He was not a man to complain and mope around protesting the grievances that had been bestowed upon African Americans at the hands of the South. There was, for him, a need to go forward as a people in the hope that the white South would see the humanity in themselves and become less inhumane in the treatment of their neighbor: African Americans. Being a pragmatic man, combined with idealism, he endeavored to view the best in people. His critics would consider this weakness, but actually there is great strength in releasing any form of bitterness from oneself. Washington felt that resentment can only breed further hopelessness that leads to perpetual hatred, therefore everyone's losing out. Someone has to offer an olive branch in order to create peace and well-being; this was Washington's style. He was at heart a peacemaker who tried hard to make peace with the most vicious and cruel of enemies. He won many friends, and in another generation would have deserved the Nobel Peace Prize, but like with the Arab-Israeli conflict, during Washington's era whites in the South in relation to African Americans were a volatile mix of desire and aversion, with the latter being most prominent in the awkward relationship.

Although this biography has added a fuller analysis of Washington and his African affairs (see chapter 6), there is a need to emphasize some points. Even the perceptive essay by Dagbovie did not cover Washington's impact on African affairs during the late nineteenth century and early twentieth century. Primary documents have already been alluded to provide evidence, but a word on foundations in liberation theory should be noted. First, there is not one scholar-activist or political-activist from the African continent or African Diaspora who is without flaws. Name anyone from Martin Delany or Bishop McNeal Turner through to W. E. B Du Bois or Marcus Garvey, and all beyond or in between. Each had in their philosophical armory a "civilizing mission" for Africa. Take Du Bois, for example: he was drenched in the philosophy and canons of European thought and even his clothing style was so influenced. He has become a "Teflon Man" when it comes to critique in the Africana world, because nothing sticks to him; it is as if it is sacrilege to disagree with him. Yet closer scrutiny reveals a man with a massive ego, a penchant for mendacity when related to Washington, and a manipulator of historical fact through pleasing prose.

In terms of scholarship, Du Bois never once cited Washington, but Washington often quoted him. In completing this biography there could not be found in Du Bois's work one mention Washington's work in Africa. Even Du Bois's *The World and Africa* published in 1946 says nothing about Washington's support for Liberia, his work to fight the atrocities in the Belgian Congo under King Leopold II, his contact with South African Black nationalists, and his work in Togo directly linking Tuskegee Institute and African and African American exchange students. Washington even had an international conference at Tuskegee Institute in April 1912, bringing ideas from the continent of Africa and the Caribbean and South American regions. This has been underplayed by Marable (1974) who was a Du Bois scholar and an Aptheker mentee. If Africa was ever mentioned in relation to Washington, it would be couched in terms of him "working with the European colonizers" and "Missionaries" so to take the gloss off his Pan African activities. He could never be overtly Pan African with the eyes of white supremacy watching his every move; he was wily, savvy, and yes, sometimes he wore the mask. In order to secure a foothold in African affairs during this era one had no choice but to work with European colonizers in some capacity. The key here for future scholars is to comprehend that "footholds" are mere stepping stones to greater liberation. Without the first step on a journey of a thousand miles there is no journey. If Washington had, for example, spoke stronger words of "Africa for the Africans" then he would not have got a foothold in Africa. This is what happened to Marcus Garvey; he was a strong advocate for Africa and wanted to establish an African homeland in Liberia. Garvey, however, was thwarted by Du Bois and others (Martin 1976, 329). Du Bois had the ear of President Charles King (1875–1961) of Liberia and did what he could to block

Garvey's impact on the African continent—especially his entry into Liberia to develop a settlement for Africans in the Diaspora.

Amy Jacques Garvey explained it this way: "In June 1924 the U.N.I.A. [Universal Negro Improvement Association] sent out a team of experts to prepare camps for the colonists. They were: O'Meally, commissioner; William Strange, mining and civil engineer; Roberts, electrical engineer; Walcott, shipwright and builder; Hurley, carpenter and builder; Nicholas, mechanical engineer, and [George] Rupert Christian, Secretary. With these men went thousands of dollars of material for ready use on landing. Additional shipments on a later ship were contracted to be sent for, when there were storage facilities" (Garvey 1970, 151). Overall, as with Washington, Du Bois used the power of his pen to ridicule Garvey and his followers. It was underhand and rather sad that the so-called Pan Africanist had a large part in the downfall of Marcus Garvey (Martin 1976). It is worth recalling that the younger Garvey had been inspired by Washington's notions of self-help and property ownership coupled with thrift and hard work—then, and only then, could there be widespread uplift among peoples of African heritage.

Another element of Washington's Pan African legacy that's unexplored by his critics is his development of a study abroad program with African and African Caribbean students coming to Tuskegee Institute to learn from the late nineteenth century through to his death in 1915. This was Pan Africanism in motion, in action, and it has largely been ignored by scholars or undermined because it does not fit the staid narrative that has fossilized Washington for over a century. He was a master of his own fate, a captain of his own ship, who while under the most brutal era of white supremacy did what he could to help his people whenever and wherever he could. Washington should be remembered as one of the African American leaders who reached out to Africa, and in this sense he should be regarded as someone who participated in the origins of Pan Africanism (Wright 2015). It is unfair in a scholarly sense, or certainly bereft of decency, to ignore his protests and lobbying for social justice while Europeans were running ragged across the continent of Africa. His protest work in regard to the colonial Belgian Congo alone should put him in the annals of Pan African history. The current scholarship from Zimmerman (2010) and Wright (2015) demands a closer look at his African relationships, and if there follows a panoramic view of Tuskegee Institute in its interaction then it should be clear that Washington's approach was sincere and in the best interest of both Tuskegee Institute and African affairs.

Washington was a man of peace and his legacy should emphasize this fact. Dagbovie (2007) points out that Harlan (1972, 1983) employed "psychohistory" when trying to understand the essence of who the man was. This should stretch further into the realm of facetiousness because chapter titles in his first biography include "Boy," "Great White Father," and

"Master of the Tuskegee Plantation." Now if these chapter titles do not give the reader a sense of where the mind of the biographer is at, then maybe a critical reading class is in order, because this author finds them implicitly related to white supremacy. Indeed, the patronizing of Washington is evident throughout Harlan's work; though subtle in many ways and hidden beneath a veneer of "academic objectivity," it is implicit if one reads between his lines. With all due respect, most critical readers of color would comprehend the imbedded signs of indirect racism in the work of Harlan (1972, 1983). What is appalling for future generations is that Washington's legacy still largely emanates from Harlan's two-volume biography and his editing of Washington's papers. This is something future biographers will need to address in assessing Washington's legacy.

On a more positive yet insightful point, the poet Washington most admired was Paul Laurence Dunbar (1872–1906), an African American who was born in Dayton, Ohio. He wrote a poem that still resonates today, first published in 1895 titled "We Wear the Mask," and it reveals a part of the lives of many human beings:

> We wear the mask that grins and lies,
> It hides our cheeks and shades our eyes,—
> This debt we pay to human guile;
> With torn and bleeding hearts we smile,
> And mouth with myriad subtleties.
>
> Why should the world be overwise,
> In counting all our tears and sighs?
> Nay, let them only see us, while
> We wear the mask.
>
> We smile, but, O great Christ, our cries
> To thee from tortured souls arise.
> We sing, but oh the clay is vile
> Beneath our feet, and long the mile;
> But let the world dream otherwise,
> We wear the mask!

(Dunbar cited in Gates and Smith 2014, 906)

Washington has been depicted as a man who "wore a mask" in his life. This is rather an erroneous concept because all humans wear masks, which are *personas*, in public in some form or other (Goffman 1959). In African American culture, however, to "wear the mask" is to hide oneself from the white world, to give a false impression of yourself by laughing when you do not really want to, and smiling when really you want to scowl. This is the essence; it can also relate to telling lies in order to win favor with the white world. Again, who in this world has ever truly been honest about one's feelings when there is an authority in the midst? The entire idea of an African American being truly honest with one's feelings in the white world is an oxymoron, a cruel kindness. In other words, there is an inherent contradiction in the phrase; it is an obvious matter that would be assumed by the majority. It is contended here that Washington was a diplomat, a statesman, who chose his words carefully especially around potential enemies.

As stated, Washington was a very thoughtful man; he read the white world around him masterfully and knew instinctively what would rile or beguile his audiences. Did he wear a mask? Of course! But did he grin and shuffle like Stepin' Fetchit from the 1930s movies? No. The persona of Washington was sincere; he actually wanted conciliation with white Southerners. He wanted the best for all in the South, and across the United States. He was a humble man, who admired everything about ordinary African Americans. He did all he could for his students, many of who were mired in poverty. On Washington's genuine care for students, Emmett Scott, his trusted secretary, arguably knew him better than most and wrote, "He constantly insisted that the welfare of the students should be at all times the dominant consideration in the conduct of the institution. . . . To the delight of the students he would occasionally call a mass-meeting where he would call upon them one by one to get up and tell him of anything that was wrong, of anything that was keeping them from being as happy as he wanted them to be" (Scott and Stowe 2009, 174). In addition, if one reads Washington's *Character Building* (1903) there is wisdom and philosophical grounding in much of his words. Kindness to fellow human beings, looking out for each other, giving back, and staying focused on one's goals are just some of the themes he would discuss Sunday evenings with his students and faculty. This is a man who cared deeply about the welfare of his students above all else.

It is stated that he could be hard and meticulous with those subordinates who did not work 100 percent to the best of their ability. He was a tough leader, yet he never asked of anyone what he would not do himself. In essence, it was all about having a successful institution that would be an example of African American competence. Something that no one could deny was in the manner of which he led Tuskegee Institute without a hint of bureaucratic corruption. His persona was upright, though extremely cautious in the company of white Southerners who he knew detested his success and that of the students under his wing. Therefore the "mask" was necessary, and words of conciliation were often required. Historians have taken these parts of Washington and blown them up to conflate all that he stood for without examining him holistically. The most successful African American male, the most famous globally, between 1895 and 1915, had to walk like a fox on ice. For the majority of his life, he was able to do so, but there was one incident that remains a conundrum on his character.

In March 1911, he was in New York City for business, and he got caught up in situation that went viral at the time. Apparently he was in the wrong neighborhood, looking for a person on a Sunday evening in the Central Park region of West 63rd Street. In brief, he appeared to be loitering outside the home of what he deemed an acquaintance, but a white man, Henry Ulrich, saw things differently. He saw an African American hanging about and decided to beat him unmercifully; Washington fled but took repeated blows to the head that needed over a dozen stitches. If not for a plainclothes policeman, he may have been killed that evening near Central Park. At the police station they realized it was Booker T. Washington, and the assailant was arrested. This incident caught the attention of the newspapers, and Washington found himself in a potential scandal due to the area he was in being one frequented by ladies of the night. He denied any wrongdoing and that he was simply given the wrong address to meet a businessman. Washington was just under the age of fifty-five years when this incident happened to mar his unblemished career.

Although rumors circled, he managed to overcome the glare of publicity, and with the man who assaulted him being a person who had abandoned his family, he was deemed unfit as a character. Washington did not press charges, and the event disappeared from the public radar. However, this was a traumatic experience for the middle-aged Washington; he took a severe physical beating that evening, and it is assumed that the psychological scars ran even deeper. He was already a man suffering from poor health due to his unrelenting schedule. It is only fair to state that this experience in New York City did not aid in his recuperation. Regardless of this experience, he continued to work on persistently, driving himself on by sheer will and determination.

By 1913, with the advent of the Woodrow Wilson administration, the influence of Washington waned in politics. He had been an adviser to both Roosevelt and Taft, but when Wilson took office racism once again raised its ugly head. Segregation in the White House and policies that further stifled African American progress were implemented. Wilson was a Southerner and a thoroughly converted white supremacist; he had dangled a carrot toward African Americans before he attained office to secure votes, but once in he turned his back on social equality issues. Du Bois was one such African American who had supported Wilson and now was left forlorn at the prospect of his time in office. It seems that Washington was correct in not backing Wilson. As mentioned throughout this biography, Washington had a deep perception of those he could work or not work with. Wilson was not a Southerner who wanted African Americans to grow and prosper beyond mediocrity. Whereas Roosevelt, though racist himself, could work with Washington on certain projects that benefited African American empowerment, there was no chance of such with Wilson.

In his book published in 1935, *Black Reconstruction in America*, Du Bois has an insightful chapter titled "The Propaganda of History" whereby he assails the manner in which white historians distorted the era of Reconstruction in order to devalue African Americans and make them appear delinquent, corrupt, and unfit for freedom (Du Bois 1995, 711–729). No one could seriously disagree with the great scholar, but it does strike as a tad hypocritical given his distorting and fossilizing of Booker T. Washington through his historical accounts of their relationship. It seems in reading this account by Du Bois that he was fully aware of how historians can contort and twist facts and interpretations of the past to suit specific purposes. Therefore one may ask, Why did Du Bois persist in distorting the legacy of Washington? Unfortunately, Du Bois is no longer here to answer this question directly but there is a response from Washington that we can turn to.

The noted writer Ishmael Reed has written one of the best introductions to the many editions of *Up from Slavery*, and in his essay he cites Washington responding to Du Bois's charge that he did not advocate liberal arts education for African Americans. Washington complained in 1903 to the editor of the Indianapolis *Star*, stating, "He [Du Bois] knows perfectly well I am not seeking to confine the [African American] race to industrial education nor make them hewers of wood and drawers of water, but I am trying to do the same thing for the [African American] which is done for all races of the world, and that is to make the masses of them combine brains with hand work to make the masses of the extent that their services will be wanted in the communities where they live" (See Reed 2010, xv). Du Bois did know because he visited and spoke at Tuskegee Institute, because he was part of publications that explained the full extent of the curriculum, and because Washington recruited faculty from both Fisk and Harvard Universities, the schools where Du Bois was educated.

It is time to reevaluate Booker T. Washington's legacy. Studies have begun to do so, but this biography has opened up the fact that Du Bois took many liberties with the historical truth. He managed to control Washington's legacy through his interpretation and with the aid of scholars from generations that followed. There was a particular anti-Washington sentiment due to his Atlanta Exposition address in 1895 coupled with his publication of *Up from Slavery*. These two sources have fossilized his legacy with few scholars taking into account the many other primary documents that could give a more holistic view of his life—and thankfully provided in this volume. The essence of this biography offers a perspective that brings to light evidence that has been buried or at least overlooked by generations of scholars. It is hoped that the existing generation of young scholars and those not yet born will at least find an alternative to the Du Bois viewpoint on the Tuskegee Institute builder.

Washington was fundamentally an institution builder and sustainer, and at the time of his death in November 1915, he was on a tour to raise funds for Tuskegee Institute. He fell ill after a speaking engagement and was taken to hospital in New York, where the doctors let him know he only had hours to live. Immediately he made plans to return to Tuskegee; the historical record states that he told the physicians, "I was born in the South, I have lived and labored in the South, and I expect to die and be buried in the South" (Scott and Stowe 2009, 237). After an arduous train journey, he finally reached his beloved home, The Oaks, on the Tuskegee Institute campus, where he passed away in the early hours of November 14, 1915. Ultimately, though he had been suffering from physical exhaustion, his death was due to severe high blood pressure. At the time of his death, it was 225 over 145; the normal count should be 120 over 80. Ironically, it is a disease that still afflicts African Americans in the present day due to the daily stress and pressures of life in a racist society.

Given the context of this biography, it would be relevant to conclude with some encouraging words from Booker T. Washington. The outlook emanates from his book *Character Building*, and the chapter is titled "Don't be Discouraged." He wrote, "Make up your minds that you are not going to allow anything to discourage you. . . . Those of you who have been inclined to be moody and morose, or have been inclined to feel that the whole world is against you, that there is no use to try and elevate yourselves, make up your minds that your future is just as bright as that of anybody else. Do this, and you will find that you have it in your own power to make your future bright or gloomy, just as you desire" (Washington 1903, 55–56). Thousands attended his funeral to bid farewell to a wonderful life in the history of African America. He was laid to rest on the grounds of his beloved Tuskegee Institute campus in a simple grave, no fanfare, just how he requested it to be.

Today on a beautiful campus Tuskegee University still thrives with nearly three thousand students and an endowment of almost $127 million (2018). The institution is international in reputation, offering undergraduate and graduate degrees up to the doctoral level. Booker T. Washington would be pleased to know that his legacy is wrapped up in a successful university that continues to offer both vocational and liberal arts opportunities. Tuskegee University has one of the best veterinary schools in the nation, along with agricultural, nutritional, engineering, nursing, business, and architectural studies, to name just some of the areas of study. When considering the life of a man who started this institution on July 4, 1881, with just thirty students in a dilapidated shanty, this is the story of dreams. Long live the spirit and legacy of Booker T. Washington, and may his life be *fully* comprehended and taught to future generations. Indeed, his life matters—as all Black lives continue to matter.

Timeline

1856
Booker T. Washington is born on April 5 in Franklin County, Virginia, on the plantation of James Burroughs.

1861
He is valued at $400 in the Burroughses' inventory of plantation property.

1861–1865
He lives through the Civil War and listens to stories from the elders regarding its progress.

1865
After Emancipation, his family moves to Malden, West Virginia. His mother, Jane, his brother, John, and his sister, Amanda, make the arduous journey to meet up with Booker's stepfather, Washington Ferguson.

1868–1871
Washington works during the day in the salt mine, and after some time he is allowed to attend an evening primary school for the first time. He is taught by William Davis.

1872
Aged 16 years he leaves home to make an arduous five-hundred-mile trek to enroll in Hampton Institute.

1875
He graduates with honors from Hampton Institute and is regarded as the best student of his mentor, General Samuel Chapman Armstrong.

1875–1878
He returns home to teach school in Malden, West Virginia.

1878
He spends eight months at Wayland Seminary in Washington, D.C.

1879–1881
He joins Hampton Institute as a faculty member and takes charge of a teaching program for newly arrived Native Americans.

1881
He becomes the first principal of Tuskegee Normal and Industrial Institute, which opens on July 4.

1882
He marries his childhood sweetheart from Malden, Fanny N. Smith.

1883
He completes the first permanent building structure at Tuskegee Institute, naming it Porter Hall after its main benefactor, Alfred Haynes Porter (1828–1902).

1883
June 6: Daughter Portia, his first child, is born.

1884
May 4: Fanny dies from lingering complications after most likely a fall from a stagecoach; she was approximately 26 years old.

1884
Marking his first major public speaking engagement, Washington gives a speech entitled "The Educational Outlook in the South" for the National Education Association in Madison, Wisconsin.

1885
The first class of Tuskegee Institute graduates.

1885
Washington marries Olivia A. Davidson.

1887
May 29: Booker T. Washington Jr. is born.

1889
June 2: Ernest Davidson is born.

1889
May 9: Olivia A. Davidson dies at the age of thirty-four years after being frail for some years.

1892
Washington establishes Farmer's Annual Conference at Tuskegee Institute in order to share agricultural techniques and best practices.

1892
He marries Margaret Murray; she outlives her husband by ten years and dies in 1925.

1895
September 18: He delivers the renowned "Atlanta Compromise" speech at the Cotton States International Exposition in Atlanta, Georgia.

1896
Supreme Court decision on *Plessy v. Ferguson* decides "separate but equal" public amenities and institutions are Constitutional—bringing federal segregation into law for almost seventy years.

1896
Washington becomes the first African American to receive a master's honorary degree from Harvard University.

1898
President William McKinley visits Tuskegee Institute.

1899
Washington publishes *The Future of the American Negro*.

1899
Construction of The Oaks, the family residence on the Tuskegee Institute campus, begins; the family moves in at the outset of the twentieth century.

1899
July 7: While on a European trip, the Washingtons attend a garden party at Windsor Castle with the host, Queen Victoria, and other guests.

1900
Washington's first autobiography *The Story of My Life* is published.

1900
August 23: National Negro Business League is established.

1900
Washington sends three Tuskegee graduates to Togo (Africa) to establish a cotton farm, having made contact with African dignitaries who had visited the Tuskegee Institute to learn about the teaching methods. A steady number of Africans and African Caribbean students enroll for classes as students abroad.

1901
He publishes his highly successful autobiography, *Up from Slavery*.

1901
October 16: He is the guest of President Theodore Roosevelt for dinner at the White House. This causes strife for both men due to the virulent racism and segregationist sentiment.

1903
July 30: At the "Boston Riot" Booker T. Washington is heckled by William Monroe Trotter at the local branch meeting of the National Negro Business League (NNBL). Trotter is arrested during the mayhem.

1903
Washington publishes *Character Building*, a collection of his Sunday evening talks to students at Tuskegee Institute that would hopefully inspire them to stay on track with their studies and life ambitions.

1904
January 6–8: Carnegie Hall Conference in New York takes place. It brings African American and white leaders from the North and South to discuss the "future of the race," largely in terms of business, education, and community.

1904
Washington lobbies President Roosevelt and Congress for the Congolese/Africans in their oppression under colonial Belgian rule and King Leopold.

1905
President Theodore Roosevelt visits Tuskegee Institute.

1907–1914
Washington works with President Roosevelt and President Taft administrations, U.S. State Department, and government officials from Liberia/Africa to aid in the African nation's development.

1907
The Negro in the South is published with two chapters from both Booker T. Washington and W. E. B. Du Bois. This is the first time they are both joint authors of a book, though Washington is the main energy behind its publication.

1907
Washington publishes a biography of *Frederick Douglass*. There is a chance W. E. B. Du Bois may have published this work, but the editor of the series, Ellis P. Oberholtzer, makes an error in contacting Du Bois after he has already negotiated with Washington the biography on Frederick Douglass.

1908
With the blessing and support of the U.S. State Department, Washington hosts the British explorer, colonizer, and exploiter of African territories and her peoples, Harry Johnston, at The Oaks in Tuskegee. They discuss the best way to aid Liberia and her future independence.

1909
He publishes *The Story of the Negro: The Rise of the Race from Slavery*, arguably the first comprehensive Black History survey book of its kind.

1911
He publishes *My Larger Education* and brings up to date his life and thoughts on education and the problems facing African Americans.

1911
March 19: Washington is violently assaulted in New York near Central Park by a white man; the National Association for the Advancement of Colored People (NAACP) has a resolution condemning the attack.

1912
Washington publishes *The Man Farthest Down: A Record of Observation and Study in Europe*, an extraordinary work, as it depicts the poor of Europe and states that African Americans in many ways were progressing much better.

1912
April 17–19: The International Conference on the Negro is held at Tuskegee Institute, covering African continental affairs and African Diaspora, in terms of the Caribbean, North and South American regions.

1912
September: Washington uses his influence to help his protégé, Alain Leroy Locke, gain an assistant professorship at Howard University. Locke would become renowned in his field of Africana philosophy being the editor of *The New Negro* (1925). This is largely hidden history because it does not fit the stereotyped version of Washington. Locke's career was mainly spent in higher education, in the field of liberal arts.

1915
March: Washington establishes an annual Negro Health Week, covering health and other social issues impacting the African American experience.

1915
While on a speaking engagement in New York, he suffers a debilitating illness caused by high blood pressure. His poor health has built up over a

number of years, largely due to physical and mental exhaustion. He insists on returning to Tuskegee by train against medical advice and dies in the early morning hours of November 14 at his home.

1915

At the time of his passing, November 14, 1915, Tuskegee Institute has over 200 faculty and 100 buildings, offers 40 different professions and trades to study, and has an endowment of $2 million (equivalent to over $50 million in 2020). Today, Tuskegee University continues his legacy with a $129 million endowment (2018) and a student body population over 3,000.

PRIMARY DOCUMENTS

Booker T. Washington, "Atlanta Compromise" Speech, 1895

In Atlanta on September 18, 1895, at the Atlanta Cotton States and International Exposition, Booker T. Washington gave what is now deemed his "Atlanta Compromise" address. The speech effectively catapulted him into national and international fame as the leading spokesperson for African Americans. Frederick Douglass had died seven months earlier in February, and symbolically it was suggested Washington would be the natural successor to lead African Americans into the twentieth century.

The speech itself is famous for yielding political power to whites in the Southern states in exchange for allowing African Americans freedom to educate their masses for skilled labor and to build their communities positively with land ownership and property. Washington stated: "In all things that are purely social we can be as separate as the fingers, yet one as the hand in all things essential to mutual progress." Effectively, he endorsed segregation and the slow march toward social equality for his people. It was better to "cast down your bucket where you are" and toil for a better future by building up education and skills required for industrial work and the maintenance of property ownership. He believed in self-help, self-determination, and self-pride—while developing greater harmony with the white hegemony. It was a speech largely lauded at the time, but in due course many African American intellectuals and leaders regretted his seeming capitulation to white supremacy—though this is a harsh criticism.

Mr. President and Gentlemen of the Board of Directors and Citizens:

One-third of the population of the South is of the Negro race. No enterprise seeking the material, civil, or moral welfare of this section can disregard this element of our population and reach the highest success. I but convey to you, Mr. President and Directors, the sentiment of the masses of my race when I say that in no way have the value and manhood of the American Negro been more fittingly and generously recognized than by the managers of this magnificent Exposition at every stage of its progress. It is a recognition that will do more to cement the friendship of the two races than any occurrence since the dawn of our freedom.

Not only this, but the opportunity here afforded will awaken among us a new era of industrial progress. Ignorant and inexperienced, it is not strange that in the first years of our new life we began at the top instead of at the bottom; that a seat in Congress or the state legislature was more sought than real estate or industrial skill; that the political convention or stump speaking had more attractions than starting a dairy farm or truck garden.

A ship lost at sea for many days suddenly sighted a friendly vessel. From the mast of the unfortunate vessel was seen a signal, "Water, water; we die of thirst!" The answer from the friendly vessel at once came back, "Cast down your bucket where you are." A second time the signal, "Water, water; send us water!" ran up from the distressed vessel, and was answered, "Cast down your bucket where you are." And a third and fourth signal for water was answered, "Cast down your bucket where you are." The captain of the distressed vessel, at last heeding the injunction, cast down his bucket, and it came up full of fresh, sparkling water from the mouth of the Amazon River. To those of my race who depend on bettering their condition in a foreign land or who underestimate the importance of cultivating friendly relations with the Southern white man, who is their next-door neighbor, I would say: "Cast down your bucket where you are"—cast it down in making friends in every manly way of the people of all races by whom we are surrounded.

Cast it down in agriculture, mechanics, in commerce, in domestic service, and in the professions. And in this connection it is well to bear in mind that whatever other sins the South may be called to bear, when it comes to business, pure and simple, it is in the South that the Negro is given a man's chance in the commercial world, and in nothing is this Exposition more eloquent than in emphasizing this chance. Our greatest danger is that in the great leap from slavery to freedom we may overlook the fact that the masses of us are to live by the productions of our hands, and fail to keep in mind that we shall prosper in proportion as we learn to dignify and glorify common labour, and put brains and skill into the common occupations of life; shall prosper in proportion as we learn to draw the line between the superficial and the substantial, the ornamental gewgaws of life and the useful. No race can prosper till it learns that there is as much dignity in tilling a field as in writing a poem. It is at the bottom of life we must begin, and not at the top. Nor should we permit our grievances to overshadow our opportunities.

To those of the white race who look to the incoming of those of foreign birth and strange tongue and habits for the prosperity of the South, were I permitted I would repeat what I say to my own race, "Cast down your bucket where you are." Cast it down among the eight millions of Negroes whose habits you know, whose fidelity and love you have tested in days when to have proved treacherous meant the ruin of your firesides. Cast down your bucket among these people who have, without strikes and labour wars, tilled your fields, cleared your forests, built your railroads and cities, and brought forth treasures from the bowels of the earth, and helped make possible this magnificent representation of the progress of the South. Casting down your bucket among my people, helping and encouraging them as you are doing on these grounds, and to education of head, hand, and heart, you will find that they will buy your surplus land, make blossom the waste places in your fields, and run your factories. While doing this, you can be sure in the future, as in the past, that you and your families will be surrounded by the most patient, faithful, law-abiding, and unresentful people that the world has seen. As we have proved our loyalty to you in the past, in nursing your children, watching by the sick-bed of your mothers and fathers, and often following them with tear-dimmed eyes to their graves, so in the future, in our humble way, we shall stand by you with a devotion that no foreigner can approach, ready to lay down our lives, if need be, in defense of yours, interlacing our industrial, commercial, civil, and religious life with yours in a way that shall make the interests of both races one. In all things that are purely social we can be as separate as the fingers, yet one as the hand in all things essential to mutual progress.

There is no defense or security for any of us except in the highest intelligence and development of all. If anywhere there are efforts tending to curtail the fullest growth of the Negro, let these efforts be turned into stimulating, encouraging, and making him the most useful and intelligent citizen. Effort or means so invested will pay a thousand per cent interest. These efforts will be twice blessed—blessing him that gives and him that takes. There is no escape through law of man or God from the inevitable:

The laws of changeless justice bind Oppressor with oppressed;

And close as sin and suffering joined We march to fate abreast...

Nearly sixteen millions of hands will aid you in pulling the load upward, or they will pull against you the load downward. We shall constitute one-third and more of the ignorance and crime of the South, or one-third [of] its intelligence and progress; we shall contribute one-third to the business and industrial prosperity of the South, or we shall prove a veritable body of death, stagnating, depressing, retarding every effort to advance the body politic.

Gentlemen of the Exposition, as we present to you our humble effort at an exhibition of our progress, you must not expect overmuch. Starting thirty years ago with ownership here and there in a few quilts and pumpkins and chickens (gathered from miscellaneous sources), remember the path that has led from these to the inventions and production of agricultural implements, buggies, steam-engines, newspapers, books, statuary, carving, paintings, the management of drug stores and banks, has not been trodden without contact with thorns and thistles. While we take pride in what we exhibit as a result of our independent efforts, we do not for a moment forget that our part in this exhibition would fall far short of your expectations but for the constant help that has come to our educational life, not only from the Southern states, but especially from Northern philanthropists, who have made their gifts a constant stream of blessing and encouragement.

The wisest among my race understand that the agitation of questions of social equality is the extremest folly, and that progress in the enjoyment of all the privileges that will come to us must be the result of severe and constant struggle rather than of artificial forcing. No race that has anything to contribute to the markets of the world is long in any degree ostracized. It is important and right that all privileges of the law be ours, but it is vastly more important that we be prepared for the exercise of these privileges. The opportunity to earn a dollar in a factory just now is worth infinitely more than the opportunity to spend a dollar in an opera-house.

In conclusion, may I repeat that nothing in thirty years has given us more hope and encouragement, and drawn us so near to you of the white race, as this opportunity offered by the Exposition; and here bending, as it were, over the altar that represents the results of the struggles of your race and mine, both starting practically empty-handed three decades ago, I pledge that in your effort to work out the great and intricate problem which God has laid at the doors of the South, you shall have at all times the patient, sympathetic help of my race; only let this be constantly in mind, that, while from representations in these buildings of the product of field, of forest, of mine, of factory, letters, and art, much good will come, yet far above and beyond material benefits will be that higher good, that, let us pray God, will come, in a blotting out of sectional differences and racial animosities and suspicions, in a determination to administer absolute justice, in a willing obedience among all classes to the mandates of law. This, coupled with our material prosperity, will bring into our beloved South a new heaven and a new earth.

Source: Washington, Booker T. "Address By Booker T. Washington, Principal Tuskegee Normal and Industrial Institute, Tuskegee, Alabama, at

Opening of Atlanta Exposition." African American Perspectives collection, Library of Congress, September 18, 1895.

James Creelman, "South's New Epoch," *New York World*, 1895

The following description of Booker T. Washington's Atlanta Cotton and International Exposition speech is a contemporary account by a journalist from a New York newspaper. It is important because it gives the modern reader an insight not readily found in previous biographies. For example, those African Americans in the audience that day were seen to be in awe of Washington's speech and did not view it is a bad thing to accept that "in all things that are purely social we can be as separate as the fingers, yet one as the hand in all things essential to mutual progress." The journalist describes one "ragged, ebony giant" African American in the audience as having "watched the orator with burning eyes and tremulous face until the supreme burst of applause came, and then the tears ran down his face." This is the depiction of awe and reverence for Washington's speech by his people that is not often taken into account. What biographers and historians have failed to do is consider more deeply the time and place, and that segregation was a matter of fact; therefore he could not do much in the form of a compromise other than implicitly secure less violence and intimidation from white Southerners.

Hence, was it really a "compromise" to suggest that African Americans would be comfortable with segregation as long as it was fair in scope, and that viciousness would cease against them? The essence of Washington's address was to promote peace and conciliation between white Southerners and African Americans; he did not give up the right to vote, but he did suggest that African Americans could take a step back in politics in order to focus on education, skilled trades, property accumulation, and overall economic stability. The following account gives a strong indication that he was convincing to both whites and African Americans, and maybe whites being pleased is the reason it has been too often misinterpreted out of social context.

Atlanta, September 18, 1895

While President Cleveland was waiting at Gray Gables to-day, to send the electric spark that started the machinery of the Atlanta Exposition, a Negro Moses stood before a great audience of white people and delivered an oration that marks a new epoch in the history of the South; and a body of Negro troops marched in a procession with the citizen soldiery of Georgia and Louisiana. The whole city is thrilling to-night with a realization of the extraordinary significance of these two unprecedented events. Nothing has happened since Henry Grady's immortal speech before the New England society in New York that indicates so profoundly the spirit of the New South, except, perhaps, the opening of the Exposition itself.

When Professor Booker T. Washington, Principal of an industrial school for coloured people in Tuskegee, Ala. stood on the platform of the Auditorium, with the sun shining over the heads of his auditors into his eyes, and with his whole face lit up with the fire of prophecy, Clark Howell, the successor of Henry Grady, said to me, "That man's speech is the beginning of a moral revolution in America."

It is the first time that a Negro has made a speech in the South on any important occasion before an audience composed of white men and women. It electrified the audience, and the response was as if it had come from the throat of a whirlwind.

Mrs. Thompson had hardly taken her seat when all eyes were turned on a tall tawny Negro sitting in the front row of the platform. It was Professor Booker T. Washington, President of the Tuskegee (Alabama) Normal and Industrial Institute, who must rank from this time forth as the foremost man of his race in America. Gilmore's Band played the "Star-Spangled Banner," and the audience cheered. The tune changed to "Dixie" and the audience roared with shrill "hi-yis." Again the music changed, this time to "Yankee Doodle," and the clamour lessened.

All this time the eyes of the thousands present looked straight at the Negro orator. A strange thing was to happen. A black man was to speak for his people, with none to interrupt him. As Professor Washington strode to the edge of the stage, the low, descending sun shot fiery rays through the windows into his face. A great shout greeted him. He turned his head to avoid the blinding light, and moved about the platform for relief. Then he turned his wonderful countenance to the sun without a blink of the eyelids, and began to talk.

There was a remarkable figure; tall, bony, straight as a Sioux chief, high forehead, straight nose, heavy jaws, and strong, determined mouth, with big white teeth, piercing eyes, and a commanding manner. The sinews stood out on his bronzed neck, and his muscular right arm swung high in the air, with a lead-pencil grasped in the clinched brown fist. His big feet were planted squarely, with the heels together and the toes turned out. His voice range out clear and true, and he paused impressively as he made each point. Within ten minutes the multitude was in an uproar of enthusiasm -- handkerchiefs were waved, canes were flourished, hats were tossed in the air. The fairest women of Georgia stood up and cheered. It was as if the orator had bewitched them.

And when he held his dusky hand high above his head, with the fingers stretched wide apart, and said to the white people of the South on behalf of his race, "In all things that are purely social we can be as separate as the fingers, yet one as the hand in all things essential to mutual progress," the great wave of sound dashed itself against the walls, and the whole audience was on its feet in a delirium of applause, and I thought at that moment of the night when Henry Grady stood among the curling wreaths of tobacco-smoke in Delmonico's banquet-hall and said, "I am a Cavalier among Roundheads."

I have heard the great orators of many countries, but not even Gladstone himself could have pleased a cause with most consummate power than did this angular Negro, standing in a nimbus of sunshine, surrounded by the men who once fought to keep his race in bondage. The roar might swell ever so high, but the expression of his earnest face never changed.

A ragged, ebony giant, squatted on the floor in one of the aisles, watched the orator with burning eyes and tremulous face until the supreme burst of applause came, and then the tears ran down his face. Most of the Negroes in the audience were crying, perhaps without knowing just why.

At the close of the speech Governor Bullock rushed across the stage and seized the orator's hand. Another shout greeted this demonstration, and for a few minutes the two men stood facing each other, hand in hand.

Source: Creelman, James. "South's New Epoch." *New York World*, September 18, 1895.

Booker T. Washington, Address before the National Educational Association, 1900

This address to the National Educational Association in July 1900 explains Washington's philosophy on education succinctly. In the first few paragraphs one can glean that he is putting his predominant white audience at ease, mainly Southerners. He indirectly ingratiates by claiming the African American was "rescued from heathen Africa" and has learned the culture of European Americans. *This is rather difficult to stomach, but the fact remains that all the great thinkers could at times be disparaging to the African continent: W. E. B. Du Bois and Marcus Garvey to some extent were both inculcated with what could be deemed "Western arrogance" when it came to their thoughts on the African continent. The negative effect of European education could impact the greatest of African thinkers. So do not be put off entirely by Washington's perspective, and remember too he was talking to a rather intellectually hostile, racially speaking, audience as an African American leader.*

That stated, if one reads the address very carefully as a rhetorical lesson it is very insightful, the way he employs short tales that are imbued with common idiom and folklore emanating from the African American Southern experience. Basically, he explains to his audience that it is not in the interest of the South to keep the African American mired in poverty and ignorance. Without his upliftment there will be no genuine prosperity. Moreover, to keep a people down only keeps the oppressor down too. The need is to foster good relations, industrial education that meets the needs of the South, coupled with academic knowledge. He does not dismiss liberal arts, he simply states it is important to build from the bottom up, not top down. That is, African Americans, of which there were ten million in 1900, need to build their economic power and property to develop a strong base for higher education pursuit. In other words, without the strength of a viable economic base there can be no hope for long-term prosperity that is commonplace. Crucially, the white South should be open to allowing the African American the space to develop their world without interference and social injustice. In turn, there is a need for helping each other build a broad and prosperous South that can compete with the North and West in agriculture and other industries.

Charleston, S.C. July 11, 1900

Ladies and Gentlemen: We stand tonight on historic ground. Charleston and South Carolina have made history—history that will always occupy a prominent place in the annals of our country. But South Carolina was never greater or prouder than tonight, when, with open arms and generous hospitality, she extends a welcome to the educators of America, regardless of race or color. The world is moving forward, not backward. Under the shadow of Fort Sumter we find ourselves tonight. If history be true, I think that it was nearly forty years ago that a little company of men, moved by a different spirit, clad in different uniforms, armed with different weapons, came to this vicinity to bring cheer, comfort, food, and reinforcement to an endangered, suffering, starving garrison. The army that comes into

Charleston today comes with guns beaten into plowshares, and swords into pruning hooks. It comes with no special regalia. Already we find that Fort Sumter has surrendered and Charleston is ours. It is in this spirit and with this object we come to you—to bring relief, the relief that comes from the spreading of education and intelligence, kindness and brotherly love, among all nations and all classes. It is when we witness such scenes as this that our belief in the ability of our country to work out all its problems becomes stronger, and that the education of all the people, in heart, head, and hand, will be the solution of all the trying problems that surround and confront this southland, where both races have had difficulties to contend with which no other people have ever met.

When we disarm ourselves of prejudices and passions, we must acknowledge that the white South owes much to the Negro, and that the Negro owes much to the white South. The Negro has a right to cherish love for the South. It was here that we came centuries ago in our heathenism, and here we were taught the religion of Christ; here we came without a language, and here we were taught the Anglo-Saxon tongue; here we came without habits of thrift, and here we were taught industry and economy. The Negro has a right to cherish memories of the South. In a large degree it has been the brawn and muscle of the black man that have cleared the forests, opened the mines, and built the railroads; that have grown the rice and cotton and the sugar—cane; that have made the South rich and prosperous.

In all discussion and legislation bearing upon this subject we must keep in mind that the Negro has a peculiar claim upon the conscience, the intelligence, and the hearts of the American people. You must remember that you are dealing with a race not only forced to come into this country against its will, but in the face of its most earnest protest. These people have a claim upon your intelligence and your sympathies that perhaps no other people can have. And, now that we are here, the great problem is that is confronting us is how to solve this problem in justice to southern white men, among whom the Negro must live, and in justice to the Negro himself.

During the last thirty—five years quite a number of suggestions have been made looking to a solution of this problem. A few years ago some six hundred of our people sailed from Savannah, Ga., bound for Liberia, and people said all at once: "We have found a way to solve this problem; our people have sailed for Africa, and the problem is solved." But those people forgot that on the same morning, here in the black belt of the South, perhaps before breakfast, about six hundred more black children came into the world.

I have a good friend in the state of Georgia who is very earnest in his belief that the way to solve this difficulty is to set aside some territory in the far West and put the Negro in it, and let him grow up there a distant race. There is difficulty in that way. In the first place, you would have to build a wall about that territory to keep the black man in it, and, in the second place, you would have to build a wall about it—and I suspect a much higher one—to keep the white man out of it.

I was on the train not very long ago with a gentleman who had a third suggestion. He contended that the problem was solving itself, because the Negro was so fast becoming a part of other races that there soon would be no Negro race in this country. There is a difficulty about that. If it is proven that a man has even 1 per cent. of African blood, he becomes a Negro every time; the 99 per cent. of Anglo—Saxon blood counts for nothing—the man always falls to our pile in the count of races. It takes 100 per cent. to make a white man, and 1 per cent. to make a Negro every time. So, you see, we are a stronger race than the white man.

The problem will not be solved in any of these ways. There is only one way to solve it—by treating the Negro with humanity and justice, just as I find the people of Charleston treating the black man today. When you go still farther in the study of this question, you will find that the Negro is the only race that has ever had the rare privilege of coming to America by reason of having a very special and very pressing invitation to come here. The unfortunate white race come here against the protests of the leading citizens of this country in 1492 and later; while, for some reason, we seem to have been so important to the business prosperity of this country that we had to be sent for, and sent for at great cost and inconvenience on the part of our white friends. And now we have the reputation of being rather an obliging and polite race; after having put our white friends to so much trouble, expense, and inconvenience to get us here, it would be rather unkind and ungracious on our part not to stay here.

At one time an old colored man in South Carolina sold a hog to a white man for $5. The white man paid his money, took the hog, and went on his way. When he got about half way home the hog got out of the pen and went back home to the old Negro, Uncle Zeke. About noon another white man came along and wanted to buy a hog; and Uncle Zeke sold him the same hog for another $5. The second white man went on his way home, and met the first coming back to Uncle Zeke's house for his hog. He said, "Mister, where did you get that hog? Uncle Zeke sold me that hog this morning for $5, and he got away from me and went back." "Well," said the other, "he sold him to me this afternoon." "How are we going to settle this thing?" said the first purchaser. "Let's go back and see Uncle Zeke about it," said the other. They went back to Uncle Zeke's and the first one said: "How about this hog? Didn't you sell him to me this morning for $5?" "I sure did," said Uncle Zeke. "Didn't you sell him to me this afternoon for $5" said the other man. "I sure did," said Uncle Zeke. "Well, how about this thing?" they said, "we don't understand it." Uncle Zeke said: "For Gawd, can't you white people go settle that thing among yourselves?"

Now, for thirty—five years, my friends, you white people of the North and of the South have been contending as to which one of you is responsible for bringing the black man into this country. Now that you are here face to face, I want you to get together and settle this thing among yourselves.

But I assure you, my friends, I am not here this evening to plead for education merely on behalf of the Negro. Those of you who understood slavery and what it meant will agree with me when I say that slavery wrought almost as much permanent injury to the white man during its existence as to the black man. And those of you who understand conditions as they are today in the South will agree with me that so long as the rank and file of our people are in poverty and ignorance, so long will there be a millstone about the nice of progress in the South. So I plead, not for the Negro alone, but in a higher spirit, that you will remove the burden of poverty and ignorance from both races throughout the South.

In a larger degree, if we would work out our problem as black people, we have got to consider the immediate needs that surround and confront us as a race; and in a brief, earnest manner get down to the bottom facts of our conditions.

At one time, in Alabama, an old colored man, teaching a Sunday—school class, was trying to cross the Red Sea without getting wet, and how the forces of Pharaoh got into the water. He said: "It was this way: When the first party came along it was early in the morning, and it was cold, and the ice as hard and thick, and they had no trouble in crossing. But when the next party came along it was 12 o'clock in the day, and the ice had begun to melt, and when they went on it, it broke and they went down." There was in the class a man who have been going to school, and he said: "I don't understand that kind of an explanation. I have been studying that kind of thing, and my geography teaches me that ice does not form so near the equator." The old minister said: "I was expecting just that sort of a question. The time I am speaking 'bout was before they had any gografys or 'quators there." That old minister, in his straightforward way, was simply trying to brush aside all the artificiality and get to the bedrock of common—sense; and that is what we have to do to lift our people up.

I claim that, in the present condition of our people, industrial education will have a special place in helping us out of our present state. We find that in many cases it is a positive sin to take a black boy from an agricultural district and send him to a school or a city where he is educated in everything in heaven and earth and has no connection with agricultural life, with the result that he remains in the city in an attempt to live by his wits. And again, my friends, you will find that in proportion as we give industrial training in connection with academic training, there go with it a knowledge and a feeling that there is a dignity, a civilizing power, in intelligent labor. And you will find at those institutions where industrial education is emphasized, and the student enable to work out his own expenses, that the very effort gives him a certain amount of self—reliance or backbone he would not get without such effort on his own part. When the Bible says, "Work out your own salvation with fear and trembling," I am tempted to believe it means about what it says. I believe it is largely possible for a race as well as an individual to work out his own salvation in a large measure in the field, in the college, in the shop, and with the hammer and the saw.

Once, in the South, and old colored man was very anxious to have turkey for his Christmas dinner, and he prayed for it night after night: "Lord, please send this darkey a turkey"; but no turkey came. So one night, when it near Christmas time, he prayed: "Lord, please send this darkey *to* a turkey"; and he got it that same night. I don't know how white people get hold of turkeys, but, my friends, we don't get hold of much, as a race or as individuals, unless we put forth something of the kind of effort that old black man put forth. There are three things as a race we have to learn to do if we want to get on our feet. We have to learn to put skill and dignity and brains into all our occupations. A few days ago a gentleman asked me in what way the North could protect the Negro in the exercise of his rights in the South. Help him to do things so well that no one can do them better. Help him to do a common thing in an uncommon manner, and that will in a large measure help to solve our problem.

The black man, in connection with all this, has to learn that we have to pay the price; that a race, like an individual, must pay the price for anything that it gets. No individual or race can get hold of something for nothing, it has got to pay the price—starting at the bottom, and gradually, earnestly, thru a series of years, working up toward the highest civilization. One of the hardest lessons for a race, like an individual, to learn is that it will grow strong and powerful in proportion as it learns to do well the little things about its doors. The race that learns this lesson may be retarded in its upward progress, but it can never be defeated. In a larger measure throughout this country the black man should seek to make himself, not a burden, but a helper to the community in which he lives; not a receiver, but a giver; not a destroyer, but a producer in the highest sense I want to see the Negro put that intelligence into labor which will dignify it, and lift it out of the atmosphere of sloth and drudgery into that atmosphere where people will feel that labor is glorified and dignified.

A short time ago I was in the state of Iowa, and I saw a white man out there planting corn, and this white man was sitting down upon some kind of machine. All the work this white man seemed to do was to hold back two fine spirited horses and keep them from working themselves to death. He was not only sitting down planting corn, but he had a big red umbrella hoisted over him. When it went over the ground, I think that machine plowed up the ground, and I think it made all the furrows; I am sure it dropped the corn in the furrows and covered the corn. I was in one or our southern states later, and I saw a black man planting corn. I saw him competing in the market with this white man in Iowa. He had a mule going about a mile an hour. He had a pole on the plow. The mule would go a step or two and stop, and he would get the pole and hit him to make him start again. He would go on again and stop, and the old fellow would go and get a stone and knock the old plow together. He would go on a little farther, and then the old fellow would have to stop and fix up the harness—made partly of rages and partly of leather. He would go on a little farther, and have to stop and fix his "galluses" before he got to the end of the row. He was what we call a "One gallus farmer"—had only a strap across one shoulder. He would go on in that fashion and plow up the ground, and other black man, with the same kind of mule, would come behind and put in the corn, and a fourth would come behind and cover the corn. Under no conceivable circumstances is it possible for that black man, following that mule in the South, to compete with that white man in Iowa sitting under that red umbrella. You are going to buy your corn every time from the individual who can produce it cheapest, no matter what his color; all you want is the cheapest and best corn. My object is emphasizing industrial education is to help the give the Negro boy in the South so much brain and skill that he can sit under a red umbrella, so as to make the forces of nature in a large degree work for him. When that is down we shall cease to buy our corn, and to compete as we do now in so large a degree with the West and the North. We will free the poor white boy and free the poor black boy in the South at the same time.

I was in Boston some time ago, and I saw a white man washing shirts; and, as usual, this white man was sitting down. You don't see a white man doing much work unless he is sitting down. But he "gets there"—he gets results, and results are what the world is looking for. When it wants corn and cotton, it does not care whether it is made by a black man standing up or a white man sitting down; all it wants is the best and cheapest corn and cotton. You must put brains and skill into all these common but important occupations if we would hold our own as a race in this country.

All this pertains to the material side, and not to the ethical, higher growth of the Negro, you say. I do not overlook or undervalue that side of our development. But show me a race that is living from day to day on the outer edges of the industrial world; show me a race living on the skimmed milk of other people, and I will show you a race that is a football for political parties. The black man, like the white man, must have this industrial, commercial foundation upon which to rest his higher life. The black man in the South is very emotional; but, my friends, it is hard to make a Christian out of a hungry man, whether black or white. I have tried that, but always failed. In proportion as the black man gets into habits of thrift and industry, in the same proportion he improves in his moral and industrial life. Would you think the average black man can feel as much in ten minutes as the white man can in an hour? In our religion we feel more than you do. When the black man gets religion he is expected to shout and jump around. If he does not, we get skeptical, and we say he has the white man's religion. This emotional side of our nature puts us in awkward circumstances sometimes. Some time ago a good colored woman in some southern city went to the Episcopal Church and they gave her a seat in the gallery. When the good preacher got warmed up in his sermon, the old woman got "happy" and got to groaning and singing. One of the officers of the church heard her going on and went to her. "What is the matter" he asked; "why do you disturb us?" She said: "I am happy; I got religion." "Why," he said, "this is no place to get religion."

But gradually throughout the South, as we watch the influence of this industrial education as it strikes the rank and file of our people in the corners of the South, it not only changes them into habits of industry, but it is helping them in that moral and religious life. Some time ago I met an old colored man going to camp meeting. I asked: "Where are you going?" "I am going to camp meeting," he said. "I haven't been in eight years, and now I am going. I heard you tell us some time ago to buy land and stop mortgaging crops. I followed your advice. I ain't been to camp—meeting in eight years, but I am going now, sure. I bought fifty acres of land, and I done paid the last dollar on it—ain't no man got a mortgage on it, and the wagon got a right to go to camp—meeting too this year. Do you see these two big mules? They belong to Sam. I paid the last dollar on them, and they got a right to go to camp' meeting. Do you see this bread in the basket? My old woman cooked the bread; I raised it, and the old woman cooked it. We are going to camp meeting, and are going to shout and have a big time. We have food in our stomachs and religion in our hearts."

Gradually we are changing the moral condition of the colored people throughout the South. We are making progress in the settlement of these problems. The black man is gradually buying land and teaching schools in every party of the South. The Negro is not only getting an education, but is fast converting the white man to believe in the education of the black man throughout this country. And in proportion as we can convince the white men in every part of the South that the education makes black men more useful citizens, in the same proportion will our problem as a race be solved. And I want you to remember that when you hear of crime being committed in the South, this crime is not being committed by the educated black men of the race. It is very seldom, if ever, that anyone has heard of a black man who has been thoroughly educated in industrial schools or in colleges committing any of these heinous crimes so often charged up against our race. In a larger degree you must learn to judge us by those in the schoolroom, and not by those in the penitentiary; by those who are in the field and in the shop, not by those on the streets in idleness; by those who have bought homes and are taxpayers, not by those in dens of misery and crime; by those who have learned the laws of health and are dying out. Keep the searchlights constantly focused upon the weaker elements of any race, and who among them can be called successful people? You judge the English by Gladstone, the Germans by Bismarck, the French by Loubet—by those who have succeeded, not by those who have failed.

We are making progress in another direction, and the Negro is not unappreciative of the opportunity the South gives him in this respect. Go out here about a mile from the center of this city, and I will show you a spectacle that perhaps no other city, in the North or West, can present—the spectacle of the white South giving to the black boy and the black girl an opportunity to work in a cotton factory. In proportion as we get these business opportunities, in the same proportion shall we go forward as a race.

At one time, in a certain part of the South, there was a white man who wanted to cross a river, and he went to a colored man nearby and asked him to lend him 3 cents to pay his way across the ferry. The colored man said: "Boss, how much money have you got?" The white man replied: "I haven't got any today. I am broke and in bad circumstances, and I want to borrow 3 cents to pay my way across the ferry." "Boss," said the colored man, "I know you are a white man, and I expect you got some sense than this old 'nigger,' but I ain't going to loan you no 3 cents. The man that ain't got no money is just as well off on one side of the river as on t'other." Now in reference to our race, I would say that a race that is without bank accounts, or property, or business standing, is just as well off on one side of the river as on the other. Whether we live in the North or the South, we have got to enter into the industries and enterprises of the community in which we live. And in proportion as we do that the whites will respect us more, not matter where we live.

Whenever a black man has $500 to loan there is never any trouble getting a white man to borrow it from him. I never heard of any such thing. A short time ago one of our men at Tuskegee tried to find how many bushels of sweet potatoes he could produce on a single acre of land. He got a yield last year of 266 bushels. The average production in that community before had been forty-nine bushels. When he produced those 266 bushels, you should have seen the white men coming to see how he did that thing. They forgot all about the color of his skin; they did not have any prejudice against those potatoes; they simply know there was a Negro who by his knowledge of improved methods of agriculture could produce more potatoes than they could. Every white man there was ready to take off his hat to that black man. Put such a black man in every community in the South, and you will find that the race problem will begin to disappear.

In discussing this problem further, I thank God that I have come to a point in the struggle where I can sympathize with the white man as much as I can sympathize with the black man. And I thank God further—and I make a statement here which I have make in our northern cities—that I have grown to the point where I can sympathize with even a southern white man as much as I can with a northern white man. To me "a man is a man for a' than and' that." And in exchanging this sympathy I believe as a race, we shall strengthen ourselves at every point; for no race, black or white, can go on cherishing hatred or ill—will toward one another race without itself being narrowed and drawn down in everything that builds character and manhood and womanhood. I propose that no race shall drag down and narrow my soul by making me hate it. I propose that the Negro, if possible, shall be bigger in his sympathies than even the white man, and if the white man in any part this country would hate us, let us love him; if he would treat us cruelly let us extend to him the hand of mercy; if he would push us down, let us help to push him up.

No race has ever made such immense progress, under similar conditions, as the black race of this country. You must not, however, measure us by the distance we have traveled so much as by the obstacles we have overcome in traveling that distance.

In conclusion, my friends of the white race, this problem concerns nearly ten millions of my people and sixty millions of yours. We rise as you rise, fall as you fall. Where we are strong you are strong. There is no power that can separate our destiny. No member of your race in any part of this country can harm the weakest member of mine without the proudest and bluest blood in your civilization being degraded. I believe the time has come in the history of this problem when the culture, the education, the refinement of the white South is going to take hold and help life the black man up as it has never done before. No race can oppress or neglect a weaker race without that race itself being degraded and injured. No strong race can help a weaker race without the stronger race being made stronger. Oppression degrades, assistance elevates. But you as white people and we as black people must remember that mere material, visible accumulation alone will not solve our problem, and that education of the white people and of the black people will be a failure unless we keep constantly before us the fact that the final aim of all education, whether industrial or academic, must be that influence which softens the heart, and brings to it a spirit of kindness and generosity; that influence which makes us seek the elevation of all men, regardless of race or color. The South will prosper in proportion as with development in agriculture, in mines, in domestic arts, in manufacture there goes that education which brings respect for law, which broadens the heart, sweetens the nature, and makes us feel that we are our "brother's keeper," whether that broader was born in England, Italy, Africa, or the Islands of the Sea.

Source: National Educational Association. *Proceedings and Addresses, 1900*. Washington, DC: Government Printing Office, 1900, 114–123.

Booker T. Washington, "Industrial Education for the Negro," 1903

In 1903, Booker T. Washington brought together a group of African American intellectuals and artists in order to cover the social problems facing their people. Among the thinkers, who each participated in active in political thought, were: W. E. B. Du Bois, T. Thomas Fortune, Paul Laurence Dunbar, and Charles W. Chestnutt. Washington brought them together and published an edited volume titled The Negro Problem. *What is significant about this book is that it was largely ignored by prominent scholars; even Du Bois himself failed to cite it. Perhaps it did not fit the historical narrative that Washington did not work with those who disagreed with him. Washington provides a careful explanation of his preferred education model (known as Industrial Education), while not dismissing academic skills, encouraging "the Negro to secure all the mental strength, all the mental culture—whether gleaned from science, mathematics, history, language or literature that his circumstances will allow."*

What is also significant about this edited volume is that the chapter directly following Washington's is Du Bois's notion of the Talented Tenth, a rather elitist view of there being ten percent of highly educated African Americans to teach the ninety percent ignorant masses. The fact that Washington's chapter preceded means he was comfortable having Du Bois's chapter respond to his perspective that related to teaching the masses. Other writers speak to the social issues they deem paramount facing African Americans at the dawn of the twentieth century. Crucially, this important book has been relatively lost in history. It needs to recirculate among scholars and be considered fully within its contemporary context. This is a book that was published the same year as Du Bois's The Souls of Black Folk *and deserves to be accounted for in terms of scholarly balance. Washington wrote the following chapter in regard to his view of industrial education.*

One of the most fundamental and far-reaching deeds that has been accomplished during the last quarter of a century has been that by which the Negro has been helped to find himself and to learn the secrets of civilization—to learn that there are a few simple, cardinal principles upon which a race must start its upward course, unless it would fail, and its last estate be worse than its first.

It has been necessary for the Negro to learn the difference between being worked and working—to learn that being worked meant degradation, while working means civilization; that all forms of labor are honorable, and all forms of idleness disgraceful. It has been necessary for him to learn that all races that have got upon their feet have done so largely by laying an economic foundation, and, in general, by beginning in a proper cultivation and ownership of the soil.

Forty years ago my race emerged from slavery into freedom. If, in too many cases, the Negro race began development at the wrong end, it was largely because neither white nor black properly understood the case. Nor is it any wonder that this was so, for never before in the history of the world had just such a problem been presented as that of the two races at the coming of freedom in this country.

For two hundred and fifty years, I believe the way for the redemption of the Negro was being prepared through industrial development. Through all those years the Southern white man did business with the Negro in a way that no one else has done business with him. In most cases if a Southern white man wanted a house built he consulted a Negro mechanic about the plan and about the actual building of the structure. If he wanted a suit of clothes made he went to a Negro tailor, and for shoes he went to a shoemaker of the same race. In a certain way every slave plantation in the South was an industrial school. On these plantations young colored men and women were constantly being trained not only as farmers but as carpenters, blacksmiths, wheelwrights, brick masons, engineers, cooks, laundresses, sewing women and housekeepers.

I do not mean in any way to apologize for the curse of slavery, which was a curse to both races, but in what I say about industrial training in slavery I am simply stating facts. This training was crude, and was given for selfish purposes. It did not answer the highest ends, because there was an absence of mental training in connection with the training of the hand. To a large degree, though, this business contact with the Southern white man, and the industrial training on the plantations, left the Negro at the close of the war in possession of nearly all the common and skilled labor in the South. The industries that gave the South its power, prominence and wealth prior to the Civil War were mainly the raising of cotton, sugar cane, rice and tobacco. Before the way could be prepared for the proper growing and marketing of these crops forests had to be cleared, houses to be built, public roads and railroads constructed. In all these works the Negro did most of the heavy work. In the planting, cultivating and marketing of the crops not only was the Negro the chief dependence, but in the manufacture of tobacco he became a skilled and proficient workman, and in this, up to the present time, in the South, holds the lead in the large tobacco manufactories.

In most of the industries, though, what happened? For nearly twenty years after the war, except in a few instances, the value of the industrial training given by the plantations was overlooked. Negro men and women were educated in literature, in mathematics and in the sciences, with little thought of what had been taking place during the preceding two hundred and fifty years, except, perhaps, as something to be escaped, to be got as far away from as possible. As a generation began to pass, those who had been trained as mechanics in slavery began to disappear by death, and gradually it began to be realized that there were few to take their places. There were young men educated in foreign tongues, but few in carpentry or in mechanical or architectural drawing. Many were trained in Latin, but few as engineers and blacksmiths. Too many were taken from the farm and educated, but educated in everything but farming. For this reason they had no interest in farming and did not return to it. And yet eighty-five per cent. of the Negro population of the Southern states lives and for a considerable time will continue to live in the country districts. The charge is often brought against the members of my race—and too often justly, I confess—that they are found leaving the country districts and flocking into the great cities where temptations are more frequent and harder to resist, and where the Negro people too often become demoralized. Think, though, how frequently it is the case that from the first day that a pupil begins to go to school his books teach him much about the cities of the world and city life, and almost nothing about the country. How natural it is, then, that when he has the ordering of his life he wants to live it in the city.

Only a short time before his death the late Mr. C. P. Huntington, to whose memory a magnificent library has just been given by his widow to the Hampton Institute for Negroes, in Virginia, said in a public address some words which seem to me so wise that I want to quote them here:

"Our schools teach everybody a little of almost everything, but, in my opinion, they teach very few children just what they ought to know in order to make their way successfully in life. They do not put into their hands the tools they are best fitted to use, and hence so many failures. Many a mother and sister have worked and slaved, living upon scanty food, in order to give a son and brother a 'liberal education,' and in doing this have built up a barrier between the boy and the work he was fitted to do. Let me say to you that all honest work is honorable work. If the labor is manual, and seems common, you will have all the more chance to be thinking of other things, or of work that is higher and brings better pay, and to work out in your minds better and higher duties and responsibilities for yourselves, and for thinking of ways by which you can help others as well as yourselves, and bring them up to your own higher level."

Some years ago, when we decided to make tailoring a part of our training at the Tuskegee Institute, I was amazed to find that it was almost impossible to find in the whole country an educated colored man who could teach the making of clothing. We could find numbers of them who could teach astronomy, theology, Latin or grammar, but almost none who could instruct in the making of clothing, something that has to be used by every one of us every day in the year. How often have I been discouraged as I have gone through the South, and into the homes of the people of my race, and have found women who could converse intelligently upon abstruse subjects, and yet could not tell how to improve the condition of the poorly cooked and still more poorly served bread and meat which they and their families were eating three times a day. It is discouraging to find a girl who can tell you the geographical location of any country on the globe and who does not know where to place the dishes upon a common dinner table. It is discouraging to find a woman who knows much about theoretical chemistry, and who cannot properly wash and iron a shirt.

In what I say here I would not by any means have it understood that I would limit or circumscribe the mental development of the Negro student. No race can be lifted until its mind is awakened and strengthened. By the side of industrial training should always go mental and moral training, but the pushing of mere abstract knowledge into the head means little. We want more than the mere performance of mental gymnastics. Our knowledge must be harnessed to the things of real life. I would encourage the Negro to secure all the mental strength, all the mental culture—whether gleaned from science, mathematics, history, language or literature that his circumstances will allow, but I believe most earnestly that for years to come the education of the people of my race should be so directed that the greatest proportion of the mental strength of the masses will be brought to bear upon the every—day practical things of life, upon something that is needed to be done, and something which they will be permitted to do in the community in which they reside. And just the same with the professional class which the race needs and must have, I would say give the men and women of that class, too, the training which will best fit them to perform in the most successful manner the service which the race demands.

I would not confine the race to industrial life, not even to agriculture, for example, although I believe that by far the greater part of the Negro race is best off in the country districts and must and should continue to live there, but I would teach the race that in industry the foundation must be laid—that the very best service which any one can render to what is called the higher education is to teach the present generation to provide a material or industrial foundation. On such a foundation as this will grow habits of thrift, a love of work, economy, ownership of property, bank accounts. Out of it in the future will grow practical education, professional education, positions of public responsibility. Out of it will grow moral and religious strength. Out of it will grow wealth from which alone can come leisure and the opportunity for the enjoyment of literature and the fine arts.

In the words of the late beloved Frederick Douglass: "Every blow of the sledge hammer wielded by a sable arm is a powerful blow in support of our cause. Every colored mechanic is by virtue of circumstances an elevator of his race. Every house built by a black man is a strong tower against the allied hosts of prejudice. It is impossible for us to attach too much importance to this aspect of the subject. Without industrial development there can be no wealth; without wealth there can be no leisure; without leisure no opportunity for thoughtful reflection and the cultivation of the higher arts."

I would set no limits to the attainments of the Negro in arts, in letters or statesmanship, but I believe the surest way to reach those ends is by laying the foundation in the little things of life that lie immediately about one's door. I plead for industrial education and development for the Negro not because I want to cramp him, but because I want to free him. I want to see him enter the all—powerful business and commercial world.

It was such combined mental, moral and industrial education which the late General Armstrong set out to give at the Hampton Institute when he established that school thirty years ago. The Hampton Institute has continued along the lines laid down by its great founder, and now each year an increasing number of similar schools are being established in the South, for the people of both races.

Early in the history of the Tuskegee Institute we began to combine industrial training with mental and moral culture. Our first efforts were in the direction of agriculture, and we began teaching this with no appliances except one hoe and a blind mule. From this small beginning we have grown until now the Institute owns two thousand acres of land, eight hundred of which are cultivated each year by the young men of the school. We began teaching wheelwrighting and blacksmithing in a small way to the men, and laundry work, cooking and sewing and housekeeping to the young women. The fourteen hundred and over young men and women who attended the school during the last school year received instruction—in addition to academic and religious training—in thirty-three trades and industries, including carpentry, blacksmithing, printing, wheelwrighting, harness-making, painting, machinery, founding, shoemaking, brickmasonry and brickmaking, plastering, sawmilling, tinsmithing, tailoring, mechanical and architectural drawing, electrical and steam engineering, canning, sewing, dressmaking, millinery, cooking, laundering, housekeeping, mattress making, basketry, nursing, agriculture, dairying and stock raising, horticulture.

Not only do the students receive instruction in these trades, but they do actual work, by means of which more than half of them pay some part or all of their expenses while remaining at the school. Of the sixty buildings belonging to the school all but four were almost wholly erected by the students as a part of their industrial education. Even the bricks which go into the walls are made by students in the school's brick yard, in which, last year, they manufactured two million bricks.

When we first began this work at Tuskegee, and the idea got spread among the people of my race that the students who came to the Tuskegee school were to be taught industries in connection with their academic studies, were, in other words, to be taught to work, I received a great many verbal messages and letters from parents informing me that they wanted their children taught books, but not how to work. This protest went on for three or four years, but I am glad to be able to say now that our people have very generally been educated to a point where they see their own needs and conditions so clearly that it has been several years since we have had a single protest from parents against the teaching of industries, and there is now a positive enthusiasm for it. In fact, public sentiment among the students at Tuskegee is now so strong for industrial training that it would hardly permit a student to remain on the grounds who was unwilling to labor.

It seems to me that too often mere book education leaves the Negro young man or woman in a weak position. For example, I have seen a Negro girl taught by her mother to help her in doing laundry work at home. Later, when this same girl was graduated from the public schools or a high school and returned home she finds herself educated out of sympathy with laundry work, and yet not able to find anything to do which seems in keeping with the cost and character of her education. Under these circumstances we cannot be surprised if she does not fulfill the expectations made for her. What should have been done for her, it seems to me, was to give her along with her academic education thorough training in the latest and best methods of laundry work, so that she could have put so much skill and intelligence into it that the work would have been lifted out from the plane of drudgery. The home which she would then have been able to found by the results of her work would have enabled her to help her children to take a still more responsible position in life.

Almost from the first Tuskegee has kept in mind—and this I think should be the policy of all industrial schools—fitting students for occupations which would be open to them in their home communities. Some years ago we noted the fact that there was beginning to be a demand in the South for men to operate dairies in a skillful, modern manner. We opened a dairy department in connection with the school, where a number of young men could have instruction in the latest and most scientific methods of dairy work. At present we have calls—mainly from Southern white men—for twice as many dairymen as we are able to supply. What is equally satisfactory, the reports which come to us indicate that our young men are giving the highest satisfaction and are fast changing and improving the dairy product in the communities into which they go. I use the dairy here as an example. What I have said of this is equally true of many of the other industries which we teach. Aside from the economic value of this work I cannot but believe, and my observation confirms me in my belief, that as we continue to place Negro men and women of intelligence, religion, modesty, conscience and skill in every community in the South, who will prove by actual results their value to the community, I cannot but believe, I say, that this will constitute a solution to many of the present political and social difficulties.

Many seem to think that industrial education is meant to make the Negro work as he worked in the days of slavery. This is far from my conception of industrial education. If this training is worth anything to the Negro, it consists in teaching him how not to work, but how to make the forces of nature—air, steam, water, horse—power and electricity—work for him. If it has any value it is in lifting labor up out of toil and drudgery into the plane of the dignified and the beautiful. The Negro in the South works and works hard; but too often his ignorance and lack of skill causes him to do his work in the most costly and shiftless manner, and this keeps him near the bottom of the ladder in the economic world.

I have not emphasized particularly in these pages the great need of training the Negro in agriculture, but I believe that this branch of industrial education does need very great emphasis. In this connection I want to quote some words which Mr. Edgar Gardner Murphy, of Montgomery, Alabama, has recently written upon this subject:

"We must incorporate into our public school system a larger recognition of the practical and industrial elements in educational training. Ours is an agricultural population. The school must be brought more closely to the soil. The teaching of history, for example, is all very well, but nobody can really know anything of history unless he has been taught to see things grow—has so seen things not only with the outward eye, but with the eyes of his intelligence and conscience. The actual things of the present are more important, however, than the institutions of the past. Even to young children can be shown the simpler conditions and processes of growth—how corn is put into the ground—how cotton and potatoes should be planted—how to choose the soil best adapted to a particular plant, how to improve that soil, how to care for the plant while it grows, how to get the most value out of it, how to use the elements of waste for the fertilization of other crops; how, through the alternation of crops, the land may be made to increase the annual value of its products—these things, upon their elementary side are absolutely vital to the worth and success of hundreds of thousands of these people of the Negro race, and yet our whole educational system has practically ignored them.

"Such work will mean not only an education in agriculture, but an education through agriculture and education, through natural symbols and practical forms, which will educate as deeply, as broadly and as truly as any other system which the world has known. Such changes will bring far larger results than the mere improvement of our Negroes. They will give us an agricultural class, a class of tenants or small land owners, trained not away from the soil, but in relation to the soil and in intelligent dependence upon its resources."

I close, then, as I began, by saying that as a slave the Negro was worked, and that as a freeman he must learn to work. There is still doubt in many quarters as to the ability of the Negro unguided, unsupported, to hew his own path and put into visible, tangible, indisputable form, products and signs of civilization. This doubt cannot be much affected by abstract arguments, no matter how delicately and convincingly woven together. Patiently, quietly, doggedly, persistently, through summer and winter, sunshine and shadow, by self—sacrifice, by foresight, by honesty and industry, we must re—enforce argument with results. One farm bought, one house built, one home sweetly and intelligently kept, one man who is the largest tax payer or has the largest bank account, one school or church maintained, one factory running successfully, one truck garden profitably cultivated, one patient cured by a Negro doctor, one sermon well preached, one office well filled, one life cleanly lived—these will tell more in our favor than all the abstract eloquence that can be summoned to plead our cause. Our pathway must be up through the soil, up through swamps, up through forests, up through the streams, the rocks, up through commerce, education and religion!

Source: Washington, Booker T. *The Negro Problem*. New York: James Pott & Company, 1903, 9–29.

"Thousands Pay Tribute to William H. Baldwin," *The New York Times*, 1905

The following journalist account of the memorial for William H. Baldwin indicates the depth of friendship between Booker T. Washington and the late president of the Long Island Railroad. Washington was among the white and rich elites on the platform. What is important about this description from the New York Times *is that it acknowledges Washington as an equal and a friend of Baldwin and his family. The long list of famous men and women in attendance is also important for the reader to note.*

Too often Washington has been deemed as a "puppet" being manipulated by the rich whites of the North, and this could not be further from the truth. However, his work was greatly admired and it was backed by some genuine philanthropic souls in the white community because it was helping African Americans gain education and opportunity. William H. Baldwin also had a house available for Washington and his family whenever he visited New York. This was an unpretentious friendship between two men who cared for each other beyond their racialized lives. The entire article is left intact for the reader; Washington's part in the service is at the latter part of the piece. The names printed in attendance are some of the most powerful individuals in society during this era—1912.

Thousands Pay Tribute to William H. Baldwin
Long Island Road Wheels Stop as Memorial Service Begins.
LIFE CALLED A VICTORY
Throng of Friends Hears Eulogies of Railroad President at Church of the Messiah.

The Church of the Messiah was filled yesterday afternoon with one of the most representative bodies of men ever brought together in this city at the memorial service to the memory of William H. Baldwin, Jr., President of the Long Island Railroad Company and philanthropist.

It was 4 o'clock when a string orchestra intoned "Nearer, My God, to Thee" and the Rev. Robert Collyer, the Rev. Dr. Minot J. Savage, Dr. Felix Adler, and Booker T. Washington walked to their places on the platform. At that moment every wheel upon the Long Island Railroad system, every stroke of the hammer in the shops and wheels of the ferryboats in midstream or at their docks stopped and remained still for two minutes out of respect to the dead President. Meanwhile the hat of every employee was off. The offices of the Pennsylvania Railroad Company and the shops had closed at noon, that delegations from the railroad might attend the services.

When the services began the church was crowded in every part, and many hundreds stood through the services. Men in every walk of life were there—lawyers, merchants, capitalists, laborers, and many negroes, whose staunch friend Mr. Baldwin had been. There were present the full Board of Directors of the Long Island Railroad, delegations of Trustees from the John F. Slater Fund, the General Education Board, Hampton Institute

Board, Metropolitan Security Company, American Surety Company, Armstrong Association, Corn Exchange Bank, East Side Civic Club, Colored Republican Club of New York, Negro Business League, Atlantic Avenue Engineer Corps, and John D. Rockefeller, Jr.'s Bible class of the Fifth Avenue Baptist Church.

Occupying front pews were Mrs. Baldwin and her children and the five brothers and three sisters of the deceased. The ushers were H. M. Atkinson of Atlanta, Paul Bowles of Springfield, Mass.; Kane S. Greene of Philadelphia, Henry M. Williams of Boston, and James H. Hamilton, Eliot Norton, Walter H. Page, Oswald Garrison Villard, and William F. Potter of New York, the latter being Vice President of the Long Island Road and Mr. Baldwin's probable successor in the Presidency.

HIS FRIENDS' EULOGIES

The eulogies were all made by men who had known Mr. Baldwin intimately and with whom he had in various ways been closely associated. The Rev. Dr. Samuel A. Eliot, son of the President of Harvard University and a schoolmate of Mr. Baldwin, was to have spoken of his old friend from the viewpoint of intimate personal association with him, but Dr. Savage announced that Dr. Eliot was ill. Dr. Savage spoke in Dr. Eliot's place.

Dr. Felix Adler said that he had been chosen to speak of Mr. Baldwin's relations to the larger civic and social movements. It was impossible, he said, to single out isolated instances for special consideration, especially in the life of a man like Mr. Baldwin, the virtue of whose private life was so conspicuous in his public conduct. Just as the wheels of a great railway system were stopping at that instant, Dr. Adler said, so it was fitting that a great audience like that he was addressing should pause for a while to consider the life and the sterling virtues of so great and good a man as Mr. Baldwin, and while accepting piously and philosophically the inevitable, lift up their hearts in thought of what he had been to them.

Wherever the friends of Mr. Baldwin met in the weeks past, Dr. Adler said, and the subject of the incurable malady of the dead railroad President came up, it was quickly dropped, for his friends could not bear the thought that he was soon to be taken from them.

"He seemed to me," said Dr. Adler, "to be a man typical of the best influences of modern democracy on manhood. He was a typical American, because he rose through his own effort from the lower ranks to high places through his Odyssean resource and energy.

THE GLORY HE LIKED

"I remember saying to him some time ago what a glorious city this would be to live in when all the improvements going forward had been completed—glorious in its inner and spiritual life as well as in its physical, and his reply was how much more glorious it was to think of things that were to be accomplished and to have been one of the factors in making it better for others, to be in and a part of the life and heart of the change.

"William H. Baldwin's democratic attitude also proclaimed him the typical American. His was one of the safest and strongest voices in the present debate between labor and capital. His heart was full of sympathy for the struggling multitude. To him there was no line between classes and masses. He was a believer in organized labor. 'As an employer,' he once said, 'I need an organization among my employees, because they best know their own needs, and their knowledge is one of the safeguards upon which I must depend to keep me from error': but he allowed no encroachment by his employees upon the rights of their fellow workers. His life was typical of the manhood that seeks not first for personal success and retires to a life of philanthropy near its close, but he combined constant devotion to public causes with his striving for personal success.

"Inflexible as he was in principle, and in his devotion to all things pure and good, he did not set himself up as above his fellows, but his manner showed the beautiful flower of the finest moral sense. I have heard him say that while he might see light in one direction there were others who might see light in another direction that he could not see. He never assumed to judge between man and man, or between man and woman, either.

BOY AND MAN BLENDED.

"His life was the blending of opposites, the sanguineness of optimism, his perennial youth, his manner like that of a boy combined with the fullness and ripeness of thought of the mature man.

"Last week I spoke of Baldwin to some school children, and they listened in rapt attention to his deeds. I wish that he might be spoken of in all the schools; that his life might be held up as a shining example to our youth, and that they might know that worth does not exist only in the dusty tomes of the past, but that it is here with us to-day. I wish that his features might be commemorated in council chamber or in a civic hall of fame, and I am glad to know that a memorial to him has been contemplated. But the finest and most intimate memorial is the effect he produced in those associated with him. His picture is enshrined in the hearts of his friends forever."

Booker T. Washington said that he met Mr. Baldwin some years ago when he was connected with the Southern Railroad. He sought to interest him in Tuskegee Institute, and Mr. Baldwin replied that he would help, if after investigation he found that they were doing "the real thing" down there.

BOOKER T. WASHINGTON'S TRIBUTE.

"In these words, 'the real thing,' we have in a large degree the keynote to the character of Mr. Baldwin," said Mr. Washington. "It has been my privilege to meet many men in various walks of life. Never have I met one who could detect more quickly the sham in words, dress, or actions, or one whose whole nature revolted more quickly against pretense or superficiality."

Mr. Washington told of Mr. Baldwin's visit to the institute and of his close investigation. He said he would never forget how, when he had looked the place over thoroughly, Mr. Baldwin said in his almost childlike simplicity and tender earnestness: "I believe in this; I want to help you." Mr. Washington said further:

"May we not all reverently thank God that such a soul has been permitted to come among us—that we have been permitted even in a slight degree to touch and share his life? Because he lived we shall live, and our lives will be stronger, more unselfish, and more useful, now and evermore."

Dr. Savage said that Mr. Baldwin had been one of the very small circle of men whom he loved. Many he had reverenced and respected, but few had been able to create the love that William H. Baldwin had created.

"But we are not here," said Dr. Savage, "to mourn and to be gloomy and sad, not to memorialize a death, but to show that we understand that his life was a victory, and it is that victory which we celebrate to-day."

Dr. Savage then announced that it was Mrs. Baldwin's express wish that Mr. Baldwin's favorite hymn should be sung. At his request the entire audience rose and joined in the singing, which rolled out in great chorus. The hymn was "Then and Now," by John Greenleaf Whittier, the first verse of which is:

Oh, something gleams upon our sight,
Through present wrong, the Eternal Right,
And step by step, since time began,
We see the steady gain of man.

DR. COLLYER'S TRIBUTE

Dr. Savage then introduced the Rev. Dr. Collyer as one who had known Mr. Baldwin's mother and father and had seen the Younger Baldwin grow to manhood.

"What can I say better than 'amen' to what has already been said?" asked Dr. Collyer. "I knew William Baldwin in that lovely home where I was ever a welcome guest. I saw him prepare for college and go forth into the world. There for a while our paths converged, but I remember the glad letter I got from his father on the occasion of his first promotion. It was no surprise to me later, knowing the boy as I had, to hear how he was taking hold of life. It was my privilege to see him grow also to the full realization of many of his hopes and ambitions, and while he was taken from us all too early, we and the world are better that he has lived."

Dr. Collyer then pronounced the benediction and the services were at an end.

Prominent among the great throng in the church were:

Andrew Carnegie	Robert Frier Monroe,
H. H. Rogers	St. Clair McKelway,
Seth Low,	Carl Schurz,
Howard Veiller,	A. J. Cassatt,
Rev. Dr. Thomas R. Slicer,	George H. Daniels,
Rev. Dr. S. D. McConnell,	William H. Newman,
Austen G. Fox	H. C. Duval,
Dr. H. M. Leipziger	James Stillman
Robert W. de Forest,	Hamilton Fish,
H. H. Vreeland,	George W. Perkins,
Thomas J. Ryan,	John A. McCall,
John R. Parsons,	James H. Hyde,
Edward M. Shepard,	John De Witt Warner,
Robert Ogden,	George L. Rives,
Lowell M. Palmer,	Alexander E. Orr,
Wheeler H. Peckham,	John Claflin,
Rev. Dr. Lyman Abbott,	Woodbury Langdon,
John D. Cimmins,	Charles Stewart Smith
George F. Bacon,	Jacob H. Schiff,
William K. Vanderbilt.	

One of the features of the service was the attendance of members of the Class of '85 of Harvard, with which Mr. Baldwin graduated. These were: Henry M. Williams, John R. McArthur, Amos T. French, J. M. G. Goodale, Edward C. Thayer, F. Winthrop White, Everett V. Abbot, James K. Paulding, Henry Simpson, Edmund S. Middleton, L. W. Batten, Theodore Dunham, Charles F. Brandt, Chauncey G. Parker, J. Victor Onativia, and Edgerton R. Winthrop, Jr.

Source: *New York Times*, January 12, 1905. https://www.nytimes.com/1905/01/12/archives/thousands-pay-tribute-to-william-h-baldwin-long-island-road-wheels.html.

Alain LeRoy Locke, Letter to Booker T. Washington, 1912

Dated September 16, 1912, the following letter is from the renowned Harlem Renaissance philosopher Alain Locke to Booker T. Washington. It reveals evidence that proves beyond doubt that Washington was not only a friend of higher education, but would help any young scholar of African American heritage who wanted to have a career in the liberal arts. Washington has been castigated as basically anti–liberal arts and higher education, but this letter confirms that one of the famous scholars from the Harlem Renaissance was indebted to Washington for the help he received in getting his appointment as a professor at Howard University. Locke would go on to be a celebrated liberal arts scholar who edited and published the famous Harlem Renaissance book, The New Negro, *in 1925.*

What is particularly fascinating is the fact it appears that Locke had also spent some time teaching at Tuskegee Institute, which supposedly did not teach liberal arts classes—another bogus claim by Washington's critics. Moreover, what is unfair to the legacy of Booker T. Washington is the point that generations of scholars and readers were not aware of the connection he had with Locke. Given the stereotyping of Washington's character by his critics, specifically Du Bois, this connection with the young Alain Locke would not fit. For a scholar, this is an important find in the Booker T. Washington archives that should change the way he has been considered historically. Clearly, Alain Locke was more than indebted for the help he received at the outset of his career from the man who was supposed to be averse to liberal arts. Lastly, as mentioned within the book, Washington was also a trustee of Howard University—hence his being able to help secure Locke an academic position at the university.

Camden, N.J. September 16, 1912

Personal.

My dear Doctor Washington, I was just on the point of writing you when I received your kindly letter of the 12th inst. Saturday, the14th, I was elected an assistant Professor at Howard, in English and Philosophy, upon the recommendation of Dean Moore, but with work in the College Dept. as well as in Teachers' College, and therefore with Dean Miller's consent. I was about to write you news of this, and to thank you for your very valuable and timely help in the Howard matter, when your letter with its still greater willingness to assist me in getting placed arrives to put me still more in your debt. I shall see to it that I myself and certain of the Howard authorities appreciate the fine disinterestedness of your willingness to assist me in locating at Howard when you were yourself able to use me at Tuskegee. I shall hope and expect to serve your very best interests at Howard and elsewhere, until I more than repay you for your deep personal interest.

I really believe that until I have an opportunity to serve a direct apprenticeship under you in your peculiar field of organized race work and propaganda, as I fervently hope someday to have opportunity, I may perhaps be very well able to justify your good wishes and expectations in the field of journalism and college teaching which is now, and partly through your kind offices, open before me. You will be interested to know that through the Civil Service, I have also been appointed an assistant organizer of the New Jersey Emancipation Commission, in charge of the statistical side of the work, a post that I can very well keep in conjunction with the work at Howard. This, with other journalistic matters, which I plan to discuss with you at my earliest opportunity, will keep me in touch with the larger world of affairs that I wish at all costs to keep contact with.

Believe me, Doctor Washington, until I have chance to see you and thank you personally, most deeply and acceptably indebted and grateful; and if you have taken any of your officers at Tuskegee into your council, acquaint them please with my present situation, and assure them of my willingness to serve you and them always in whatever way I may be able.

With best thanks and respects, Sincerely yours,

Alain LeRoy Locke

Source: Locke, Alain L. "Letter to Washington, September 16, 1912." Alain Locke Papers, MSRC, Box 164–91, Folder 55 (Washington, Booker T.).

Booker T. Washington, "A National Negro Business League Address," 1913

The National Negro Business League (NNBL) was established by Washington in 1900. The idea originally came out of the research of W. E. B. Du Bois while he was at Atlanta University. However, Washington was able to put theory into practice and he created a rather substantial network of African American businessmen and women across the United States, with chapters in most major cities. They met annually for a conference on best practices in business. Washington was the president from 1900 up to his death in 1915.

What is significant about this address in August of 1913 is in the Woodrow Wilson presidency being rather harsh toward African Americans. Wilson was a white supremacist who segregated the White House in terms of staff quarters and job allocation, giving clear notice that African Americans were not going to receive any upliftment from his presidency. Washington responded to Wilson's wickedness by stating, while not naming him outright, "Those who treat us unjustly are losing more than we are. So often the keeper of the prison is on the outside, but the free man is on the inside. As I said in the beginning, we have more friends both North and South than enemies. Let us advertise our friends more and our enemies less." Washington always left his audience in a positive mood regardless of how hard the times and experience were. He did not know how to be negative; the glass for him was always half-full as opposed to being half-empty. The following address specifies his optimism toward the scope and breath of African American businesses in 1913.

Academy of Music, Philadelphia, PA
This the fourteenth meeting of the National Negro Business League marks also the fiftieth anniversary of our freedom as a race. It is, then, both timely and fitting that this great gathering of the representatives of the backbone and progress of our race should be held in Philadelphia. It is most appropriate that this meeting should take place after fifty years of freedom in the city where 137 years ago that immortal document, the Declaration of Independence, was issued.

Whether the American Negro was meant at the time to be included within the scope and meaning of the words of the Declaration of Independence has been a debatable question. However that may be decided, we mean as a race through this and similar organizations to make ourselves such a useful and potent part of American citizenship so that in all the future no one will dare question our right to be included in any declaration that relates to any portion of the body politic.

During the fifty years of our freedom we have been subjected to some pretty severe tests. First, there were not a few who raised the question as to whether or not the American Negro could survive in a state of freedom. We answer that question by showing that when freedom came to us we were 4,000,000 in number; now we have grown to over 10,000,000 free American citizens. This means that we have a population of American Negroes that is more than twice as large as the population of Australia, one and a half times as large as the whole population of Canada, and nearly twice as large as the combined population of Norway, Sweden, Switzerland and Denmark. These facts should put an end for all time to doubt about our ability to survive in a state of freedom.

One other question was debated fifty years ago, and that was the question as to our ability to support ourselves from a physical and personal point of view. There were not a few who fifty years ago predicted that this newly freed race would become a perpetual burden upon the pocketbook of the nation. It was freely predicted that we would neither feed, clothe nor shelter ourselves. Every year the American Congress is asked to appropriate between ten and twelve millions of dollars to be used largely in providing food, clothes and shelter for about 300,000 American Indians. While this is true of the American Indian (and I have nothing but the highest respect for the Indians) ever since the days of Reconstruction the American Negro has not called upon Congress to appropriate a single dollar to be used in providing either clothes, shelter or food for our race. Absolutely in all these personal matters we have supported ourselves and mean to do so in all the future, and it is very seldom that in any part of this country does one find a Black hand reached from corner of a street asking for any man's personal charity. Within fifty years, then, we have proven that we can survive from a physical point of view, and we have proven that we could not only support ourselves but could contribute taxes from $700,000,000, worth of property toward the support of local, state and national government.

With the fifty years of our freedom we have been subjected to a third test that is one of the conditions of growth and permanency under the conditions of freedom. This third test embraces our ability to combine, to work in harness in the capacity of organized human beings. There can be little civilization and little progress without the capacity and willingness to work together in organized groups.

Fifty years ago we had almost no experience in working together as organized groups. During the past half-century we have proven our ability to organize. We now have 62 banks under the control of black organizations. Fifty years ago we had few religious organizations. Now we have four great religious branches to say nothing of smaller ones having a total membership of 3,113,900 members or about 33 percent of the race.

Our capacity to organize has been shown too in the case of the National Negro Business League with its numerous local branches, and more especially in the numerous secret and beneficial societies which have been originated and are being sustained by Negroes. A rough study indicates that we have at least 13 of these organizations with distinct aims and purposes, and which is either local, state wide or national in their scope. A study of these organizations reveals the fact that these organizations have a total membership of at least 3,000,000 persons. These figures take no account of the fact that not a few individuals belong to many different organizations.

So much for indications of progress in the past. What about the present, and our duty in the immediate future?

First and foremost I call the attention of the race through this League to the fact that there are at least 200,000,000 acres of unused and unoccupied land in the Southern States. This means a territory as large as

Australia, France, Germany, Italy and Spain. I am glad to say that we already own and occupy 20,000,000 acres, but this is only about two acres for each individual. All this means one thing, that the time has come when this Business League and other organizations should send forth a voice which can be heard everywhere and cannot be misunderstood, for a larger proportion of our race to leave the towns and cities and plant themselves in the country districts on the soil before it is too late. Verily it is true that right here in the United States the words of the prophet of old are fulfilled, when he said there was a land awaiting the occupation of the people that was "flowing with milk and honey." In our case as a race, the milk will come from our own Jersey cows and the honey from our own well-kept bees. Forward to the land should be our motto everywhere. Instead of owning 20,000,000 acres, we should own within the next quarter of a century 40,000,000 acres. To the man or the race who owns the soil all good things come in time. Let us leave the fleeting and often deceiving easy life of the cities and get on God's green earth. I want to see members of my race that are now in too large numbers flocking to the cities, join the great world movement "back to the land," or better still "forward to the land."

While the millions of Negroes in the South are largely an ignorant people so far as letters are concerned, they are not as a rule degraded people. Some of the finest specimens of physical and moral manhood to be found anywhere in the world can be found among the country people of our race. There is a vast difference between ignorance and degradation.

In order to get ourselves planted on the soil, for a season we shall have to forebear the enjoyment of some of the things that make life inviting in the cities. In the cities it is with our race in a large measure as with others in the same relative position of civilization. There is tremendous temptation in the cities for us to get the signs of civilization instead of the substance itself. In the city the temptation is to get an automobile before we get a house, to get a dress suit before we get a bank account, to spend all that we get in for rent, food and dress and lay up for old age or for those dependent upon us. In the city the temptation is to be dependent instead of independent, to let someone else think and plan for us instead of thinking and planning for ourselves. If any one doubts the truth of this statement, let him go through the streets of one of our Northern cities early in the morning and note the large number of colored people that are washing someone else's windows or sweeping someone else's floor. No disgrace in this, but the White man will have more respect for us in proportion as we are able to create positions for ourselves. We must learn to sacrifice today that we may enjoy tomorrow, to do without today that we may possess tomorrow.

Now as to our program for the future. We should make up our minds thoroughly that there is a permanent place in the country for us, and that we have more friends both in the North and the South than we have enemies.

We should make up our minds that we are to use material gain and prosperity not as an end but as a means toward securing and enjoying the best things in our American life.

What are our chances and what is the outlook? The large number of independent, prosperous and law-abiding Black people right here in Philadelphia partly answers this question. What hundreds in Philadelphia have done others can do throughout the United States.

Remember, as I have said, that we have a race of ten millions with whom to do business and in the South especially our commercial activity is not confined to our race. In a Southern city when I was spending a half-hour in a Negro bank, I noted that one-fourth of the people who came in to do business with that bank were White people. Young men, young women, there are openings in this great country of ours for Negroes to establish and maintain many additional and various kinds of business concerns.

There is a place for at least 900,000 independent, self-supporting Negro farmers. When I was recently in the Far West, nothing impressed me more than to note the large number of educated White men who were beginning life as farmers. Often they started in a little hut or "dug-out" and suffered privations, but they were sticking to it. Those are people who in the future make the great kings of industry.

There are openings in the South for 1000 more sawmills and 1000 brickyards.

It is easily possible to find inviting places North and South w[h]ere 4,000 more grocery stores can be opened.

We need 2000 additional dry goods stores, and 1500 shoe stores.

Our race needs 1000 more good restaurants and hotels.

White women in all parts of the world are opening millinery shops. I want to see a larger number our bright ambitious colored women do the same thing. There are opportunities for starting 1500 millinery Stores.

We already have over 350 drug stores, but 1000 more could be started and would be sustained.

We already have over 60 banks, but 150 additional banks should be organized. In cities like Philadelphia, New York, Baltimore, Washington, Memphis, New Orleans, Atlanta, Charleston, Savannah and Mobile three or four banks properly and conducted can be supported.

Now is the time to seize hold of these golden opportunities and use them before it is too late. These great chances are at our door. Shall we use them? Too many of our well-educated young men and women are content to be merely salary drawers or wage earners, depending on someone else to think and plan for them.

Activity and success in all these economic directions lay the foundation for the most enduring success in all professional directions. For our race like others must be built upon an economic foundation as well as an intellectual, moral and religious one. Work more and more in these directions and neither we nor our children will be dependent upon the uncertainties of seeking and holding political office for ourselves - but positions which no man can give us nor take from us.

The land, the forests, the minerals, the streams, sun and rain from which original wealth come draw no color line.

Of the ten million at least who belong to the ordinary, hard working classes, in all our planning for business success we will not, cannot succeed unless we get close to these hard working masses. They are the backbone of our race. We must feel we are not a part of them nor must we ever get above. I beg of you that in your local leagues that you get hold of the man who works with his pick and plow and the woman, who washes, irons or sews. These will be money into your banks and support your other commercial enterprises.

Finally, as a race we must not be discouraged. There will come to us as to all races, seasons of depression and gloom. Once in a while even those in high places may seem to seek to insult and humiliate and harass us, but this cannot last. "The morning cometh." Those who treat us unjustly are losing more than we are. So often the keeper of the prison is on the outside but the free man is on the inside. As I said in the beginning, we have more friends both North and South than enemies. Let us advertise our friends more and our enemies less.

We must not lose faith in our White friends and above all this we must have constant and unvarying faith in our own race. We must have pride of race. We must be as proud of being a Negro as the Japanese is of being Japanese. Let us go from this great meeting filled with a spirit of race pride, rejoicing in the fact that we belong to a race that has made greater progress within fifty years than any race has made history, and let each dedicate themselves to the task of doing his part in making the ten millions of Black citizens in America an example for all the world in usefulness, law abiding habits and high character.

Source: Washington, Booker T. "A National Negro Business League Address." *The Indianapolis Freeman,* Booker T. Washington Papers, Library of Congress, August 23, 1913.

Booker T. Washington, Letter to the Editor of the *New York World,* 1915

The following article is evidence of Booker T. Washington's advocacy in African affairs. It is his protest letter to the United States Congress about a proposed immigration bill to ban peoples of African heritage from entering the nation. Washington had a vestige interest in stopping this potential law because he had a vibrant study abroad program that took African Americans to Africa and brought African and African Caribbean students to study at Tuskegee Institute. Again, this was a part of Washington's legacy that gets overlooked. He was what this author deems a "quiet Pan Africanist" who worked between the American and European powers to the benefit of African people.

It was not a perfect scenario because he had to be careful in how he spoke of empowering Africans from the continent and Caribbean regions. Maybe this is why the African and Caribbean regions that are part of his work have been severely under-researched. Or if it was considered, it was not fully comprehended due to the ideological make-up of the scholars assessing Washington. But this article pulls no punches; his appeal and advocacy for African and Caribbean migrants is clear. What is also important is the fact that he was successful in his appeal. The bill was defeated and foreign visitors of African heritage were able to continue to visit, and of course Washington was able to sustain his study abroad program for Africans who would continue to come to Tuskegee Institute to learn and be inspired by African American talent in education. Note, this was a time of extreme racism, and to find an institution run by and for African Americans must have been empowering for those foreign visitors of African heritage.

To the Editor of The World: Through your newspaper I desire to appeal to the American congress and to the people of the United States in favor of fair play and justice in connection with the immigration bill now pending before the United States Senate, which by amendment excludes from coming into this country any person of African descent.

The bill, in my opinion, is unjust, unreasonable and unnecessary. It is unnecessary because only a few thousand people of African descent enter this country annually. Practically all of these that do come are mainly from the West Indies and almost none from the continent of Africa. It is evident that many of those who come into this country do not remain permanently, but I find, according to the census of 1910, there were in the United States only 40,319 Negroes who were foreign born, and only 473 of these had come from Africa.

The bill puts an unnecessary slight upon colored people by classing them with alien criminals.

The bill in its present form would seem to prohibit citizens from the republics of Liberia, Cuba and Hayti, and also from Porto Rico and Santo Domingo, entering this country, thus placing an unnecessary hardship upon these smaller countries, which would not be done, in my opinion, if they were stronger.

In a personal conversation with a high officer of the Panama Canal Commission he told me that the services of the Jamaican Negroes were invaluable in building the Panama Canal. Now that we are celebrating the completion of this great canal, it seems most unjust and unreasonable that the people who contributed in so large a measure toward it should be slapped in the face and told that they cannot enter this country even when they meet the requirements of our Government.

An investigation will show that the colored people who have come to this country from the West Indian Islands and from other foreign countries have proved as a whole to be a law-abiding, intelligent, industrious class. They have never become Anarchists or as a class given trouble to the Government.

Let me repeat that it is unfair at this time, when we are all striving to bring about racial harmony and peace, to raise a question which is calculated to stir up needless strife, and I cannot feel that the best people In the South approve of any such bill.

Lastly, the passing of such an unjust law will cripple the missionary and educational work which we are trying to do In Africa and elsewhere. For a number of years some of the brightest young people from Africa and elsewhere have been coming to this country to receive training to fit them to go back and help their people, and this they have done in an effective manner. All this, I understand, will be stopped by the passing of this law.

This measure is not political or sectional, and I hope that all people will see the justice of asking Congress to refrain from perpetrating this unjust act upon my race. Certainly we have enough to contend with already without having this additional handicap and discouragement placed in our pathway.

BOOKER T. WASHINGTON.

Source: *New York World*, January 6, 1915, 8. Letter dated January 2, 1915, in Booker T. Washington Papers, Vol. 13, p. 209.

Bibliography

Adi, Hakim, and Marika Sherwood. *Pan-African History: Political Figures from Africa and the Diaspora since 1787.* London: Routledge, 2003.
Aiello, Thomas. *The Battle for the Souls of Black Folk: W.E.B. Du Bois, Booker T. Washington and the Debate that Shaped the Course of the Civil Rights Movement.* Santa Barbara, CA: Praeger, 2016.
Alexander, Shawn Leigh, ed. *T. Thomas Fortune: The Afro-American Agitator.* Gainesville: University Press of Florida, 2008.
Allen, James, et al. *Without Sanctuary: Lynching Photography in America.* Santa Fe, NM: Twin Palms Publishers, 2004.
Anderson, James D. *The Education of Blacks in the South, 1860–1935.* Chapel Hill: University of North Carolina Press, 1988.
Angell, Stephen W. *Bishop Henry McNeal Turner and African-American Religion in the South.* Knoxville: University of Tennessee Press, 1992.
Appiah, Kwame Anthony. *Lines of Descent: W.E.B. Du Bois and the Emergence of Identity.* Cambridge, MA: Harvard University Press, 2014.
Aptheker, Herbert, ed. *The Correspondence of W.E.B. Du Bois, Selections, 1877–1934.* Vol. 1. Amherst: University of Massachusetts Press, 1973.
Aptheker, Herbert, ed. "Introduction" (i–xx) to Booker T. Washington and W. E. B. Du Bois, *The Negro in the South.* New York: University Books, 1970.
Asante, Molefi K. *History of Africa: The Quest for Eternal Harmony.* London: Routledge, 2007.
Asante, Molefi K., and Abu S. Abarry, eds. *African Intellectual Heritage: A Book of Sources.* Philadelphia, PA: Temple University Press, 1996.
Bailey, Thomas Pearce. *Race Orthodoxy in the South, and Other Aspects of the Negro Question.* New York: Neale Publishing, 1914.

Bast, Diane Carol, S. T. Karnick, and Lee Walker, eds. *Booker T. Washington: A Re-Examination.* Chicago: The Heartland Institute, 2008.

Bennett, Lerone, Jr. *Forced into Glory: Abraham Lincoln's White Dream.* Chicago: Johnson Publishing Company, 1999.

Bennett, Lerone, Jr. *Pioneers of Protest.* Chicago: Johnson Publishing Company, 1968.

Bieze, Michael. *Booker T. Washington and the Art of Self-Representation.* New York: Peter Lang, 2008.

Bieze, Michael Scott, and Marybeth Gasman, eds. *Booker T. Washington Rediscovered.* Baltimore, MD: John Hopkins University Press, 2012.

Blackmon, Douglas A. *Slavery by Another Name: The Re-Enslavement of Black Americans from the Civil War to World War II.* New York: Anchor Books, 2008.

Blight, David W. *Frederick Douglass: Prophet of Freedom.* New York: Simon & Schuster, 2018.

Brooks, John Graham. *An American Citizen: The Life of William Henry Baldwin, Jr.* New York: Houghton Mifflin Company, 1910.

Brundage, W. Fitzhugh, ed. *Booker T. Washington: Up from Slavery 100 Years Later.* Gainesville: University Press of Florida, 2003.

Carnegie, Andrew. *The Autobiography of Andrew Carnegie and The Gospel of Wealth.* New York: Renaissance Classics, 2012.

Carroll, Rebecca, ed. *Uncle Tom or New Negro? Booker T. Washington and Up from Slavery 100 Years Later.* New York: Harlem Moon, 2006.

Carson, Clayborne, and Kris Shepard, eds. *A Call to Conscience: Landmark Speeches of Dr. Martin Luther King, Jr.* New York: Grand Central Publishing, 2002.

Christian, Mark. "An African Centered Perspective on White Supremacy." *Journal of Black Studies* 33, no. 2 (November 2002a): 179–198.

Christian, Mark, ed. *Black Identity in the 20th Century: Expressions of the US and UK African Diaspora.* London: Hansib Publications Ltd., 2002b.

Christian, Mark, ed. *Integrated but Unequal: Black Faculty in Predominately White Space.* Trenton, NJ: Africa World Press, 2012.

Christian, Mark, ed. "Marcus Garvey and the UNIA: New Perspectives on Philosophy, Religion, Micro-Studies, Unity, and Practice." Special Issue, *Journal of Black Studies* 39, no. 2 (November 2008): 163–331.

Christian, Mark. "Marcus Garvey and the Universal Negro Improvement Association (UNIA): With Special Reference to the 'Lost' Parade in Columbus, Ohio, September 25, 1923." *Western Journal of Black Studies* 28, no. 3 (2004): 424–434.

Christian, Mark. *Multiracial Identity: An International Perspective.* London: Palgrave, 2000.

Christian, Mark. "Who's Afraid of the Black Male Scholar? A Voice from Within the Walls of Academia." In *RIP Jim Crow: Fighting Racism through Higher Education Policy, Curriculum, and Cultural Interventions*, edited by Virginia Stead, 19–35. New York, Peter Lang, 2016.

Christian, Mark, and Stephanie Y. Evans, eds. "Africana/Black Studies at the Graduate Level: A Twenty-First Century Perspective." Special Issue, *Western Journal of Black Studies* 34, no. 2 (Summer 2010): 231–304.

Clarke, John Henrik. *African World Revolution: Africa at the Crossroads.* Trenton, NJ: Africa World Press, 1991.

Clarke, John Henrik, and Amy Jacques Garvey, eds. *Marcus Garvey and the Vision of Africa.* New York: Vintage, 1974.

Cox, Oliver C. "The Leadership of Booker T. Washington." *Social Forces* 30, no. 1 (1951): 91–97.

Crummell, Alex. *Africa and America: Addresses and Discourses.* Springfield, MA: Willey & Co., 1891.

Cruse, Harold. *The Crisis of the Negro Intellectual: A Historical Analysis of the Failure of Black Leadership.* New York: Quill, 1984.

Dagbovie, Pero Gaglo. "Exploring a Century of Historical Scholarship on Booker T. Washington." *Journal of African American History* 92, no. 2 (Spring 2007): 239–264.

Davidson, Basil. *The Lost Cities of Africa.* Revised Edition. New York: Little Brown & Co., 1987.

Davis, Deborah. *Guest of Honor: Booker T. Washington, Theodore Roosevelt, and the White House Dinner That Shocked a Nation.* New York: Atria Books, 2012.

Deutsch, Stephanie. *You Need a Schoolhouse: Booker T. Washington, Julius Rosenwald, and the Building of Schools for the Segregated South.* Evanston, IL: Northwestern University Press, 2011.

Diangelo, Robin. *White Fragility: Why It's So Hard for White People to Talk about Racism.* Boston, MA: Beacon, 2018.

Dixon, Thomas, Jr. *The Leopard's Spots: A Romance of the White Man's Burden.* New York: Doubleday & Page, 1902 [reprint].

Douglass, Frederick. *Frederick Douglass Autobiographies: Narrative of the Life of Frederick Douglass, an American Slave, My Bondage and My Freedom, Life and Times of Frederick Douglass.* New York: The Library of America, 1994.

Du Bois, W. E. B. *The Autobiography of W.E.B. Du Bois: A Soliloquy on Viewing My Life from the Last Decade of Its First Century.* New York: International Publishers, 1968.

Du Bois, W. E. B. *Black Reconstruction in America: 1860–1880.* New York: Touchstone, 1995; first published in 1935.

Du Bois, W. E. B. *Dusk of Dawn: An Essay toward an Autobiography of a Race Concept.* New Brunswick, NJ: Transaction, 1992; first published in 1940.

Du Bois, W. E. B. *The Souls of Black Folk.* 100th Anniversary ed. Boulder, CO: Paradigm, 2004; first published in 1903.

Du Bois, W. E. B. "The Talented Tenth." In *The Negro Problem: A Series of Articles by Representative Negroes of Today,* edited by Booker T. Washington, 13–32. Middletown, DE: Renaissance Classics, 2020; first published in 1903.

Du Bois, W. E. B. *The World and Africa: An Inquiry into the Part Which Africa Has Played in World History.* New York: International Publishers, 1965; first published in 1946.

Duster, Alfreda M., ed. *Crusade for Justice: The Autobiography of Ida B. Wells.* Chicago: The University of Chicago Press, 1970.

Ellis, Reginald, K. *Between Washington and Du Bois: The Racial Politics of James Edward Shepard.* Gainesville: University Press of Florida, 2017.

Ellison, Ralph. *Invisible Man.* London: Penguin, 1965.

Equal Justice Initiative. *Lynching in America: Confronting the Legacy of Racial Terror.* 2nd ed. Montgomery, AL: Equal Justice Initiative, 2015.

Esedebe, Olisanwuche P. *Pan-Africanism: The Idea and the Movement, 1776–1991.* 2nd ed. Washington, DC: Howard University, 1994.

Essien-Udom, E. U. *Black Nationalism: A Search for Identity in America.* Chicago: University of Chicago Press, 1971.

Feagin, Joe R. *Racist America: Roots, Current Realities, and Future Reparations.* New York: Routledge, 2014.

Foner, Philip S. *W.E.B. Du Bois Speaks: Speeches and Addresses 1890–1919.* New York: Pathfinder, 1970.

Fortune, T. Thomas. *Black & White: Land, Labor, and Politics in the South.* New York: Washington Square Press, 2007.

Foster, William Z. *The Negro People in American History.* New York: International Publishers, 1954.

Franklin, John Hope, and Evelyn B. Higginbotham. *From Slavery to Freedom: A History of African Americans.* 9th ed. New York: McGraw-Hill, 2011.

Franklin, John Hope, and August Meir, eds. *Black Leaders of the 20th Century.* Urban: University of Illinois Press, 1982.

Frazier, Franklin E. *Black Bourgeoisie: The Rise of a New Middle Class in the United States.* New York: Collier Books, 1962.

Frederickson, George M. *White Supremacy: A Comparative Study in American & South African History.* New York: Oxford University Press, 1981.

Garvey, Amy Jacques. *Garvey & Garveyism.* London: Collier Books, 1970.

Garvey, Marcus. *The Philosophy & Opinions of Marcus Garvey, Or Africa for the Africans*. Vols. I & II. Compiled by Amy Jacques Garvey. Dover, MA: The Majority Press, 1986.

Gates, Henry Louis, Jr. *Stony the Road: Reconstruction, White Supremacy, and the Rise of Jim Crow*. New York: Penguin, 2019.

Gates, Henry Louis, Jr., and Valerie A. Smith, eds. *The Norton Anthology of African American Literature*. 3rd ed. Vol. 1. New York: W.W. Norton, 2014.

Ginzburg, Ralph. *100 Years of Lynchings*. Baltimore, MD: Black Classic Press, 1988.

Goffman, Erving. *The Presentation of Self in Everyday Life*. New York: Anchor Books, 1959.

Greenidge, Kerri K. *Black Radical: The Life and Times of William Monroe Trotter*. Liveright: New York, 2020.

Haley, Alex. *Autobiography of Malcolm X*. New York: Ballantine Books, 1992.

Hamilton, Kenneth M. *Booker T. Washington in American Memory*. Urbana, IL: University of Illinois Press, 2017.

Hare, Nathan. *The Black Anglo-Saxons*. Chicago: Third World Press, 1991.

Harlan, Louis R. "The Southern Education Board and the Race Issue in Public Education." *Journal of Southern History* 23, no. 2 (May 1957): 189–202.

Harlan, Louis R. "Booker T. Washington and the White Man's Burden." In *Booker T. Washington in Perspective: Essays of Louis R. Harlan*, edited by Raymond W. Smock, 68–97. Jackson: University Press of Mississippi, 1988.

Harlan, Louis R. *Booker T. Washington: The Making of a Black Leader, 1856–1901*. New York: Oxford University Press, 1972.

Harlan, Louis R. *Booker T. Washington: The Wizard of Tuskegee, 1901–1915*. New York: Oxford University Press, 1983.

Harlan, Louis R., and Raymond W. Stock, eds. *The Booker T. Washington Papers*. 14 Vols. Urbana: University of Illinois, 1972–89.

Harris, Joseph E. *Africans and Their History*. 2nd ed. New York: Meridian, 1972.

Hawkins, Hugh. *Booker T. Washington and His Critics*. 2nd ed. Lexington, KY: D.C. Heath and Co., 1974.

Herskovits, Melvin J. *The Myth of the Negro Past*. New York: Harper & Bros. Pub., 1941.

Hill, Robert A., ed. *The Marcus Garvey and Universal Negro Improvement Association Papers*. Vol. 1 (1826–August 1919). Los Angeles: University of California Press, 1983.

Hodes, Martha. *White Women, Black Men: Illicit Sex in the 19th-Century South*. New Haven, CT: Yale University Press, 1997.

Holmes, William F. *The White Chief: James Kimble Vardaman.* Baton Rouge: Louisiana State University Press, 1970.

Holt, Rackham. *George Washington Carver: An American Biography.* New York: Doubleday, Doran and Co., 1943.

Isenberg, Nancy. *White Trash: The 400-Year Untold History of Class in America.* New York: Penguin, 2016.

Jackson, David H. *Booker T. Washington and the Struggle against White Supremacy: The Southern Educational Tours, 1908–1912.* New York: Palgrave, 2008.

Kantrowitz, Stephen. *Ben Tillman and the Reconstruction of White Supremacy.* North Carolina: University of North Carolina Press, 2000.

Karenga, Maulana. *Introduction to Black Studies.* 4th ed. Los Angeles, CA: University of Sankore Press, 2010.

Kelley, Robin D. G., and Lewis Earl, eds. *To Make Our World Anew: A History of American Americans.* New York: Oxford University Press, 2000.

Kimmel, Michael S., and Abby L. Ferber, eds. *White Privilege: A Reader.* 4th ed. Boulder, CO: Westview Press, 2017.

King, Martin Luther, Jr. *Where Do We Go From Her: Chaos or Community?* Boston, MA: Beacon Press, 1968.

Kirkland, Avon. "Booker-Chapter VII." In *Uncle Tom or Negro*, edited by Rebecca Carroll, 57–67. New York: Harlem Moon, 2006.

Kitwana, Bakari. "Booker-Chapter IX." In *Uncle Tom or New Negro*, edited by Rebecca Carroll, 76–84. New York: Harlem Moon, 2006.

Kitwana, Bakari. *The Hip Hop Generation: Young Blacks and the Crisis in African-American Culture.* New York: Basic Books, 2002.

Lake, Marilyn. *Progressive New World: How Settler Colonialism and Transpacific Exchange Shaped American Reform.* Cambridge, MA: Harvard University Press, 2019.

Lemelle, Sid. *Pan Africanism for Beginners.* New York: Writers and Readers, 1992.

Levering Lewis, David. *W.E.B. Du Bois: Biography of a Race: 1868–1919.* New York: Henry Holt and Co., 1993.

Locke, Alain L. *The New Negro: Voices of the Harlem Renaissance.* New York: Touchstone, 1997.

Locke, Alain L. "Letter to Booker T. Washington, September 16, 1912." In *Booker T. Washington Papers.* Vol. 12, edited by Louis R. Harlan and Raymond W. Stock, 9–10. Urbana: University of Illinois, 1982.

Logan, Rayford W. *The Betrayal of the Negro: From Rutherford B. Hayes to Woodrow Wilson.* New York: Da Capo Press, 1997.

Malcolm X, with Alex Haley. *The Autobiography of Malcolm X.* New York: Ballantine Books, 1992a.

Malcolm X, with ed. Steve Clark. *The Final Speeches: February 1965.* New York: Pathfinder, 1992b.

Mansfield, Stephen. *Then Darkness Fled: The Liberating Wisdom of Booker T. Washington.* Nashville, Tennessee: Highland Books, 1999.

Marable, Manning. *Black Leadership: Four Great American Leaders and the Struggle for Civil Rights.* New York: Penguin, 1999.

Marable, Manning. "Booker T. Washington and the Political Economy of Black Education in the United States, 1880–1915." *Education with Production* 4, no. 2 (February 1986): 10–37.

Marable, Manning. *W.E.B. Du Bois: Black Radical Democrat.* Boston, MA: Twayne, 1986.

Marable, Manning W. "Booker T. Washington and African Nationalism." *Phylon* 35, no. 4 (4th Qtr. 1974): 398–406.

Martin, Tony. *Race First: The Ideological and Organizational Struggles of Marcus Garvey and the Universal Negro Improvement Association.* Dover, MA: The Majority Press, 1976.

Mathews, Basil. *Booker T. Washington: Educator and Interracial Interpreter.* Cambridge, MA: Harvard University Press, 1948.

McMillen, Neil R. *Dark Journey: Black Mississippians in the Age of Jim Crow.* Urbana: University of Illinois Press, 1990.

Meier, August. *Negro Thought in America, 1880–1915: Racial Ideologies in the Age of Booker T. Washington.* Ann Arbor: The University of Michigan Press, 1970.

Mills, C. Wright. *The Sociological Imagination.* London: Oxford University Press, 1959.

Morrison, Toni. *The Origin of Others.* Cambridge, MA: Harvard University Press, 2017.

Moses, Wilson Jeremiah. *Alexander Crummell: A Study of Civilization and Discontent.* New York: Oxford University Press, 1989.

Moss, Alfred A., Jr. *The American Negro Academy: Voice of the Talented Tenth.* Baton Rouge: Louisiana State University Press, 1981.

Myrdal, Gunnar. *An American Dilemma: The Negro Problem and Modern Democracy.* New York: Harper and Bros., 1944.

Norrell, Robert J. "Understanding the Wizard: Another Look at the Age of Booker T. Washington" In *Booker T. Washington: Up from Slavery 100 Years Later,* edited by W. Fitzhugh Brundage, 58–80. Gainesville: University Press of Florida, 2003.

Norrell, Robert J. *Up from History: The Life of Booker T. Washington.* Cambridge, MA: Harvard University Press, 2009.

Phillips, Ulrich B. *American Negro Slavery: A Survey of the Supply, Employment and Control of Negro Labor as Determined by Plantation Regime.* New York: D. Appleton and Company, 1929.

Reed, Ishmael. "Introduction: Booker vs. the Negro-Saxons." In *Up from Slavery*, edited by Booker T. Washington, vii–xxii. London: Signet Classics, 2010.

Rogers, Joel A. *World's Great Men of Color*. Vol. I. New York: Touchstone, 1996.

Rogers, Joel A. *World's Great Men of Color* Vol. II. New York: Touchstone, 1996.

Scott, Emmett J., and Lyman Beecher Stowe, eds. *Booker T. Washington: Builder of a Civilization*. Gloucestershire, UK: Dodo Press, 2009.

Seraile, William. *Angels of Mercy: White Women and the History of New York's Colored Orphan Asylum*. New York: Fordham University Press, 2011.

Smock, Raymond W. *Booker T. Washington: Black Leadership in the Age of Jim Crow*. Chicago: Ivan R. Dee, 2009.

Smock, Raymond W., ed. *Booker T. Washington in Perspective: Essay of Louis R. Harlan*. Jackson: University of Mississippi Press, 1988.

Snyder, Jeffrey Aaron. *Making Black History: The Color Line, Culture, and Race in the Age of Jim Crow*. Athens: University of Georgia Press, 2018.

Spencer, Samuel R, Jr. *Booker T. Washington and the Negro's Place in American Life*. Boston, MA: Little Brown and Co., 1955.

Stampp, Kenneth M. *The Peculiar Institution: Slavery in the Ante-Bellum South*. New York: Vintage, 1956.

Stelly-Burden, Charisse, and Gerald Horne. *W.E.B. Du Bois: A Life in American History*. Santa Barbara, CA: ABC-CLIO, 2019.

Stewart, Ruth Ann. *Portia: The Life of Portia Washington Pitman, the Daughter of Booker T. Washington*. New York: Doubleday & Co., 1977.

Sundquist, Eric J., ed. *The Oxford W.E.B. Du Bois Reader*. New York: Oxford University Press, 1996.

Terrell, Mary Church. *A Colored Woman in a White World*. New York: Humanity Books, 2005.

"Thousand Pay Tribute to William H. Baldwin." *New York Times*, January 12, 1905.

Trotter, William Monroe. "A Critique of Booker T. Washington's Plan." In *African Intellectual Heritage: A Book of Sources*, edited by Molefi K. Asante and Abu S. Abarry, 500–502. Philadelphia, PA: Temple University Press, 1996.

Twain, Mark. *King Leopold's Soliloquy*. New York: UNO Press, n.d.; First published 1905.

Washington, Booker T. *Character Building: Addresses Delivered on Sunday Evenings to the Students of Tuskegee Institute.* Amsterdam, Holland: Fredonia Books, 1903.
Washington, Booker T. *The Future of the Negro.* Gloucestershire, UK: Dodo Press, 2010.
Washington, Booker T. *Frederick Douglass.* Honolulu, HI: University Press of the Pacific, 2003; first published in 1907.
Washington, Booker T. *The Man Farthest Down: A Record of Observation and Study in Europe.* London: Forgotten Books, 2015; first published in 1912.
Washington, Booker T. *My Larger Education.* New York: Dover, 2013; first published in 1911.
Washington, Booker T. *The Negro in Business.* Wichita, KS: Devore and Sons, Inc., 1992; first published in 1907.
Washington, Booker T., ed. *The Negro Problem.* Middletown, DE: n/p, 2020; first published in 1903.
Washington, Booker T. *The Story of My Life and Work.* Cincinnati, OH: W.H. Ferguson, Co., 1900.
Washington, Booker T. *The Story of the Negro: The Rise of the Race from Slavery.* Gloucestershire, UK: Nonsuch, 2007; first published in 1909.
Washington, Booker T. *Tuskegee & Its People: Their Ideals and Achievements, Illustrated Edition.* New York: D. Appleton and Co., 1906.
Washington, Booker T. *Up from Slavery.* New York: Penguin, 1986; first published in 1901.
Washington, Booker T. *Working with the Hands.* London: Alexander Moring, 2007; first published in 1904.
Washington, Booker T., and W. E. B. Du Bois. *The Negro in the South.* New York: University Books, 1970; first published in 1907.
Weber, Max. *The Protestant Ethic and the Spirit of Capitalism.* London: Routledge, 1992.
Weisberger, Bernard A. *Booker T. Washington.* New York: Mentor, 1972.
Wells-Barnett, Ida B. *On Lynchings.* New York: Humanity Books, 2002.
West, Michael R. *The Education of Booker T. Washington: American Democracy and the Idea of Race Relations.* New York: Columbia University Press, 2006.
Woodson, Carter G. *The Education of the Negro: An Essential Preface for Understanding the Mis-Education of the Negro.* New York: A&B Books Publishers, 1992.
Woodson, Carter G. *The Mis-Education of the Negro.* Trenton, NJ: Africa World Press, 1990.

Woodward, C. Vann. *Origins of the New South, 1877–1913*. Revised edition. Baton Rouge: Louisiana State University, 1971.
Woodward, C. Vann. *The Strange Career of Jim Crow*. 3rd revised ed. New York: Oxford University Press, 1974.
Wright, Tyrene. *Booker T. Washington and Africa: The Making of a Pan Africanist*. New York: Global Africa, 2015.
Zimmerman, Andrew. *Alabama in Africa: Booker T. Washington, the German Empire, & the Globalization of the New South*. Princeton, NJ: Princeton University Press, 2010.

Index

Note: Page numbers in *italics* indicate photos.

Abolitionist movement, 2–7, 9–10, 20, 24, 146
Accommodation, 72, 90, 93, 104, 119, 126–127, 145, 168, 176, 179, 183, 199
Adams, Lewis, 43, 44–45, 48, 133
American Colonization Society (ACS), 10, 11, 122, 145, 146
African Communities League (ACL), 169, 192
African Diaspora, 123, 143–144, 149, 154, 160, 166, 168–170, 173, 192, 203–204, 215
African Methodist Episcopal (AME) Church, 121–122, 123, 154
African National Congress (ANC), 160–162
African Times and Orient Review, 158, 192
Aiello, Thomas, 182, 183–184
Ali, Duse Mohamed, 158, 192
American Colonization Society (ACS), 10, 11, 122, 145, 146
American Dream, 16, 87
American Negro Academy (ANA), 124–125
Aptheker, Herbert, 72, 110, 134–135, 136, 137, 139, 141, 149–150, 163, 196, 199, 200, 203
Armstrong, Samuel Chapman, *31*, 31–34, 37, 38–39, 41–42, 44, 52, 85–86, 200, 211, 238

Asante, Molefi K., 162, 164
"Atlanta Compromise" speech (Washington), 69–71, 213
background to, 65–68
"cast down your bucket where you are," 70, 122, 217, 218–219
conclusion, 220
content and delivery, 68
impact and legacy, 72–90
journalist's description of, 221–223
reception to, 71–73
"separate as the fingers, yet one as the hand," 71, 73, 152, 217, 219
text of, 217–221

Bailey, Thomas Pearce, 74–75, 76, 77
Baldwin, William H., Jr., 57, 83, 85–86, 116–117, 138. *See also* "Thousands Pay Tribute to William H. Baldwin"
Bantu Business League, 160
Belgian Congo, 147, 203, 204
Berea College, 85
Birth of a Nation (film), 77, 151, 168
Black Belt South, 50, 65, 107, 185, 190, 225
Black codes, 10, 14–16, 71
Black Nationalism, 155, 169
Black Power, 135, 192
Blyden, Edward Wilmot, 169

Boer War, 159
Booker T. Washington Institute (Liberia), 173
"Boston Riot," 214
Brown, John, 6–7, 9
Brown v. Board of Education, 76
Brownsville Affair, 167
Burroughs, Elizabeth, 20
Burroughs, James, 20–21, 24
Burroughs, Jane (Washington's mother), 13, 20, 22, 24, 26, 211
Burroughs plantation, 20–24, 211

Calloway, James Nathan, 158
Campbell, George W., 44, 48
Carnegie, Andrew, 83, 86, 87–89, 93, 112–113, 138, 176, 182, 183, 189, 246
Carnegie Hall Conference, 214
Carroll, Rebecca, 193–194
Carver, George Washington, 58–59, 62, 112, 142, 187
"Cast down your bucket where you are," 70, 122, 217, 218–219
Chesnutt, Charles W., 130
Civil War, 8–14
　abolitionism and, 2–7
　causes of, 4, 8–11
　onset of, 8
　See also Reconstruction Era
Clarke, John Henrik, 191
Cleveland, Grover, 80–81, 221
Coleridge-Taylor, Samuel, 57, 120, 148
Congo, 157, 162, 165, 214
Congo Free State, 154
Congo Reform Association, 147
Cotton States International Exposition, 66–90, 95, 108, 213. *See also* "Atlanta Compromise" speech (Washington)
Cox, Oliver Cromwell, 187–188, 200
Creelman, James. *See* "South's New Epoch" (Creelman)
Crisis, The (NAACP publication), 127
Crisis of the Negro Intellectual, The (Cruse), 190, 191
Crummell, Alexander, 122–123
Cruse, Harold, 190–191

Dagbovie, Pero Gaglo, 199–204
Davis, William, 211
Delany, Martin R., 3, 123, 154, 156, 203
Dixon, Thomas, Jr., 77, 151–152, 156, 167, 168, 177
Douglass, Frederick, 3, 108
　abolitionist movement and, 2–3
　on African repatriation, 122, 145, 146, 154, 156
　autobiographical writings of, 8
　biography of, 214
　birthdate of, 20
　Brown, John, and, 6–7
　commencement address at Tuskegee Institute, 2, 65
　death of, 66, 95, 217
　Du Bois, W. E. B., on, 133
　education of, 132
　Garrison, William Lloyd, and, 3
　Lincoln, Abraham, and, 10, 11
　profile of, 2
　Washington and, 73–74, 83
　Washington on, 237–238
Dred Scott v. Sandford, 4–5, 6, 9
Du Bois, W. E. B., *101*
　birth of, 99–100
　Black Reconstruction in America, 157, 208
　collaborations with Washington, 130–139, 214
　contrasted with Washington, 99–103, 106–107, 129, 203
　correspondence with Washington, 181
　critiques of Washington, 107–119, 140–141, 186–187, 190–191, 198, 199–200
　on Douglass, Frederick, 133
　The Dusk of Dawn, 116, 117–118, 140–141, 181
　on faculty at University of Pennsylvania, 104–105, 124
　on faculty at Wilberforce University, 102, 103–105

fundraising of, 183
German Romanticism and, 106
National Negro Business League
    and, 88, 248
The Negro in the South, 134–135,
    137, 138–139, 214
"Of Mr. Booker T. Washington and
    Others," 99, 108, 115, 140–142, 163
Pan Africanism and, 160–161, 162,
    164, 165–166, 168, 170, 174–175,
    176, 182, 203–204
The Philadelphia Negro, 105
president of American Negro
    Academy, 124, 125
profile of, 100
*A Soliloquy on Viewing My Life from
    the Last Decade of Its First
    Century,* 181
The Souls of Black Folk, 99, 100, 108,
    116, 123, 130, 132, 134–135, 162,
    181, 184, 188, 234
student at Fisk University, 102, 104
student at Harvard, 79, 100,
    102–103, 111
*The Suppression of the African
    Slave-Trade to the United States of
    America, 1638–1870,* 102
"The Talented Tenth," 131–132
Talented Tenth concept, 110, 119,
    123, 131–134, 137, 139, 170, 191,
    195, 234
on the Tuskegee Institute, 89,
    103–104, 140, 147, 180
on Washington's "Atlanta
    Compromise" speech, 72
The World and Africa, 203
Dube, John Langalibalele, 160–163
Dunbar, Paul Laurence, 130, 139, 185,
    205, 233

Ellison, Ralph, 196
Emancipation Proclamation, 10, *11,* 15,
    16

Farmer's Annual Conference, 212
Federal Freedman's Bureau, 13, 16, 29, 32

Ferguson, Washington (Washington's
    stepfather), 20, 21, 26, 27–28, 211
Fifteenth Amendment, 13
Finlay, Robert, 122, 146
Fisk University, 55, 59, 90, 102, 104,
    106, 109, 120, 131–132, 140, 151,
    158, 198, 208
Fortune, T. Thomas, 127–130, 131, 133,
    145, 233
Foster, Wilbur F., 43, 44
Fourteenth Amendment, 13
Frazier, E. Franklin, 188–189
Freedman's Bureau, 13, 16, 29, 32

Garnet, Henry Highland, 144–145, 146
Garrison, William Lloyd, 2–4, *4*
    The Liberator (newspaper), 3, 4
    profile of, 3
Garvey, Marcus, 144, 154, *155,*
    155–156, 163, 191, 203–204, 224
    Ali, Duse Mohamed, and, 158, 192
    correspondence with Washington,
        175–176
    Fortune, T. Thomas, and, 128
    Malcolm X and, 201
    profile of, 192
Ghana, 135, 165, 167, 172
Griffith, D. W., 168
Guardian (African American
    newspaper), 119, 127

Haley, Alex, 201
Hampton Normal and Agricultural
    Institute, 93, 190, 236, 242–243
    Armstrong, Samuel Chapman, and,
        31, 31–34, 37, 38–39, 41–42, 44,
        52, 85–86, 200, 211, 238
    Fanny (Washington's first wife) as
        student at, 43
    as model for Tuskegee Institute, 34,
        42, 51, 98
    Olivia (Washington's second wife) as
        student at, 49, 50
    Washington as faculty member at
        Hampton Institute, 37–39,
        102–103, 212

Hampton Normal and Agricultural
Institute (*cont.*)
Washington graduates with honors
from Hampton Institute, 34, 211
Washington as student at Hampton
Institute, 29–37, 101, 184–185,
211
Harlan, Louis R., 31, 93, 104, 108–109,
116, 126, 128, 133, 138, 147,
153–154, 157, 160, 161–162, 169,
172, 185, 194–195, 199–201,
204–205
Harper's Ferry rebellion, 5–7, 9
Harris, Thomas, 115–116
Hayes, Rutherford B., 15, 17
Hayford, J. E. Casely, 169
Herskovits, Melvin, 27
Historically Black colleges and
universities, 104, 112, 131,
183–184
Fisk University, 55, 59, 90, 102, 104,
106, 109, 120, 131–132, 140, 151,
158, 198, 208
Hampton Normal and Agricultural
Institute, 29–43, 49–52, 85–86,
93, 101–103, 184–185, 190, 200,
211, 212, 236, 238, 242–243
Howard University, 104, 106, 109,
120, 124–126, 128, 132, 140, 151,
215, 247–248
Wilberforce University, 102,
103–105, 123, 183
See also Tuskegee Normal and
Industrial Institute
Hodes, Martha, 82
Horne, Gerald, 106
Howard University, 104, 106, 109, 120,
124–126, 128, 132, 140, 151, 215,
247–248
Hughes, Langston, 139, 185
Hurston, Zora Neale, 139, 185

"Industrial Education for the Negro"
(Washington), 233–241
on abstract knowledge, 237, 241
on agricultural education, 240–241
on book education, 239
on Hampton Institute, 238
on mental and moral culture, 238
on overlooking value of industrial
training, 235–236
on slavery, 234–236, 240
on work training, 238–239
Invisible Man (Ellison), 196

Jamaica, *155*, 163, 169, 175–176, 192,
255
Johnson, Andrew, 10
Johnson, James Weldon, 124
Johnston, Harry, 215

Karenga, Maulana, 190
King, Charles, 203–204
King, Martin Luther, Jr., 4, 100, 163,
165, *193*
assassination of, 163
"I Have a Dream" address, 66, 179
Pan-Africanism and, 160, 172
profile of, 180
on Washington, 192–193, 196, 197
Kirkland, Avon, 194–196
Ku Klux Klan (KKK), 16, 35, *36*, 77,
168, 201

Leopold II, King of Belgium, 146–147,
150, 162, 165, 203, 214
Liberia, 122–123, 145–146, 152,
154–158, 165, 167, 169, 173,
203–204, 214, 215
Lincoln, Abraham, *11*
Emancipation Proclamation, 10, *11*,
15, 16
as Great Emancipator, 12–13
profile of, 10
support for ACS, 145, 146
Locke, Alain LeRoy, 125–126, 215
letter to Booker T. Washington,
246–248
Lynching, 35, 70, 71, 76, 81, 82, 109,
115, 116, 120, 127, 131, 197
anti-lynching movement, 55, 57, 129,
198

Malcolm X, 100, 132, 163, 170, 201
Marable, Manning, 141, 149, 150, 152, 154–157, 163, 174, 199–200, 203
Marx, Karl, 136–137, 157
Marxism, 135–137, 152, 157, 187–189
Mathews, Basil, 27
McKinley, William, 83–84, 95, 213

Nation of Islam, 201
National Association for the Advancement of Colored People (NAACP), 113, 119, 127, 140, 215
National Council for Black Studies (NCBS), 45, 114
National Educational Association, Washington's address before
  on emotions and religion, 230
  in industrial education, 227–230
  on Liberia, 225
  on need for humanity and justice, 226–227
  on need to pay the price, 228–229
  on rescue of African Americans from "heathen Africa," 225
  on sympathizing with white men, 232
  tale of Christmas dinner, 228
  tale of crossing the river, 231–232
  tale of planting corn, 228–229
  tale of sale of hog, 226–227
  tale of Sunday-school class, 227
  text of, 223–233
National Negro Business League (NNBL), 88–90, 91, 92, 96, 118–119, 127, 129, 136, 149, 160, 164, 189, 195, 213, 214
"National Negro Business League Address, A" (Washington), 248–254
  on ability to work together, 250
  on the future, 252–254
  on land and agriculture, 250–251
  on Philadelphia, 249
  on self-sufficiency, 249–250
Negro Health Week, 215

Negro Problem, The, 130–135
  "Industrial Education for the Negro," 233–241
New Negro, The (Locke), 126, 215, 247
New York Age (African American newspaper), 127, 128
New York World, Washington's letter to the editor of, 254–256
Niagara Movement, 113, 119, 126–127
Nkrumah, Kwame, 165, 167, 172
Norrell, Robert J., 72, 146, 153, 161–162, 202
North Star (newspaper), 3

Oberholtzer, Ellis P., 214
Ogden, Robert C., 85–86, 93

Pan Africanism, 106–107, 111, 143, 146, 149–150, 152, 154, 158–177, 192, 203–204, 254
Phillips, U. B., 7–8
Plessy, Homer, 76
Plessy v. Ferguson, 75–76, 213
Porter, Alfred Haynes, 212

Race massacres, 196–197
Reconstruction Era, 13–17, 35, 70–77, 135, 153
Reed, Ishmael, 208
Roosevelt, Theodore
  visit to Tuskegee Institute, 167, 214
  Washington as advisor to, 57, 89, 95–97, 126, 142, 147, 152, 157–158, 166–168, 181, 207
  Washington's dinner at the White House, 96–97, 142, 152, 197, 214
Rosenwald, Julius, 92, 93–95, 171, 183, 188–189
Ruffner, Lewis, 29, 30–31, 35

Scott, Dred, 4–5, 6, 9
Scott, Emmett J., 98, 138, 171–172, 177, 200, 206
"Separate as the fingers, yet one as the hand," 71, 73, 152, 217, 219
"Separate but equal" doctrine, 213

Slave narratives, 8, 20
South Africa, 152, 154, 157, 159–161, 173, 203
"South's New Epoch" (Creelman), 221–223
Spencer, Herbert, 88
Stanley, Henry, 147
Stelly-Burden, Charisse, 106
Stereotypes
  of Africa and Africans, 144
  in *Gone with the Wind* (film), 20
  in scholarship, 7–8, 75, 189
  sexual, 82
  of Washington, 93, 137, 189, 196, 215, 247
  Washington's responses to, 95, 104
  of women, 199
Stokes, Caroline Phelps, 85
Stokes, Olivia Phelps, 85
Stowe, Harriet Beecher, 194

Taft, William Howard, 89, 93, 120, 159, 181, 207, 214
Talented Tenth, 110, 119, 123, 131–134, 137, 139, 170, 191, 195, 234
Taney, Roger B., 5, 6, 9
Taylor, Robert R., 85
Thirteenth Amendment, 2, 10, 13, 15, 16
"Thousands Pay Tribute to William H. Baldwin," 241–246
  on blending of opposites, 244
  Collyer's tribute, 245–246
  on friends' eulogies, 243
  on the glory he liked, 243–244
  Washington's tribute, 245
Tillman, Benjamin R., 76–77, 96–97
Togo, 154, 155–158, 162, 164, 165–166, 173, 177, 203, 213
Trotter, William Monroe, 99, 118–120, 121, 126–127, 142, 153, 183, 214
Turner, Henry McNeal, 121–123, 144, 146, 154, 155, 166, 203
Tuskegee Normal and Industrial Institute, 41–63
  Adams, Lewis, and, 43, 44–45, 48
  Carver, George Washington, and, 58–59, 62
  commencement address by Frederick Douglass, 2, 65
  Creelman, James, on, 222
  critiques of, 89, 103–104, 140, 147, 180, 188–189, 200
  curriculum and pedagogy at, 49–54, 90, 103–104, 106, 151, 184–187, 189, 200
  Ellison, Ralph, at, 196
  endowment of, 190, 209, 216
  Farmer's Annual Conference, 212
  first class graduates from, 212
  fundraising for, 51–57, 112–113, 183–184, 185, 189, 209
  Hampton Institute as model for, 34, 42
  "Industrial Education for the Negro" (Washington) on, 236, 238–240
  International Conference on the Negro, 215
  legacy of Washington and, 175–177, 199–200, 203–206, 208–209
  Locke, Alain LeRoy, on, 246–248
  Margaret (Washington's third wife) and, 55, 55–58
  The Oaks (family residence), 57, 209, 213, 215
  Olivia (Washington's second wife) and, 49–50, 51, 53–56, 57
  Phelps Hall, 85
  Porter Hall, 212
  student body population, 209, 216
  study abroad program, 158, 175–177, 203–204, 254
  Sunday evening talks by Washington, 60–63, 206, 214
  Togo expedition, 155–158, 162, 164, 165–166, 173, 177, 203, 213
  "Tuskegee Machine," 89–91, 118, 126–127, 129, 140, 142, 147, 180, 182
  visit by President McKinley to, 83–84, 213
  visit by President Roosevelt to, 167, 214
  Washington becomes first principal of, 41–42, 212
  women at, 199
Twain, Mark, 146–147

"Uncle Tom," 192–196
Uncle Tom's Cabin (Stowe), 194
Universal Negro Improvement Association (UNIA), 128, 169, 192, 204
Up from Slavery (Washington)
  on the Civil War, 12
  on date of Washington's birth, 19
  on death of his mother, 34
  on General Armstrong, 33, 41
  on "'grape-vine' telegraph," 11–12
  impact of, 95, 97, *155*, 159–160, 192
  publication of, 213
  reception to, 87, 95
  on reception to "Atlanta Compromise" speech, 80
  Uncle Tom or New Negro? and, 194

Vardaman, James K., *77*, 78
Victoria, Queen, 89, 95, 213
Victorian era, 57, 58, 198–199

Washington, Booker T.
  assaulted near Central Park, 207, 215
  attends garden party at Windsor Castle, 89, 213
  birth of, 19–20, 211
  birthdate of, 19–20
  childhood, 8–17
  collaborations with Du Bois, 130–139, 214
  contrasted with Du Bois, 99–103, 106–107, 129, 203
  contributions to education and pedagogy, 184–185
  correspondence with Du Bois, 181
  courage of, 180–181
  critiqued by Du Bois, 107–119, 140–141, 186–187, 190–191, 198, 199–200
  death of, 209, 215–216
  death of Fanny (first wife), 43, 212
  death of mother, 34–35
  death of Olivia (second wife), 212
  dinner at the White House, 96–97, 142, 152, 197, 214
  as faculty member at Hampton Institute, 37–39, 102–103, 212
  final illness of, 209, 215–216
  fundraising skills, 51–57, 112–113, 183–184, 185, 189, 209
  graduates with honors from Hampton Institute, 34, 211
  honorary degrees, 133–134, 213
  marries Fanny N. Smith, 43, 212
  marries Margaret Murray, 213
  marries Olivia A. Davidson, 212
  name of, 26–27
  oratorical skills, 185
  in Pine Bluff, Arkansas, *180*
  principal of Tuskegee Institute, 43–44, 212
  as student at Hampton Institute, 29–37, 101, 184–185, 211
  value of as plantation property, 20–21, 211
  at Wayland Seminary, 36–37, 102, 212
  work ethic, 185–186
  work in salt mines, 27–28
  See also Tuskegee Normal and Industrial Institute
Washington, Booker T., published works
  Character Building, 61, 206, 209, 214
  The Future of the American Negro, 213
  The Man Farthest Down: A Record of Observation and Study in Europe, 176, 215
  My Larger Education, 202, 215
  The Negro in Business, 91
  The Negro in the South, 134–135, 137, 138–139, 214
  The Negro Problem, 130–135, 233–241
  The Story of My Life, 213
  The Story of the Negro: The Rise of the Race from Slavery, 143, 147–149, 153, 165–166, 170–171, 177–178, 215
  Working with the Hands, 186, 198
  See also Up from Slavery (Washington)

Washington, Booker T., speeches
  "The Educational Outlook in the South," 212
  "The Force That Wins," 37
  "The Highest Education," 61–62
  See also "Atlanta Compromise" speech (Washington)
Washington, Booker T. Washington, Jr. (Washington's son), 50, 53–54, 56, 58, 69, 120, 131, 212
Washington, Ernest Davidson (Washington's son), 50, 53, 54, 56, 69, 120, 212
Washington, Fanny Norton Smith (Washington's wife), 42, 43, 50, 51, 52–53, 56, 212
Washington, Margaret Murray (Washington's wife), 55, 55–58, 69, 82, 106, 131, 195, 198–199, 213
Washington, Olivia America Davidson (Washington's wife), 49–50, 51, 53–56, 57, 212
Washington, Portia Marshall (Washington's daughter), 43, 52–53, 54–58, 69, 104, 120, 138, 169, 189–190, 212
"We Wear the Mask" (Dunbar), 205
Wilberforce University, 102, 103–105, 123, 183
Williams, Henry Sylvester, 149, 158, 164, 169
Williams, John Sharp, 78–79
Wilson, Woodrow, 77, 151, 168, 191, 207, 248
World War II, 15, 72
Wright, Tyrene, 149–150, 152, 156, 158, 164, 174, 177, 202, 204

Zimmerman, Andrew, 159, 165, 176–177, 204
Zulu Christian Industrial School, 160

About the Author

Mark Christian, PhD, is a full and tenured professor in Africana Studies at the City University of New York. He was educated in the United Kingdom and the United States and is a former research fellow at the University of London's Commonwealth Institute. A senior Fulbright Scholar, he is author of *Multiracial Identity: An International Perspective* (Palgrave, 2000) and editor of *Black Identity in the 20th Century: Expressions of the US and UK African Diaspora* (Hansib, 2002) as well as *Integrated but Unequal: Black Faculty in Predominately White Space* (Africa World Press, 2012). His latest book is *The 20th Century Civil Rights Movement: An Africana Studies Perspective* (Kendall & Hunt, 2021).

www.ingramcontent.com/pod-product-compliance
Lightning Source LLC
Chambersburg PA
CBHW060945230426
43665CB00015B/2071